Advanced Node.js Development

Master Node.js by building real-world applications

Andrew Mead

BIRMINGHAM - MUMBAI

Advanced Node.js Development

Acquisition Editor: Ben Renow-Clarke
Content Development Editor: Monika Sangwan
Technical Editor: Gaurav Gavas
Copy Editor: Tom Jacob
Project Coordinator: Suzanne Coutinho
Proofreader: Safis Editing
Indexer: Rekha Nair
Production Coordinator: Shantanu N. Zagade

First published: March 2018

Production reference: 1290318

Published by Packt Publishing Ltd.
Livery Place
35 Livery Street
Birmingham
B3 2PB, UK.

ISBN 978-1-78839-393-5

www.packtpub.com

Contributors

About the author

Andrew Mead is a full-stack developer living in beautiful Philadelphia! He launched his first Udemy course in 2014 and had a blast teaching and helping others. Since then, he has launched three courses with over 21,000 students and over 1,900 5-star reviews.

Andrew currently teaches Node.js, Gulp, and React. Before he started teaching, he created a web app development company. He has helped companies of all sizes launch production web applications to their customers. He has had the honor of working with awesome companies such as Siemens, Mixergy, and Parkloco. He has a Computer Science degree from Temple University, and he has been programming for just over a decade. He loves creating, programming, launching, learning, teaching, and biking.

Packt is searching for authors like you

If you're interested in becoming an author for Packt, please visit authors.packtpub.com and apply today. We have worked with thousands of developers and tech professionals, just like you, to help them share their insight with the global tech community. You can make a general application, apply for a specific hot topic that we are recruiting an author for, or submit your own idea.

Table of Contents

Preface

Welcome to *Advanced Node.js Development*. This book is packed with a ton of content, projects, challenges, and real-world examples, all designed to teach you Node by *doing*. This means you'll be getting your hands dirty early on in the upcoming chapters writing some code, and you'll be writing code for every project. You will be writing every line of code that powers our applications. Now, we would require a text editor for this book.

All the projects in the book are fun to build and they were designed to teach you everything required to launch your own Node app, from planning to development and testing to deploying. Now, as you launch these different Node applications and move through the book, you will run into errors, which is bound to happen. Maybe something doesn't get installed as expected, or maybe you try to run an app and instead of getting the expected output, you get a really long obscure error message. Don't worry, I am there to help. I'll show you tips and tricks to get pass through those errors in the chapters. Let's go ahead and get to it.

Who this book is for

This book targets anyone looking to launch their own Node applications, switch careers, or freelance as a Node developer. You should have a basic understanding of JavaScript in order to follow this book.

What this book covers

Chapter 1, *Getting Set Up*, will be a very basic setup for your local environments. We'll learn to install MongoDB and Robomongo.

Chapter 2, *MongoDB, Mongoose, and REST APIs – Part 1*, will help you learn how to connect your Node applications to the MongoDB database you've been running on your local machine.

Chapter 3, *MongoDB, Mongoose, and REST APIs – Part 2*, will help you start playing with Mongoose and connect to our MongoDB database.

Chapter 4, *MongoDB, Mongoose, and REST APIs – Part 3*, will resolve queries and ID validation after playing with Mongoose.

Chapter 5, *Real-Time Web Apps with Socket.io*, will help you learn in detail about Socket.io and WebSockets, help you and create real-time web applications.

Chapter 6, *Generating newMessage and newLocationMessage*, discusses how to generate text and gelocation messages.

Chapter 7, *Styling Our Chat Page as a Web App*, continues our discussion on styling our chat page and make it look more like a real web application.

Chapter 8, *The Join Page and Passing Room Data*, continues our discussion about the chat page and look into the join page and passing room data.

Chapter 9, *ES7 classes*, will help you learn the ES6 class syntax and using it creating user's class and some other methods.

Chapter 10, *Async/Await Project Setup*, will walk you through the process of learning how async/await works.

To get the most out of this book

To run the projects in this book, you will need the following:

- The latest version of Node.js (9.x.x at the time of writing this book)
- Express
- MongoDB
- Mongoose
- Atom

We'll see the rest of the requirements along the course of the book.

Download the example code files

You can download the example code files for this book from your account at www.packtpub.com. If you purchased this book elsewhere, you can visit www.packtpub.com/support and register to have the files emailed directly to you.

You can download the code files by following these steps:

1. Log in or register at www.packtpub.com.
2. Select the **SUPPORT** tab.
3. Click on **Code Downloads & Errata**.
4. Enter the name of the book in the **Search** box and follow the onscreen instructions.

Once the file is downloaded, please make sure that you unzip or extract the folder using the latest version of:

- WinRAR/7-Zip for Windows
- Zipeg/iZip/UnRarX for Mac
- 7-Zip/PeaZip for Linux

The code bundle for the book is also hosted on GitHub at https://github.com/PacktPublishing/Advanced-Node.js-Development. We also have other code bundles from our rich catalog of books and videos available at https://github.com/PacktPublishing/. Check them out!

Download the color images

We also provide a PDF file that has color images of the screenshots/diagrams used in this book. You can download it here: http://www.packtpub.com/sites/default/files/downloads/AdvancedNode.jsDevelopment_ColorImages.pdf.

Conventions used

There are a number of text conventions used throughout this book.

CodeInText: Indicates code words in text, database table names, folder names, filenames, file extensions, pathnames, dummy URLs, user input, and Twitter handles. Here is an example: "Mount the downloaded WebStorm-10*.dmg disk image file as another disk in your system."

A block of code is set as follows:

```
html, body, #map {
  height: 100%;
  margin: 0;
  padding: 0
}
```

When we wish to draw your attention to a particular part of a code block, the relevant lines or items are set in bold:

```
[default]
exten => s,1,Dial(Zap/1|30)
exten => s,2,Voicemail(u100)
exten => s,102,Voicemail(b100)
exten => i,1,Voicemail(s0)
```

Any command-line input or output is written as follows:

```
$ cd css
```

Bold: Indicates a new term, an important word, or words that you see onscreen. For example, words in menus or dialog boxes appear in the text like this. Here is an example: "Select **System info** from the **Administration** panel."

 Warnings or important notes appear like this.

 Tips and tricks appear like this.

Get in touch

Feedback from our readers is always welcome.

General feedback: Email feedback@packtpub.com and mention the book title in the subject of your message. If you have questions about any aspect of this book, please email us at questions@packtpub.com.

Errata: Although we have taken every care to ensure the accuracy of our content, mistakes do happen. If you have found a mistake in this book, we would be grateful if you would report this to us. Please visit www.packtpub.com/submit-errata, selecting your book, clicking on the Errata Submission Form link, and entering the details.

Piracy: If you come across any illegal copies of our works in any form on the Internet, we would be grateful if you would provide us with the location address or website name. Please contact us at copyright@packtpub.com with a link to the material.

If you are interested in becoming an author: If there is a topic that you have expertise in and you are interested in either writing or contributing to a book, please visit authors.packtpub.com.

Reviews

Please leave a review. Once you have read and used this book, why not leave a review on the site that you purchased it from? Potential readers can then see and use your unbiased opinion to make purchase decisions, we at Packt can understand what you think about our products, and our authors can see your feedback on their book. Thank you!

For more information about Packt, please visit packtpub.com.

Getting Set Up 1

In this chapter, you'll get your local environment set up for the rest of the book. Whether you're on macOS, Linux, or Windows, we'll install MongoDB and Robomongo.

More specifically, we'll cover the following topics:

- MongoDB and Robomongo installation for Linux and macOS
- MongoDB and Robomongo installation for Windows

Installing MongoDB and Robomongo for Linux and macOS

This section is for macOS and Linux users. If you are on Windows, I have written a separate section for you.

The first thing we'll do is to download and set up MongoDB, as this will be the database we will use. We'll be using a third-party service to host our database when we eventually deploy it to Heroku, but on our local machine we'll need to download MongoDB so that we can start up a database server. This will let us connect to it via our Node applications to read and write data.

In order to grab the database, we'll head over to mongodb.com. Then we can go to the **Download** page and download the appropriate version.

On this page, scroll down and select **Community Server**; this is the one we'll be using. Also, there are options for different operating systems, whether it's Windows, Linux, macOS, or Solaris. I'm on macOS, so I'll use this download:

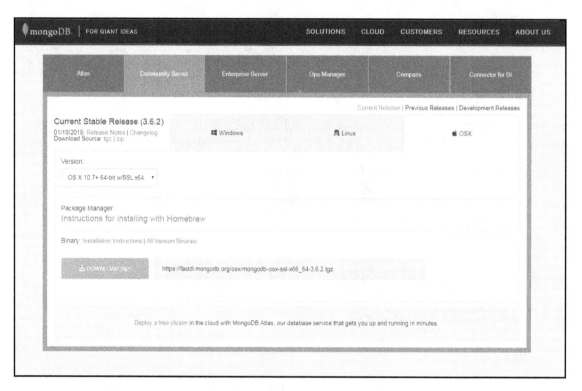

If you're on Linux, click on **Linux**; then go to the **Version** drop down and select the appropriate version. For example, if you're on Ubuntu 14.04, you can download the correct one from the **Linux** tab. Then, you can simply click on the **Download** button and follow along.

Next you can open it up. We'll just extract the directory, creating a brand new folder in the Downloads folder. If you're on Linux, you might need to manually extract the contents of that archive into the Downloads folder.

Now this folder contains a `bin` folder, and in there we have all of the executables that we need in order to do things such as connecting to the database and starting a database server:

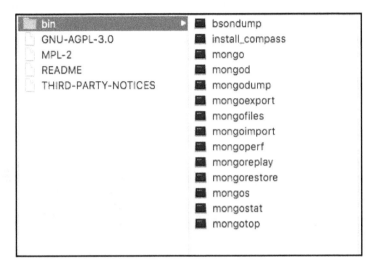

Before we go ahead and run any of them. We'll rename this directory to `mongo` and then move it into the `user` directory. You can see that now in the `user` directory, I have the `mongo` folder. We'll also create a brand new directory alongside of `mongo` called `mongo-data`, and this will store the actual data inside of the database:

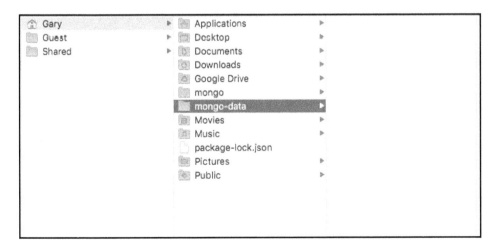

So when we insert a new record into the `Todos` table, for example, that will live in the `mongo-data` folder. Once you have the `mongo` folder moved into the `user` directory and you have the new `mongo-data` folder, you are ready to actually run the database server from Terminal. I'll go into Terminal and navigate into that brand new `mongo` folder that is in the `user` directory, where I currently am, so I can `cd` into `mongo`, then I'll `cd` into the `bin` directory by tacking it on right there:

```
cd mongo/bin
```

From here, we have a bunch of executables that we can run:

We have things such as **bisondump** and **mongodump**. In this section, we'll focus on: **mongod**, which will start up the database server, and **mongo**, which will let us connect to the server and run some commands. Just like when we type `node` we can run some JavaScript commands right in Terminal, when we type `mongo`, we'll be able to run some Mongo commands to insert, fetch, or do anything we like with the data.

First up though, let's start up the database server. I'll use `./` to run a file in the current directory. The file we'll run is called `mongod`; also, we do need to provide one argument: the `dbpath` argument. The `dbpath` argument will get set equal to the path of the directory we just created, the `mongo-data` directory. I'll use ~ (the tilde) to navigate to the user directory, and then to `/mongo-data`, as shown here:

```
./mongod --dbpath ~/mongo-data
```

Running this command will start up the server. This will create an active connection, which we can connect to for manipulating our data. The last line that you see when you run the command should be, **waiting for connections on port 27017**:

```
● ○ ○                    bin — mongod --dbpath ~/mongo-data — 108×15
2018-02-16T09:49:01.298+0530 I CONTROL  [initandlisten] **             server with --bind_ip 127.0.0.1 to disab
le this warning.
2018-02-16T09:49:01.298+0530 I CONTROL  [initandlisten]
2018-02-16T09:49:01.298+0530 I CONTROL  [initandlisten]
2018-02-16T09:49:01.298+0530 I CONTROL  [initandlisten] ** WARNING: soft rlimits too low. Number of files is
  256, should be at least 1000
2018-02-16T09:49:01.433+0530 I STORAGE  [initandlisten] createCollection: admin.system.version with provided
  UUID: 06c8d421-ee05-4193-9a5a-5a402e6cf505
2018-02-16T09:49:02.315+0530 I COMMAND  [initandlisten] setting featureCompatibilityVersion to 3.6
2018-02-16T09:49:02.341+0530 I STORAGE  [initandlisten] createCollection: local.startup_log with generated U
UID: 4b2b58cb-16d8-4198-a20f-a713e2435608
2018-02-16T09:49:02.920+0530 I FTDC     [initandlisten] Initializing full-time diagnostic data capture with
directory '/Users/Gary/mongo-data/diagnostic.data'
2018-02-16T09:49:02.921+0530 I NETWORK  [initandlisten] waiting for connections on port 27017
```

If you see this, it means that your server is up and running.

Next up, let's open a new tab, which starts in the exact same directory, and this time around, instead of running `mongod`, we'll run the `mongo` file:

```
./mongo
```

When we run `mongo`, we open up a console. It connects to the database server we just started, and from here, we can start running some commands. These commands are just to test that things are working as expected. We'll be going over all of this in detail later in this section. For now though, we can access `db.Todos`, and then we'll call `.insert` to create a brand new Todo record. I'll call it like a function:

```
db.Todos.insert({})
```

Next, inside of `insert`, we'll pass in our document. This will be the MongoDB document we want to create. For now, we'll keep things really simple. On our object, we'll specify one attribute, `text`, setting it equal to a string. Inside of quotes, type anything you want to do. I'll say `Film new node course`:

```
db.Todos.insert({text: 'Film new node course'})
```

With your command looking just like this, you can press *enter*, and you should get back a **WriteResult** object with an **nInserted** property, which is short for the number inserted: a value set to **1**. This means that one new record was created, and that is fantastic!

```
> db.Todos.insert({text: 'Film new node course'})
WriteResult({ "nInserted" : 1 })
>
```

Now that we've inserted a record, let's fetch the record just to make sure that everything worked as expected.

Instead of calling `insert`, we'll call `find` without any arguments. We want to return every single item in the `Todos` collection:

db.Todos.find()

When I run this, what do we get? We get one object-looking thing back:

```
> db.Todos.find()
{ "_id" : ObjectId("5a865ca621c9df6d2a3ea59a"), "text" : "Film new node course" }
>
```

We have our `text` attribute set to the text that we provided, and we have an `_id` property. This is the unique identifier for each record, which we'll talk about later. As long as you're seeing the **text** property coming back to what you set, you are good to go.

We can shut down the `mongo` command. However, we will still leave the `mongod` command running because there's one more thing I want to install. It's called Robomongo, and it's a graphic user interface for managing your Mongo database. This will be really useful as you start playing around with Mongo. You'll be able to view the exact data saved in the database; you can manipulate it and do all sorts of stuff.

Over in **Finder**, we have our `mongo-data` directory, and you can see that there is a ton of stuff in here. This means that our data was successfully saved. All of the data is in this `mongo-data` directory. To download and install Robomongo, which is available for Linux, Windows and macOS, we'll head over to `robomongo.org` and grab the installer for our operating system:

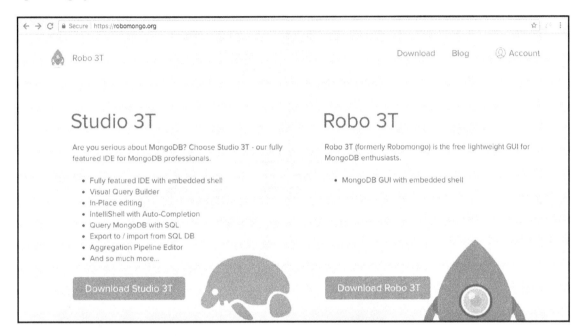

We can click on **Download Robo 3T** and download the most recent version; it should automatically detect your OS. Download the installer for either Linux or macOS. The one for macOS is really simple. It's one of those installers where you take the icon and drag it into the `Applications` folder. For Linux, you'll need to extract the archive and run the program in the `bin` directory. This will start up Robomongo on your Linux distribution.

Since I'm using macOS, I'll just quickly drag the icon over to **Applications**, and then we can play around with the program itself. Next, I'll open it up inside the Finder. When you first open up Robomongo, you might get a warning like the following on macOS, since it's a program that we downloaded and it's not from an identified macOS developer:

This is fine; most programs you download from the web will not be official since they did not come from the App Store. You can right-click on the downloaded package, select **Open**, and then click on **Open** again to run that program. When you first open it, you'll see some screens like the following:

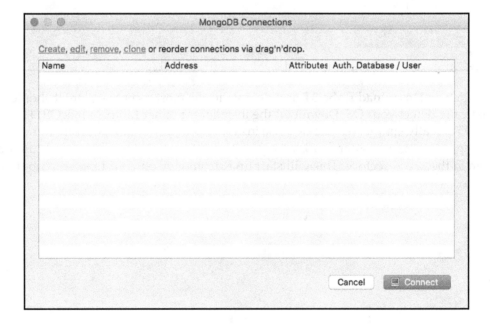

We have a little screen in the background and a list of connections; currently that list is empty. What we need to do is to create a connection for our local MongoDB database so that we can connect to it and manipulate that data. We have **Create**. I'll click on this, and the only thing we'll need to update is **Name**. I'll give it a more descriptive name, such as `Local Mongo Database`. I'll set **Address** to `localhost` and the `27017` port is correct; there's no need to change these. So, I'll click on **Save**:

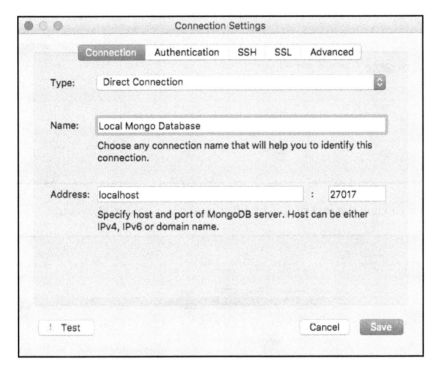

Next, I'll double-click on the database to connect to it. Inside the tiny window, we have our database. We are connected to it; we can do all sorts of things to manage it.

We can open up the `test` database, and in there, we should see one `Collections` folder. If we expand this folder, we have our `Todos` collection, and from there, we can right-click on the collection. Next, click on **View Documents**, and we should get our one Todo item, the one that we created over inside the Mongo console:

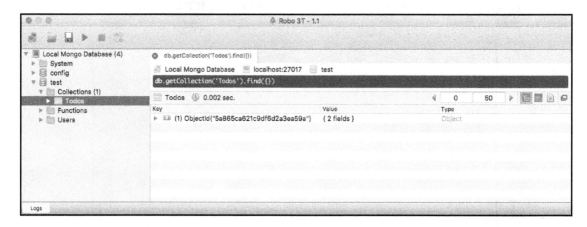

I can expand it to view the **text** property. **Film new node course** shows up:

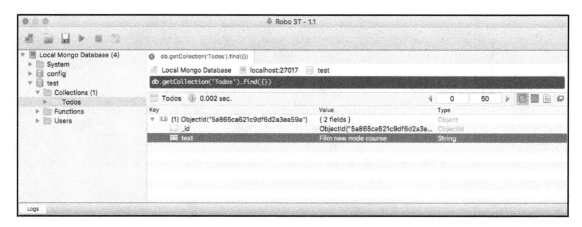

If you're seeing this, then you are done.

The next section is for Windows users.

Installing MongoDB and Robomongo for Windows

If you're on Windows, this is the installation section for you. If you're on Linux or macOS, the previous section was for you; you can skip this one. Our goal here is to install MongoDB on our machines, which will let us create a local MongoDB database server. We'll be able to connect to that server with Node.js, and we'll be able to read and write data to the database. This will be fantastic for the Todo API, which will be responsible for reading and writing various Todo-related information.

To get started, we'll grab the MongoDB installer by going over to mongodb.com. Here we can click on the big green **Download** button; also, we can see several options on this page:

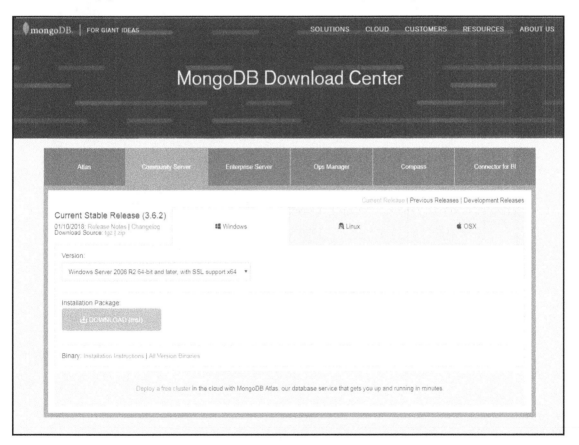

We'll use **Community Server** and for Windows. If you go to the **Version** drop down, none of the versions there will look right for you. The top one is what we want: **Windows Server 08 R2 64-bit and later with SSL support**. Let's start to download this. It is slightly big; just a tad over 100 MB, so it will take a moment for the download to begin.

I'll start it up. It's one of those basic installers, where you click on **Next** a few times and you agree to a license agreement. Click on the **Custom** option for a second, although we will be following through with the **Complete** option. When you click on **Custom**, it will show you where on your machine it's going to be installed, and this is important. Here, you can see that for me it's on C:\Program Files\MongoDB\Server, then in the 3.2 directory:

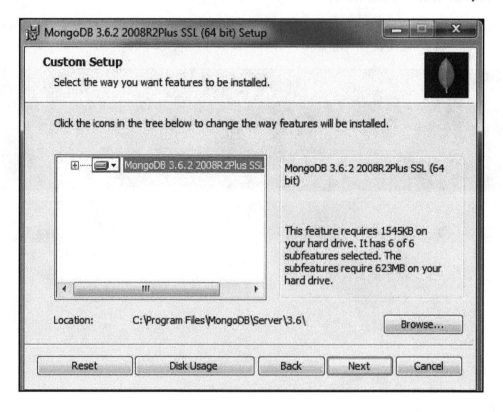

This is going to be important because we'll need to navigate into this directory in order to start up the MongoDB server. I will go back though, and I will be using the **Complete** option, which installs everything we need. Now we can actually start the installation process. Usually, you have to click on **Yes**, verifying that you want to install the software. I'll go ahead and do that, and then we are done.

Now once it's installed, we'll navigate into Command Prompt and boot up a server. The first thing we need to do is to navigate into that `Program Files` directory. I'm in Command Prompt. I recommend that you use Command Prompt and not Git Bash. Git Bash will not work for starting up the MongoDB server. I'll navigate to the root of my machine using `cd/`, and then we can start navigating to that path using the following command:

```
cd Program Files/MongoDB/Server/3.2
```

This is the directory where MongoDB was installed. I can use `dir` to print out the contents of this directory, and what we care about here is the `bin` directory:

```
C:\Windows\system32\cmd.exe

C:\Program Files\MongoDB\Server\3.6>dir
 Volume in drive C has no label.
 Volume Serial Number is 8671-22D7

 Directory of C:\Program Files\MongoDB\Server\3.6

20-02-2018  12:30    <DIR>          .
20-02-2018  12:30    <DIR>          ..
20-02-2018  12:30    <DIR>          bin
10-01-2018  19:15            35,181 GNU-AGPL-3.0
10-01-2018  19:15            17,099 MPL-2
10-01-2018  19:15             2,195 README
10-01-2018  19:15            58,403 THIRD-PARTY-NOTICES
               4 File(s)        112,878 bytes
               3 Dir(s)  230,676,480,000 bytes free

C:\Program Files\MongoDB\Server\3.6>
```

We can navigate into `bin` using `cd bin`, and print its contents out using `dir`. Also, this directory contains a whole bunch of executables that we'll use to do things such as starting up our server and connecting to it:

```
C:\Windows\system32\cmd.exe

C:\Program Files\MongoDB\Server\3.6>cd bin

C:\Program Files\MongoDB\Server\3.6\bin>dir
 Volume in drive C has no label.
 Volume Serial Number is 8671-22D7

 Directory of C:\Program Files\MongoDB\Server\3.6\bin

20-02-2018  12:30    <DIR>          .
20-02-2018  12:30    <DIR>          ..
10-01-2018  19:16         6,937,280 bsondump.exe
10-01-2018  19:40             1,041 InstallCompass.ps1
19-12-2016  18:30         2,000,384 libeay32.dll
10-01-2018  19:28        14,100,992 mongo.exe
10-01-2018  19:41        30,839,296 mongod.exe
10-01-2018  19:42       327,274,496 mongod.pdb
10-01-2018  19:18         9,060,710 mongodump.exe
10-01-2018  19:17         7,204,660 mongoexport.exe
10-01-2018  19:17         7,118,475 mongofiles.exe
10-01-2018  19:17         7,298,763 mongoimport.exe
10-01-2018  19:41        26,096,640 mongoperf.exe
10-01-2018  19:18        10,407,232 mongorestore.exe
10-01-2018  19:33        16,472,064 mongos.exe
10-01-2018  19:33       174,788,608 mongos.pdb
10-01-2018  19:16         7,268,696 mongostat.exe
10-01-2018  19:19         7,072,066 mongotop.exe
19-12-2016  18:30           325,120 ssleay32.dll
              17 File(s)    654,266,523 bytes
               2 Dir(s)  230,676,242,432 bytes free

C:\Program Files\MongoDB\Server\3.6\bin>
```

The first executable we'll run is this **mongod.exe** file. This will start our local MongoDB database. Before we can go ahead and run this EXE, there is one more thing we need to do. Over in the generic File Explorer, we need to create a directory where all of our data can be stored. To do this, I'll put mine in my user directory by going to the `C:/Users/Andrew` directory. I'll make a new folder, and I'll call this folder `mongo-data`. Now, the `mongo-data` directory is where all of our data will actually be stored. This is the path that we need to specify when we run the `mongod.exe` command; we need to tell Mongo where to store the data.

Over in Command Prompt, we can now start this command. I'll run `mongod.exe`, passing in as the `dbpath` argument, the path to that folder we just created. In my case, it's `/Users/Andrew/mongo-data`. Now if your username is different, which it obviously is, or you put the folder in a different directory, you'll need to specify the absolute path to the `mongo-data` folder. Once you have that though, you can start up the server by running the following command:

```
mongod.exe --dbpath /Users/Andrew/mongo-data
```

You'll get a long list of output:

The only thing you need to care about is that, at the very bottom, you should see **waiting for connections on port 27017**. If you see this, then you are good to go. But now that the server is up, let's connect to it and issue some commands to create and read some data.

Creating and reading data

To do this, we'll open up a second Command Prompt window and navigate into that same `bin` directory using `cd/Program Files/MongoDB/Server/3.2/bin`. From here, we'll run `mongo.exe`. Note that we're not running the `mongod` command; we're running `mongo.exe`. This will connect to our local MongoDB database, and it will put us in sort of a Command Prompt view of our database. We'll be able to issue various Mongo commands to manipulate the data, kind of like we can run Node from Command Prompt to run various JavaScript statements right inside the console. When we run this, we're going to connect to the database. Over in the first console window, you can see that **connection accepted** shows up. We do have a new connection. In the first console window now, we can run some commands to create and read data. Now I don't expect you to take away anything from these commands. We'll not talk about the ins and outs of MongoDB just yet. All I want to do is to make sure that when you run them, it works as expected.

To get started, let's create a new Todo from the console. This can be done via `db.Todos`, and on this Todos collection, we'll call the `.insert` method. Also, we'll call `insert` with one argument, an object; this object can have any properties we want to add to the record. For example, I want to set a `text` property. This is the thing I actually need to do. Inside quotes, I can put something. I'll go with `Create new Node course`:

```
db.Todos.insert({text: 'Create new Node course'})
```

Now when I run this command, it will actually make the insert into our database and we should get a `writeResult` object back, with an `nInserted` property set to 1. This means that one record was inserted.

Now that we have one Todo in our database, we can try to fetch it using `db.Todos` once again. This time, instead of calling `insert` to add a record, we'll call `find` with no arguments provided. This will return every single Todo inside of our database:

```
db.Todos.find()
```

When I run this command, We get an object-looking thing where we have a `text` property set to `Create new Node course`. We also have an `_id` property. The `_id` property is MongoDB's unique identifier, and this is the property that they use to give your document; in this case, a Todo, a unique identifier. We'll be talking more about `_id` and about all of the commands we just ran, a little later. For now, we can close this using *Ctrl + C*. We've successfully disconnected from Mongo, and now we can also close the second Command Prompt window.

Before we move on, there is one more thing I want to do. We'll be installing a program called Robomongo—a GUI for MongoDB. It will let you connect to your local database as well as real databases, which we'll be talking about later. Also, it'll let you view all the data, manipulate it and do anything you could do inside a database GUI. It's really useful; sometimes you just need to dive into a database to see exactly what the data looks like.

In order to get this started, we'll head over to a new tab and go to `robomongo.org`:

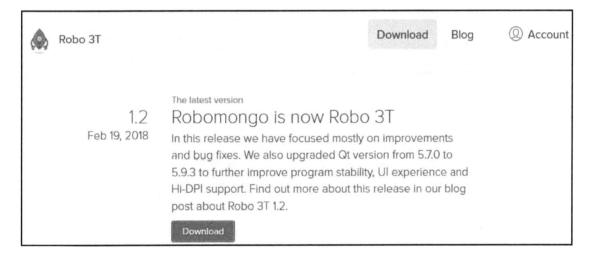

Here we can grab the installer by going to **Download**. We'll download the latest version, and I'm on Windows. I want the installer, not the portable version, so I'll click on the first link here:

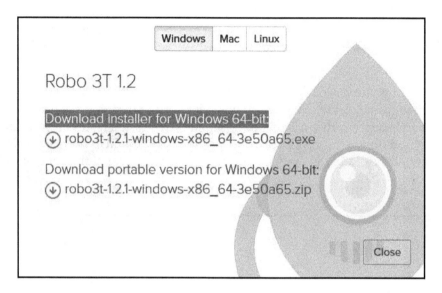

This is going to start a really small download, just 17 MB, and we can click on **Next** a few times through this one to get Robomongo installed on our machines.

I'll start the process, confirming installation and clicking on **Next** just a couple of times. There's no need to do anything custom inside the settings. We'll run the installer with all of the default settings applied. Now we can actually run the program by finishing all the steps in the installer. When you run Robomongo, you'll be greeted with a **MongoDB Connections** screen:

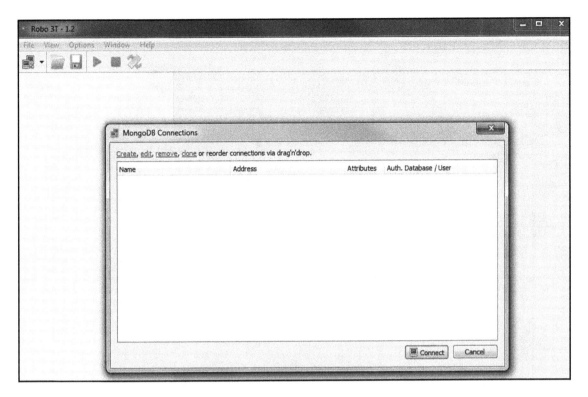

This screen lets you configure all of the connections for Robomongo. You might have a local connection for your local database, and you might have a connection to a real URL where your actual production data is stored. We'll get into all that later.

For now, we'll click on **Create**. By default, your `localhost` address and your `27017` port do not need to be changed:

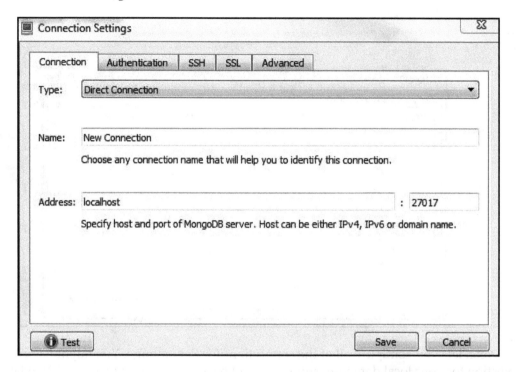

All I'm going to do is to change the name so that it's a little easier to identify. I'll go with `Local Mongo Database`. Now, we can save our new connection and actually connect to the database by simply double-clicking on it. When we do that, we get a little tree view of our database. We have this `test` database; this is the one that's created by default, which we can expand. Then we can expand our `Collections` folder and see the `Todos` collection. This is the collection we created inside the console. I'll right-click on this and go to **View Documents**. When I view the documents, I actually get to view the individual records:

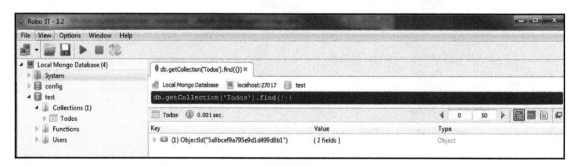

Here, I see my **_id** and **text** properties that have **Create new Node course** sitting in the above image.

If you are seeing this, then this means that you have a local Mongo server running, and it also means that you've successfully inserted data into it.

Summary

In this chapter, you downloaded and ran the MongoDB database server. This means that we have a local database server we can connect to from our Node application. We also installed Robomongo, which lets us connect to our local database so that we can view and manipulate data. This comes in handy when you're debugging or managing data, or doing anything else with your Mongo database. We'll be using it throughout the book, and you'll begin to see why it's valuable in the later chapters. For now though, you are all set up. You are ready to continue on and start building the Todo API.

2
MongoDB, Mongoose, and REST APIs – Part 1

In this chapter, you're going to learn how to connect your Node applications to the MongoDB database you've been running on your local machine. This means that we'll be able to issue database commands right inside of our Node apps to do stuff like insert, update, delete, or read data. This is going to be critical if we're ever going to make that Todo REST API. When someone hits one of our API endpoints, we want to manipulate the database, whether it's reading all of the Todos or adding a new one. Before we can do any of that though, we have to learn the basics.

Connecting to MongoDB and writing data

To connect to our MongoDB database from inside of Node.js, we're going to be using an npm module created by the MongoDB team. It's called node-mongodb-native, but it includes all of the features you'll need to connect to and interact with your database. To get to it, we're going to Google `node-mongodb-native`:

The GitHub repo, which should be the first link, is the one we want—the node-mongodb-native repository—and if we scroll down, we can take a look at a few important links:

MongoDB Node.JS Driver

what	where
documentation	http://mongodb.github.io/node-mongodb-native
api-doc	http://mongodb.github.io/node-mongodb-native/3.0/api
source	https://github.com/mongodb/node-mongodb-native
mongodb	http://www.mongodb.org

Bugs / Feature Requests

Think you've found a bug? Want to see a new feature in `node-mongodb-native` ? Please open a case in our issue management tool, JIRA:

- Create an account and login jira.mongodb.org.
- Navigate to the NODE project jira.mongodb.org/browse/NODE.
- Click **Create Issue** - Please provide as much information as possible about the issue type and how to reproduce it.

First up we have **documentation**, and we also have our **api-docs**; these are going to be critical as we start exploring the features that we have inside of this library. If we scroll down further on this page, we'll find a ton of examples on how to get started. We'll be going through a lot of this stuff in this chapter, but I do want to make you aware of where you can find other resources because the mongodb-native library has a ton of features. There are entire courses dedicated to MongoDB, and they don't even begin to cover everything that's built-in to this library.

We're going to be focusing on the important and common subset of MongoDB that we need for Node.js apps. To get started, let's go ahead and open up the documentations, which are shown in the preceding image. When you go to the docs page, you have to pick your version. We'll be using version 3.0 of the driver, and there's two important links:

- **The Reference link:** This includes guide-like articles, things to get you started, and other various references.
- **The API link:** This includes the details of every single method available to you when you're working with the library. We'll be exploring some of the methods on this link as we start creating our Node Todo API.

For now though, we can get started by creating a new directory for this project, and then we're going to go ahead and install the MongoDB library and connect to the database we have running. I am going to assume that you have your database running for all the sections in this chapter. I have it running in a separate tab in my Terminal.

If you're on Windows, refer to the instructions in the Windows installation section to start your database if you forget. If you're on a Linux or macOS operating system, use the instructions I have already mentioned, and don't forget to also include that `dbpath` argument, which is essential for booting up your MongoDB server.

Creating a directory for the project

To kick things off, I'm going to make a new folder on the Desktop for the Node API. I'll use `mkdir` to create a new folder called `node-todo-api`. Then, I can go ahead and use `cd` to go into that directory, `cd node-todo-api`. And from here, we're going to run `npm init`, which creates our `package.json` file and lets us install our MongoDB library. Once again, we're going to be using enter to skip through all of the options, using the defaults for each:

```
● ● ●                node-todo-api — npm TERM_PROGRAM=Apple_Terminal TERM=xterm-256color — 108×23
description:
entry point: (index.js)
test command:
git repository:
keywords:
author:
license: (ISC)
About to write to /Users/Gary/Desktop/node-todo-api/package.json:

{
  "name": "todo-api",
  "version": "1.0.0",
  "description": "",
  "main": "index.js",
  "scripts": {
    "test": "echo \"Error: no test specified\" && exit 1"
  },
  "author": "",
  "license": "ISC"
}

Is this ok? (yes) □
```

Once we get to the end we can confirm our selections, and now our `package.json` file is created. The next thing we're going to do is open up this directory inside of Atom. It's on the Desktop, `node-todo-api`. Next up, inside of the root of the project we're going to create a new folder, and I'm going to call this folder `playground`. Inside of this folder, we'll store various scripts. They're not going to be scripts related to the Todo API; they'll be scripts related to MongoDB, so I do want to keep them in the folder, but I don't necessarily want them to be part of the app. We'll use the `playground` folder for that, like we have in the past.

In the `playground` folder, let's go ahead and make a new file, and we'll call this file `mongodb-connect.js`. Inside of this file, we're going to get started by loading in the library and connecting to the database. Now in order to do that, we have to install the library. From the Terminal, we can run `npm install` to get that done. The new library name is `mongodb`; all lowercase, no hyphens. Then, we're going to go ahead and specify the version to make sure we're all using the same functionality, `@3.0.2`. This is the most recent version at the time of writing. After the version number, I am going to use the `--save` flag. This is going to save it as a regular dependency, which it already is:

```
npm install mongodb@3.0.2 --save
```

We're going to need this to run the Todo API application.

Connecting the mongodb-connect file to the database

With MongoDB now installed, we can move it to our `mongodb-connect` file and start connecting to the database. The first thing we need to do is pull something out of the library that we just installed, which is the `mongodb` library. What we're looking for is something called the `MongoClient` constructor. The `MongoClient` constructor lets you connect to a Mongo server and issue commands to manipulate the database. Let's go ahead and kick things off by creating a constant called `MongoClient`. We're going to set that equal to `require`, and we're going to require the library we just installed, `mongodb`. From that library, we're going to pull off `MongoClient`:

```
const MongoClient = require('mongodb').MongoClient;
```

With the `MongoClient` now in place, we can call `MongoClient.connect` to connect to the database. This is a method, and it takes two arguments:

- The first argument is a string, and this is going to be the URL where your database lives. Now in a production example, this might be an Amazon Web Services URL or a Heroku URL. In our case, it's going to be a localhost URL. We'll talk about that later.
- The second argument is going to be a callback function. The callback function will fire after the connection has either succeeded or failed, and then we can go ahead and handle things appropriately. If the connection failed, we'll print a message and stop the program. If it succeeded, we can start manipulating the database.

Adding a string as the first argument

For the first argument in our case, we're going to start off with `mongodb://`. When we connect to a MongoDB database, we want to use the mongodb protocol like this:

```
MongoClient.connect('mongodb://')
```

Next up, it's going to be at localhost since we're running it on our local machine, and we have the port, which we have already explored: `27017`. After the port, we need to use / to specify which database we want to connect to. Now, in the previous chapter, we used that test database. This is the default database that MongoDB gives you, but we could go ahead and create a new one. After the /, I'm going to call the database `TodoApp`, just like this:

```
MongoClient.connect('mongodb://localhost:27017/TodoApp');
```

Adding the callback function as the second argument

Next up, we can go ahead and provide the callback function. I'm going to use an ES6 arrow (=>) function, and we're going to get past two arguments. The first one is going to be an error argument. This may or may not exist; just like we've seen in the past, it'll exist if an error actually happened; otherwise it won't. The second argument is going to be the `client` object. This is what we can use to issue commands to read and write data:

```
MongoClient.connect('mongodb://localhost:27017/TodoApp', (err, client) => {

});
```

Error handling in mongodb-connect

Now, before we write any data, I'm going to go ahead and handle any potential errors that come about. I'll do that using an `if` statement. If there is an error, we're going to print a message to the console, letting whoever is looking at the logs know that we were unable to connect to the database server, `console.log`, then inside of quotes put something like `Unable to connect to MongoDB server`. After the `if` statement, we can go ahead and log out a success message, which will be something like `console.log`. Then, inside of quotes, we'll use `Connected to MongoDB server`:

```
MongoClient.connect('mongodb://localhost:27017/TodoApp', (err, client) => {
  if(err){
    console.log('Unable to connect to MongoDB server');
  }
  console.log('Connected to MongoDB server');
});
```

Now, when you're handling errors like this, the success code is going to run even if the error block runs. What we want to do instead is add a `return` statement right before the `console.log('Unable to connect to MongoDB server');` line.

This `return` statement isn't doing anything fancy. All we're doing is using it to prevent the rest of the function from executing. As soon as you return from a function, the program stops, which means if an error does occur, the message will get logged, the function will stop, and we'll never see this `Connected to MongoDB server` message:

```
if(err) {
    return console.log('Unable to connect to MongoDB server');
  }
```

An alternative to using the `return` keyword would be to add an `else` clause and put our success code in an `else` clause, but it's unnecessary. We can just use the `return` syntax, which I prefer.

Now, before we run this file, there is one more thing I want to do. At the very bottom of our callback function, we're going to call a method on db. It's called `client.close`:

```
MongoClient.connect('mongodb://localhost:27017/TodoApp', (err, client) => {
  if(err) {
    return console.log('Unable to connect to MongoDB server');
  }
  console.log('Connected to MongoDB server');
  const db = client.db('TodoApp');
```

```
    client.close();
});
```

This closes the connection with the MongoDB server. Now that we have this in place, we can actually save the `mongodb-connect` file and run it inside of the Terminal. It doesn't do much yet, but it is indeed going to work.

Running the file in the Terminal

Inside the Terminal, we can run the file using `node playground` as the directory, with the file itself being `mongodb-connect.js`:

node playground/mongodb-connect.js

When we run this file, we get `Connected to MongoDB server` printing to the screen:

```
Gary:node-todo-api Gary$ node playground/mongodb-connect.js
Connected to MongoDB server
Gary:node-todo-api Gary$ ▊
```

If we head over into the tab where we have the MongoDB server, we can see we got a new connection: **connection accepted.** As you can see in the following screenshot, that connection was closed down, which is fantastic:

```
UID: a9091af0-74bb-4884-9c1e-f7cde3723cce
2018-02-16T11:27:05.137+0530 I FTDC     [initandlisten] Initializing full-time diagnostic data capture with
directory '/Users/Gary/mongo-data/diagnostic.data'
2018-02-16T11:27:05.166+0530 I NETWORK  [initandlisten] waiting for connections on port 27017
2018-02-16T11:28:27.997+0530 I NETWORK  [listener] connection accepted from 127.0.0.1:50744 #1 (1 connection
 now open)
2018-02-16T11:28:28.017+0530 I NETWORK  [conn1] received client metadata from 127.0.0.1:50744 conn: { driver
: { name: "nodejs", version: "3.0.2" }, os: { type: "Darwin", name: "darwin", architecture: "x64", version:
"17.4.0" }, platform: "Node.js v9.3.0, LE, mongodb-core: 3.0.2" }
2018-02-16T11:28:28.027+0530 I NETWORK  [conn1] end connection 127.0.0.1:50744 (0 connections now open)
▯
```

Using the Mongo library we were able to connect, print a message, and disconnect from the server.

Now, you might have noticed that we changed the database name in the `MongoClient.connect` line in Atom, and we never actually did anything to create it. In MongoDB, unlike other database programs, you don't need to create a database before you start using it. If I want to kick up a new database I simply give it a name, something like `Users`.

Now that I have a `Users` database, I can connect to it and I can manipulate it. There is no need to create that database first. I'm going to go ahead and change the database name back to `TodoApp`. If we head into the Robomongo program and connect to our local database, you'll also see that the only database we have is `test`. The `TodoApp` database was never even created, even though we connected to it. Mongo is not going to create the database until we start adding data into it. We can go ahead and do that right now.

Adding data to the database

Inside of Atom, before our call to `db.close`, we're going to insert a new record into a collection. This is going to be the Todo application. We're going to have two collections in this app:

- a `Todos` collection
- a `Users` collection

We can go ahead and start adding some data to the `Todos` collection by calling `db.collection`. The `db.collection` method takes the string name for the collection you want to insert into as its only argument. Now, like the actual database itself, you don't need to create this collection first. You can simply give it a name, like `Todos`, and you can start inserting into it. There is no need to run any command to create it:

```
db.collection('Todos')
```

Next, we're going to use a method available in our collection called `insertOne`. The `insertOne` method lets you insert a new document into your collection. It takes two arguments:

- The first one is going to be an object. This is going to store the various key-value pairs we want to have in our document.
- The second one is going to be a callback function. This callback function will get fired when things either fail or go well.

You're going to get an error argument, which may or may not exist, and you'll also get the result argument, which is going to be provided if things went well:

```
const MongoClient = require('mongodb').MongoClient;

MongoClient.connect('mongodb://localhost:27017/TodoApp', (err, client) => {
  if(err){
    console.log('Unable to connect to MongoDB server');
  }
  console.log('Connected to MongoDB server');
  const db = client.db('TodoApp');
  db.collection('Todos').insertOne({
    text: 'Something to do',
    completed: false
  }, (err, result) => {
  });
  client.close();
});
```

Inside of the error callback function itself, we can add some code to handle the error, and then we'll add some code to print the object to the screen if it was added successfully. First up, let's add an error handler. Much like we have done previously, we're going to check if the error argument exists. If it does, then we'll simply print a message using the `return` keyword to stop the function from executing. Next, we can use `console.log` to print `Unable to insert todo`. The second argument I'm going to pass to the `console.log` is going to be the actual `err` object itself, so if someone's looking at the logs, they can see exactly what went wrong:

```
db.collection('Todos').insertOne({
  text: 'Something to do',
  completed: false
}, (err, result) => {
  if(err){
    return console.log('Unable to insert todo', err);
  }
```

Next to our `if` statement, we can add our success code. In this case, all we're going to do is pretty-print something to the `console.log` screen, and then I'm going to call `JSON.stringify`, where we're going to go ahead and pass in `result.ops`. The `ops` attribute is going to store all of the docs that were inserted. In this case, we used `insertOne`, so it's just going to be our one document. Then, I can add my other two arguments, which are `undefined` for the filter function, and `2` for the indentation:

```
db.collection('Todos').insertOne({
  text: 'Something to do',
  completed: false
}, (err, result) => {
  if(err){
    return console.log('Unable to insert todo', err);
  }

  console.log(JSON.stringify(result.ops, undefined, 2));
});
```

With this in place, we can now go ahead and execute our file and see what happens. Inside of the Terminal, I'm going to run the following command:

```
node playground/ mongodb-connect.js
```

When I execute the command, we get our success message: `Connected to MongoDB server`. Then, we get an array of documents that were inserted:

```
Gary:node-todo-api Gary$ node playground/mongodb-connect.js
Connected to MongoDB server
[
  {
    "text": "Something to do",
    "completed": false,
    "_id": "5a867e78c3a2d60bef433b06"
  }
]
Gary:node-todo-api Gary$
```

Now as I mentioned, in this case we just inserted one document, and that shows up as shown in the preceding screenshot. We have the `text` property, which gets created by us; we have the `completed` property, which gets created by us; and we have the `_id` property, which gets automatically added by Mongo. The `_id` property is going to be the topic of the following section. We're going to talk in depth about what it is, why it exists and why it's awesome.

For now, we're going to go ahead and just note that it's a unique identifier. It's an ID given to just this document. That is all it takes to insert a document into your MongoDB database using Node.js. We can view this document inside of Robomongo. I'm going to right-click the connection, and click **Refresh**:

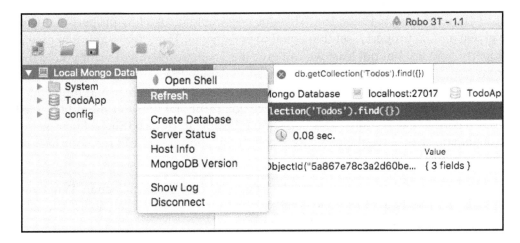

This reveals our brand new `TodoApp` database. If we open that up, we get our `Collections` list. We can then go into the `Collections`, view the documents, and what do we get? We get our one **Todo** item. If we expand it, we can see we have our _id, we have our **text** property, and we have our **completed** Boolean:

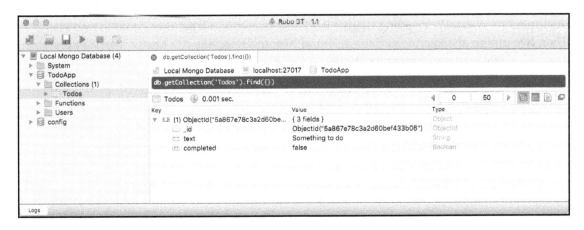

In this case, the Todo is not completed, so the **completed** value is **false**. Now, what I want you to do is add a new record into a collection. This is going to be your challenge for the section.

Adding a new record into a collection

Inside of Atom, what I'd like you to do is take the code all the way from `db.collection` down to the bottom of our callback, and comment it out. Then, we're going to go ahead and add something following it. Right previous `db.close()`, you're going to type `Insert new doc into the Users collection`. This doc is going to have a few properties. I want you to give it a `name` property; set that equal to your name. Then, we're going to give it an `age` property, and last but not least we can give it a `location` string. I want you to insert that doc using `insertOne`. You're going to need to pass in the new collection name into the collection method. Then, further down, you're going to add some error-handling code, and you're going to print the ops to the screen. Once you rerun the file, you should be able to view your record in the Terminal and you should be able to refresh things. Over in Robomongo, you should see the new Users collection, and you should see your user with the name, age, and location you specified.

Hopefully, you were able to insert a new document into the Users collection. What you needed to do in order to get this done is call `db.collection` so we can access the collection we want to insert into, which in this case is `Users`:

```
//Insert new doc into Users(name, age, location)
db.collection('Users')
```

Next up, we have to call a method to manipulate the `Users` collection. We want to insert a new document, so we're going to use `insertOne`, just like we did in the previous sub-section. We're going to pass our two arguments into `insertOne`. The first one is the document to insert. We're going to give it a `name` property; I'll set that equal to `Andrew`. Then, we can go ahead and set the `age` equal to something like `25`. Lastly, we'll set the `location` equal to my current location, `Philadelphia`:

```
//Insert new doc into Users(name, age, location)
db.collection('Users').insertOne({
  name: 'Andrew',
  age: 25,
  location: 'Philadelphia'
}
```

The next argument we want it to pass in is our callback function, which is going to get called with the error object as well as the results. Inside of the callback function itself, we're going to first handle the error. If there was an error, we're going to go ahead and log it to the screen. I'm going to return `console.log`, and then we can put the message: `Unable to insert user`. Then, I'll add the error argument as the second argument for `console.log`. Next up, we can add our success case code. If things go well, all I'm going to do is use `console.log` to print `result.ops` to the screen. This is going to show us all of the records that were inserted:

```
//Insert new doc into Users(name, age, location)
db.collection('Users').insertOne({
  name: 'Andrew',
  age: 25,
  location: 'Philadelphia'
}, (err, result) => {
  if(err) {
    return console.log('Unable to insert user', err);
  }
  console.log(result.ops);
});
```

We can now go ahead and rerun the file inside of the Terminal using the *up* arrow key and the *enter* key:

```
Gary:node-todo-api Gary$ node playground/mongodb-connect.js
Connected to MongoDB server
[ { name: 'Andrew',
    age: 25,
    location: 'Philadelphia',
    _id: 5a868fa51a01c50c6ac3c1b3 } ]
Gary:node-todo-api Gary$
```

We get our array of inserted documents, and we just have one. The `name`, `age`, and `location` properties all come from us, and the `_id` property comes from MongoDB.

Next up, I want you to verify that it was indeed inserted by viewing it in Robomongo. In general, when you add a new collection or a new database, you can just right-click the connection itself, click **Refresh**, and then you should be able to see everything that was added:

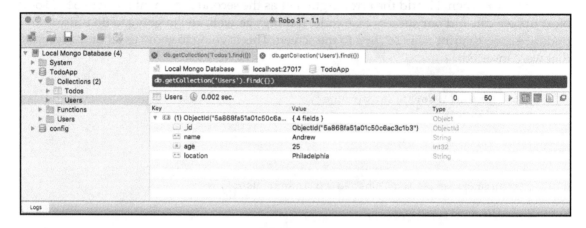

As shown in the preceding screenshot, we have our **Users** collection. I can view the documents for Users. We get our one document with the name set to **Andrew**, age set to **25**, and location set to **Philadelphia**. With this in place, we are now done. We've been able to connect to our MongoDB database using Node.js, and we've also learned how to insert documents using this mongo-native library. In the next section, we're going to take an in-depth look at ObjectIds, exploring exactly what they are and why they're useful.

The ObjectId

Now that you have inserted some documents into your MongoDB collections, I want to take a moment to talk about the `_id` property in the context of MongoDB because it's a little different than the IDs that you're probably used to if you've used other database systems, like Postgres or MySQL.

The _id property in the context of MongoDB

To kick off our discussion of the _id property, let's go ahead and rerun the mongodb-connect file. This is going to insert a new document into the Users collection, like we've defined in the db.collection line. I'm going to go ahead and do that by running the file through the node. It's in the playground folder, and the file itself is called mongodb-connect.js:

```
node playground/mongodb-connect.js
```

I'm going to run the command, and we're going to print out the document that got inserted:

```
Gary:node-todo-api Gary$ node playground/mongodb-connect.js
Connected to MongoDB server
[ { name: 'Andrew',
    age: 25,
    location: 'Philadelphia',
    _id: 5a868fa51a01c50c6ac3c1b3 } ]
Gary:node-todo-api Gary$
```

As we've seen in the past, we get our three attributes as well as the one added by Mongo.

The first thing you'll notice about this is that it is not an auto incrementing integer, kind of like it is for Postgres or MySQL, where the first record has an ID of 1 and the second one has an ID of 2. Mongo does not use this approach. Mongo was designed to scale out really easily. Scaling out means that you can add on more database servers to handle that extra load.

Imagine you have a web app that gets about 200 users a day and your current servers are ready for that traffic. Then, you get picked up by some news outlet and 10,000 people flood your site. With MongoDB, it's really easy to kick up new database servers to handle that extra load. When we use a randomly generated ID, we don't need to constantly communicate with the other database servers to check what the highest incrementing value is. Is it 7? Is it 17? It doesn't really matter; we're simply going to generate a new random ObjectId and use that for the document's unique identifier.

Now, the ObjectId itself is made up of a few different things. It's a 12-byte value. The first four bytes are a timestamp; we'll talk about that later. That means that we have a timestamp built into the data that refers to the moment in time the ID was created. This means that in our documents, we don't need to have a createdAt field; it's already encoded in the ID.

The next three bytes are machine identifiers. This means that if two computers generate ObjectIds, their machine ID is going to be different, and this is going to ensure that the ID is unique. Next up, we have two bytes, the process ID, which is just another way to create a unique identifier. Last up, we have a 3-byte counter. This is similar to what MySQL would do. This is only 3 bytes of the ID. As we have already mentioned, we have a timestamp which is going to be unique; a machine identifier; a process ID; and lastly, just a random value. That is what makes up an ObjectId.

The ObjectId is the default value for `_id`. If nothing is provided, you can indeed do whatever you like with that property. For example, inside of the `mongodb-connect` file, I can specify an `_id` property. I'm going to give it a value, so let's go with `123`; add a comma at the end; and that is perfectly legal:

```
db.collection('Users').insertOne({
  _id: 123,
  name: 'Andrew',
  age: 25,
  location: 'Philadelphia'
}
```

We can save the file, and rerun the script using the *up* arrow key and the *enter* key:

```
Gary:node-todo-api Gary$ node playground/mongodb-connect.js
Connected to MongoDB server
[ { _id: 123, name: 'Andrew', age: 25, location: 'Philadelphia' } ]
Gary:node-todo-api Gary$
```

We get our record, where the `_id` property is `123`. The `ObjectId` is the default way MongoDB creates IDs, but you can do anything you like for ID creation. Inside of Robomongo, we can give our **Users** collection a refresh, and we get our documents:

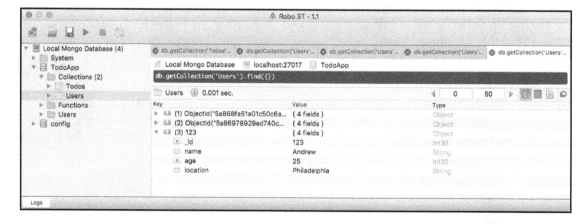

We have the one we created in the previous section and the two we just made now, all with a unique identifier. This is why unique IDs are really important. In this example, we have three properties: **name**, **age** and **location**, and they're the same for all the records. This is a reasonable thing to do. Imagine two people need to do the same thing, like buy groceries. That string alone is not going to be enough to uniquely identify a Todo. ObjectIds, on the other hand, are going to be unique, and that is what we're going to use to associated things like Todos with things like Users.

Next up, I want to take a look at some things we can do with the ID inside of our code. As I mentioned earlier, a timestamp is embedded inside of here, and we can actually pull that out. Inside of Atom, what we're going to do is remove the _id property. The timestamp is only going to be available when you're using the ObjectId. Then, inside of our callback, we can go ahead and print the timestamp to the screen.

```
db.collection('Users').insertOne({
  name: 'Andrew',
  age: 25,
  location: 'Philadelphia'
}, (err, result) => {
  if(err) {
    return console.log('Unable to insert user', err);
  }

  console.log(result.ops);
});
```

If you remember, result.ops is an array of all the documents that got inserted. We're only inserting one, so I'm going to access the first item in the array, and then we're going to access the _id property. This is going to do exactly what you might think:

```
console.log(result.ops[0]._id);
```

If we save the file and rerun the script over from the Terminal, all we get is the ObjectId printing to the screen:

```
[Gary:node-todo-api Gary$ node playground/mongodb-connect.js
Connected to MongoDB server
5a8698e47bcb000cb63cb05a
Gary:node-todo-api Gary$ 
```

Now though, we can call a method on the _id property.

Calling the .getTimestamp function

What we're going to call is `.getTimestamp`. The `getTimestamp` is a function, but it doesn't take any arguments. It simply returns the timestamp that the ObjectId was created at:

```
console.log(result.ops[0]._id.getTimestamp());
```

Now, if we go ahead and rerun our program, we get a timestamp:

```
Gary:node-todo-api Gary$ node playground/mongodb-connect.js
Connected to MongoDB server
2018-02-16T08:41:27.000Z
Gary:node-todo-api Gary$
```

In the preceding screenshot, I can see that the ObjectId was created on February 16th 2016 at 08:41 Z, so this timestamp is indeed correct. This is a fantastic way to figure out exactly when a document was created.

Now, we don't have to rely on MongoDB to create our ObjectIds. Inside of the MongoDB library, they actually give us a function we can run to make an ObjectId whenever we like. For the moment, let's go ahead and comment out our call to insert one.

At the very top of the file, we're going to change our import statement to load in something new off of MongoDB, and we're going to do this using an ES6 feature known as object destructuring. Let's take a quick second to talk about that before we actually go ahead and use it.

Using object destructuring ES6

Object destructuring lets you pull out properties from an object in order to create variables. This means that if we have an object called `user` and it's set equal to an object with a `name` property set to `andrew` and an age property set to `25`, as shown in the following code:

```
const MongoClient = require('mongodb').MongoClient;

var user = {name: 'andrew', age: 25};
```

We can easily pull out one of these into a variable. Let's say, for example, we want to grab name and create a `name` variable. To do that using object destructuring in ES6, we're going to make a variable and then we're going to wrap it inside of curly braces. We're going to provide the name we want to pull out; this is also going to be the variable name. Then, we're going to set it equal to whatever object we want to destructure. In this case, that is the `user` object:

```
var user = {name: 'andrew', age: 25};
var {name} = user;
```

We have successfully destructured the `user` object, pulling off the `name` property, creating a new `name` variable, and setting it equal to whatever the value is. This means I can use the `console.log` statement to print `name` to the screen:

```
var user = {name: 'andrew', age: 25};
var {name} = user;
console.log(name);
```

I'm going to rerun the script and we get `andrew`, which is exactly what you'd expect because that is the value of the `name` property:

```
Gary:node-todo-api Gary$ node playground/mongodb-connect.js
andrew
Connected to MongoDB server
Gary:node-todo-api Gary$
```

ES6 destructuring is a fantastic way to make new variables from an object's properties. I'm going to go ahead and delete this example, and at the top of the code, we're going to change our `require` statement so that it uses destructuring.

Before we add anything new, let's go ahead and take the MongoClient statement and switch it to destructuring; then, we'll worry about grabbing that new thing that's going to let us make ObjectIds. I'm going to copy and paste the line and comment out the old one so we have it for reference.

```
// const MongoClient = require('mongodb').MongoClient;
const MongoClient = require('mongodb').MongoClient;
```

What we're going to do is remove our `.MongoClient` call after `require`. There's no need to pull off that attribute because we're going to be using destructuring instead. That means over here we can use destructuring, which requires us to add our curly braces, and we can pull off any property from the MongoDB library.

```
const {MongoClient} = require('mongodb');
```

In this case, the only property we had was `MongoClient`. This creates a variable called `MongoClient`, setting it equal to the `MongoClient` property of `require('mongodb')`, which is exactly what we did in the previous `require` statement.

Creating a new instance of objectID

Now that we have some destructuring in place, we can easily pull more things off of MongoDB. We can add a comma and specify something else we want to pull off. In this case, we're going to pull off uppercase, `ObjectID`.

```
const {MongoClient, ObjectID} = require('mongodb');
```

This `ObjectID` constructor function lets us make new ObjectIds on the fly. We can do anything we like with them. Even if we're not using MongoDB as our database, there is some value in creating and using ObjectIds to uniquely identify things. Next, we can make a new ObjectId by first creating a variable. I'll call it `obj`, and we'll set it equal to `new ObjectID`, calling it as a function:

```
const {MongoClient, ObjectID} = require('mongodb');

var obj = new ObjectID();
```

Using the `new` keyword, we can create a new instance of `ObjectID`. Next up, we can go ahead and log that to the screen using `console.log(obj)`. This is a regular ObjectId:

```
console.log(obj);
```

If we rerun the file over from the Terminal, we get exactly what you'd expect:

```
Gary:node-todo-api Gary$ node playground/mongodb-connect.js
5a869c6a8353400cd9161760
Connected to MongoDB server
Gary:node-todo-api Gary$
```

We get an ObjectId-looking thing. If I rerun it again, we get a new one; they are both unique:

```
Gary:node-todo-api Gary$ node playground/mongodb-connect.js
5a869cbe9c794c0ce0597329
Connected to MongoDB server
Gary:node-todo-api Gary$
```

Using this technique, we can incorporate ObjectIds anywhere we like. We could even generate our own, setting them as the `_id` property for our documents, although I find it much easier to let MongoDB handle that heavy lifting for us. I'm going to go ahead and remove the following two lines since we won't actually be using this code in the script:

```
var obj = new ObjectID();
console.log(obj);
```

We have learned a bit about ObjectIds, what they are, and why they're useful. In the following sections, we're going to be taking a look at other ways we can work with MongoDB. We'll learn how to read, remove, and update our documents.

Fetching data

Now that you know how to insert data into your database, let's go ahead and talk about how we can fetch data out of it. We're going to be using this technique in the Todo API. People are going to want to populate a list of all the Todo items they need, and they might want to fetch the details about an individual Todo item. All of this is going to require that we can query the MongoDB database.

Fetching todos in Robomongo file

Now, we're going to create a new file based off of `mongodb-connect`. In this new file, instead of inserting records, we'll fetch records from the database. I'm going to create a duplicate, calling this new file `mongodb-find`, because `find` is the method we're going to use to query that database. Next, we can go ahead and remove all of the commented-out code that currently inserts records. Let's get started by trying to fetch all of the Todos out of our Todos collection. Now, if I head over to Robomongo and open up the `Todos` collection, we have just one record:

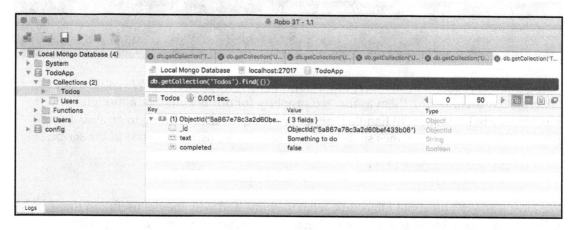

In order to make this querying a little more interesting, we're going to go ahead and add a second one. Right in the Robomongo window, I can click **Insert Document**. Robomongo can delete, insert, update, and read all of your documents, and this makes it a fantastic tool for debugging. We can add a new document on the fly, with a `text` property equal to `Walk the dog`, and we can also tack on a `completed` value. I'm going to set `completed` equal to `false`:

```
{
    text : "Walk the dog",
    completed : false
}
```

Now by default, we're not going to provide an _id prop. This is going to let MongoDB automatically generate that ObjectId, and right here we have our two Todos:

With this in place, let's go ahead and run our first query inside of Atom.

The find method

In Atom, what we're going to do is access the collection, just like we did inside of the mongodb-connect file using db.collection, passing in the collection name as the string. This collection is going to be the Todos collection. Now, we're going to go ahead and use a method available on collections called find. By default, we can call find with no arguments:

```
db.collection('Todos').find();
```

This means we're not providing a query, so we're not saying we want to fetch all Todos that are completed or not completed. We're just saying we want to fetch all Todos: everything, regardless of its values. Now, calling find is only the first step. find returns a MongoDB cursor, and this cursor is not the actual documents themselves. There could be a couple of thousand, and that would be really inefficient. It's actually a pointer to those documents, and the cursor has a ton of methods. We can use those methods to get our documents.

One of the most common cursor methods we're going to be using is `.toArray`. It does exactly what you think it does. Instead of having a cursor, we have an array of the documents. This means we have an array of objects. They have ID properties, text properties, and completed properties. This `toArray` method gets us exactly what we want back, which is the documents. `toArray` returns a promise. This means we can tack on a `then` call, we can add our callback, and when things go right, we can do something like print those documents to the screen.

```
db.collection('Todos').find().toArray().then((docs) => {
});
```

We're going to get the documents as the first and only argument here, and we can also add an error handler. We'll get passed an error argument, and we can simply print something to the screen like `console.log(Unable to fetch todos);` as the second argument, we'll pass in the `err` object:

```
db.collection('Todos').find().toArray().then((docs) => {
}, (err) => {
  console.log('Unable to fetch todos', err);
});
```

Now, for the success case, what we're going to do is print the documents to the screen. I'm going to go ahead and use `console.log` to print a little message, `Todos`, and then I'll call `console.log` again. This time, we'll be using the `JSON.stringify` technique. I'll be passing in the documents, `undefined` for our filter function and 2 for our spacing.

```
db.collection('Todos').find().toArray().then((docs) => {
  console.log('Todos');
  console.log(JSON.stringify(docs, undefined, 2));
}, (err) => {
  console.log('Unable to fetch todos', err);
});
```

We now have a script that is capable of fetching the documents, converting them into an array, and printing them to the screen. Now, for the time being, I'm going to comment out the `db.close` method. Currently, that would interfere with our previous bit of code. Our final code would look as follows:

```
//const MongoClient = require('mongodb').MongoClient;
const {MongoClient, ObjectID} = require('mongodb');

MongoClient.connect('mongodb://localhost:27017/TodoApp', (err, client) => {
  if(err){
    console.log('Unable to connect to MongoDB server');
  }
```

```
console.log('Connected to MongoDB server');
const db = client.db('TodoApp');
db.collection('Todos').find().toArray().then((docs) => {
  console.log('Todos');
  console.log(JSON.stringify(docs, undefined, 2));
}, (err) => {
  console.log('Unable to fetch todos', err);
});
//client.close();
});
```

Save the file and run it from the Terminal. Inside of the Terminal, I'm going to go ahead and run our script. Obviously, since we connected to the database with Robomongo, it is running somewhere; it's running in this other tab. In the other tab, I can run the script. We're going to run it through `node`; it's in the `playground` folder, and the file itself is called `mongodb-find.js`:

node playground/mongodb-find.js

When I execute this file, we're going to get our results:

```
Gary:node-todo-api Gary$ node playground/mongodb-find.js
Connected to MongoDB server
Todos
[
  {
    "_id": "5a867e78c3a2d60bef433b06",
    "text": "Something to do",
    "completed": false
  },
  {
    "_id": "5a869ebdbaa6685dd161d2e5",
    "text": "Walk the dog",
    "completed": false
  }
]
```

We have our `Todos` array with our two documents. We have our `_id`, our `text` properties, and our `completed` Boolean values. We now have a way to query our data right inside of Node.js. Now, this is a very basic query. We fetch everything in the `Todos` array, regardless of whether or not it has certain values.

Writing a query to fetch certain values

In order to query based on certain values, let's go ahead and switch up our `Todos`. Currently, both of them have a `completed` value equal to `false`. Let's go ahead and change the `Walk the dog` completed value to `true` so we can try to just query items that aren't completed. Over in Robomongo, I'm going to right-click the document and click **Edit Document**, and there we can edit the values. I'm going to change the `completed` value from `false` to `true`, and then I can save the record:

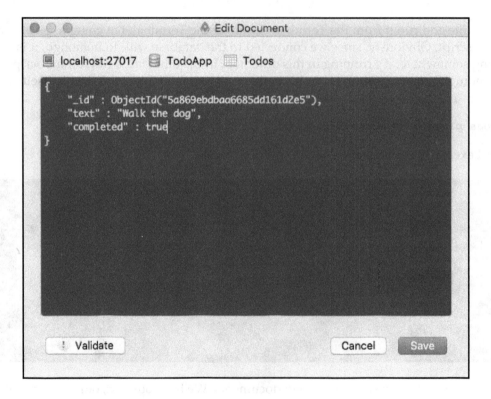

Inside of the Terminal, I can rerun the script to prove that it has changed. I'm going to shut down the script by running *control + C*, and then I can rerun it:

```
Gary:node-todo-api Gary$ node playground/mongodb-find.js
Connected to MongoDB server
Todos
[
  {
    "_id": "5a867e78c3a2d60bef433b06",
    "text": "Something to do",
    "completed": false
  },
  {
    "_id": "5a869ebdbaa6685dd161d2e5",
    "text": "Walk the dog",
    "completed": true
  }
]
```

As shown in the preceding screenshot, we have our two `Todos`, one with a `completed` value of `false` and one with a `completed` value of `true`. By default, a Todo app is probably only going to show you the `Todos` collection you haven't completed. The ones you have completed, like `Walk the dog`, will probably be hidden, although they could be accessible if you clicked a button like **Show all Todos**. Let's go ahead and write a query that just fetches the `Todos` collection that have a `completed` status set to `false`.

Writing a query to fetch completed todos

To get this done, inside of Atom, we're going to make a change to how we call find. Instead of passing in 0 arguments, we're going to pass in 1. This is what's known as our query. We can start specifying how we want to query the `Todos` collection. For example, maybe we want to query only `Todos` that have a `completed` value equal to `false`. All we have to do to query by value is set up the key-value pairs, as shown here:

```
db.collection('Todos').find({completed: false}).toArray().then((docs) => {
```

If I rerun our script over in the Terminal after shutting it down, we get just our one Todo item:

```
Gary:node-todo-api Gary$ node playground/mongodb-find.js
Connected to MongoDB server
Todos
[
  {
    "_id": "5a867e78c3a2d60bef433b06",
    "text": "Something to do",
    "completed": false
  }
]
```

We have our item with the `text` equal to `Something to do`. It has a `completed` status of `false`, so it shows up. Our other Todo with a `text` property of `Walk the dog` is not showing up because that one has been completed. It doesn't match the query, so MongoDB does not return it. This is going to come in handy as we start querying our documents based off of completed values, text properties, or IDs. Let's take a quick moment to look at how we can query one of our `Todos` by ID.

Qureying todos by id

The first thing we need to do is remove everything from our query object; we no longer want to query by the `completed` value. Instead, we're going to query by the `_id` property.

Now, in order to illustrate this, I'm going to grab the ID of the Todo with the `completed` value of `false` from the Terminal. I'm going to copy it using *command + C*. If you're on Windows or Linux, you might need to right-click after highlighting the ID, and click **Copy text**. Now that I have the text inside of the clipboard, I can head over to the query itself. Now, if we try to add the ID like this:

```
db.collection('Todos').find({_id: ''}).toArray().then((docs) => {
```

It is not going to work as expected because what we have inside of the ID property is not a string. It's an ObjectId, which means that we need to use the `ObjectID` constructor function that we imported previously in order to create an ObjectId for the query.

To illustrate how that's going to happen, I'm going to go ahead and indent our object. This is going to make it a little easier to read and edit.

```
db.collection('Todos').find({
    _id: '5a867e78c3a2d60bef433b06'
}).toArray().then((docs) => {
```

Now, I'm going to remove the string and call `new ObjectID`. The `new ObjectID` constructor does take an argument: the ID, in this case, we have it stored as a string. This is going to work as expected.

```
db.collection('Todos').find({
    _id: new ObjectID('5a867e78c3a2d60bef433b06');
})
```

What we're doing here is we're querying the Todos collection, looking for any records that have an `_id` property equal to the ID we have. Now, I can go ahead and save this file, give things a refresh by running the script again, and we'll get the exact same Todo:

```
Gary:node-todo-api Gary$ node playground/mongodb-find.js
Connected to MongoDB server
Todos
[
  {
    "_id": "5a867e78c3a2d60bef433b06",
    "text": "Something to do",
    "completed": false
  }
]
```

I can go ahead and change it for the `Walk the dog` Todo by copying the string value, pasting that inside of the ObjectID constructor function, and rerunning the script. When I do this, I get the `Walk the dog` Todo returned because that was the ObjectId I queried.

Now, querying in this fashion is one of the ways we'll be using find, but there are other methods other than `toArray` that are available on our cursors. We can explore other ones by heading over to the docs for the native driver. Inside of Chrome, have the MongoDB docs pulled up—these are the docs I showed you how to access in the previous chapter—and on the left-hand side, we have the **Cursor** section.

If you click that, we can view a list of all the methods available to us on that cursor:

This is what comes back from find. At the very bottom of the list, we have our `toArray` method. The one that we're going to look at right now is called count. From previous, you can go ahead and click **count**; it's going to bring you to the documentation; the documentation for the native driver is actually really good. There is a complete list of all the arguments that you can provide. Some of them are optional, some of them are required, and there is usually a real-world example. Next, we can figure out exactly how to use `count`.

Implementing the count method

Now, we're going to go ahead and implement count over inside of Atom. What I'm going to do is take the current query, copy it to the clipboard, and then comment it out. I'm going to go ahead and replace our call to `toArray` with a call to `count`. Let's go ahead and remove the query that we pass in to find. What we're going to do here is count up all of the Todos in the `Todos` collection. Instead of having a call to `toArray`, we're going to have a call to count instead.

```
db.collection('Todos').find({}).count().then((count) => {
```

As you saw inside of the examples for count, they call count like this: calling count, passing in a callback function that gets called with an error, or the actual count. You can also have a promise as a way to access that data, which is exactly what we did with `toArray`. In our case, instead of passing a callback function like this, we're going to use the promise instead. We already have the promise set up. All we need to do to fix this is change `docs` to `count`, and then we're going to remove the `console.log` caller where we print the docs to the screen. Right after we print Todos, we're going to print `Todos count`, with a colon passing in the value.

```
db.collection('Todos').find({}).count().then((count) => {
    console.log('Todos count:');
}, (err) => {
    console.log('Unable to fetch todos', err);
});
```

This is not a template string, but I am going to go ahead and swap it out with one, replacing the quotes with `` ` ``. Now, I can pass in the `count`.

```
db.collection('Todos').find({}).count().then((count) => {
    console.log(`Todos count: ${count}`);
}, (err) => {
    console.log('Unable to fetch todos', err);
});
```

Now that we have this in place, we have a way to count up all of the Todos in the `Todos` collection. Inside the Terminal, I'm going to go ahead and shut down our previous script and rerun it:

```
[Gary:node-todo-api Gary$ node playground/mongodb-find.js
Connected to MongoDB server
Todos count: 2
```

We get `Todos count` too, which is correct. The cursor that we have, a call to find, returns everything in the Todos collection. If you count all of that up, you're going to get those two Todo items.

Once again, these are `count` and `toArray`; they're just a subset of all of the awesome methods you have available to you. We will be using other methods, whether it be the MongoDB native driver or, as you'll see later, the library Mongoose, but for now let's go ahead and do a challenge, given what you know.

Querying users collection

To get started, let's head into Robomongo, open up the **Users** collection, and take a look at all the documents we have inside of there. We currently have five. If you don't have the exact same number or yours are a little different, that's fine. I'm going to highlight them, right-click them, and click **Expand Recursively**. This is going to show me all of the key-value pairs for each document:

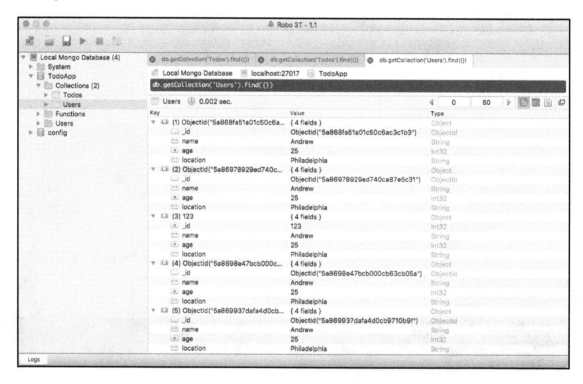

Currently, aside from the ID, they're all identical. The name's Andrew, the age is 25, and the location is Philadelphia. I'm going to tweak the name property for two of them. I'm going to right-click the first document, and change the name to something like `Jen`. Then, I'll go ahead and do the same thing for the second document. I'm going to edit that document and change the name from `Andrew` to `Mike`. Now I have one document with a name of `Jen`, one with `Mike`, and three with `Andrew`.

We're going to query our users, looking for all of the users with the name equal to the name that you provided in the script. In this case, I'm going to try to query for all documents in the `Users` collection where the name is `Andrew`. Then, I'm going to print them into the screen, and I will expect to get three back. The two with the names `Jen` and `Mike` should not show up.

The first thing we need to do is fetch from the collection. This is going to be the `Users` collection as opposed to the `Todos` collection we've used in this chapter. In the `db.collection`, we're looking for the `Users` collection and now we're going to go ahead and call `find`, passing in our query. We want a query, fetching all documents where the name is equal to the string `Andrew`.

```
db.collection('Users').find({name: 'Andrew'})
```

This is going to return the cursor. In order to actually get the documents, we have to call `toArray`. We now have a promise; we can attach a `then` call onto `toArray` to do something with the docs. The documents are going to come back as the first argument in our success handler, and right inside of the function itself we can print the docs to the screen. I'm going to go ahead and use `console.log(JSON.stringify())`, passing in our three classic arguments: the object itself, `docs`, `undefined`, and 2 for formatting:

```
db.collection('Users').find({name: 'Andrew'}).toArray().then((docs) => {
  console.log(JSON.stringify(docs, undefined, 2));
});
```

With this in place, we have now done. We have a query, and it should work. We can test it by running it from the Terminal. Inside the Terminal, I'm going to go ahead and shut down the previous connection and rerun the script:

```
Gary:node-todo-api Gary$ node playground/mongodb-find.js
Connected to MongoDB server
[
  {
    "_id": 123,
    "name": "Andrew",
    "age": 25,
    "location": "Philadelphia"
  },
  {
    "_id": "5a8698e47bcb000cb63cb05a",
    "name": "Andrew",
    "age": 25,
    "location": "Philadelphia"
  },
  {
    "_id": "5a869937dafa4d0cb9710b9f",
    "name": "Andrew",
    "age": 25,
    "location": "Philadelphia"
  }
]
```

When I do this, I get my three documents back. All of them have a `name` equal to `Andrew`, which is correct because of the query we set up. Notice the documents with a name equal to `Mike` or `Jen` are nowhere to be found.

We now know how to insert and query data from the database. Up next, we're going to take a look at how we can remove and update documents.

Setting up the repo

Before we go any further, I do want to add version control to this project. In this section, we're going to create a new repo locally, make a new GitHub repository, and push our code to that GitHub repository. If you're already familiar with Git or GitHub, you can go ahead and do that on your own; you don't need to go through this section. If you're new to Git and it doesn't make sense just yet, that's also fine. Simply follow along, and we'll go through the whole process.

This section is going to be really simple; nothing MongoDB- related here. To get started, I am going to go ahead and initialize a new Git repository from the Terminal by using `git init`. This is going to initialize a new repository, and I can always run `git status` like this to take a look at the files that are untracked:

```
[Gary:node-todo-api Gary$ git init
Initialized empty Git repository in /Users/Gary/Desktop/node-todo-api/.git/
[Gary:node-todo-api Gary$ git status
On branch master

No commits yet

Untracked files:
  (use "git add <file>..." to include in what will be committed)

        node_modules/
        package-lock.json
        package.json
        playground/

nothing added to commit but untracked files present (use "git add" to track)
Gary:node-todo-api Gary$
```

Here we have our `playground` folder, which we want to add under version control, and we have `package.json`. We also have `node_modules`. We do not want to track this directory. This contains all of our npm libraries. To ignore `node_modules`, in Atom we're going to make the `.gitignore` file in the root of our project. If you remember, this lets you specify files and folders that you want to leave out of your version control. I'm going to create a new file called `.gitignore`. In order to ignore the `node_modules` directory, all we have to do is type it exactly as it's shown here.

```
node_modules/
```

I'm going to save the file and rerun `git status` from the Terminal. We get the `.gitignore` folder showing up, and the `node_modules` folder is nowhere in sight:

```
[Gary:node-todo-api Gary$ git status
On branch master

No commits yet

Untracked files:
  (use "git add <file>..." to include in what will be committed)

        .gitignore
        package-lock.json
        package.json
        playground/

nothing added to commit but untracked files present (use "git add" to track)
Gary:node-todo-api Gary$
```

The next thing we're going to do is make our first commit, using two commands. First up, I'm going to use `git add .` to add everything to the next commit. Then, I can make the commit using `git commit` with the -m flag. A good message for this commit would be `Init commit`:

```
git add .
git commit -m 'Init commit'
```

Now before we go, I do want to make a GitHub repository and get this code up there. This is going to require me to open up the browser and go to `github.com`. Once you're logged in we can make a new repo. I'm going to make a new repo and give it a name:

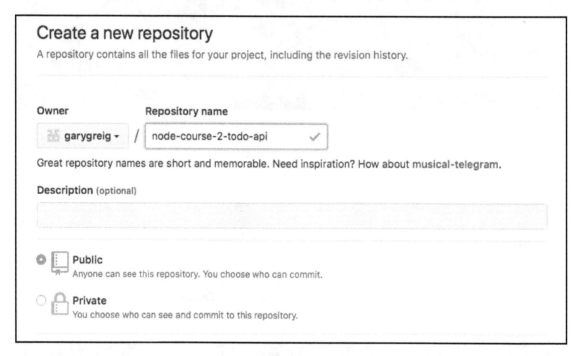

I'm going to go with `node-course-2-todo-api`. You can name yours something else if you wish. I'm going to go with this one to keep the course files organized. Now I can go ahead and create this repository, and as you may recall, GitHub actually gives us a few helpful commands:

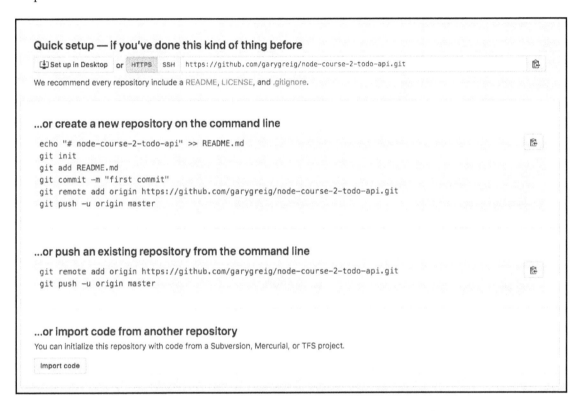

In this case, we're pushing an existing repository from the command line. We already went through the steps of initializing the repository, adding our files and making our first commit. That means I can take the following two lines, copy them, head over to the Terminal, and paste them in:

```
git remote add origin
https://github.com/garygreig/node-course-2-todo-api.git
git push -u origin master
```

You might need to do these one at a time, depending on your operating system. On the Mac, when I try to paste in multiple commands it's going to run all but the last, and then I just have to hit enter to run the last one. Take a moment to knock that out for your operating system. You might need to run it as one command, or you might be able to paste it all in and hit *enter*. Either way, what we have here is our code pushed up to GitHub. I can prove that it's pushed up by refreshing the repository page:

Right there we have all of our source code, the `.gitignore` file, `package.json`, and we have our `playground` directory with our MongoDB scripts.

That's it for this section. We'll explore how to delete data from a MongoDB collection in the next section.

Deleting documents

In this section, you're going to learn how to delete documents from your MongoDB collections. Before we get into that, in order to explore the methods that let us delete multiple documents or just one, we want to create a few more Todos. Currently, the `Todos` collection only has two items, and we're going to need a few more in order to play around with all these methods involving deletion.

Now, I do have two. I'm going to go ahead and create a third by right-clicking and then going to **Insert Document....** We'll make a new document with a `text` property equal to something like `Eat lunch`, and we'll set `completed` equal to `false`:

```
{
    text: 'Eat lunch',
    completed: false
}
```

Now before we save this, I am going to copy it to the clipboard. We're going to create a few duplicate Todos so we can see how we can delete items based off of specific criteria. In this case, we're going to be deleting multiple Todos with the same text value. I'm going to copy that to the clipboard, click **Save**, and then I'll create two more with the exact same structure. Now we have three Todos that are identical except for the ID, and we have two that have unique **text** properties:

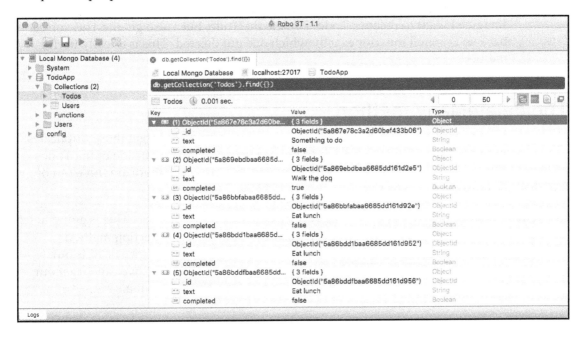

Let's go ahead and move into Atom and start writing some code.

Exploring methods to delete data

I'm going to duplicate the `mongodb-find` file, creating a brand-new file called `mongodb-delete.js`. In here, we'll explore the methods for deleting data. I'm also going to remove all of the queries that we set up in the previous section. I am going to keep the `db.close` method commented out, as once again we don't want to close the connection just yet; it's going to interfere with these statements we're about to write.

Now, there are three methods that we'll be using in order to remove data.

- The first one is going to be `deleteMany`. The `deleteMany` method will let us target many documents and remove them.
- We'll also be using `deleteOne`, which targets one document and removes it.
- And finally, we'll be using `findOneAndDelete`. The `findOneAndDelete` method lets you remove an individual item and it also returns those values. Imagine I want to delete a Todo. I delete the Todo, but I also get the Todo object back so I can tell the user exactly which one got deleted. This is a really useful method.

The deleteMany method

Now, we're going to start off with `deleteMany`, and we're going to target those duplicates we just created. The goal in this section, is to delete every single Todo inside of the Todos collection that has a `text` property equal to `Eat lunch`. Currently, there are three out of five that fit that criteria.

In Atom, we can go ahead and kick things off by doing `db.collection`. This is going to let us target our Todos collection. Now, we can go ahead and use the collection method `deleteMany`, passing in the arguments. In this case, the only argument we need is our object, and this object is just like the object we passed to find. With this, we can target our Todos. In this case, we're going to delete every Todo where the `text` equals `Eat lunch`.

```
//deleteMany
db.collection('Todos').deleteMany({text: 'Eat lunch'});
```

We didn't use any punctuation in RoboMongo, so we're also going to avoid punctuation over in Atom; it needs to be exactly the same.

Now that we have this in place, we could go ahead and tack on a `then` call to do something when it either succeeds or fails. For now, we'll just add a success case. We are going to get a result argument passed back to the callback, and we can print that to the `console.log(result)` screen, and we'll take a look at exactly what is in this result object a bit later.

```
//deleteMany
db.collection('Todos').deleteMany({text: 'Eat lunch'}).then((result) => {
  console.log(result);
});
```

With this in place, we now have a script that deletes all Todos where the text value is `Eat lunch`. Let's go ahead and run it, and see exactly what happens. In the Terminal, I'm going to run this file. It's in the `playground` folder, and we just called it `mongodb-delete.js`:

node playground/mongodb-delete.js

Now when I run it, we get a lot of output:

```
Gary:node-todo-api Gary$ node playground/mongodb-delete.js
Connected to MongoDB server
CommandResult {
  result: { n: 3, ok: 1 },
  connection:
   Connection {
     domain: null,
     _events:
      { error: [Function],
        close: [Function],
        timeout: [Function],
        parseError: [Function] },
     _eventsCount: 4,
     _maxListeners: undefined,
     options:
      { host: 'localhost',
        port: 27017,
        size: 5,
```

A really important piece of output, the only important piece actually, is up at the very top. If you scroll to the top, what you're going to see is this `result` object. We get `ok` set to 1, which means things did go as expected, and we get n set to 3. n is the number of records that were deleted. In this case, we had three Todos that match that criteria, so three Todos were deleted. This is how you can target and delete many Todos.

The deleteOne Method

Now, aside from `deleteMany`, we have `deleteOne`, and `deleteOne` works exactly the same as `deleteMany`, only it deletes the first item it sees that matches the criteria and then it stops.

To illustrate exactly how this works, we're going to create two items inside of our collection. If I give things a refresh, you will see that we now only have two documents:

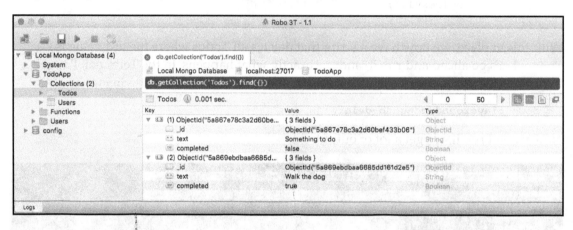

These are the ones we started with. I'm going to insert documents again using the same data that's already in my clipboard. This time we'll just make two document, two that are identical.

The deleteOne method

The goal here is to use `deleteOne` to delete the document where the text equals `Eat lunch`, but since we're using `deleteOne` and not `deleteMany`, one of these should stay around and one of them should go away.

Back inside of Atom, we can go ahead and get started by calling `db.collection` with the collection name we want to target. In this case it's `Todos` again, and we're going to use `deleteOne`. The `deleteOne` method takes that same criteria. We're going to target documents where `text` equals `Eat lunch`.

This time though, instead of deleting multiple documents we're just going to delete the one, and we are still going to get that same exact result. To prove it, I'll just print to the screen like we did previously with `console.log(result)`:

```
//deleteOne
db.collection('Todos').deleteOne({text: 'Eat lunch'}).then((result) => {
  console.log(result);
});
```

With this in place, we can now rerun our script and see what happens. In the Terminal, I'm going to shut down our current connection and rerun it:

```
Gary:node-todo-api Gary$ node playground/mongodb-delete.js
Connected to MongoDB server
CommandResult {
  result: { n: 1, ok: 1 },
  connection:
  Connection {
    domain: null,
    _events:
    { error: [Function],
      close: [Function],
      timeout: [Function],
      parseError: [Function] },
    _eventsCount: 4,
    _maxListeners: undefined,
    options:
    { host: 'localhost',
      port: 27017,
      size: 5,
```

We get a similar-looking object, a bunch of junk we don't really care about, but once again if we scroll to the top we have a `result` object, where `ok` is `1` and the number of deleted documents is also `1`. Even though multiple documents did pass this criteria it only deleted the first one, and we can prove that by going over to Robomongo, right-clicking up above, and viewing the documents again. This time around, we have three Todos.

We do still have one of the Todos with the `Eat lunch` text:

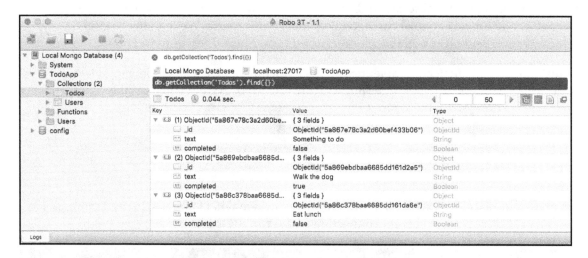

And now that we know how to use these two methods, I want to take a look at my favorite method. This is `findOneAndDelete`.

The findOneAndDelete method

Most of the time, when I'm deleting a document, I only have the ID. This means that I don't exactly know what the text is or the completed status, and that can be really useful depending on your user interface. For example, if I delete a Todo, maybe I want to show that next, saying *You deleted the Todo that says Eat lunch*, with a little undo button in case they didn't mean to take that action. Getting the data back as well as deleting it can be really useful.

In order to explore `findOneAndDelete`, we're going to once again target the Todo where the `text` equals `Eat lunch`. I'm going to go ahead and comment out `deleteOne`, and next we can get started by accessing the appropriate collection. The method is called `findOneAndDelete`. The `findOneAndDelete` method takes a very similar set of arguments. The only thing we need to pass in is the query. This is going to be identical to the ones we have in the previous screenshot. This time though, let's go ahead and target Todos that had a `completed` value set to `false`.

Now there are two Todos that fit this query, but once again we're using a `findOne` method, which means it's only going to target the first one it sees, the one with a `text` property of `Something to do`. Back in Atom, we can get this done by targeting Todos where `completed` equals `false`. Now, instead of getting back a result object with an `ok` property and an `n` property, the `findOneAndDelete` method actually gets that document back. This means we can tack on a `then` call, we can get our result, and we can print it to the screen once again with `console.log(result)`:

```
//findOneAndDelete
db.collection('Todos').findOneAndDelete({completed: false}).then((result)
=> {
  console.log(result);
});
```

Now that we have this in place, let's test things out over in the Terminal. In the Terminal, I'm going to shut down the script and start it up again:

```
Gary:node-todo-api Gary$ node playground/mongodb-delete.js
Connected to MongoDB server
{ lastErrorObject: { n: 1 },
  value:
   { _id: 5a867e78c3a2d60bef433b06,
     text: 'Something to do',
     completed: false },
  ok: 1 }
```

We get a few different things in our result object. We do get an `ok` set to 1, letting us know things went as planned. We have a `lastErrorObject`; we'll talk about that in just a second; and we have our `value` object. This is the actual document we deleted. This is why the `findOneAndDelete` method is super handy. It gets that document back as well as deleting it.

Now in this particular case, the `lastErrorObject`, once again just has our `n` property, and we can see the number of Todos that were deleted. There is other information that could potentially be in `lastErrorObject`, but that's only going to happen when we use other methods, so we'll look at that when the time comes. For now, when you delete a Todo, we just get the number back.

With this in place, we now have three different ways we can target our MongoDB documents and remove them.

Using the deleteMany and findOneAndDelete methods

We're going to go ahead and go over a quick challenge to test your skills. Inside of Robomongo, we can look at the data we have in the `Users` collection. I'm going to open it up, highlight all the data, and expand it recursively so we can view it:

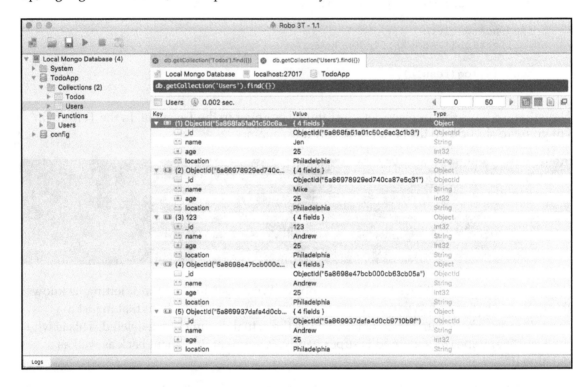

We have the name **Jen**; we have **Mike**; we have **Andrew**, **Andrew** and **Andrew**. This is perfect data. Yours might look a little different, but the goal is to use two methods. First up, look for any duplicates, anything that has a name set to the name of another document. In this case, I have three documents where the **name** is **Andrew**. What I want to do is use `deleteMany` to target all of these documents and remove them. I also want to use `findOneAndDelete` to delete another document; it doesn't matter which one. And I want you to delete it by ID.

In the end, both statements should show their effect over inside of Robomongo. When I'm done, I'm hoping to see these three documents deleted. They all have the name **Andrew**, and I'm hoping to see the document where the name **Mike** is deleted, because I'm going to target this one by ID in my `findOneAndDelete` method call.

First up, I'm going to write my scripts, one for deleting users where the name is `Andrew` and one for deleting the document with the ID. In order to grab the ID, I am going to go ahead and edit it and simply grab the text inside of quotes, and then I can cancel the update and move into Atom.

Removing duplicate documents

First up, we're going to go ahead and try to remove the duplicate users, and I'm going to do this by using `db.collection`. We're going to target the `Users` collection, and in this particular case, we're going to be using the `deleteMany` method. Here, we're going to try to delete all of the users where the `name` property equals `Andrew`.

```
db.collection('Users').deleteMany({name: 'Andrew'});
```

Now I could tack on a then call to check for success or errors, or I could just leave it like this, which is what I'm going to do. If you use a callback or the promise then method, that is perfectly fine. As long as the deletion happens, you're good to go.

Targeting the documents using ID

Next up, I'm going to write the other statement. We're going to target the `Users` collection once again. Now, we're going to go ahead and use the `findOneAndDelete` method. In this particular case, I am going to be deleting the Todo where the `_id` equals the ObjectId I have copied to the clipboard, which means I need to create a `new ObjectID`, and I also need to go ahead and pass in the value from the clipboard inside of quotes.

```
db.collection('Users').deleteMany({name: 'Andrew'});

db.collection('Users').findOneAndDelete({
  _id: new ObjectID("5a86978929ed740ca87e5c31")
})
```

Either single or double would work. Make sure the capitalization of `ObjectID` is identical to what you have defined, otherwise this creation will not happen.

Now that we have the ID created and passed in as the `_id` property, we can go ahead and tack on a `then` callback. Since I'm using `findOneAndDelete`, I am going to print that document to the screen. Right here I'll get my argument, `results`, and I'm going to print it to the screen using our pretty- printing method,`console.log(JSON.stringify())`, passing in those three arguments, the `results`, `undefined`, and the spacing, which I'm going to use as 2.

```
db.collection('Users').deleteMany({name: 'Andrew'});

db.collection('Users').findOneAndDelete({
  _id: new ObjectID("5a86978929ed740ca87e5c31")
}).then((results) => {
  console.log(JSON.stringify(results, undefined, 2));
});
```

With this in place, we are now ready to go.

Running the findOneAndDelete and deleteMany statements

Let's go ahead and comment out `findOneAndDelete` first. We'll run the `deleteMany` statement. Over in the Terminal, I can shut down the current connection, start it up again, and if we go over to Robomongo, we should see that those three documents were deleted. I'm going to right-click on `Users` and view the documents:

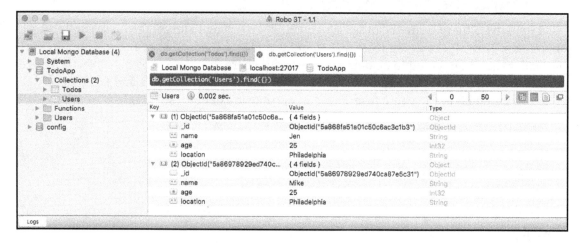

We just get the two documents back. Anything where the name was Andrew is now removed, which means our statement worked as expected, and this is fantastic.

Next up, we can run our findOneAndDelete statement. In this case, we're expecting that that one document, the one where the name equals Mike, gets removed. I'm going to go ahead and make sure I save the file. Once I do, I can move into the Terminal and rerun the script. This time around, we get the document back where the name is Mike. We did target the correct one, and it does appear that one item was deleted:

```
|Gary:node-todo-api Gary$ node playground/mongodb-delete.js
Connected to MongoDB server
{
  "lastErrorObject": {
    "n": 1
  },
  "value": {
    "_id": "5a86978929ed740ca87e5c31",
    "name": "Mike",
    "age": 25,
    "location": "Philadelphia"
  },
  "ok": 1
}
```

I can always go ahead and verify this by refreshing the collection inside of Robomongo:

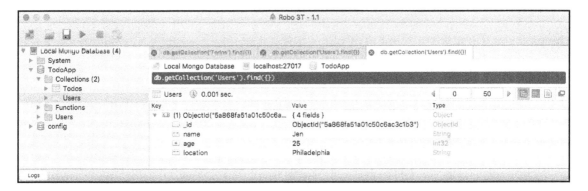

I get my collection with just one document inside of it. We are now done. We know how to delete documents from our MongoDB collections; we can delete multiple documents; we can target just one, or we can target one and get its value back.

Making commit for the deleting documents methods

Before we go, let's go ahead and make a commit, pushing it up to GitHub. In the Terminal, I can shut down the script and I can run `git status` to see what files we have untracked. Here, we have our `mongodb-delete` file. I can add it using `git add .` and then I can commit, using `git commit` with the `-m` flag. Here, I can go ahead and provide a commit message, which is going to be `Add delete script`:

```
git commit -m 'Add delete script'
```

I'm going to make that commit and I am going to push it up to GitHub using `git push`, which will default to the origin remote. When you only have one remote, the first one is going to be called origin. This is the default name, just like master is the default branch. With this in place, we are now done. Our code is up on GitHub. The topic of the next section is updating, which is where you're going to learn how to update documents inside of a collection.

Updating data

You know how to insert, delete, and fetch documents out of MongoDB. In this section, you're going to learn how to update documents in your MongoDB collections. To kick things off, as usual, we're going to duplicate the last script we wrote, and we'll update it for this section.

I'm going to duplicate the `mongodb-delete` file, renaming it to `mongodb-update.js`, and this is where we'll write our update statements. I'm also going to delete all of the statements we wrote, which is the deleted data. Now that we have this in place, we can explore the one method we'll be looking at in this section. This one is called `findOneAndUpdate`. It's kind of similar to `findOneAndDelete`. It lets us update an item and get the new document back. So if I update a Todo, set it as `completed` equal to `true`, I will get that document back in the response. Now in order to get started, we're going to be updating one of the items that we have inside of our Todos collection. If I view the documents, we currently have two. The goal here is going to be to update the second item, the one where `text` equals `Eat lunch`. We're going to try to set the `completed` value to `true`, which would be a pretty common action.

If I check off a Todo item, we want to toggle that completed Boolean value. Back inside of Atom, we're going to kick things off by accessing the appropriate collection. That'll be db.collection. The collection name is Todos, and the method we'll be using is findOneAndUpdate. Now, findOneAndUpdate is going to take the most arguments we've used so far, so let's go ahead and look up the documentation for it for future reference.

Over inside of Chrome, we currently have the **Cursor** tab open. This is where we have the count method defined. If we scroll next the **Cursor** tab, we have our other tabs. The one we're looking for is Collection. Now, inside of the **Collection** section, we have our **typedefs** and our **methods**. We're looking at methods here, so if I scroll down, we should be able to find findOneAndUpdate and click it. Now, findOneAndUpdate takes quite a few arguments. The first one is the filter. The update argument lets us target the document we want to update. Maybe we have the text, or most likely we have the ID of the document. Next up is the actual updates we want to make. We don't want to update the ID, we just want to filter by ID. In this case, the updates are going to be updating the completed Boolean. Then we have some options, which we are going to define. We'll use just one of them. We also have our callback. We're going to leave off the callback as we've been doing so so far, in favor of promises. As you can see on the documentation page, it returns a promise if no callback is passed in, and that's exactly what we expect. Let's go ahead and start filling out the appropriate arguments for findOneAndUpdate, kicking things off with the filter. What I'm going to do is filter by ID. In Robomongo, I can grab the ID of this document. I'm going to edit it and copy the ID to the clipboard. Now, in Atom, we can start querying the first object, filter. We're only looking for documents where the _id equals new ObjectID with the value that we copied to the clipboard. This is all we need for the filter argument. Next up is going to be the actual updates we want to apply, and this is not exactly straightforward. What we have to do here is learn about the MongoDB update operators.

We can view a complete list of these operators and exactly what they are by googling `mongodb update operators`. When I do this, we're looking for the `mongodb.com` documentation:

Now this documentation is specific to MongoDB, which means it's going to work with all of the drivers. In this case, it is going to work with our Node.js driver. If we scroll down further, we can look at all of the update operators we have access to. The most important, and the one we're going to get started with, is the `$set` operator. This lets us set a field's value inside of our update, which is exactly what we want to do. There's other operators, like increment. This one, `$inc`, lets you increment a field's value, like the age field in our `Users` collection. Although these are super useful, we're going to get started with `$set`. In order to use one of these operators, what we need to do is type it out, `$set`, and then set it equal to an object. In this object, these are the things that we're actually going to be setting. For example, we want to set `completed` equal to `true`. If we tried to put `completed` equal to `true` at the root of the object like this, it would not work as expected. We have to use these update operators, which means we need this. Now that we have our updates in place using the set update operator, we can go ahead and provide our third and final argument. If you head over to the documentation for `findOneAndUpdate`, we can take a look at the `options` real quick. The one we care about is `returnOriginal`.

The `returnOriginal` method is defaulted to `true`, which means that it returns the original document, not the updated one, and we don't want that. When we update a document, we want to get back that updated document. What we're going to do is set `returnOriginal` to `false`, and that's going to happen in our third and final argument. This one is also going to be an object, `returnOriginal`, which is going to be setting equal to `false`.

With this in place, we are done. We can tack on a `then` call to do something with the results. I'll get my result back and I can simply print it to the screen, and we can take a look at exactly what comes back:

```
db.collection('Todos').findOneAndUpdate({
  _id: new ObjectID('5a86c378baa6685dd161da6e')
}, {
  $set: {
    completed:true
  }
}, {
  returnOriginal: false
}).then((result) => {
  console.log(result);
});
```

Now, let's go ahead and run this from the Terminal. I'm going to save my file inside the Terminal. We're going to be running `node`. The file is in the `playground` folder, and we will call it `mongodb-update.js`. I'm going to run the following script:

node playground/mongodb-update.js

We get back the value prop, just like we did when we used `findOneAndDelete`, and this has our document with the completed value set to true, which is the brand-new value we just set, which is fantastic:

```
[Gary:node-todo-api Gary$ node playground/mongodb-update.js
Connected to MongoDB server
{ lastErrorObject: { n: 1, updatedExisting: true },
  value:
   { _id: 5a86c378baa6685dd161da6e,
     text: 'Eat lunch',
     completed: true },
  ok: 1 }
```

If we head over to Robomongo, we can confirm that the value was indeed updated. We can see this in the old document, where the value is false. I'm going to open up a new view for Todos:

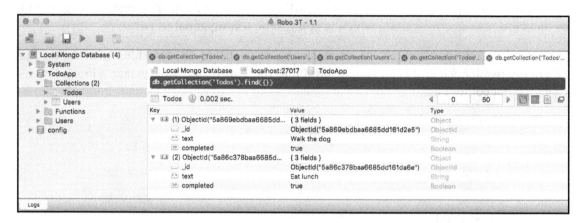

We have **Eat lunch**, with a **completed** value of **true**. Now that we have this in place, we know how to insert, delete, update, and read documents from our MongoDB collections. To wrap this section up, I want to give you a quick challenge. Over inside of the Users collection, you should have a document. It should have a name. It's probably not Jen; it's probably something that you set. What I want you to do is update this name to your name. Now if it's already your name, that's fine; you can change it to something else. I also want you to use $inc, the increment operator that we talked about, to increment this by 1. Now I'm not going to tell you exactly how increment works. What I want you to do is head over to the docs, click on the operator, and then scroll down to see the examples. There's examples for each operator. It's going to become really useful for you to learn how to read documentation. Now, documentation for libraries is not always going to be the same; everyone does it a little differently; but once you learn how to read the docs for one library, it gets a lot easier to read the docs for others, and I can only teach so much in this course. The real goal of this course is to get you writing your own code, doing your own research, and looking up your own documentation, so your goal once again is to update this document, setting the name to something other than what it's currently set to, and incrementing the age by 1.

To kick things off, I'm going to grab the ID of the document in Robomongo, since this is the document I want to update. I'll copy the ID to the clipboard, and now we can focus on writing that statement in Atom. First up, we'll update the name, since we already know how to do that. In Atom, I'm going to go ahead and duplicate the statement:

```
db.collection('Todos').findOneAndUpdate({
  _id: new ObjectID('57bc4b15b3b6a3801d8c47a2')
}, {
  $set: {
    completed:true
  }
}, {
  returnOriginal: false
}).then((result) => {
  console.log(result);
});
```

I'll copy it and paste it. Back inside of Atom, we can start swapping things out. First up, we're going to swap out the old ID for the new one, and we're going to change what we passed to set. Instead of updating `completed`, we want to update `name`. I'm going to set the `name` equal to something other than `Jen`. I'm going to go ahead and use my name, `Andrew`. Now, we are going to keep `returnOriginal` set to `false`. We want to get the new document back, not the original. Now, the other thing that we need to do is increment the age. This is going to be done via the increment operator, which you should have explored using the documentation over inside of Chrome. If you click on `$inc`, it's going to bring you to the `$inc` part of the documentation, and if you scroll down, you should be able to see an example. Right here, we have an example of what it looks like to increment:

```
db.products.update(
   { sku: "abc123" },
   { $inc: { quantity: -2, "metrics.orders": 1 } }
)
```

We set $inc just like we set set. Then, inside of the object, we specify the things we want to increment, and the degree to which we want to increment them. It could be -2, or in our case, it would be positive, 1. In Atom, we can implement this, as shown in the following code:

```
db.collection('Users').findOneAndUpdate({
  _id: new ObjectID('57abbcf4fd13a094e481cf2c')
}, {
  $set: {
    name: 'Andrew'
  },
  $inc: {
    age: 1
  }
}, {
  returnOriginal: false
}).then((result) => {
  console.log(result);
});
```

I'll set $inc equal to an object, and in there, we'll increment the age by 1. With this in place, we are now done. Before I run this file, I am going to comment out to the other call to findOneAndUpdate, just leaving the new one. I also need to swap out the collection. We're no longer updating the Todos collection; we're updating the Users collection. Now, we are good to go. We're setting the name equal to Andrew and we're incrementing the age by 1, which means that we would expect the age in Robomongo to be 26 instead of 25. Let's go ahead and run this by restarting the script over in the Terminal:

```
Gary:node-todo-api Gary$ node playground/mongodb-update.js
Connected to MongoDB server
{ lastErrorObject: { n: 1, updatedExisting: true },
  value:
   { _id: 5a868fa51a01c50c6ac3c1b3,
     name: 'Andrew',
     age: 26,
     location: 'Philadelphia' },
  ok: 1 }
```

We can see our new document, where the name is indeed `Andrew` and the age is indeed `26`, and this is fantastic. Now that you know how to use the increment operator, you can also go off and learn all of the other operators you have available to you inside of your update calls. I can double-check that everything worked as expected in Robomongo. I'm going to go ahead and refresh the `Users` collection:

We have our updated document right here. Well, let's wrap this section up by committing our changes. In the Terminal, I'm going to run `git status` so we can view all of the changes to the repository:

```
Gary:node-todo-api Gary$ git status
On branch master
Your branch is up-to-date with 'origin/master'.

Untracked files:
  (use "git add <file>..." to include in what will be committed)

    playground/mongodb-update.js

nothing added to commit but untracked files present (use "git add" to track)
Gary:node-todo-api Gary$
```

Here, we just have one untracked file, our `mongodb-update` script. I'm going to use `git add .` to add that to the next commit, and then I'll use `git commit` to actually make the commit. I am going to provide the `-m` argument for `message` so we can specify a message, which is going to be `Add update script`:

```
git add .
git commit -m 'Add update script'
```

And now we can run the commit command and push it up to GitHub, so our code is backed up on our GitHub repository:

```
git push
```

With updating in place, we now have all of the basic CRUD (Creating, Reading, Updating, and Deleting) operations down. Up next, we're going to talk about something called Mongoose, which we'll be using for the Todo API.

Summary

In this chapter, we started with connecting to MongoDB and writing data. We then went ahead to understand the `id` property in the context of MongoDB. After learning more about fetching data, we explored different methods to delete data in the documents.

In the next chapter, we will continue to play more with Mongoose, MongoDB, and REST APIs.

3
MongoDB, Mongoose, and REST APIs – Part 2

In this chapter, you're finally going to move out of the `playground` folder, and we're going to start playing with Mongoose. We'll be connecting to our MongoDB database, creating a model, talking about what exactly a model is, and finally, we'll be saving some data to the database using Mongoose.

Setting up Mongoose

We're not going to need any of the files we currently have open in the `playground` directory, so we can go ahead and close them. We're also going to wipe the `TodoApp` database using Robomongo. The data inside of Robomongo is going to be a little different than the data we'll be using going forward, and it's best to start with a clean slate. There is no need to create the database after you drop it because if you remember, MongoDB is going to automatically create the database once you start writing data to it. With this in place, we can now explore Mongoose, and the first thing I always like to do is check out the website.

You can check the website out by going to `mongoosejs.com`:

Here, you can find examples, guides, a full list of plugins, and a ton of great resources. The **read the docs** resource is the one I use the most. It includes tutorial-like guides that have examples, as well as documentation covering every single feature of the library. It really is a fantastic resource.

 If you ever want to learn about something or want to use a feature we don't cover in the book, I highly recommend coming to this page, taking the examples, copying and pasting some code, playing around with it, and figuring out how it works. We're going to be covering most of the essential Mongoose features right now.

Setting up root of the project

The first thing we need to do before we can actually use Mongoose in our project is install it. Over in the Terminal, I'm going to install it using `npm i`, which is short for `npm install`. The module name itself is called `mongoose`, and we'll be installing the most recent version, which is going to be version `5.0.6`. We're going to tack on the `--save` flag since we will need Mongoose for both production and testing purposes:

```
npm i mongoose@5.0.6 --save
```

Once we run this command, it's going to go off and do its thing. We can move into Atom and start creating the files we're going to need to run our application.

First up, let's make a folder in the root of the project. This folder is going to be called `server`, and everything related to our server is going to get stored in the `server` folder. The first file we're going to create is going to be called `server.js`. This is going to be the root of our application. When you want to start up your Node app, you're going to run this file. This file will get everything ready to go.

The first thing we need to do inside of `server.js` is load in Mongoose. We're going to make a variable called `mongoose`, and we're going to acquire it from the `mongoose` library.

```
var mongoose = require('mongoose');
```

Now that we have the mongoose variable in place, we need to go ahead and connect to the database because we can't start writing data to the database until Mongoose knows how to connect.

Connecting mongoose to database

The process of connecting is going to be pretty similar to what we did inside of our MongoDB scripts; for example, the `mongodb-connect` script. Here, we called `MongoClient.connect`, passing in a URL. What we're going to do for Mongoose is call `mongoose.connect`, passing in the exact same URL; `mongodb` is the protocol, call in `//`. We're going to be connecting to our `localhost` database on port `27017`. Next up is going to be our `/`, followed by the database name, and we'll continue to use the `TodoApp` database, which we used over in the `mongodb-connect` script.

```
var mongoose = require('mongoose');

mongoose.connect('mongodb://localhost:27017/TodoApp');
```

This is where the two functions differ. The `MongoClient.connect` method takes a callback, and that is when we have access to the database. Mongoose is a lot more complex. This is good, because it means our code can be a lot simpler. Mongoose is maintaining the connection over time. Imagine I try to save something, `save new something`. Now obviously, by the time this save statement runs, `mongoose.connect` is not going to have had time to make a database request to connect. That's going to take a few milliseconds at least. This statement is going to run almost right away.

Behind the scenes, Mongoose is going to be waiting for the connection before it ever actually tries to make the query, and this is one of the great advantages of Mongoose. We don't have to micromanage the order in which things happen; Mongoose takes care of that for us.

There is one more thing I want to configure just above `mongoose.connect`. We've been using promises in this course, and we're going to continue using them. Mongoose supports callbacks by default, but callbacks really aren't how I like to program. I prefer promises as they're a lot simpler to chain, manage, and scale. Right above the `mongoose.connect` statement, we're going to tell Mongoose which promise library we want to use. If you're not familiar with the history of promises, it didn't have to always be something built into JavaScript. Promises originally came from libraries like Bluebird. It was an idea a developer had, and they created a library. People started using it, so much so that they added it to the language.

In our case, we need to tell Mongoose that we want to use the built-in promise library as opposed to some third-party one. We're going to set `mongoose.Promise` equal to `global.Promise`, and this is something we're only going to have to do once:

```
var mongoose = require('mongoose');

mongoose.Promise = global.Promise;
mongoose.connect('mongodb://localhost:27017/TodoApp');
```

We're just going to put these two lines in `server.js`; we don't have to add them anywhere else. With this in place, Mongoose is now configured. We've connected to our database and we've set it up to use promises, which is exactly what we want. The next thing we're going to do is create a model.

Creating the todo model

Now, as we have already talked about, inside of MongoDB, your collections can store anything. I could have a collection with a document that has an age property, and that's it. I could have a different document in the same collection with a property name; that's it. These two documents are different, but they're both in the same collection. Mongoose likes to keep things a little more organized than that. What we're going to do is create a model for everything we want to store. In this example, we'll be creating a Todo model.

Now, a Todo is going to have certain attributes. It's going to have a `text` attribute, which we know is a string; it's going to have a `completed` attribute, which we know is a Boolean. These are things we can define. What we're going to do is create a Mongoose model so Mongoose knows how to store our data.

Right below the `mongoose.connect` statement, let's make a variable called `Todo`, and we're going to set that equal to `mongoose.model`. The `model` is the method we're going to use to create a new model. It takes two arguments. The first one is the string name. I'm going to match the variable name on the left, `Todo`, and the second argument is going to be an object.

```
mongoose.connect('mongodb://localhost:27017/TodoApp');
var Todo = mongoose.model('Todo', {
});
```

This object is going to define the various properties for a model. For example, the Todo model is going to have a `text` property, so we can set that up. Then, we can set text equal to an object, and we can configure exactly what text is. We can do the same thing for `completed`. We're going to have a completed property, and we're going to want to specify certain things. Maybe it's required; maybe we have custom validators; maybe we want to set the type. We're also going to add one final one, `completedApp`, and this is going to let us know when a Todo was completed:

```
var Todo = mongoose.model('Todo', {
  text: {

  },
  completed: {

  },
  completedAt: {

  }
});
```

A `createdApp` property might sound useful, but if you remember the MongoDB `ObjectId`, that already has the `createdAt` timestamp built in, so there's no reason to add a `createdApp` property here. `completedAt`, on the other hand, is going to add value. It lets you know exactly when you have completed a Todo.

From here, we can start specifying the details about each attribute, and there's a ton of different options available inside of the Mongoose documentation. For now though, we're going to keep things really simple by specifying the type for each, for example, `text`. We can set `type` equal to `String`. It's always going to be a string; it wouldn't make sense if it was a Boolean or a number.

```
var Todo = mongoose.model('Todo', {
  text: {
    type: String
  },
```

Next, we can set a type for `completed`. It needs to be a Boolean; there's no way around that. We're going to set `type` equal to `Boolean`.

```
  completed: {
    type: Boolean
  },
```

The last one we have is `completedAt`. This is going to be a regular old Unix timestamp, which means it's just a number, so we can set the `type` for `completedAt` equal to `Number`:

```
  completedAt: {
    type: Number
  }
});
```

With this in place, we now have a working Mongoose model. It's a model of a Todo that has a few properties: `text`, `completed`, and `completedAt`.

Now in order to illustrate exactly how we create instances of this, we're going to go ahead and just add one Todo. We're not going to worry about fetching data, updating data, or deleting data, although that is stuff that Mongoose supports. We'll be worrying about that in the following sections, as we start building out the individual routes for our API. For now, we're going to go over just a very quick example of creating a brand-new Todo.

Creating a brand-new Todo

I'm going to make a variable called `newTodo`, although you could call it anything you like; the name here is not important. What is important though is that you run the Todo function. This is what comes back from `mongoose.model` as a constructor function. We want to add the `new` keyword in front of it because we're creating a new instance of `Todo`.

Now, the `Todo` constructor function does take an argument. It's going to be an object where we can specify some of these properties. Maybe we know that we want `text` to equal something like `Cook dinner`. Right in the function, we can specify that. `text` equals a string, `Cook dinner`:

```
var newTodo = new Todo({
  text: 'Cook dinner'
});
```

We haven't required any of our attributes, so we could just stop here. We have a `text` property; that's good enough. Let's go ahead and explore how to save this to the database.

Saving the instance to the database

Creating a new instance alone does not actually update the MongoDB database. What we need to do is call a method on `newTodo`. This is going to be `newTodo.save`.
The `newTodo.save` method is going to be responsible for actually saving `text` to the MongoDB database. Now, `save` returning a promise, which means we can tack on a `then` call and add a few callbacks.

```
newTodo.save().then((doc) => {

}, (e) => {

});
```

We'll add the callbacks for when the data either gets saved or when an error occurs because it can't save for some reason. Maybe the connection failed, or maybe the model is not valid. Either way, for now we'll just print a little string, `console.log(Unable to save todo)`. Up above, in the success callback, we're actually going to get that Todo. I can call the argument `doc`, and I can print it to the screen, `console.log`. I'll print a little message first: `Saved todo`, and the second argument will be the actual document:

```
newTodo.save().then((doc) => {
  console.log('Saved todo', doc);
}, (e) => {
  console.log('Unable to save todo');
});
```

We've configured Mongoose, connecting to the MongoDB database; we've created a model, specifying the attributes we want Todos to have; we created a new Todo; and finally, we saved it to the database.

Running the Todos script

We're going to run the script from the Terminal. I'm going to kick things off by running `node`. The file we're running is in the `server` directory, and it's called `server.js`:

```
node server/server.js
```

```
Gary:node-todo-api Gary$ node server/server.js
Saved todo { text: 'Cook dinner', _id: 5a86f7e5ec5b92416115f4d1, __v: 0 }
```

When we run the file, we get `Saved todo`, meaning that things went well. We have an object right here with an `_id` property as expected; the `text` property, which we specified; and the `__v` property. The `__v` property means version, and it comes from Mongoose. We'll talk about it later, but essentially it keeps track of the various model changes over time.

If we open up Robomongo, we're going to see the exact same data. I'm going to right-click the connection and refresh it. Here, we have our `TodoApp`. Inside of the `TodoApp` database, we have our `todos` collection:

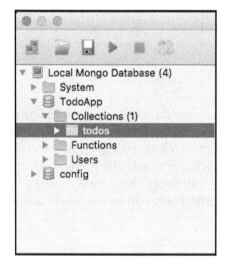

Notice that Mongoose automatically lowercased and pluralized Todo. I'm going to view the documents:

We have our one document with the **text** equal to **Cook dinner**, exactly what we created over inside of Atom.

Creating a second Todo model

We have one Todo created using our Mongoose model. What I want you to do is make a second one, filling out all three values. This means you're going to make a new Todo with a `text` value, a `completed` Boolean; go ahead and set that to `true`; and a `completedAt` timestamp, which you can set to any number you like. Then, I want you to go ahead and save it; print it to the screen if it saves successfully; print an error if it saves poorly. Then, finally, run it.

The first thing I would have done is made a new variable down below. I'm going to make a variable called `otherTodo`, setting it equal to a `new` instance of the `Todo` model.

```
var otherTodo = new Todo ({
});
```

From here, we can pass in our one argument, which is going to be the object, and we can specify all of these values. I can set text equal to whatever I like, for example, Feed the cat. I can set the completed value equal to true, and I can set completedAt equal to any number. Anything lower than 0, like -1, is going to go backwards from 1970, which is where 0 is. Anything positive is going to be where we're at, and we'll talk about time-stamps more later. For now, I'm going to go with something like 123, which would basically be two minutes into the year 1970.

```
var otherTodo = new Todo ({
    text: 'Feed the cat',
    completed: true,
    completedAt: 123
});
```

With this in place, we now just need to call save. I'm going to call otherTodo.save. This is what's actually going to write to the MongoDB database. I am going to tack on a then callback, because I do want to do something once the save is complete. If the save method worked, we're going to get our doc, and I'm going to print it to the screen. I'm going to use that pretty-print system we talked about earlier, JSON.stringify, passing in the actual object, undefined, and 2.

```
var otherTodo = new Todo ({
    text: 'Feed the cat',
    completed: true,
    completedAt: 123
});

otherTodo.save().then((doc) => {
    console.log(JSON.stringify(doc, undefined, 2));
})
```

You don't need to do this; you can print it in any way you like. Next up, I'm going to print a little message if things go poorly: console.log('Unable to save', e). It'll pass along that error object, so if someone's reading the logs, they can see exactly why the call failed:

```
otherTodo.save().then((doc) => {
    console.log(JSON.stringify(doc, undefined, 2));
}, (e) => {
    console.log('Unable to save', e);
});
```

With this in place, we can now comment out that first Todo. This is going to prevent another one from being created, and we can rerun the script, running our brand-new Todo creation calls. In the Terminal, I'm going to shut down the old connection and start up a new one. This is going to create a brand-new Todo, and we have it right here:

```
Gary:node-todo-api Gary$ node server/server.js
Saved todo { text: 'Cook dinner', _id: 5a86f94dfd8d484195ee05b7, __v: 0 }
{
  "text": "Feed the cat",
  "completed": true,
  "completedAt": 123,
  "_id": "5a86f94dfd8d484195ee05b8",
  "__v": 0
}
```

The text property equals Feed the cat. The completed property sets to the Boolean true; notice there's no quotes around it. The completedAt equals the number 123; once again, no quotes. I can also go into Robomongo to confirm this. I'm going to refetch the Todos collection, and now we have two Todos:

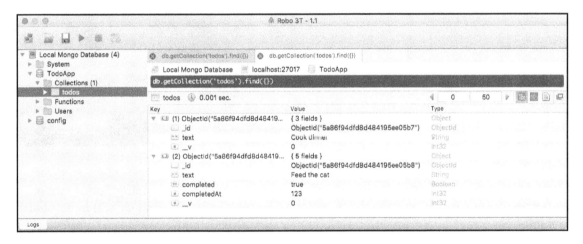

On the right-hand side of the **Values** column, you'll also notice the **Type** column. Here, we have **int32** for **completedAt** and the **__v** property. The **completed** property is a Boolean, **text** is a **String**, and the **_id** is an **ObjectId** type.

There's a lot of useful information hidden inside of Robomongo. If you want something, they most likely have it built in. That's it for this one. We now know how to use Mongoose to make a connection, create a model, and finally save that model to the database.

Validators, Types, and Defaults

In this section, you're going to learn how to improve your Mongoose models. This is going to let you add things like validation. You can make certain properties be a requirement, and you can set up smart defaults. So, if something like completed is not provided, you can have a default value that gets set. All of this functionality is built into Mongoose; we just have to learn how to use it.

To illustrate why we'd want to set this stuff up, let's scroll to the bottom of our server file and remove all of the properties on the new Todo we created. Then, we're going to save the file and move into the Terminal, running the script. That's going to be node in the server directory, and the file is going to be called server.js:

```
node server/server.js
```

When we run it, we get our new Todo, but it only has the version and ID properties:

```
Gary:node-todo-api Gary$ node server/server.js
{
  "_id": "5a870175dc9e6341c1613265",
  "__v": 0
}
```

All of the properties we specified in the model, text, completed, and completedAt, are nowhere to be found. That's a pretty big problem. We should not be adding Todos to the database if they don't have a text property, and things like completed should have smart defaults. No-one's going to create a Todo item if they already completed it, so completed should default to false.

Mongoose validators

Now in order to get started, we're going to pull up two pages in the Mongoose documentation, just so you know where this stuff lives if you ever want to dive deeper in the future. First up, we're going to look up the validators. I'm going to google `mongoose validators`, and this is going to show us all of the default validation properties we have built in:

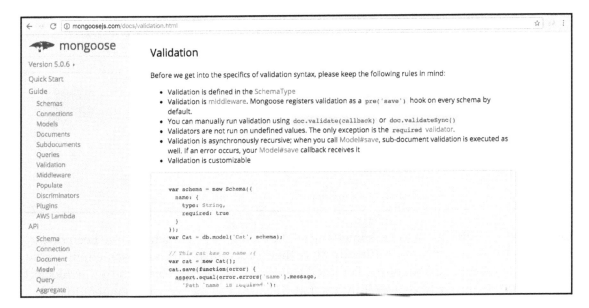

For example, we can set something as `required`, so if it's not provided it's going to throw an error when we try to save that model. We can also set up validators for things like numbers and strings, giving a `min` and `max` value or a `minlength`/`maxlength` value for a string.

The other page we're going to look at is the Schemas page. To get to this, we're going to google `mongoose schemas`. This is the first one, the `guide.html` file:

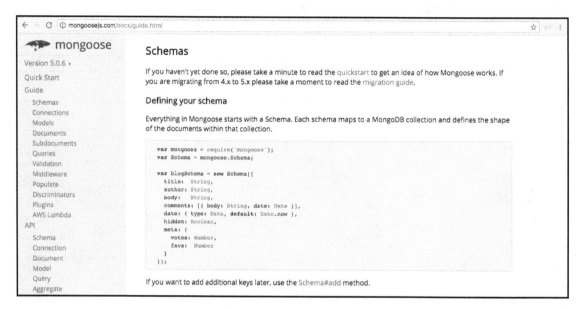

On this page, you're going to see something slightly different from what we've been doing so far. They call `new Schema`, setting up all of their properties. This is not something we've done yet, but we will in the future. For now, you can consider this object, the `Schema` object, identical to the one we have over in Atom that we pass in as the second argument to our `mongoose.model` call.

Customizing the Todo text property

To kick things off, let's customize how Mongoose treats our `text` property. Currently, we tell Mongoose that we want it to be a string, but we don't have any validators. One of the first things we can do for the `text` property is set `required` equal to `true`.

```
var Todo = mongoose.model('Todo', {
  text: {
    type: String,
    required: true
  },
```

When you set `required` equal to `true`, the value must exist, so if I were to try to save this Todo it would fail. And we can prove this. We can save the file, head over to the Terminal, shut things down, and restart it:

```
at /Users/Gary/Desktop/node-todo-api/node_modules/mongoose/lib/document.js:1570:9
at process._tickCallback (internal/process/next_tick.js:150:11)
at Function.Module.runMain (module.js:703:11)
at startup (bootstrap_node.js:194:16)
at bootstrap_node.js:618:3
    message: 'Path `text` is required.',
    name: 'ValidatorError',
    properties: [Object],
    kind: 'required',
    path: 'text',
    value: undefined,
    reason: undefined,
    '$isValidatorError': true } },
  _message: 'Todo validation failed',
  name: 'ValidationError' }
```

We get an unreadable error message. We'll dive into this in a second, but for now all you need to know is that we're getting a validation error: **Todo validation failed**, and that is fantastic.

Now, aside from just making sure the `text` property exists, we can also set up some custom validators. For strings, for example, we have a `minlength` validator, which is great. You shouldn't be able to create a Todo whose text is an empty string. We can set `minlength` equal to the minimum length, which we're is going to be `1` in this case:

```
var Todo = mongoose.model('Todo', {
  text: {
    type: String,
    required: true,
    minlength: 1
  },
```

Now, even if we do provide a `text` property in the `otherTodo` function, let's say we set `text` equal to an empty string:

```
var otherTodo = new Todo ({
  text: ''
});
```

It's still going to fail. It is indeed there but it does not pass the minlength validator, where the `minlength` validator must be 1. I can save the `server` file, restart things over in the Terminal, and we still get a failure.

Now aside from `required` and `minlength`, there are a couple other utilities that are around in the docs. One good example is something called `trim`. It's fantastic for strings. Essentially, `trim` trims off any white space in the beginning or end of your value. If I set `trim` equal to `true`, like this:

```
var Todo = mongoose.model('Todo', {
  text: {
    type: String,
    required: true,
    minlength: 1,
    trim: true
  },
```

It's going to remove any leading or trailing white space. So if I try to create a Todo whose `text` property is just a bunch of spaces, it's still going to fail:

```
var otherTodo = new Todo ({
  text: '         '
});
```

The `trim` property is going to remove all of the leading and trailing spaces, leaving an empty string, and if I rerun things, we still get a failure. The text field is invalid. If we do provide a valid value, things are going to work as expected. Right in the middle of all of the spaces in `otherTodo`, I'm going to provide a real Todo value, which is going to be `Edit this video`:

```
var otherTodo = new Todo ({
  text: '    Edit this video    '
});
```

When we try to save this Todo, the first thing that's going to happen is the spaces in the beginning and the end of the string are going to get trimmed. Then, it's going to validate that this string has a minimum length of 1, which it does, and finally, it will save the Todo to the database. I'm going to go ahead and save `server.js`, restart our script, and this time around we get our Todo:

```
[Gary:node-todo-api Gary$ node server/server.js
{
  "text": "    Edit this video    ",
  "_id": "5a8704bfbc6d00424c6ef266",
  "__v": 0
}
```

The `Edit this video` text shows up as the `text` property. Those leading and trailing spaces have been removed, which is fantastic. Using just three properties, we were able to configure our `text` property, setting up some validation. Now, we can do similar stuff for `completed`.

Mongoose defaults

For `completed`, we're not going to `require` it because the completed value is most likely going to default to `false`. What we can do instead is set the `default` property, giving this `completed` field a default value.

```
completed: {
  type: Boolean,
  default: false
},
```

Now `completed`, as we talked about earlier in the section, should default to `false`. There's no reason to create a Todo if it's already done. We can do the same thing for `completedAt`. If a Todo starts off not completed, then `completedAt` is not going to exist. It is only going to exist when the Todo has been completed; it's going to be that timestamp. What I'm going to do is set `default` equal to `null`:

```
completed: {
  type: Boolean,
  default: false
},
completedAt: {
  type: Number,
  default: null
}
```

Awesome. Now, we have a pretty good schema for our Todo. We're going to validate that the text is set up properly by the user, and we are going to set up the `completed` and `completedAt` values by our-self since we can just use defaults. With this in place, I can now rerun our `server` file, and here we get a better default Todo:

```
[Gary:node-todo-api Gary$ node server/server.js
{
  "text": "Edit this video",
  "completed": false,
  "completedAt": null,
  "_id": "5a8706434892b94255667bf7",
  "__v": 0
}
```

We have the `text` property and the user provided, which has been validated and trimmed. Next, we have `completed` set to `false` and `completedAt` set to `null`; this is fantastic. We now have a foolproof schema that has good defaults and validation.

Mongoose types

If you've been playing around with the various types, you might have noticed that if you set a `type` equal to something other than the type you specified, in certain cases it does still work. For example, if I try to set `text` equal to an object, I'm going to get an error. It's going to say hey, you tried to use a string, but an object showed up instead. However, if I try to set `text` equal to something like a number, I'm going to go with `23`:

```
var otherTodo = new Todo ({
  text: 23
});
```

This is going to work. That's because Mongoose is going to cast your number into a string, essentially wrapping it in quotes. The same thing is going to be true with the Boolean. If I pass in a Boolean like this:

```
var otherTodo = new Todo ({
  text: true
});
```

The resulting string is going to be `"true"`. I'm going to go ahead and save the file after setting `text` equal to `true`, and run the script:

```
Gary:node-todo-api Gary$ node server/server.js
{
  "text": "true",
  "completed": false,
  "completedAt": null,
  "_id": "5a8706b30fe427425be3d99e",
  "__v": 0
}
```

When I do it, I get `text` equal to `true`, as shown in the preceding screenshot. Notice it is indeed wrapped in quotes. It's important to be aware that typecasting does exist inside of Mongoose. It can easily trip you up and cause some unexpected errors. For now though, I am going to set `text` equal to a proper string:

```
var otherTodo = new Todo ({
  text: 'Something to do'
});
```

Creating a Mongoose user model for authentication

Now, we're going to create a brand-new Mongoose model. First up, you're going to make a new User model. Eventually, we're going to use this for authentication. It's going to store stuff like an email and a password, and the Todos are going to be associated with that User so when I create one, only I can edit it.

We'll look into all these, but for now, we're going to keep things really simple. On the User model, the only property that you need to set up is the email property. We'll set up others like password later, but it's going to be done a little differently since it needs to be secure. For now, we'll just stick with email. I want you to require it. I also want you to trim it, so if someone adds spaces before or after, those spaces go away. Last but not least, go ahead and set the type equal to a String, set type, and set minlength of 1. Now, obviously, you'll be able to pass in a string that's not an email. We'll explore custom validation a little later. This is going to let us validate that the email is an email, but for now this is going to get us on the right track.

Once you have your Mongoose model created, I want you to go ahead and try to create a new User. Create one without the email property, and then make one with the email property, making sure that when you run the script, the data shows up as expected over in Robomongo. This data should show up in the new Users collection.

Setting up the email property

The first thing I'm going to do is make a variable to store this new model, a variable called User, and I'm going to set that equal to mongoose.model, which is how we can make our new User model. The first argument, as you know, needs to be the string model name. I'm going to use the exact same name as I specified over in the variable, although it could be different. I just like to keep things using this pattern, where the variable equals the model name. Next up, as the second argument, we can specify the object where we configure all the properties a User should have.

```
var User = mongoose.model('User', {

});
```

Now as I mentioned previously, we'll be adding others later, but for now, adding support for an `email` property will be good enough. There's a few things I want to do on this email. First up, I want to set the `type`. An email is always going to be a string, so we can set that `type` equal to `String`.

```
var User = mongoose.model('User', {
  email: {
    type: String,


  }
});
```

Next up, we're going to `require` it. You can't make a user without an email, so I'll set `required` equal to `true`. After required, we're going to go ahead and `trim` that email. If someone adds spaces before or after it, it's clearly a mistake, so we'll go ahead and remove those for the `User` model, making our application just a little more user-friendly. Last but not least, what we want to do is set up a `minlength` validator. We'll be setting up custom validation later, but for now `minlength` of 1 is going to get the trick done.

```
var User = mongoose.model('User', {
  email: {
    type: String,
    required: true,
    trim: true,
    minlength: 1
  }
});
```

Now, I am going to go ahead and create a new instance of this `User` and save it. Before I run the script though, I will be commenting out our new Todo. Now, we can make a new instance of this `User` model. I'm going to make a variable called `user` and set it equal to `new User`, passing in any values we want to set on that user.

```
var User = mongoose.model('User', {
  email: {
    type: String,
    required: true,
    trim: true,
    minlength: 1
  }
});

var user = new User({

});
```

I'm going to run it with nothing at first, just to make sure the validation is working. Next to the user variable, I can now call `user.save`. The `save` method returns a promise, so I can tack on a `then` callback. I'm going to add a success case for this one, and an error handler. The error handler will get that error argument, and the success case will get the doc. If things go well, I'll print a message using `console.log('User saved', doc)`, followed by the `doc` argument. No need to format it for this example. I'll do the same thing for the error handler, using `console.log('Unable to save user')` followed by the error object:

```
var user = new User({

});

user.save().then((doc) => {
  console.log('User saved', doc);
}, (e) => {
  console.log('Unable to save user', e);
});
```

Since we're creating a user with no properties, we would expect the error to print. I'm going to save `server.js` and restart the file:

```
errors:
  { email:
    { ValidatorError: Path `email` is required.
    at new ValidatorError (/Users/Gary/Desktop/node-todo-api/node_modules/mongoose/lib/error/validator.js:25
:11)
    at validate (/Users/Gary/Desktop/node-todo-api/node_modules/mongoose/lib/schematype.js:782:13)
    at /Users/Gary/Desktop/node-todo-api/node_modules/mongoose/lib/schematype.js:831:11
    at Array.forEach (<anonymous>)
    at SchemaString.SchemaType.doValidate (/Users/Gary/Desktop/node-todo-api/node_modules/mongoose/lib/schem
atype.js:791:19)
    at /Users/Gary/Desktop/node-todo-api/node_modules/mongoose/lib/document.js:1570:9
    at process._tickCallback (internal/process/next_tick.js:150:11)
    at Function.Module.runMain (module.js:703:11)
    at startup (bootstrap_node.js:194:16)
```

We get our error. It's a validation error called **Path 'email' is required**. Mongoose is letting us know that we do indeed have an error. The email does need to exist, since we set `required` equal to `true`. I'm going to go ahead and put a value, setting `email` to my email, `andrew@example.com`, and I'll put a few spaces afterwards:

```
var user = new User({
    email: 'andrew@example.com '
});
```

This time around, things should go as expected and `trim` should be trimming the end of that email, removing all of the spaces, and that's exactly what we get:

```
Gary:node-todo-api Gary$ node server/server.js
User saved { email: 'andrew@example.com',
  _id: 5a8708e0e40b324268c5206c,
  __v: 0 }
```

The `User` was indeed saved, which is great, and the `email` has been properly formatted. Now obviously, I could have put a string in like `123`, and it would have worked because we don't have custom validation set up just yet, but we have a pretty good starting point. We have the `User` model, and we have our `email` property set up and ready to go.

With this in place, we are now going to start creating the API. In the next section, you're going to install a tool called **Postman**, which is going to help us test our HTTP requests, and then we're going to create our very first route for our Todo REST API.

Installing Postman

In this section, you're going to learn how to use Postman. Postman is an essential tool if you're building a REST API. I have never worked with a team or on a project where Postman was not heavily used by every developer involved. Postman lets you create HTTP requests and fire them off. This makes it really easy to test that everything you're writing is working as expected. Now obviously, we will also be writing automated tests, but using Postman lets you play around with data and see how things work as you move through your API. It really is a fantastic tool.

We're going to head over to the browser and go to `getpostman.com`, and here we can grab
their application:

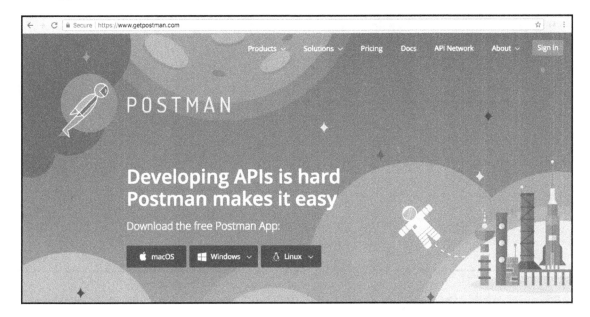

Now I'm going to be using the Chrome application. To install it, all you have to do is install
the Chrome app from the Chrome store, click **Add to Chrome**, and it should bring you over
to the page where you can open up the application. Now, to open up Chrome apps, you
have to go to this kind of weird URL. It's `chrome://apps`. Here, you can view all of your
apps, and we can just open up Postman by clicking it.

Now as I mentioned previously, Postman lets you make HTTP requests, so we're going to
go ahead and make a few to play around with the user interface. You do not need to make
an account, and you do not need to sign up for a paid plan. The paid plans are targeted
towards teams of developers who need advanced features. We are just making basic
requests on our machine; we don't need cloud storage or anything like that. I'm going to
skip account creation, and we can go right to the application.

Here, we can set up our request; this is what happens in the panel:

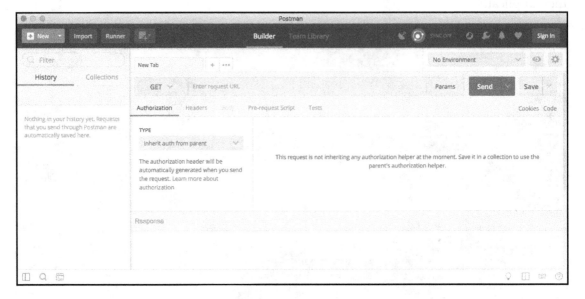

And, in the white space, we'll be able to view the result. Let's go ahead and make a request to Google.

Making an HTTP request to Google

In the URL bar, I'm going to type `http://google.com`. We can click **Send** to send off that request. Make sure you have **GET** chosen as your HTTP method. When I fire off the request, it comes back, and all of the data that comes back is shown in the white space:

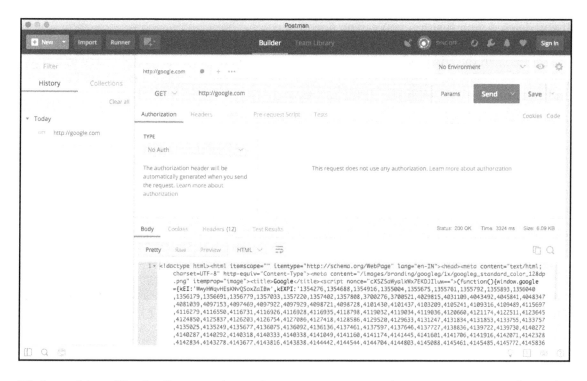

We have things like the **Status** code; we have a **200**, meaning things went great; we have the **Time**, which took about a quarter of a second; we have **Headers**, which are coming back from Google; we have **Cookies**, but there's none in this case; and we have our **Body** data. The body for google.com is an HTML website. For the most part, the bodies that we'll be sending and getting in Postman are going to be JSON since we're building out the REST API.

Illustrating working of the JSON data

So to illustrate how JSON data works, we're going to make a request to the geocoding URL that we used earlier in the course. If you remember, we were able to pass in a location and we got some JSON back, describing things like the latitude and longitude, and the formatted address. Now this should still be in your Chrome history.

If you deleted your history, you can go ahead and
put `https://maps.googleapis.com/maps/api/geocode/json?address=1301+lombard+st+p hiladelphia` in the address bar. This is the URL I'll be using; you can simply copy it, or you can grab any JSON API URL. I'm going to copy it to the clipboard, head back into Postman, and swap out the URL with the URL I just copied:

Now, I can go ahead and fire off the request. We get our JSON data, which is fantastic:

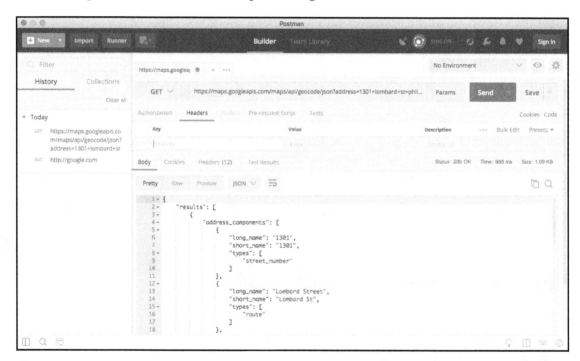

We're able to see exactly what comes back when we make this request, and this is how we're going to be using Postman.

We'll use Postman to make requests, add Todos, delete Todos, get all of our Todos, and log in; all of that stuff is going to happen right in here. Remember, APIs don't necessarily have a frontend. Maybe it's an Android app; maybe it's an iPhone app or a web app; maybe it's another server. Postman gives us a way to interact with our API, making sure it works as expected. We have all of the JSON data that comes back. In the **Raw** view, which is under **Body**, we have the raw data response. Essentially, it's just unprettified; there is no formatting, there is no colorization. We also have a **Preview** tab. The **Preview** tab is pretty useless for JSON. When it comes to JSON data., I always stick with the **Pretty** tab, which should be the default.

Now that we have Postman installed and we know a little bit about how to use it, we're going to move on to the next section, where we will actually create our first request. We'll be firing off a Postman request to hit the URL we're going to create. This is going to let us make new Todos right from Postman or any other application, whether it's a web app, a mobile app, or another server. That's all coming up next, so just make sure you have Postman installed. If you were able to do everything in this section, you are ready to continue.

Resource Creation Endpoint - POST /todos

In this section, you're going to create your HTTP POST route for adding new Todos. Before we dive into that, we're first going to refactor everything we have in server.js. We have database configuration stuff which should live somewhere else and we have our models, which should also live in separate files. The only thing we want in server.js is our Express route handlers.

Refactoring the server.js file to create POST todos route

To get started, inside of the `server` folder, we're going to make a new folder called `db`, and inside of the `db` folder we'll make a file where all of this Mongoose configuration will happen. I'm going to call that file `mongoose.js`, and all we need to do is take our Mongoose configuration code right here:

```
var mongoose = require('mongoose');
mongoose.Promise = global.Promise;
mongoose.connect('mongodb://localhost:27017/TodoApp');
```

Cut it out, and to move it over into `mongoose.js`. Now, we need to export something. What we're going to export is the `mongoose` variable. So essentially, when someone requires the mongoose.js file, they're going to have Mongoose configured and they're going to get it —they're going to get back the `mongoose` variable that comes from the library. I'm going to set `module.exports` equal to an object, and on that object we'll set `mongoose` equal to `mongoose`:

```
mongoose.connect('mongodb://localhost:27017/TodoApp');

module.exports = {
  mongoose: mongoose
};
```

Now as we know, in ES6, this can be simplified. If you have a property and a variable with the same name you can shorten it, and we can take things a step further and put it all on one line:

```
module.exports = {mongoose};
```

Now we have the Mongoose configuration in a separate file, and that file can be required in the `server.js` file. I'm going to pull off the mongoose property using ES6 destructuring. Essentially, we're creating a local variable called `mongoose` equal to the mongoose property on the object, and that object is going to be the return result from requiring the file we just created. It's in the `db` directory and it's called `mongoose.js`, and we can leave off that extension:

```
var mongoose = require('./db/mongoose');
```

Now that Mongoose lives in its own place, let's do the same thing for `Todo` and `User`. This is going to happen in a new folder in a server called `models`.

Configuring the Todo and Users file

Inside of models, we're going to create two files, one for each model. I'm going to make two new files called todo.js, and user.js. We can take the todos and Users models from the server.js file and simply copy and paste them into their appropriate files. Once the model's copied, we can remove it from server.js. The Todos model is going to look like this:

```
var Todo = mongoose.model('Todo', {
  text: {
    type: String,
    required: true,
    minlength: 1,
    trim: true
  },
  completed: {
    type: Boolean,
    default: false
  },
  completedAt: {
    type: Number,
    default: null
  }
});
```

The user.js model is going to look like this.

```
var User = mongoose.model('User', {
  email: {
    type: String,
    required: true,
    trim: true,
    minlength: 1
  }
});
```

I'm also going to remove everything we have so far, since those examples in server.js aren't necessary anymore. We can simply leave our mongoose import statement up at the top.

Inside of these model files, there are a few things we need to do. First up, we will call the `mongoose.model` in both Todos and Users files, so we still need to load in Mongoose. Now, we don't have to load in the `mongoose.js` file we created; we can load in the plain old library. Let's make a variable. We'll call that variable `mongoose`, and we're going to `require('mongoose')`:

```
var mongoose = require('mongoose');

var Todo = mongoose.model('Todo', {
```

The last thing that we need to do is export the model, otherwise we can't use it in files that require this one. I'm going to set `module.exports` equal to an object, and we'll set the `Todo` property equal to the `Todo` variable; this is exactly what we did over in `mongoose.js`:

```
module.exports = {Todo};
```

And we're going to do the exact same thing in `user.js`. Inside of `user.js`, up at the top, we'll create a variable called `mongoose` requiring `mongoose`, and at the bottom we'll export the `User` model, `module.exports`, setting it equal to an object where `User` equals `User`:

```
Var mongoose = require('mongoose');

var User = mongoose.model('User', {
  email: {
    type: String,
    required: true,
    trim: true,
    minlength: 1
  }
});

module.exports = {User};
```

Now, all three of our files have been formatted. We have our three new files and our one old one. The last thing left to do is load in `Todo` and `User`.

Loading Todo and User file in server.js

In the `server.js` file, let's make a variable using destructuring call `Todo`, setting it equal to `require('./models/todo')`, and we can do the exact same thing for `User`. Using ES6 destructuring, we're going to pull off that `User` variable, and we're going to get it from the object that comes back from a call to `require`, requiring `models/user`:

```
var {mongoose} = require('./db/mongoose');
var {Todo} = require('./models/todo');
var {User} = require('./models/user');
```

With this in place, we are now ready to get going. We have the exact same setup, only it's been refactored, and this is going to make it a lot easier to test, update, and manage. The `server.js` file is just going to be responsible for our routes.

Configuring the Express application

Now, to get started, we're going to need to install Express. We've already done that in the past, so over in the Terminal all we need to do is run `npm i` followed by the module name, which is `express`. We'll be using the most recent version, `4.16.2`.

We're also going to be installing a second module, and we can actually type that right after the first one. There's no need to run `npm install` twice. This one is called the `body-parser`. The `body-parser` is going to let us send JSON to the server. The server can then take that JSON and do something with it. `body-parser` essentially parses the body. It takes that string body and turns it into a JavaScript object. Now, with `body-parser`, we're going to be installing version `1.18.2`, the most recent version. I'm also going to provide the `--save` flag, which is going to add both Express and `body-parser` to the dependencies section of `package.json`:

```
npm i express@4.16.2 body-parser@1.18.2 --save
```

Now, I can go ahead and fire off this request, installing both modules, and over inside of `server.js`, we can start configuring our app.

First up, we have to load in those two modules we just installed. As I mentioned previously, I like to keep a space between local imports and library imports. I'm going to use a variable called `express` to store the Express library, namely `require('express')`. We're going to do the same thing for `body-parser` with a variable called `bodyParser`, setting it equal to the return result from requiring `body-parser`:

```
var express = require('express');
var bodyParser = require('body-parser');

var {mongoose} = require('./db/mongoose');
var {Todo} = require('./models/todo');
var {User} = require('./models/user');
```

Now that we can set up a very basic application. We're going to make a variable called `app`; this is going to store our Express application. I'm going to set this equal to a call to `express`:

```
var {User} = require('./models/user');

var app = express();
```

And we're also going to call `app.listen`, listening on a port. We will be deploying this to Heroku eventually. For now though, we're going to have a local port, port `3000`, and we'll provide a callback function that's going to fire once the app is up. All we're going to do is use `console.log` to print `Started on port 3000`:

```
var app = express();

app.listen(3000, () => {
  console.log('Started on port 3000');
});
```

Configuring the POST route

Now, we have a very basic server. All we have to do is start configuring our routes, and as I promised, the one we're going to be focusing on in this section is the POST route. This is going to let us create new Todos. Now, inside of your REST APIs, there's the basic CRUD operations, CRUD being Create, Read, Update, and Delete.

When you want to create a resource, you use the POST HTTP method, and you send that resource as the body. This means that when we want to make a new Todo, we're going to send a JSON object over to the server. It's going to have a text property, and the server is going to get that text property, create the new model, and send the complete model with the ID, the completed property, and completedAt back to the client.

To set up a route, we need to call app.post, passing in the two arguments we've used for every single Express route, which are our URL and our callback function that get called with the req and res objects. Now, the URL for a REST API is really important, and there is a lot of talk about the proper structure. For resources, what I like to do is use /todos:

```
app.post('/todos', (req, res) => {

});
```

This is for resource creation, and this is a pretty standard setup. /todos is for creating a new Todo. Later on, when we want to read Todos, we'll use the GET method, and we will use GET from /todos to get all Todos or /todos, some crazy number, to get an individual Todo by its ID. This is a very common pattern, and it's the one we're going to be using. For now though, we can focus on getting the body data that was sent from the client.

Getting body data from the client

To do this, we have to use the body-parser module. As I mentioned previously, body-parser is going to take your JSON and convert it into an object, attaching it onto this request object. We're going to configure the middleware using app.use. The app.use takes the middleware. If we're writing custom middleware, it'll be a function; if we're using third-party middleware, we usually just access something off of the library. In this case, it's going to be bodyParser.json getting called as a function. The return value from this JSON method is a function, and that is the middleware that we need to give to Express:

```
var app = express();

app.use(bodyParser.json());
```

With this in place, we can now send JSON to our Express application. What I'd like to do inside of the `post` callback is simply `console.log` the value of `req.body`, where the body gets stored by `bodyParser`:

```
app.use(bodyParser.json());

app.post('/todos', (req, res) => {
  console.log(req.body);
});
```

We can now start up the server and test things out inside of Postman.

Testing the POST route inside Postman

In the Terminal, I'm going to use `clear` to clear the Terminal output, and then I'll run the app:

```
node server/server.js
```

The server is up on port 3000, which means we can now head into Postman:

```
[Gary:node-todo-api Gary$ node server/server.js
Started on port 3000
```

Inside of Postman, we're not going to be making a GET request like we did in the previous section. This time, what we're going to be doing is making a **POST** request, which means we need to change the HTTP method to **POST**, and type the URL. That's going to be `localhost:3000` for the port, `/todos`. This is the URL that we want to send our data to:

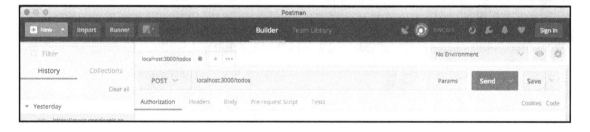

Now in order to send some data to the application, we have to go to the **Body** tab. We're trying to send JSON data, so we're going to go to **raw** and select **JSON (application/json)** from the drop-down list on the right-hand side:

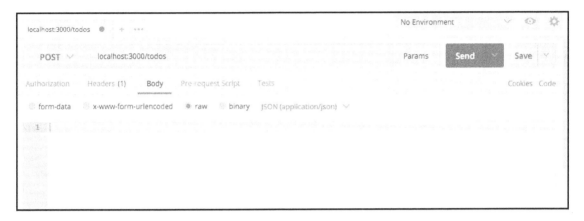

Now we have our **Header** set. This is the Content-Type header, letting the server know that JSON is getting sent. All of this is done automatically with Postman. Inside of **Body**, the only piece of information I'm going to attach to my JSON is a `text` property:

```
{
    "text": "This is from postman"
}
```

Now we can click **Send** to fire off our request. We're never going to get a response because we haven't responded to it inside of `server.js`, but if I head over to the Terminal, you see we have our data:

```
[Gary:node-todo-api Gary$ node server/server.js
Started on port 3000
{ text: 'This is from postman' }
```

This is the data we created inside of Postman. It's now showing up in our Node application, which is fantastic. We are one step closer to actually creating that Todo. The only thing left to do inside of the post handler is to actually create the Todo using the information that comes from the `User`.

Creating an instance of Mongoose model

Inside `server.js`, let's make a variable called `todo` to do what we've done previously, creating an instance of a Mongoose model. We're going to set it equal to `new Todo`, passing in our object and passing in the values we want to set. In this case, we just want to set `text`. We're going to set text to `req.body`, which is the object we have, and then we're going to access the `text` property, like so:

```
app.post('/todos', (req, res) => {
  var todo = new Todo({
    text: req.body.text
  });
```

Next up, we're going to call `todo.save`. This is going to actually save the model to the database, and we're going to be providing a callback for a success case and an error case.

```
app.post('/todos', (req, res) => {
  var todo = new Todo({
    text: req.body.text
  });

todo.save().then((doc) => {
}, (e) => {
});
```

Now if things go well, we're going to be sending back the actual Todo which is going to show up in the then callback. I'm going to get the `doc`, and right inside of the callback function, I'm going to use `res.send` to send the doc back. This is going to give the `User` really important information, things like the ID and the `completed` and `completedAt` properties, which were not set by the `User`. If things go poorly and we get an error, that's fine too. All we're going to do is use `res.send` to send that error back:

```
todo.save().then((doc) => {
  res.send(doc);
}, (e) => {
  res.send(e);
});
```

We'll be modifying how we send errors back a little later. For now, this code is going to work just great. We can also set an HTTP status.

Setting up HTTP status code

If you remember, HTTP statuses let you give someone some information about how the request went. Did it go well? Did it go poorly? That kind of thing. You can get a list of all the HTTP statuses available to you by going to `httpstatuses.com`. Here, you can view all of the statuses that you can set:

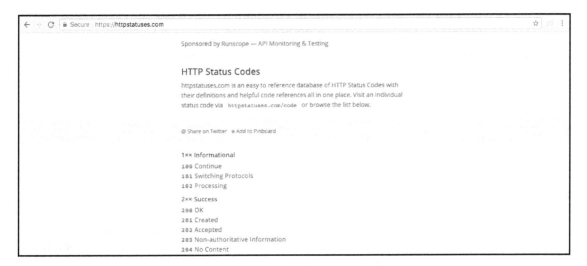

The one that's set by default by Express is `200`. This means that things went OK. What we're going to be using for an error is code `400`. A `400` status means there was some bad input, which is going to be the case if the model can't be saved. Maybe the `User` didn't provide a `text` property, or maybe the text string was empty. Either way, we want to send a `400` back, and that's going to happen. Right before we call `send`, all we're going to do is call `status`, passing in the status of `400`:

```
todo.save().then((doc) => {
  res.send(doc);
}, (e) => {
  res.status(400).send(e);
});
```

With this in place, we are now ready to test out our `POST /todos` request over inside of Postman.

Testing POST /todos inside of Postman

I'm going to restart the server in the Terminal. You could start this up with `nodemon` if you like. For the moment, I'll be manually restarting it:

```
nodemon server/server.js
```

We're now up on localhost 3000, and inside of Postman, we can make the exact same request we made earlier. I'm going to click on **Send**:

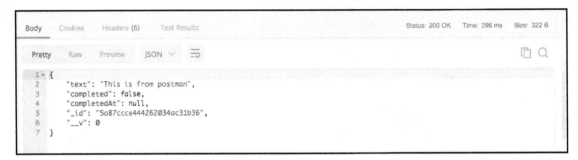

We get a **Status** of **200**. This is fantastic; it's the default status, which means things went great. The JSON response is exactly what we expected. We have our `text` that we set; we have the `_id` property which was generated; we have `completedAt`, which is set to `null`, the default; and we have `completed` set to `false`, the default.

We could also test what happens when we try to create a Todo without the proper information. For example, maybe I set a `text` property equal to an empty string. If I send this over, we now get a **400 Bad Request**:

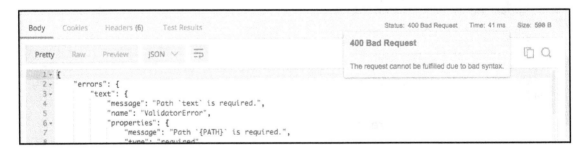

Now, we have a bunch of validation code saying that the `Todo validation failed`. Then, we can go into the `errors` object to get the specific error. Here, we can see the `text` field failed, and the `message` is `Path 'text' is required`. All of this information can help someone fix their request and make a proper one.

Now if I head over into Robomongo, I'm going to refresh the collection for `todos`. Look at the last one, and it is indeed the one we created in Postman:

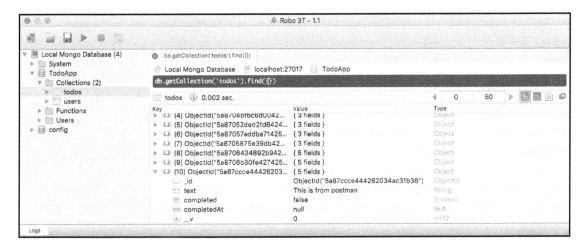

The **text** is equal to **This is from postman**. With this in place, we now have our very first HTTP endpoint set up for the Todo REST API.

Now I haven't talked exactly about what REST is. We're going to talk about that later. For now, we're going to focus on creating these endpoints. The REST version will come up a little later when we start adding authentication.

Adding more Todos to the database

Over inside of Postman, we can add a few more Todos, which is what I'm going to do. `Charge my phone`—I don't think I've ever needed to be reminded of that one—and we'll add `Take a break for lunch`. In the Pretty section, we see the `Charge my phone` Todo was created with a unique ID. I'm going to send off the second one, and we'll see that the `Take a break for lunch` Todo was created:

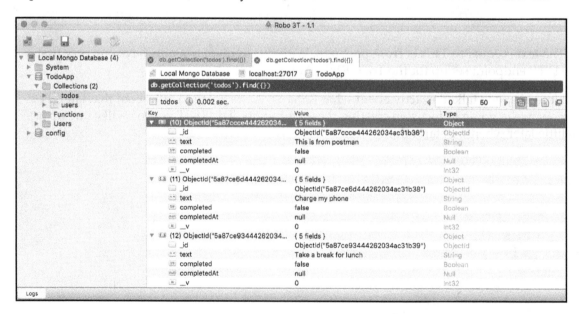

Over inside of Robomongo, we can give our `todos` collection a final refresh. I'm going to expand those last three items, and they are indeed the three items we created in Postman:

Now that we have some meaningful work done in our project, let's go ahead and commit our changes. As you can see over in Atom, the `server` directory is green, meaning that it hasn't been added to Git, and the `package.json` file is orange, which means that it's been modified, even though Git is tracking it. Over in the Terminal we can shut down the server, and I always like to run `git status` to do a sanity check:

```
[Gary:node-todo-api Gary$ git status
On branch master
Your branch is up-to-date with 'origin/master'.

Changes not staged for commit:
  (use "git add <file>..." to update what will be committed)
  (use "git checkout -- <file>..." to discard changes in working directory)

        modified:   package-lock.json
        modified:   package.json

Untracked files:
  (use "git add <file>..." to include in what will be committed)

        server/

no changes added to commit (use "git add" and/or "git commit -a")
Gary:node-todo-api Gary$
```

Here, everything does look as expected. I can it using `git add .` to add everything, followed by one more sanity check:

```
[Gary:node-todo-api Gary$ git add .
[Gary:node-todo-api Gary$ git status
On branch master
Your branch is up-to-date with 'origin/master'.

Changes to be committed:
  (use "git reset HEAD <file>..." to unstage)

        modified:   package-lock.json
        modified:   package.json
        new file:   server/db/mongoose.js
        new file:   server/models/todo.js
        new file:   server/models/user.js
        new file:   server/server.js

Gary:node-todo-api Gary$
```

Here, we have our four new files in the `server` folder, as well as our `package.json` file.

Now, it's time to make that commit. I'm going to create a quick commit. I'm using the $-am$ flag, which usually adds modified files. Since I already used add, I can simply use the $-m$ flag, like we've been doing all the way through the course. A good message for this one would be something like Add POST /todos route and refactor mongoose:

```
git commit -m 'Add POST /todos route and refractor mongoose'
```

With the commit in place, we can now wrap things up by pushing it up to GitHub, making sure it's backed up, and making sure it's available for anyone else collaborating on the project. Remember, creating a commit alone does not get it up on GitHub; you've got to push that with another command, namely git push. With that in place, it's now time to move on to the next section, where you will be testing the route you just created.

Testing POST /todos

In this section, you're going to learn how to set up the test suite for the Todo API, similar to what we did in the test section, and we'll be writing two test cases for /todos. We're going to verify that when we send the correct data as the body, we get a 200 back with the completed doc, including the ID; and, if we send bad data, we expect a 400 back with the error object.

Installing npm modules for testing POST /todos route

Now before we can do any of this, we have to install all of those modules we installed in the test section, expect for assertions, mocha for the entire test suite, supertest to test our Express routes, and nodemon. The nodemon module is going to let us create that test-watch script we had, so we can automatically restart the test suite. Now I know you have nodemon installed globally, but since we are using it inside of a package.json script, it's a great idea to install it locally as well.

We're going to run npm i with expect version 22.3.0, the most recent. Next up is going to be mocha. The most recent version is 5.0.1. After that is nodemon version 1.15.0, and last but not least is supertest at version 3.0.0. With this in place, all we have to do is tack on that --save-dev flag. We want to save these, but not as regular dependencies. They're for testing purposes only, so we're going to save them as devDependencies:

```
npm i expect@22.3.0 mocha@5.0.1 nodemon@1.15.0 supertest@3.0.0 --save-dev
```

Now, we can go ahead and run this command, and once it's done we'll be able to start setting up the test files inside of Atom.

Setting up the test files

In Atom, inside my `package.json` file, I now have my `devDependencies` listed out:

```
package.json    ✕    server.js   ✕   mongoose.js ✕   todo.js     ✕   user.js     ✕
 7          "test": "echo \"Error: no test specified\" && exit 1"
 8        },
 9        "author": "",
10        "license": "ISC",
11        "dependencies": {
12          "body-parser": "^1.18.2",
13          "express": "^4.16.2",
14          "mongodb": "^3.0.2",
15          "mongoose": "^5.0.6"
16        },
17        "devDependencies": {
18          "expect": "^22.3.0",
19          "mocha": "^5.0.1",
20          "nodemon": "^1.15.0",
21          "supertest": "^3.0.0"
22        }
23      }
```

Now, my output for this command might look a little different than yours. npm is caching some of my modules that I've installed recently, so as you can see in the preceding screenshot, it's just grabbing the local copy. They did indeed get installed though, and I can prove that by opening up the `node_modules` folder.

We're now going to create a folder inside the `server` where we can store all of our test files, and this folder is going to be called `tests`. The only file we're going to worry about creating for this section is a test file for `server.js`. I'm going to make a new file in tests called `server.test.js`. This is the extension we'll be using for test files in the chapter. Inside of the `server.test` file, we can now kick things off by requiring a lot of those modules. We're going to require the `supertest` module and `expect`. The `mocha` and `nodemon` modules do not need to be required; that's not how they're used.

The `const expect` variable we'll get will be equal to `require('expect')`, and we'll do the exact same thing for `supertest`, using `const`:

```
const expect = require('expect');
const request = require('supertest');
```

Now that we have these in place, we need to load in some of our local files. We need to load in `server.js` so we have access to the Express app since we need that for super-test, and we also want to load in our Todo model. As you'll see a little later, we're going to be querying the database, and having access to this model is going to be necessary. Now the model already exports something, but `server.js` currently exports nothing. We can fix this by adding `module.exports` to the very bottom of the `server.js` file, setting it equal to an object. On that object, all we're going to do is set the `app` property equal to the `app` variable, using the ES6 object syntax.

```
module.exports = {app};
```

With this in place, we are now ready to load those two files in.

Loading the test files

First up, let's go ahead and create a local variable called `app`, and we're going to be using ES6 destructuring to pull it off of the return result from requiring the server file. Here, we're going to start by getting the relative path. Then, we're going to go back one directory from `tests` into `server`. The filename is simply `server` without the extension. We can do the exact same thing for the Todo model as well.

We're going to make a constant called `Todo`. We're using ES6 destructuring to pull that off of the export, and the file is from the relative path, back a directory. Then we have to go into the `models` directory, and finally, the filename is called `todo`:

```
const expect = require('expect');
const request = require('supertest');

const {app} = require('./../server');
const {Todo} = require('./../models/todo');
```

And now that we have all of this loaded in, we are ready to create our `describe` block and add our test cases.

Adding describe block for the test cases

I'm going to use `describe` to group all of the routes. I'm going to have multiple test cases for some routes, and it's nice to add a `describe` block so you can quickly glance at the test output in the Terminal. The `describe` block for POST Todos will simply be called `POST /todos`. Then, we can add our arrow function (=>), and inside of here we can start laying out our test cases. The first test is going to verify that when we send the appropriate data, everything goes as expected:

```
const {Todo} = require('./../models/todo');

describe('POST /todos', () => {
  it('should create a new todo')
});
```

Now, we can add our callback function, and this function is going to take the `done` argument because this is going to be an asynchronous test. You have to specify `done`, otherwise this test is not going to work as expected. In the callback function, what we're going to do is create a variable called `text`. This is the only setup data we really need. We just need a string, and we're going to use that string throughout. Go ahead and give this any value you like. I'm going to use `Test todo text`.

```
describe('POST /todos', () => {
  it('should create a new todo', (done) => {
    var text = 'Test todo text';
  });
});
```

Now it's time to start making that request via `supertest`. We only made `GET` requests previously, but `POST` requests are just as easy.

Making the POST requests via supertest

We're going to call request, passing in the app we want to make the request on. Next up, we're going to call `.post`, which sets up a `POST` request. We're going to go to `/todos`, and the new thing we're going to do is actually send data. In order to send data along with the request as the body we have to call `send`, and we're going to pass in an object. This object is going to get converted to JSON by `supertest`, so there's no need for us to worry about that—just another great reason to use the `supertest` library. We're going to set `text` equal to the `text` variable shown previously, and we can use the ES6 syntax to get that done:

```
describe('POST /todos', () => {
  it('should create a new todo',(done) => {
    var text = 'Test todo text';

    request(app)
    .post('/todos')
    .send({text})
  })
});
```

Now that we've sent the request, we can start making assertions about the request.

Making assertions about the POST request

We'll start with the status. I'm going to `expect` that the status equals `200`, which should be the case when we send across valid data. After this, we can go ahead and make an assertion about the body that comes back. We want to make sure the body is an object and that it has the `text` property equal to the one we specified previously. That's exactly what it should be doing when it sends the body back.

Over inside of `server.test.js`, we can get that done by creating a custom `expect` assertion. If you can recall, our custom `expect` calls do get passed in the response, and we can use that response inside of the function. We're going to `expect` that the response body has a `text` property and that the `text` property equals using `toBe`, the `text` string we have defined:

```
request(app)
.post('/todos')
.send({text})
.expect(200)
.expect((res) => {
  expect(res.body.text).toBe(text);
})
```

If that's the case, great; this will pass. If not, that's fine too. We're just going to throw an error and the test will fail. The next thing we need to do is call end to wrap things up, but we're not quite done yet. What we want to do is actually check what got stored in the MongoDB collection, and this is why we loaded in the model. Instead of passing `done` into end like we did previously, we're going to pass in a function. This function will get called with an error, if any, and the response:

```
request(app)
.post('/todos')
.send({text})
.expect(200)
.expect((res) => {
  expect(res.body.text).toBe(text);
})
.end((err, res) => {

});
```

This callback function is going to allow us to do a few things. First up, let's handle any errors that might have occurred. This will be if the status wasn't `200`, or if the `body` doesn't have a `text` property equal to the `text` property we sent in. All we have to do is check if an error exists. If an error does exist, all we're going to do is pass it into `done`. This is going to wrap up the test, printing the error to the screen, so the test will indeed fail. I'm also going to `return` this result.

```
.end((err, res) => {
  if(err) {
    return done(err);
  }
});
```

Now, returning it doesn't do anything special. All it does is stop the function execution. Now, we're going to make a request to the database fetching all the Todos, verifying that our one `Todo` was indeed added.

Making a request to fetch the Todos from the database

To do that, we have to call `Todo.find`. Now, `Todo.find` is really similar to the MongoDB native `find` method we used. We can call it with no arguments to fetch everything in that collection. In this case, we'll be fetching all of the Todos. Next up, we can attach a `then` callback. We're going to get this function called with all `todos`, and we can make some assertions about that.

```
.end((err, res) => {
  if(err) {
    return done(err);
  }
}

Todo.find().then((todos) => {
})
```

In this case, we're going to assert that the Todo we created does exist. We'll get started by expecting `todos.length` to `toBe` equal to the number 1, because we've added one Todo item. We're going to make one more assertion. We're going to `expect` that that one and only item has a `text` property equal to using `toBe`, the `text` variable we have in server.test.js.

```
Todo.find().then((todos) => {
  expect(todos.length).toBe(1);
  expect(todos[0].text).toBe(text);
})
```

If both of these pass, then we can be pretty sure that everything worked as expected. The status code is correct, the response is correct, and the database looks correct as well. Now it's time to call `done`, wrapping up the test case:

```
Todo.find().then((todos) => {
  expect(todos.length).toBe(1);
  expect(todos[0].text).toBe(text);
  done();
})
```

We're not done quite yet. If either of these fail, the test is still going to pass. What we have to do is tack on a `catch` call.

Adding the catch call for the error handling

The `catch` is going to get any errors that might occur inside of our callback. Then, we're going to be able to take that error argument, and using an arrow function, we're going to be able to pass it into `done`, just like this:

```
Todo.find().then((todos) => {
    expect(todos.length).toBe(1);
    expect(todos[0].text).toBe(text);
    done();
}).catch((e) => done(e));
```

Notice here I'm using the statement syntax as opposed to the arrow function expression syntax. With this in place, our test case is now good to go. We have a great test case, and all we need to do is set up the `scripts` in `package.json` to actually run it.

Setting up test scripts in package.json

Before we run the test, we're going to set up the `scripts`, just like we did in the test section. We're going to have two: `test`, which just runs the tests; and `test-watch`, which runs the test script through `nodemon`. This means that any time we change our app, the tests will rerun.

Right in `test`, we'll be running `mocha`, and the only other argument we need to provide is the globbing pattern for the test files. We're going to fetch everything in the `server` directory, which could be in a subdirectory (which it will be later), so we'll use two stars (`**`). It can have any file name, as long as it ends with the `.test.js` extension.

```
"scripts": {
    "test": "mocha server/**/*.test.js",
    "test-watch":
},
```

Now for `test-watch`, all we're going to do is run `nodemon`. We're going to be using the `--exec` flag to specify a custom command to run inside of single quotes. The command we're going to run is `npm test`. The `test` script on its own is useful, and `test-watch` simply reruns the `test` script every time something changes:

```
"scripts": {
  "test": "mocha server/**/*.test.js",
  "test-watch": "nodemon --exec 'npm test'"
},
```

There is still a major flaw we need to fix before we can move on. As you may have noticed, inside of the `server.test` file, we make a really big assumption. We assume that there's nothing already in the database. We assume this because we expect the Todos to be a length of 1 after adding 1, which means that we assumed it started at 0. Now this assumption is not going to be correct. If I were to run the test suite right now, it would fail. I already have Todos in the database. What we're going to do is add a testing life cycle method in the `server.test` file. This one is called `beforeEach`.

Adding testing life cycle method in server.test.js file

The `beforeEach` method is going to let us run some code before every single test case. We're going to use `beforeEach` to set up the database in a way that's useful. For now, all we're going to do is make sure the database is empty. We're going to pass in a function, that function is going to get called with a `done` argument, just like our individual test cases are.

```
const {Todo} = require('./../models/todo');

beforeEach((done) => {

});
```

This function is going to run before every test case and it's only going to move on to the test case once we call `done`, which means we can do something asynchronous inside of this function. What I'm going to do is call `Todo.remove`, which is similar to the MongoDB native method. All we need to do is pass in an empty object; this is going to wipe all of our Todos. Then, we can tack on a `then` callback, and inside of the `then` callback we're going to call `done`, just like this:

```
beforeEach((done) => {
  Todo.remove({}).then(() => {
    done();
  })
});
```

Now, we can also shorten this using the expression syntax:

```
beforeEach((done) => {
  Todo.remove({}).then(() => done());
});
```

With this in place, our database is going to be empty before every request, and now our assumption is correct. We're assuming we start with 0 Todos, and we will indeed start with 0 Todos since we just deleted everything.

Running the test suite

I'm going to go ahead and move into the Terminal, clear the Terminal output, and now we can start running the test suite by using the following command:

```
npm run test-watch
```

This is going to start up `nodemon` which will start up the test suite, and right here we get one test passing, **should create a new todo**:

```
[Gary:node-todo-api Gary$ npm run test-watch

> todo-api@1.0.0 test-watch /Users/Gary/Desktop/node-todo-api
> nodemon --exec 'npm test'

[nodemon] 1.15.0
[nodemon] to restart at any time, enter `rs`
[nodemon] watching: *.*
[nodemon] starting `npm test'

> todo-api@1.0.0 test /Users/Gary/Desktop/node-todo-api
> mocha server/**/*.test.js



Started on port 3000
  POST /todos
    ✓ should create a new todo (89ms)


  1 passing (199ms)
```

We can verify that everything is working as expected by tweaking some values. I can add on `1` as follows:

```
request(app)
  .post('/todos')
  .send({text})
  .expect(200)
```

```
    .expect((res) => {
      expect(res.body.text).toBe(text + '1');
  })
```

Just to prove that it is actually doing what it says it's doing. You can see that we're getting an error because the two are not equal.

The same thing holds true with our status. If I change the status to something else, like 201, the test suite is going to rerun and it is going to fail. Last but not least, down below, if I change toBe to 3 as follows:

```
expect(todos.length).toBe(3);
```

It's going to fail because we're always wiping the database, and therefore the only correct value here would be 1. Now that we have this in place, we can add our second test case. This is going to be the test case that verifies that a Todo does not get created when we send bad data.

Test case: should not create todo with invalid body data

To get started with this one, we will be using it to create a brand-new test case. The text for this one could be something like should not create todo with invalid body data. We can pass in our callback with the done argument, and start making our super-test request.

This time around, there is no need to make a text variable since we're not going to be passing text into it. What we're going to be doing is passing in nothing at all:

```
it('should not create todo with invalid body data', (done) => {

});
```

Now, what I'd like you to do is make a request just like we did previously. You're going to make a POST request to the same URL, but instead you're going to send send as an empty object. This empty object is going to cause the test to fail because we won't be able to save the model. Then, you're going to expect we get a 400, which would be the case, we send a 400 in the server.js file. You don't need to make any assumptions about the body that comes back.

Last but not least, you are going to use the following format; we pass a callback to end, check for any errors, and then make some assumptions about the database. The assumption you're going to make is that the length of `todos` is 0. Since the preceding code block does not create a Todo, no Todos should be there. The `beforeEach` function is going to run before every test case, so the Todo that gets created in `should create a new todo` is going to get deleted before our case runs. Go ahead and set that up. Make the request and verify that the length is 0. You don't need to have the assertion in the previous test case, since this assertion asserts something about the array, and the array is going to be empty. You can also leave the following assertion off:

```
.expect((res) => {
  expect(res.body.text).toBe(text);
})
```

Since we're not going to make any assertions about the body. When you're done, save the test file. Make sure both of your tests pass.

The first thing I'm going to do is call `request`, passing in our `app`. We want to make another post request, so I'll call `.post` again, and the URL is also going to be the same. Now at this point, we are going to be calling `.send`, but we're not going to be passing invalid data. The whole point of this test case is to see what happens when we pass in invalid data. What should happen is we should get a `400`, so I'm going to `expect` that a `400` response is what comes back from the server. Now we don't need to make any assertions about the body, so we can go ahead and move on to `.end`, where we're going to pass in our function that gets called with the `err` argument, if any, and `res`, just like this:

```
it('should not create todo with invalid body data', (done) => {
  request(app)
  .post('/todos')
  .send({})
  .expect(400)
  .end((err, res) => {

  });
});
```

Now, we want to do is handle any potential errors. If there is an error we're going to return, which stops the function from executing, and we're going to call `done`, passing in that error so the test properly fails:

```
.end((err, res) => {
  if(err) {
    return done(err);
  }
});
```

Making assertions about the length of the Todos collection

Now, we can fetch from the database and make some assertions about the length of the Todos collection. I'm going to use `Todo.find` to fetch every single Todo inside of the collection. Then, I'll tack on a `then` callback, so I can do something with that data. In this case, I'll get the `todos`, and I'm going to assert something about its length. We're going to `expect` that `todos.length` equals `toBe` the number 0.

```
Todo.find().then((todos) => {
  expect(todos.length).toBe(0);
});
```

There should be no Todos in the database before this test case runs, and since we're sending in bad data, this test case should not create any Todos. We can now call `done` and we can also tack on our `catch` callback, which we're going to need to do just like we did previously. We are going to call `catch`, taking that error argument and passing it into `done`:

```
Todo.find().then((todos) => {
  expect(todos.length).toBe(0);
  done();
}).catch((e) => done(e));
```

And now, we are done. I can save the file. This is going to restart nodemon, which is going to restart our test suite. What we should see is our two test cases, both of them passing. Over in the Terminal, we get just that. We have two test cases for POST /todos, and both are indeed passing:

```
[nodemon] restarting due to changes...
[nodemon] starting `npm test`

> todo-api@1.0.0 test /Users/Gary/Desktop/node-todo-api
> mocha server/**/*.test.js



Started on port 3000
  POST /todos
    ✓ should create a new todo (85ms)
    ✓ should not create todo with invalid body data


  2 passing (130ms)
```

It took a little while to set up the basic test suite in this section, but in the future as we add more routes, testing is going to be much easier. We're not going to have to set up the infrastructure; we're not going to need to create the test scripts or install new modules.

Making commit for POST /todos route

The last thing to do is make a commit. We added some meaningful code, so we're going to want to save that work. If I run git status, you can see we have a few changed files as well as some untracked ones, so I will use git add . to add all of those to the next commit. Now, I can use git commit with the -m flag to actually make the commit. A good commit message for this one would be Test POST /todos route:

```
git commit -m 'Test POST /todos route'
```

I'm going to make the commit, and lastly, I'll be pushing this up to GitHub using git push. You can use git push for this particular case. I need to go ahead and use git push --force, which is going to overwrite everything on GitHub. This is only something I need to do in this specific situation. You should just be running git push. Once you run that, your code should get pushed up to GitHub, and you are done. We have two test cases for our route, and it's time to move on and add a new route. The next route is going to be a GET request to fetch all Todos.

List Resources - GET /todos

With our test suite in place, it's now time to create our second route, the GET /todos route, which will be responsible for returning all of your Todos. This is useful for any Todo application.

Creating the GET /todos route

The first screen you're probably going to show a user is a list of all of their Todos. This is the route you would use to get that information. It's going to be a GET request so I'm going to use app.get to register the route handler, and the URL itself is going to match the URL we have, /todos, because we want to get all of the Todos. Later on when we get an individual Todo, the URL will look something like /todos/123, but for now we're going to match it with the POST URL. Next up, we can add our callback right above app.listen in server.js; this is going to give us our request and response objects:

```
app.get('/todos', (req, res) => {

});
```

All we need to do is get all of the Todos in the collection, which we've already done in the test file. Inside of server.test.js, we used Todo.find to fetch all of the Todos. We're going to use that same technique right here, but we're not passing in a query; we want to return everything.

```
app.get('/todos', (req, res) => {
  Todo.find()
});
```

Later on when we add authentication you'll get back just the Todos you created, but for now, without authentication you're going to get everything in the Todos collection back.

Next up, we're going to attach a `then` call. This `then` call is going to take two functions, the success case function when the promise gets resolved, and a function that gets fired when the promise gets rejected. The success case will get called with all of the `todos` and all we're going to do is send that information back using `res.send`.

```
app.get('/todos', (req, res) => {
  Todo.find().then((todos) => {
    res.send()
  }, (e) => {

  })
});
```

We could pass in the `todos` array, but this is not the best way to get the job done. When you pass back an array you're kind of locking yourself down. If you want to add on another property, whether it's a custom status code or some other data, you can't because you have an array. The better solution would be to create an object, and on that object specify `todos`, setting it equal to the `todos` array using ES6:

```
app.get('/todos', (req, res) => {
  Todo.find().then((todos) => {
    res.send({todos});
  }, (e) => {

  })
});
```

This would let you add other properties later on. For example, I could add some sort of custom status code setting it equal to whatever I like. By using an object as opposed to sending an array back, we're opening ourselves up to a more flexible future. With this in place, our success case is good to go. The only thing we need to do to wrap this one up is handle errors, and the error handler is going to look exactly like the one we used previously, `res.status`. We're going to be sending back a `400` and we'll be sending back the error object that got passed into the function:

```
app.get('/todos', (req, res) => {
  Todo.find().then((todos) => {
    res.send({todos});
  }, (e) => {
    res.status(400).send(e);
  });
});
```

Now that we have this in place, we can go ahead and start up our server and test things out over inside of Postman.

Testing the GET /todos route

I'm going to fire up the server using the following command:

```
node server/server.js
```

Inside of Postman, we can get started by creating some Todos. Currently, our application and the tests for the application use the same database. The `beforeEach` method call we ran in the last section unfortunately wiped everything, which means we have no data to fetch. The first thing I'm going to do in Postman is try to fetch the data we should get back an empty array, which should still work. The URL is going to be `localhost:3000/todos` and it is indeed going to be a **GET** request. I can click **Send**, which is going to fire off the request, and we get our data back:

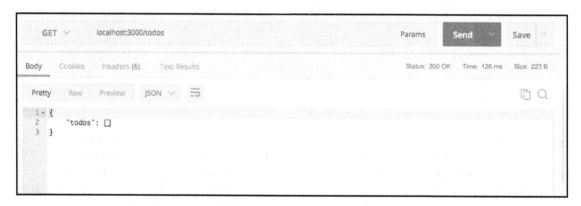

We have an object, we have our `todos` property, and we have our empty array, which is expected.

Now, as you may have noticed, manually configuring a route every single time you want to use it gets pretty tedious, and we're going to be using a lot of the same routes over and over again. With Postman, we can actually create a collection of routes so we can re-fire requests without having to manually enter all of the information. Over on the right-hand side, I can click the drop-down arrow next to **Save** and click **Save As**. Here, I can give my request a little bit of detail:

I'm going to change the **Request Name** to GET /todos; this is the naming convention I like to use, the HTTP method followed by the URL. We can leave the description blank for now, and we can create a new collection since we don't have any. The Postman Echo collection is an example collection Postman gives you to explore this feature. We're going to make one called Todo App. Now, anytime we want to run that command, all we do is we go to **Collections**, click **GET /todos**, click **Send**, and the request fires.

Let's go ahead and set up a POST request to create a Todo, and then we'll run that, save it, and rerun GET to make sure it returns the newly created Todo.

Setting up Post request to create a todo

To create the POST request, if you recall, we have to change the method to **POST** and the URL will be the same, localhost:3000/todos:

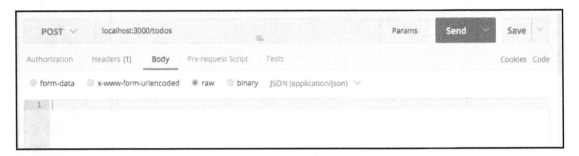

Now, in order for this request to succeed, we also have to pass along a **Body** tab. This one is going to be a raw **JSON** body. Here, we can specify the data we'd like to send. In this case, the only data property we're going to send is text, and I'll set this to Something to do from postman:

```
{
    "text": "Something to do from postman"
}
```

Now, we can go ahead and fire this off, and down below we get our newly created Todo with a **200** status code:

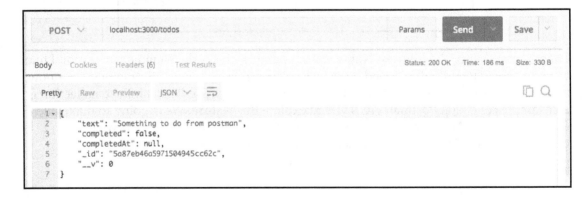

Which means everything went well. We can save this to our collections so we can easily rerun this one later. I'm going to change the **Request Name** to `POST /todos`, following that same syntax. Then, I can then select an existing collection, the **Todo App** collection, and save it:

Now I can simply click the request, using *command + enter*, or clicking the **Send** button, to fire off the request, and I get my `todos` array—everything looks great.

I can always click **POST**, add a second one, tweak it if I like, adding the number 2, and then I can use *command + enter* to fire that one off. I can rerun the GET request and I have my two `todos` in the database:

```
1 ▾ {
2 ▾     "todos": [
3 ▾        {
4              "completed": false,
5              "completedAt": null,
6              "_id": "5a87eb46a5971504945cc62c",
7              "text": "Something to do from postman",
8              "__v": 0
9          },
10 ▾       {
11             "completed": false,
12             "completedAt": null,
13             "_id": "5a87ec9ca5971504945cc62d",
14             "text": "Something to do from postman2",
15             "__v": 0
16         }
17     ]
18 }
```

With this in place, our GET /todos request is now complete. We also set up our collection in Postman, making it really easy to fire off any of these HTTP requests much faster.

I'm going to go ahead and wrap this section up by making a commit over in the Terminal. I'm going to shut the server down and run `git status`. This time around, you'll see that we just have one file and it is modified, which means instead of using `git add`, we can simply use `git commit` with the `-a` flag. The `-a` flag adds all modified files to the next commit. It does not work for new, untracked files, but modified files are perfectly fine. Then, I can tack on the `-m` flag to specify my commit message. A good one for this will be `Add GET /todos route`:

```
git commit -a -m 'Add GET /todos route'
```

Last up, we're going to push it up to GitHub using `git push`, and now we are done. In the next section, we'll write test cases for GET /todos.

Testing GET /todos

With our `GET /todos` route now in place, it is time to add a test case for it. Now, before we can actually write the test case, we have to deal with a different problem. The first thing we do inside of our `server.test` file is delete all the Todos, and this happens before every single test. The `GET /todos` route pretty much lives off the fact that there are Todos it can return. It will handle Node Todos, but for our test case, we want some data in that database.

In order to add this data, what we're going to do is modify `beforeEach`, adding some seed data. This means that our database is still going to be predictable; it's always going to look exactly the same when it starts, but it will have some items in it.

Adding seed data for the GET /todos test case

Now, in order to do that, the first thing that we're going to do is make up an array of dummy Todos. These Todos only need the `text` property since everything else is going to get populated by Mongoose. I can create a constant called `todos`, setting it equal to an array, and we're going to have an array of objects where each object has a `text` property. For example, this one could have a text of `First test todo`, and then I can add on a second object as the second item in the array, with a `text` property equal to `Second test todo`:

```
const todos = [{
  text: 'First test todo'
},{
  text: 'Second test todo'
}];
```

Now before we can actually write the test case, we have to modify `beforeEach` using a brand new Mongoose method called `insertMany`, which takes an array, as shown in the preceding code block, and inserts all of those documents into the collection. This means that we are going to need to tweak the code real quick.

Instead of having a simple arrow function that calls done, I'm going to tack on some curly braces and inside of the callback function, we're going to call `Todo.insertMany` and we're going to call `insertMany` with the array we defined in the preceding code block. This is going to insert all of the Todos in this array, our two Todos, and then we can do something like call done. I'm going to return the response, which is going to let us chain callbacks, and then I can tack on a `then` method, where I can use a really simple expression-based arrow function. All I'm going to do is call done using the expression syntax:

```
beforeEach((done) => {
  Todo.remove({}).then(() => {
    return Todo.insertMany(todos);
  }).then(() => done());
});
```

Now, let's go ahead and run the test suite. I'll warn you now, the other tests are going to have problems because the numbers that they assert are now going to be incorrect. Over in the Terminal, I'm going to start up the test suite by using the following command:

npm run test-watch

Once that test suite gets started, I'm going to move back into Atom and as you can see, as promised, both of the test cases failed. We expected 3 to be 1 and we expected 2 to be 0. Everything is now off by 2.

To fix this, we're going to use two different techniques. Inside the server.test.js file, in the Post todos test, for the first test, we're going to do is only going to find Todos where the text property equals to the Test todo text:

```
Todo.find({text}).then((todos) => {
  expect(todos.length).toBe(1);
  expect(todos[0].text).toBe(text);
  done();
}).catch((e) => done(e));
```

This means that the resulting length is still going to be 1 and the first item should still have a text property equal to the text above. For the second test, we're going to leave the find call the way it is; instead, we're going to make sure that the length of the database is 2:

```
Todo.find().then((todos) => {
  expect(todos.length).toBe(2);
  done();
}).catch((e) => done(e));
```

There should only be two documents in the Todos collection because that's all we added, and this was testing a failure so a third one should not have been added. With this in place, you can see our two test cases are now passing:

```
[nodemon] restarting due to changes...
[nodemon] starting `npm test`

> todo-api@1.0.0 test /Users/Gary/Desktop/node-todo-api
> mocha server/**/*.test.js


Started on port 3000
  POST /todos
    ✔ should create a new todo (152ms)
    ✔ should not create todo with invalid body data


  2 passing (223ms)
```

We're now ready to move on and add a new `describe` block in the test case.

Adding a describe block to the test case

I'm going to add a `describe` block, which is going to describe the GET `/todos` route, passing in our arrow function, and then we can add our single test case, `it('should get all todos', )`. Now, in this case, all `todos` refer to the two Todos we just added previously. I'm going to pass in an arrow function with the `done` argument and we are good to go. All we have to do is start the super test request—I'm going to `request` something on the express application—this is going to be a GET request so we'll call `.get`, passing in the URL `/todos`:

```
describe('GET /todos', () => {
  it('should get all todos', (done) => {
    request(app)
    .get('/todos')
  )};
});
```

With this in place, we're now ready to make our assertions; we're not sending any data in the request body, but we are going to make some assertions about what comes back.

Adding assertions to the test case

We're going to `expect` that a `200` comes back and we're also going to create a custom assertion, expecting something about the body. We'll provide our callback function with the response and we're going to `expect` that `res.body.todos` has a length of 2, `.toBe(2)`. Now that we have this in place, all we have to do is tack on an `end` call, and pass in `done` as the argument.

```
describe('GET /todos', () => {
  it('should get all todos', (done) => {
    request(app)
    .get('/todos')
    .expect(200)
    .expect((res) => {
      expect(res.body.todos.length).toBe(2);
    })
    .end(done);
  )};
});
```

There is no need to provide a function to end, because we're not doing anything asynchronously.

With this in place, we are now good to go. We can save the `server.test` file. This is going to rerun the test suite using `nodemon`; we should see our new test and it should be passing. In the Terminal, we get just that:

```
[nodemon] restarting due to changes...
[nodemon] starting `npm test`

> todo-api@1.0.0 test /Users/Gary/Desktop/node-todo-api
> mocha server/**/*.test.js



Started on port 3000
  POST /todos
    ✓ should create a new todo (86ms)
    ✓ should not create todo with invalid body data

  GET /todos
    ✓ should get all todos


  3 passing (163ms)
```

We have our section for `POST /todos`; both of these tests are passing and we have our section for `GET /todos`, and the one test is indeed passing. Now if I change the status to `201`, the test is going to fail because that's not the status that came back. If I change the length to `3`, it's going to fail because we only added 2 Todos in as the seed data.

Now that we're done, let's go ahead and make a commit, saving this code. I'm going to shut down the `test-watch` script, run a `git status` command, and we have two modified files, which means I can use `git commit` with the `-a` flag and the `-m` flag. Remember, the `-a` flag adds modified files to the next commit. A good message for this commit is going to be `Add tests for GET /todos`:

```
git commit -a -m 'Add tests for GET /todos'
```

I'm going to make the commit, push it up to GitHub, and then we are done.

Summary

In this chapter, we worked on setting up mongoose, connecting mongoose to the database. We created few Todos model and run the test script. Next, we looked into mongoose validators, Defaults and types, and customize todo model properties such as test, completed and completedAt. Then, we looked in the basics of Postman and made HTTP request to Google. We also looked into configuring some todo routes, mainly POST /todos and GET /todos. We also looked into creating test cases and testing these routes.

With this in place, we are ready to move on to adding a brand new route, which is coming up in the next chapter.

4
MongoDB, Mongoose, and REST APIs – Part 3

In this chapter, you're going to resolve the Mongoose queries and ID validation after playing with Mongoose in the previous chapter. We will get into the details of different types of todo methods followed by deploying the API to Heroku. Finally, after learning more about Postman environments and running various test cases, we will create our test database.

Mongoose queries and ID validation

In this section, you're going to learn a few alternative ways that you can use Mongoose to query your data. Now, inside of the `server.test` file, we already looked at one way, `Todo.find`. We're going to look at two more and then we're also going to explore how to validate ObjectIDs.

In order to do all of this we are going to make a new file in the `playground` folder. I'm going to call this one `mongoose-queries.js`, and the first thing we need to do is load in the `mongoose` file in the `db` folder and the `todo` file in the `models` folder. I'm going to use ES6 destructuring, like we've used for all files where this happens, then we can `require` in the local file. Using the relative path, we need to go up a directory out of `playgroundserverdb`, and finally the filename we're looking for is called `mongoose`:

```
const {mongoose} = require('./../server/db/mongoose');
```

We can do the same thing for `todo`; we're going to make that constant `Todo` from the `require`, return the result, and the file here is going to follow the same path. We need to go back a directory and into `server`, but instead of going into `db` we'll go into `models`. Then we'll get the `todo` file:

```
const {Todo} = require('./../server/models/todo');
```

Now, before we can actually do any querying, we are going to grab an ID for one of our existing Todos over in Robomongo. In the `TodoApp` database I'm going to explore all of our documents and I'll just grab the first one:

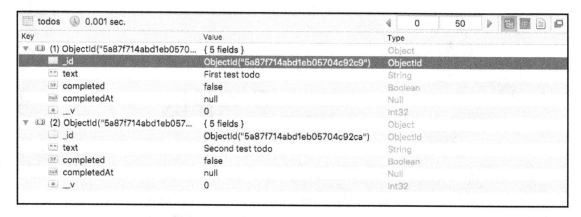

I'll right-click to edit it, then I can grab the ID excluding the quotes, parentheses, and the `ObjectId` identifier. With this ID in the clipboard back inside of Atom I can make a variable called `id` and set it equal to the ID I just copied inside of single quotes, and now we have an ID and we can use this for all of our querying.

Todo.find method

Now, I understand you've already used `Todo.find` before but we are going to talk about a few other things. So for the moment we will be starting with that. `Todo.find` lets you query as many Todos as you like. You can pass in no arguments to get all your Todos back, or you can query by anything. We're going to query by _id. Now, Mongoose is fantastic, it doesn't require you to pass in ObjectIDs, as it can actually do that for you. In this case, what we have is perfectly valid. We pass in a string as the value, and Mongoose is going to take that string, it's going to convert it to an ObjectID, and then it's going to run the query. This means we don't need to manually convert our string into an ObjectID. Now, after we make the query we can attach a `then` callback, we're going to get all of our Todos, we'll name that argument and we can go ahead and print them to the screen, `console.log('Todos',)` and the second argument will be the actual `todos` array:

```
var id = '5a87f714abd1eb05704c92c9';

Todo.find({
    _id: id
}).then((todos) => {
```

```
    console.log('Todos', todos);
});
```

Nothing new here aside from the fact that you can indeed pass in an `id` as a string.

Todo.findOne method

The next method we're going to look at is one called `Todo.findOne`. Now, `Todo.findOne` is very similar to find, the only difference is that it returns one document at most. That means it simply grabs the first one that matches the query you have. In our case we're querying by a unique ID, so it's only going to find one matching item, but if there were other results, for example, if we queried all Todos with completed false, the first doc would be the only one that returns, even though there's two that match the query. What we can do to call `findOne` is identical to what we did with find, and to prove it I'm actually going to copy the code. All we need to do is change a few things. Instead of `todos`, we get `todo`, and we're just going to get a single document not an array of documents. That means I can print a `Todo` string followed by the `todo` variable:

```
Todo.findOne({
    _id: id
}).then((todo) => {
    console.log('Todo', todo);
});
```

With this in place we now have enough examples where it makes sense to run the file and see exactly what happens.

Over inside of the Terminal I'm going to kick things off by running this file, and I'll run it using the following command:

nodemon playground/mongoose-queries.js

When we run the file, we get our `Todos` array, our array of one document, and we get our `Todo` object:

```
Gary:node-todo-api Gary$ nodemon playground/mongoose-queries.js
[nodemon] 1.14.10
[nodemon] to restart at any time, enter `rs`
[nodemon] watching: *.*
[nodemon] starting `node playground/mongoose-queries.js`
Todos [ { completed: false,
    completedAt: null,
    _id: 5a87f714abd1eb05704c92c9,
    text: 'First test todo',
    __v: 0 } ]
Todo { completed: false,
  completedAt: null,
  _id: 5a87f714abd1eb05704c92c9,
  text: 'First test todo',
  __v: 0 }
```

If you know you're just trying to fetch one individual item, I recommend using `findOne` over `find`. You get back the document as opposed to an array. This also makes it a lot easier when the ID of the Todo you're looking for doesn't exist; instead of getting an empty array as the result you'll get `null` back and you can work with that, doing whatever you like. Maybe that means you return a 404 or maybe you want to do something else if the ID is not found.

Todo.findById method

The last method we're going to look at is `Todo.findById`. Now, `findById` is fantastic if you are just looking for a document by its identifier. There is no way to query by anything else other than the ID and all you do is you pass in the id as the argument. You don't have to make a query object and you don't have to set an `_id` prompt. With this in place, we can now do the exact same thing we did with `findOne`. I'm going to prove that by taking the `then` call, pasting it inside `Todo.findById`, and just changing the print statement from `Todo` to `Todo By Id`:

```
Todo.findById(id).then((todo) => {
    console.log('Todo By Id', todo);
});
```

Now if I save the file, `nodemon` is going to rerun and we get the exact same result for both:

```
[nodemon] starting `node playground/mongoose-queries.js`
Todos [ { completed: false,
    completedAt: null,
    _id: 5a87f714abd1eb05704c92c9,
    text: 'First test todo',
    __v: 0 } ]
Todo { completed: false,
  completedAt: null,
  _id: 5a87f714abd1eb05704c92c9,
  text: 'First test todo',
  __v: 0 }
Todo By Id { completed: false,
  completedAt: null,
  _id: 5a87f714abd1eb05704c92c9,
  text: 'First test todo',
  __v: 0 }
```

If you want to find one document by something other than ID, I recommend using `findOne`. If you want to find one document by ID, I always recommend using `findById`. Now, all of this and more is available in the docs, so if you want to dive into anything I discussed here you can always go to `mongoosejs.com`. Click on the **read the docs** link, and over in the left-hand side they have a couple of links; the one that we're looking for is the one on **Queries**:

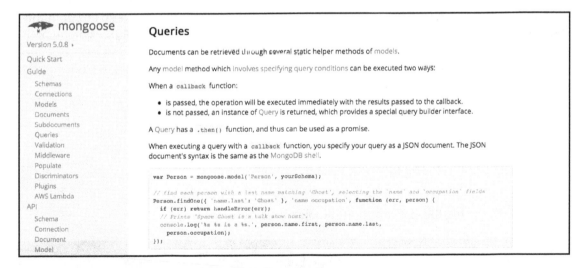

You can learn more about how to query your docs, but we pretty much covered everything this page talks about.

Handling situations where the ID doesn't exist

Now, the next thing I want to talk about is what happens when the ID isn't correct, and this is going to be the case because, remember, our API is going to be getting this ID from the user, which means that if the ID isn't correct we don't want our code to fail, we want to elegantly handle these errors. To prove this I'm going to go ahead and tweak the ID a little bit. IDs do have specific protocols so what I want you to do, for this example, is find a number in your ID. I'm going to go with the first character because it happens to be a number, and just increment it by one. I'm going to go from 5 to 6. Now we have a valid ID but the ID is not going to be in the database because I tweaked it, and obviously the other Todo in the database does not match this ID.

Now, with this in place, you can see as we restart the server we get an empty array for the find call, and we get null for both `findOne` and `findById`:

```
[nodemon] starting `node playground/mongoose-queries.js`
Todos []
Todo null
Todo By Id null
```

When your ID does not match anything in the database, an error is not going to get thrown; it's still going to fire the success case, it's just going to fire it either with an empty array or with null, which means when we want to handle that case where the ID doesn't exist in the database, all we have to do is add an `if` statement. Inside the `Todo.findById` statement, I can add an `if` statement. If there is no todo, we're going to do something, and that something is going to be to use `return` which prevents the rest of the function from executing, and we'll print a little message, `console.log('Id not found')`:

```
Todo.findById(id).then((todo) => {
    if(!todo) {
        return console.log('Id not found');
    }
    console.log('Todo By Id', todo);
});
```

Now if I save the file the last call should look a little different:

```
[nodemon] starting `node playground/mongoose-queries.js`
Todos []
Todo null
Id not found
```

As shown in the preceding screenshot, instead of getting Todo with null, we get `Id not found`, and this is perfect. Now we know how to query using `findOne` and `findById`, and we also know how to handle situations where the ID you're querying for doesn't actually exist inside of the collection. I'm going to set the ID back to its original value, changing `6` to `5`, and if I save the file, nodemon's going to restart and we're going to get our document back.

Validating an ObjectID

Now, the last thing I want to talk about is how to validate an ObjectID. What we've done so far is we've created a valid ObjectID. It's just of a value that is not in the collection, but if we were to do something like tack on two `1`s, we would actually have an invalid ID which is going to cause errors in the program. Now, you might wonder why this would ever happen, but it could happen because the user is the one specifying the ID. We're going to add a `catch` call onto `findById`. We're going to get that error and simply print it to the screen using `console.log`:

```
Todo.findById(id).then((todo) => {
  if(!todo) {
    return console.log('Id not found');
  }
  console.log('Todo By Id', todo);
}).catch((e) => console.log(e));
```

Now, to illustrate this we don't need all three queries. In order to clean up the Terminal output, I'm going to go ahead and comment out `Todo.find` and `Todo.findOne`. With this in place, our invalid ID, and the `catch` callback we can save the file, and over in the Terminal we should get a really long error message:

```
[nodemon] restarting due to changes...
[nodemon] starting `node playground/mongoose-queries.js`
{ CastError: Cast to ObjectId failed for value "5a87f714abd1eb05704c92c911" at path "_id" for model "Todo"
    at new CastError (/Users/Gary/Desktop/node-todo-api/node_modules/mongoose/lib/error/cast.js:27:11)
    at ObjectId.cast (/Users/Gary/Desktop/node-todo-api/node_modules/mongoose/lib/schema/objectid.js:158:13)
    at ObjectId.SchemaType.applySetters (/Users/Gary/Desktop/node-todo-api/node_modules/mongoose/lib/schemat
ype.js:701:12)
    at ObjectId.SchemaType._castForQuery (/Users/Gary/Desktop/node-todo-api/node_modules/mongoose/lib/schema
type.js:1072:15)
    at ObjectId.castForQuery (/Users/Gary/Desktop/node-todo-api/node_modules/mongoose/lib/schema/objectid.js
:198:15)
```

We have an error message, `CastError: Cast to ObjectId failed`, for the given value. This is warning you that your `ObjectID` doesn't just not exist in the collection, it's actually completely invalid. Now, running this with a `catch` method does let us handle the error. We could do something like tell the user, hey, the ID that you sent through is invalid, but there's also another way to get it done that I prefer. What we're going to do is load in the ObjectID off of the MongoDB native driver and that's something we did before. Right here in `mongodb-connect` we loaded in the, `ObjectID`. Inside of `mongoose-queries` we're going to do the same thing. I'm going to make a constant called `ObjectID` and we're going to get it from the `mongodb` library:

```
const {ObjectID} = require('mongodb');
```

Now, on `ObjectID` we have a lot of utility methods. We've looked at how we can create new ObjectIDs, but one thing we also have access to is a method called `ObjectId.isValid`. The `isValid` method takes the value, in this case it's our string right in `id`, and it returns true if it's valid, and false if it's not valid, which means we can add `if` conditions to validate the ID before we ever run the query.

We're going to add an `if` statement, and we're going to check if the value is not valid. I'm going to flip it using an exclamation mark, then we can call `ObjectID.isValid`. By flipping it we've essentially created a method that tests whether an ObjectID is not valid. The value I'm going to pass in is just going to be the string stored in the `id` variable, and now we can add some code to run when the ID is not valid, `console.log('ID not valid')`:

```
if(!ObjectID.isValid(id)) {
    console.log('ID not valid');
}
```

Now, if I go ahead and save the file, we should get our `ID not valid` message, and then after that we should get our error message printing to the Terminal because we do still have our `catch` call, and this query is still going to run. Over here we get just that. `ID not valid` prints to the screen:

```
[nodemon] restarting due to changes...
[nodemon] starting `node playground/mongoose-queries.js`
ID not valid
{ CastError: Cast to ObjectId failed for value "5a87f714abd1eb05704c92c911" at path "_id" for model "Todo"
    at new CastError (/Users/Gary/Desktop/node-todo-api/node_modules/mongoose/lib/error/cast.js:27:11)
    at ObjectId.cast (/Users/Gary/Desktop/node-todo-api/node_modules/mongoose/lib/schema/objectid.js:158:13)
    at ObjectId.SchemaType.applySetters (/Users/Gary/Desktop/node-todo-api/node_modules/mongoose/lib/schemat
```

But now we know how to validate IDs and that's going to come in handy in the next section.

With this in place it's now time for a challenge. Before I set up the challenge, I'm going to comment out the `id` and our `isValid` call, and down below I'll comment out `findById`. I'm going to leave them here; you can use them as a reference for what to do in the challenge. Your challenge is going to be to query the users collection. That means that you're going to want to go ahead and move into Robomongo and grab an ID from your users collection. Here I have just one document; if you have zero documents for whatever reason, you can always right-click **Insert Document**, and all you have to do is specify the email.

Now, in order to make that query over inside of Atom you are going to need to load in the user Mongoose model because currently we only have the Todo one, require. Down below I want you to use `User.findById` to query the ID that you picked over in Robomongo. Then you're going to go ahead and handle the three cases. There's going to be the case where the query works, but there is no user. In that case you're going to print something like `User not found`. You're also going to handle the case where the user was found. I want you to go ahead and print the user to the screen. Then finally you're going to handle any errors that might have occurred. You can simply print the error object to the screen for that. There's no need to use `isValid` for this one, all you have to do is fill out the `findById` call.

Now, the first thing I'm going to do is import the user file. I'm going to make a `const`, I'm going to grab the `User` variable off of the return result from require, and we're going to follow the same path we have here. We have to go out of the `playground` directory, into the `server/models` directory, and finally the filename is `user`:

```
const {User} = require('./../server/models/user');
```

Now that we have the user imported, we can query it down below. Before I write the query I am going to fetch an ID over in Robomongo:

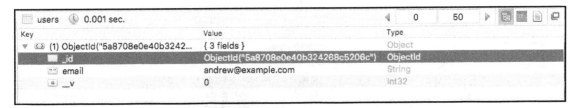

I can edit the document, highlight it, copy it, and move back into Atom. Inside of Atom I'm going to set up my `User.findById` call. All I have to do is pass in the ID; I have that in the clipboard, and I'm going to wrap it in quotes. Next up, the callbacks. I'm going to attach a `then` callback, passing in two functions. The first one is when the promise gets resolved, and the second one is when the promise gets rejected. For rejections, all we're going to do is print that error object to the screen, which means we can use `console.log(e)`. Now, if things go well, there are still a few exceptions. We want to make sure that the user actually does exist. The query is still going to pass if the ID doesn't match anything found inside of the collection. If there is no user, we are going to stop function execution using `return`, then we're going to go ahead and print using `console.log('Unable to find user')`:

```
User.findById('57bdb0fcdedf88450bfa2d66').then((user) => {
    if (!user) {
        return console.log('Unable to find user');
    }
}, (e) => {
    console.log(e);
});
```

Now, the last case we need to handle is if things actually go well, which means that the query was indeed valid and the ID was found inside of the users collection. I'm going to add `console.log` using our pretty printing technique, the `user` variable, `JSON.stringify`, passing in our three arguments, `user`, `undefined`, and the number 2:

```
User.findById('5a8708e0e40b324268c5206c').then((user) => {
    if (!user) {
        return console.log('Unable to find user');
    }
    console.log(JSON.stringify(user, undefined, 2));
}, (e) => {
    console.log(e);
});
```

With this in place I can now go ahead and save the file and open up the Terminal since it's currently hidden, we get our user showing up in the Terminal:

```
[nodemon] starting `node playground/mongoose-queries.js`
{
  "_id": "5a8708e0e40b324268c5206c",
  "email": "andrew@example.com",
  "__v": 0
}
```

This is fantastic; if you're seeing this you've successfully completed the challenge. Now I can also test that my other cases are working as expected. I'm going to change 6 at the end of my ID to a 7 and save the file:

```
[nodemon] starting `node playground/mongoose-queries.js`
Unable to find user
```

When it restarts I get `Unable to find user`, which is expected. Next up, I'm going to change it back to a 6, but I am going to tack on a few 1s, or any other characters. In this case, I'll use two 1s and two a characters. This time we do get our error, we're unable to cast that value to an ObjectId. Let's undo the change to the ID and now we're done.

I'm going to wrap this section up by committing our changes. I'm going to shut down nodemon, run a `git status` command, and we have one new file:

```
[^CGary:node-todo-api Gary$ git status
On branch master
Your branch is up-to-date with 'origin/master'.

Untracked files:
  (use "git add <file>..." to include in what will be committed)

        playground/mongoose-queries.js

nothing added to commit but untracked files present (use "git add" to track)
Gary:node-todo-api Gary$
```

I can use `git add` to add it to the next commit, then I can use `git commit` to make the commit. A good message for this one is `Add queries playground file`:

```
git commit -m 'Add queries playground file'
```

With this in place I'm going to push it up to GitHub using the `git push` command, and we are done. In the next section you will be responsible for creating an entire API request.

Getting an individual resource – GET /todos/:id

In this section, you are going to create an API route for fetching an individual Todo. Now, most of this section is going to be a challenge but there is one thing I want to show you before we get started, and that is **how to fetch a variable that's passed in via the URL.** Now, as I mentioned, the structure for this URL is going to be a GET request, /todos, then we're going to dive into the Todos, fetching an individual item where the ID gets passed, such as /todos/12345. This means that we need to make the ID part of the URL dynamic. I want to be able to fetch that value, whatever a user happens to pass in, and use it to make the query. The query that we set up in the mongoose-queries file like User.findById one to fetch the todo by Id.

Now in order to get that done, let's go ahead inside server.js file and call app.get, passing in the URL.

Taking on the challenge

The first part we already know, /todos/, but now what we need is a URL parameter. URL parameters follow this pattern: it's a colon followed by a name. Now I could call this :todoId, or anything else, but what we're going to call it for this section is :id. This is going to create an id variable; it's going to be on the request object, the one we'll set up in just a moment, and we'll be able to access that variable. That means when someone makes the GET /todos/1234324 request, the callback will fire, the one we're going to specify now, and we'll be able to query by the ID they pass in. Now, we are still going to get the request and response object, the only difference is we're now going to be using something off of request. This one is req.params. The req.params object is going to be an object, it's going to have key value pairs where the key is the URL parameter, like id, and the value is whatever value was actually put there. In order to demonstrate this, I am going to simply call res.send, sending back the req.params object:

```
//GET /todos/12345
app.get('/todos/:id', (req, res) => {
   res.send(req.params);
});
```

This is going to let us test out this route inside of Postman and see exactly how it works. Inside of the Terminal I can start up our server. I'm going to use following command to start things up:

```
nodemon server/server.js
```

Now the server's on `localhost:3000` and we can make a `GET` request to this, the `/todos/:id` URL. Over inside Postman I'm going to do just that; we have the **GET** method, the URL is `localhost`, and it's still on port `3000/todos/`, and then we can type whatever we like, for example, `123`. Now, when I send this off what we get back is that `req.params` object, and right in **Body** you can see it has an `id` property set to `123`:

GET ∨	localhost:3000/todos/123		Params	Send ∨	Save ∨
Body	Cookies	Headers (6)	Test Results	Status: 200 OK	Time: 86 ms	Size: 223 B

```
Pretty    Raw    Preview    JSON ∨

1 ▾ {
2       "id": "123"
3   }
```

That means we are able to access the value in the URL using `req.params.id`, and that is exactly what you're going to need to do for the challenge. Over inside of Atom I'll start things off by creating that variable, a `var id = req.params.id` variable.

With this in place you now know everything you need in order to complete the challenge, which is going to be to finish filling out this route. First up, you're going to validate the ID using that ObjectID `isValid` method we explored over in the `mongoose-queries` file. I'll leave a little comment, `Valid id using isValid`. Now, if it's not valid, what you're going to do is stop the function execution and you're going to respond with a `404` response code, because the ID passed in is not valid, and there's no way it's ever going to be in the collection. We're going to respond with the `404` response code letting the user know that the Todo was not found, and you can send back an empty body, which means you can just call send without passing in any value. It would be similar to the `res.status(400).send(e)` statement with no error, and you would also change `400` to `404`.

Now, after that, you're going to start querying the database and this is going to happen using `findById`. I want you to take the Id and query the `Todos` collection, looking for a matching document; there's two ways this could go. There's the success case and there is the error case. If we get an error, that one is pretty self-explanatory: all we're going to do is send back a `400` response code letting the user know that the request was not valid, and we're also going to go ahead and send back nothing. We're not going to be sending back that error argument because the error that prints for the error message could contain private information. We're going to be beefing out our error handling later. Currently, as you can see, we have the function duplicated in quite a few places. That will get moved into one location later but for now you can respond with a `400` response code and send an empty body back. This brings us to the success case. Now, if there is a Todo, `if todo`, you're going to go ahead and send it back. If there is no Todo, `if no todo`, this means the call did succeed, but the ID was not found in the collection. All you're going to do is go ahead and send back a `404` response code with an empty body.

Now, both of these statements are going to look really similar; you're sending back a `404` letting the user know that the ID they passed in does not match any ID of a document in the `Todos` collection. Now you know how to do all of this, you can use anything you need to get this done. That means you can use the `mongoose-queries` file, you can use the `mongoosejs.com` documentation, you can use Stack Overflow, Google, or anything else; it's not about memorizing exactly how to get stuff done, it's about working through those problems on your own. Eventually you will memorize a lot of these techniques as they come up again and again, but for now your goal is to just get it working. When you're done, go ahead and fire off this request over in the Postman application. That means you're going to want to grab an ID that is valid from Robomongo and paste it right in the URL. You can also test what happens with IDs that are valid, but don't exist in the database, and IDs that are invalid, such as `123`, which is not a valid ObjectID. With this in place you are ready to start the challenge.

Challenge step 1 - filling the code

The first thing I'm going to do is fill out the code. We're going to validate the ID and we're going to send back a 404 response code if it's not valid. Up at the very top of the file I do not have an ObjectID imported so I'm going to have to go ahead and do that. Just below bodyParser, I can create a variable ObjectID, and set that equal to the return result from require; we're requiring the mongodb library. Now that we have ObjectID in place, we can go ahead and use it. We'll write an if statement, if (ObjectID.isValid()). Now, obviously we only want to run this code if it's not valid, so I'm going to flip the return result using an exclamation mark, and then I'm going to pass id in. Now we have an if condition that's only going to pass if the ID, the one that got passed in as the URL parameter, was not valid. In that case we're going to use return to prevent function execution, then I'm going to go ahead and respond using res.status, setting it equal to 404, and I'm going to call send with no arguments so I can send back an empty body. There we go, our first thing is complete. With this in place we can now go ahead and move onto creating the query:

```
//GET /todos/12345
app.get('/todos/:id', (req, res) => {
    var id = req.params.id;

    if(!ObjectID.isValid(id)) {
        return res.status(404).send();
    }
});
```

At this point we actually do have something we can test: we can pass in invalid IDs and make sure we get that 404 back. Over inside of the Terminal I ran the application using nodemon so it automatically restarted in Postman. I can rerun the localhost:3000/todos/123 request and we get our **404**, which is fantastic:

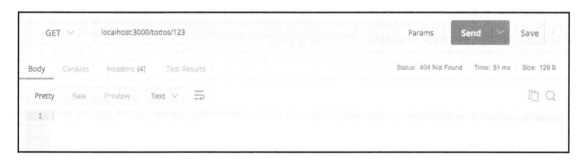

This is not a valid ObjectID, the condition failed, and the 404 was indeed returned.

Challenge step 2 - Making the query

Next up, we're going to make that query `Todo.findById`. Here we're going to pass in the ID, which we have in the `id` variable, and then we're going to attach our success and error handlers, `.then`, passing in our success callback. This is going to get called potentially with the individual Todo document, and I am going to call `catch` as well, getting the error. We can do the error handler first. If there is an error, we're going to keep things really simple, `res.status`, setting it equal to `400`, then we're going to go ahead and call `send`, leaving out the error object intentionally:

```
Todo.findById(id).then((todo) => {

}).catch((e) => {
    res.status(400).send();
});
```

With this in place the only thing left to do is fill out the success handler. The first thing we need to do is make sure that a Todo is actually found. This query, if successful, might not always result in an actual document being returned. I'm going to use an `if` statement to check if there is no Todo. If there is no Todo, we want to respond with a `404` response code, just like we did before. We're going to `return` to stop the function execution, `res.status`. The status here will be `404` and we will be using `send` to respond with no data:

```
Todo.findById(id).then((todo) => {
    if(!todo) {
        return res.status(404).send();
    }
}).catch((e) => {
    res.status(400).send();
});
```

challenge step 3 - success path

The last case is the happy path, the success case, when everything goes as planned. The ID is valid and we find a document in the Todos collection that has an ID matching the ID passed in. In that case all we're going to do is respond using `res.send`, sending back the Todo. Now, you could have sent it in like `res.todo(todo);` this will indeed work, but what I want to do is tweak it just a little bit. Instead of sending back Todo as the body, I'm going to send back an object where the Todo is attached as the `todo` property using the ES6 object definition, which is identical to this:

```
res.send({todo: todo});
```

This gives me a little flexibility down the line. I could always add other properties onto the response, like custom status codes or anything else. It's similar to the technique we used for GET /todos. Right here, res.send({todos}), instead of responding with the array, we responded with an object that has a todos property and that is the array:

```
Todo.findById(id).then((todo) => {
    if(!todo) {
        return res.status(404).send();
    }
    res.send({todo});
}).catch((e) => {
    res.status(400).send();
});
```

Now that we have this in place we are done and we can test things out. I'm going to save the file, remove all of our comments, add a semicolon where needed, and we're going to grab an ID from Robomongo. Over inside of Robomongo I can grab an ID for one of my Todos. I'm going to go with the second one. I'll edit the document and copy it to the clipboard. Now over in Postman we can go ahead and make the request, setting the ID equal to the ID value we just copied:

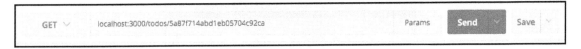

I'm going to send it off. We get our object where we have a todo property, and on that todo property we have all of the properties for the document, _id, text, completedAt, and completed:

```
1 ▾ {
2 ▾     "todo": {
3           "completed": false,
4           "completedAt": null,
5           "_id": "5a87f714abd1eb05704c92ca",
6           "text": "Second test todo",
7           "__v": 0
8       }
9   }
```

Now, the last case I want to test is what happens when we request a Todo with a valid ObjectID, but one that just happens to not exist. I'm going to do this by taking the last number in my ID and changing it from a to b:

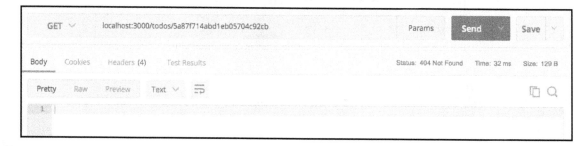

If I send this off we get our 404 response code back, which is fantastic; this is exactly what I expect to happen when I make a request for a Todo. The ObjectID is valid, it's just not in the collection. Now that we've made this request we can actually save this inside of our **Todo App** collection, so later down the line it's a lot easier to fire off this one. I'm going to save it using **Save As**:

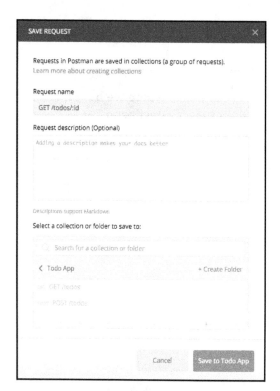

We can leave the **Request description** empty, and we can change **Request Name** to GET /todos/:id. I am going to add it to our existing collection, the **Todo App** collection. Now we have three routes; the only thing left to do for this route is to add some test cases, and that's going to be the topic of the next section.

To wrap this one up, let's commit our changes and push them up to GitHub. I'm going to shut down the server and run git status.

We can see we have our modified file; this means I can run git commit with the -a flag and the -m flag, and then I'm going to provide my commit message. Now, if you're using the -a flag and the -m flag you can actually use a shortcut, the -am flag, which does the exact same thing. It's going to add all of our modified files to the commit; it's also going to give us a place to add a message. A good message for this one would be Add GET /todos/:id:

```
git commit -am 'Add GET /todos/:id'
```

With this in place, I'm going to make the commit, push it up to GitHub, and we are done. In the next section, we are going to go ahead and write test cases for this route. It's going to be mostly a challenge like this one was.

Testing GET /todos/:id

In this section, we're going to create three test cases for this route, the one that fetches an individual Todo item. One is going to make sure that when we pass in an invalid ObjectID, we get a 404 response code. Another one is going to verify that when we pass in a valid ObjectID, but it doesn't match a doc, we get a 404 response code back, and lastly we'll write a test case that makes sure that when we pass in an ObjectID that does match a doc, that doc actually comes back in the response body.

We're going to write the test case for the valid call together, then you'll be writing two test cases on your own. That will be the challenge for this section.

Writing test cases for GET/todos/:id

Over inside of `server.test.js` we can get started down at the very bottom by adding a `describe` block. I'm going to call describe, and this `describe` block will be named GET `/todos/:id`, and we can add our arrow function (=>) as the callback function. Inside of our `describe` callback we can now set up the test case that we're going to create together, `it('should return todo doc')`. This is going to be the test that makes sure that when we pass in a valid ID that does match a doc, the doc comes back. It's going to be an asynchronous test, so we will be specifying the `done` argument:

```
describe('GET /todos/:id', () => {
  it('should return todo doc', (done) => {

  });
});
```

Now, in order to run this test case we're going to need the ID of a Todo that's actually inside of the collection, and if you remember we do add two Todos to the collection, but unfortunately we don't have the IDs. The IDs are autogenerated behind the scenes; in order to fix this what we're going to do is add the ID property, `_id`. This means we'll be able to access the ID in our test case and everything will work as expected. Now, in order to do this we do have to load an ObjectID off of MongoDB, which we've done before. I'm going to make a constant using ES6 Destructuring. I'm going to grab `ObjectID` off of the return result from requiring `mongodb`:

```
const {ObjectID} = require('mongodb');
```

Now, inside of the `todos` array we can add an `_id` property for both of our two `todos`, new `ObjectID()`, with a comma—this is for the first `todo`—and down below we can add an `_id` for the second `todo` as well, `new ObjectID()`:

```
const todos = [{
  _id: new ObjectID(),
  text: 'First test todo'
},{
  _id: new ObjectID(),
  text: 'Second test todo'
}];
```

Now that we have _ids and we can access those _ids by accessing them off the `todos` array, we're ready to write the test case.

Test 1 - Super test request

We're going to get started by creating our super test request. We're going to `request` something from the `app` express application; it is going to be a `get` request, that is, the URL we're testing, and the actual URL is going to be `/todos/id`, where `id` equals one of these `_ids` in `todos`. I'm going to go ahead and use the `_id` of the first `todo`. Down below we can fix this by changing our string to a template string, so we can inject `_id`, `/todos/` then we're going to add our syntax for injecting a value into the template string. In this case we're accessing something from the `todos` array. We want to grab the first item, this is the first `todo`, and we're looking for its `_id` property. Now, this is an ObjectID; we need to convert this into a string because that is what we're going to pass in as the URL. To convert an ObjectID to a string we can use the `toHexString` method:

```
describe('GET /todos/:id', () => {
    it('should return todo doc', (done) => {
            request(app)
            .get(`/todos/${todos[0]._id.toHexString()}`)
    });
});
```

There we go. Now we've generated the proper ID and we can start making some assertions about what should happen when this request gets fired. First up, the HTTP status code. That should be a `200`, so I can call `expect`, passing in `200`. Next step: we do want to verify that the body that comes back matches the body previous in the `todos` array, most notably that the `text` property equals the `text` property we set. I'm going to create a custom `expect` call to get that done. We'll pass in our function that gets called with the response object, and now we can make an assertion using the `expect` library. I'm going to use `expect(res.body.todo)`, which we set up in `res.send({todo})` when we used the ES6 object syntax, and that `todo` property has a `text` property that is equal to using `toBe`, the `text` property of our first `todo`. That's going to be `todos`, grabbing the first one, the zero-indexed todo, and we're going to grab its `text` property. With this in place, all of our assertions are done; we can call `end`, passing in `done`, which is going to wrap up the test case:

```
describe('GET /todos/:id', () => {
    it('should return todo doc', (done) => {
            request(app)
            .get(`/todos/${todos[0]._id.toHexString()}`)
            .expect((res) => {
                expect(res.body.todo.text).toBe(todos[0].text);
            })
```

```
                    .end(done);
        });
    });
```

Now we can go ahead and run this test over inside of the Terminal by running `npm run test-watch`. This is going to kick off our test suite and we should have our new section with our test case that is passing:

```
[nodemon] starting `npm test`

> todo-api@1.0.0 test /Users/Gary/Desktop/node-todo-api
> mocha server/**/*.test.js



Started on port 3000
  POST /todos
    ✓ should create a new todo (401ms)
    ✓ should not create todo with invalid body data

  GET /todos
    ✓ should get all todos

  GET /todos/:id
    ✓ should return todo doc


  4 passing (530ms)
```

Right here, we get `should return todo doc`, and that is passing, which is fantastic. Now it's time for you to write two test cases on your own. I'll give you the `it` calls so we're on the same page, but you are going to be responsible for filling out the actual test function, `it('should return 404 if todo not found')`. This is going to be an async test, so we'll specify the `done` argument, and your job here is going to be to make a request using a real ObjectID, and you're going to call its `toHexString` method. It is going to be a valid ID but it won't be found in the collection, so we should get a 404 back. Now, the only expectation you need to set up is the status code; make sure you get 404 back.

Test 2 - Verifying invalid ID

The second test you're going to write is going to verify that when we have an invalid ID we get back a 404 response code, it('should return 404 for non-object ids'). This is also going to be an async test, so we'll specify done. For this one, you're going to pass in a URL, something like this: /todos/123. This is indeed a valid URL, but when we try to convert 123 to an ObjectID it's going to fail, and that should trigger the return res.status(404).send() code and we should get a 404 response code back. Once again, the only expectation you need to set up for this test is that when you make the get request to the URL a 404 is the status code. Take a moment to knock out both of these test cases, making sure they work as expected when you actually have the calls set up. If all of your test cases are passing over in the Terminal when you're done, then you are ready to move on.

For the first one, I'm going to go ahead and get that HexString by creating a variable. Now, you didn't need to create a variable; you could have done it slightly differently. I'm going to make a variable called hexId, setting it equal to new ObjectID. Now on this ObjectID we do want to call that toHexString method which we used before. This takes our ObjectID and gives us a string, and we can specify that string as part of the URL. Now, it's fine if you did this inside of the get call, kind of like we do here; either way works as long as the test case passes. We're going to call request, passing in our app. Next up, we are going to make a get request, so I'll call that get method and we can set up our URL. This one is going to be /todos/ and we're going to inject in our template string that hexId value. The only expectation we need to set up is that a 404 status code comes back. We're expecting 404. We can wrap this test case up by calling end, passing in our done function:

```
it('should return 404 if todo not found', (done) => {
    var hexId = new ObjectID().toHexString();

    request(app)
    .get(`/todos/${hexId}`)
    .expect(404)
    .end(done);
});

it('should return 404 for non-object ids', (done) => {
    // /todos/123
});
```

Now we can save the file and this test case should rerun. The last test is still going to fail, but that's fine, and over here you can see we get exactly that, `should return todo doc` passes and `should return 404 if todo not found` passes:

```
Started on port 3000
  POST /todos
    ✓ should create a new todo (150ms)
    ✓ should not create todo with invalid body data

  GET /todos
    ✓ should get all todos

  GET /todos/:id
    ✓ should return todo doc
    ✓ should return 404 if todo not found
    1) should return 404 for non-object ids


  5 passing (2s)
  1 failing

  1) GET /todos/:id
       should return 404 for non-object ids:
     Error: Timeout of 2000ms exceeded. For async tests and hooks, ensure "done()" is called; if returning a
Promise, ensure it resolves.
```

And the last test to write is what happens when we have an invalid ObjectID.

Test 3 - Validating invalid ObjectID

I'm going to call `request`, passing in `app`, then I'm going to go ahead and call `get`, setting up the URL. We don't need to use template strings here since we're just going to be passing in a plain string, `/todos/123abc`. Indeed an invalid ObjectID. The ObjectIDs, as we talked about, have a very specific structure and this does not pass that criteria. To find out more about ObjectIDs you can always go back to the ObjectID section at the beginning of this chapter. Next, we're going to start setting up our assertions by calling `expect` and expecting `404` to come back, and we can wrap this test up by calling the `end` method and passing in `done`:

```
it('should return 404 for non-object ids', (done) => {
    request(app)
    .get('/todos/123abc')
    .expect(404)
    .end(done);
});
```

With this in place, our test suite for GET /todos/:id is complete. Over in the Terminal it just reran and all of the test cases passed, and this is fantastic:

```
Started on port 3000
  POST /todos
    ✓ should create a new todo (84ms)
    ✓ should not create todo with invalid body data

  GET /todos
    ✓ should get all todos

  GET /todos/:id
    ✓ should return todo doc
    ✓ should return 404 if todo not found
    ✓ should return 404 for non-object ids


  6 passing (190ms)
```

We now have a complete test suite set up for the route, which means we are done, and if the data comes back incorrectly, for example, if the body data has an extra character appended like the character 1, the test cases are going to fail. Everything is working really, really well.

The last thing left to do is commit our changes. Over inside the Terminal I'm going to shut down nodemon and run git status. Here are the only changes we have are our changes to the server.test file, which is a modified file—git is already tracking it, which means I can use git commit with the -a or -m flag or the combined -am flag, providing a message, Add test cases for GET /todos/:id:

```
git commit -am 'Add test cases for GET /todos/:id'
```

I'm going to make the commit and push it up to GitHub. In the next section, we're going to switch things up a little bit. Instead of continuing on, adding new routes, which we will do a little later, we are going to deploy our application to Heroku using a real-world MongoDB database. That means all the calls we're making in Postman we can make to a real server, and anybody can make those calls, not just people on our local machine, because the URL will no longer be on the localhost.

Deploying the API to Heroku

In this section, you're going to deploy the Todo API to Heroku so anybody with the URL can access these routes, adding and fetching Todo items. Now, before we can push it to Heroku, there are quite a few things we need to change, small tweaks to get it ready for the Heroku servers. One of the bigger tweaks is going to be to set up a real MongoDB database because currently we use a localhost database and this is not going to be available once we get our app on Heroku.

To kick things off we're going to move into the `server` file and set up the `app` variable to use the `environment` port variable that Heroku is going to set, which we did in the previous section when we deployed to Heroku. If you remember, what we did was we created a variable called `port` and we set that equal to `process.env.PORT`. This is the variable that may or may not be set; it's going to be set if the app is running on Heroku, but it won't be set if it's running locally. We can use our `||` (OR) syntax to set up a value if a port is not defined. This is going to be used on the localhost and we're going to stick with port `3000`:

```
var app = express();
const port = process.env.PORT || 3000;
```

If the `process.env.PORT` variable is there, we're going to use it; if it's not we'll use `3000`. Now, we need to swap out `3000` in `app.listen` with the `port`, which means our call to `app.listen` is going to have `port` passed in and our string below is going to get switched to a template string, so we can inject the actual port. Inside `app.listen` I'll use `Started up at port`, then I'm going to inject the actual port variable into the template string:

```
app.listen(port, () => {
    console.log(`Started on port ${port}`);
});
```

Alright, the port is set up and now we can move into the `package.json` file. There's two things we need to tweak. First up, we need to tell Heroku how to start the project. This is done via the `start` script. The `start` script is the command that Heroku is going to run to start the application. In our case it's going to be `node`, then we're going to go into the `server` directory and we're going to run the `server.js` file. I have a comma at the end and we are good to go with the `start` script:

```
"scripts": {
  "start": "node server/server.js",
  "test":"mocha server/**/*.test.js",
  "test-watch":"nodemon --exec 'npm test'"
}
```

The next thing we need to do is tell Heroku which version of Node we want to use. The default version currently is a v5 version of Node and that's going to cause some problems because we take advantage of a lot of ES6 features in this project, and those are available in v6 of Node. In order to figure out exactly what version of Node you're using, you can run node -v from the Terminal:

```
Gary:node-todo-api Gary$ node -v
v9.3.0
Gary:node-todo-api Gary$
```

Here I'm using **9.3.0**; if you're using a different v6 version that is perfectly fine. Over inside of package.json we're going to tell Heroku to use the same version we're using here. This gets done by setting up an engines property, and engines lets us specify various versions for things that Heroku lets us configure. One of these is node. The property name will be node and the value is going to be the version of Node to use, 6.2.2:

```
"engines": {
  "node": "9.3.0"
},
```

Now our package.json file is ready for Heroku. Heroku knows how to start the app and it knows exactly which version of Node we want to use, so we won't get any weird errors when we deploy.

With package.json out of the way, the last thing we need to do is set up a database, and we're going to do this with a Heroku add-on. If you go to Heroku's website and click on any of your apps, we haven't created one for this one, so click on an app from the previous section. I'm going to go ahead and click on one of mine. You're going to see a little dashboard where you can do quite a few things:

As shown in the preceding screenshot, you can see there's an **Installed add-ons** section, but what we really want is to configure our add-ons. When you configure your add-ons you're able to add all sorts of really cool tools that come built in to Heroku. Now, not all of these are free but most of them have a good free plan:

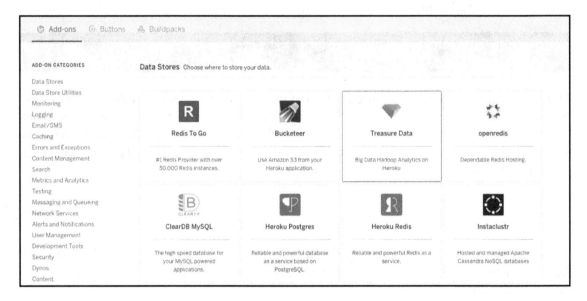

You can see we have various database-related items; down below we have **Data Store Utilities**, we have **Monitoring** tools, and a lot of really cool stuff. What we're going to be using is an add-on called **mLab**:

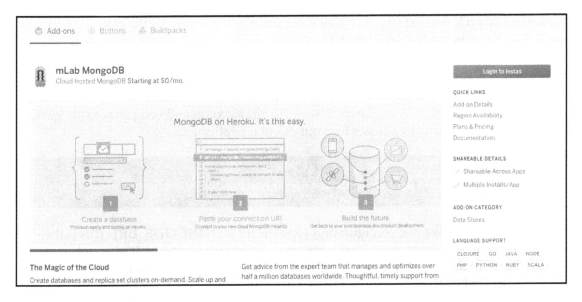

This is a MongoDB database service; it has a great free plan, and it's going to let us integrate MongoDB with our Heroku application. Now, you don't actually need to do anything from the website, as we're going to do everything from the Terminal. I just want to make you aware of exactly where this lives. Down below, you can see they do have a free **Sandbox** plan and they have plans that go all the way up to $5,000 a month. We're going to be sticking with a zero-dollar plan.

Creating a Heroku app

In order to get set up, over inside of the Terminal we're going to create a new Heroku app because currently we don't have one. `heroku create` is the command to get that done:

```
[Gary:node-todo-api Gary$ heroku create
Creating app... done, ● nameless-eyrie-97082
https://nameless-eyrie-97082.herokuapp.com/ | https://git.heroku.com/nameless-eyrie-97082.git
```

Once the application has been created we need to tell the app that we want to use `mLab`, which is short for Mongo Lab. In order to add this add-on, we're going to run the following command:

```
heroku addons:create
```

Now, the add-on is `mongolab:`, and after the `:` we're going to specify the plan we want to use. We're going to use the Sandbox plan, which is free:

```
heroku addons:create mongolab:sandbox
```

When we run this command it's going to configure `mLab` with our Heroku application and we are good to go. Now, if you run the `heroku config` command you can actually get a list of all the configuration variables for your Heroku application:

```
[Gary:node-todo-api Gary$ heroku config
=== nameless-eyrie-97082 Config Vars
MONGODB_URI: mongodb://heroku_pdgzvlvw:j5r9lbk1q75otgfh94gjgme6ti@ds113749.mlab.com:13749/heroku_pdgzvlvw
Gary:node-todo-api Gary$
```

Right now, we just have one configuration variable; it's a **MONGODB_URI**. This is the database URL that `mLab` gave us. This is the one we need to connect to, it's the only one available for our app. Now, this **MONGODB_URI** variable, this is actually on `process.env` when the app runs on Heroku, which means we can use a similar technique to what we did inside of our `mongoose.js` file. Inside of `mongoose.js`, right in our call to `connect`, we can check if `process.env.MONGODB_URI` exists. If it does, we're going to use it; if it doesn't, after our `||` statement, we are going to use the localhost URL:

```
mongoose.connect(process.env.MONGODB_URI ||
'mongodb://localhost:27017/TodoApp');
```

And this is going to make sure that our Heroku app connects to the actual database because connecting to localhost will fail, causing the app to crash. With this in place, we are now ready to get things going.

Over inside of the Terminal I'm going to run `git status` to check our changed files:

```
[Gary:node-todo-api Gary$ git status
On branch master
Your branch is up-to-date with 'origin/master'.

Changes not staged for commit:
  (use "git add <file>..." to update what will be committed)
  (use "git checkout -- <file>..." to discard changes in working directory)

        modified:   package.json
        modified:   server/db/mongoose.js
        modified:   server/server.js

Untracked files:
  (use "git add <file>..." to include in what will be committed)

        .DS_Store

no changes added to commit (use "git add" and/or "git commit -a")
Gary:node-todo-api Gary$
```

We have three; everything looks good. I can run `git commit` with the `-am` flag. This is going to let us specify our commit message, `Setup app for heroku`:

```
git commit -am 'Setup app for heroku'
```

I'm going to make the commit and push it up to GitHub. Now, we need to push our application to Heroku. I'm going to do that using the following command:

```
git push heroku master
```

Remember, when you create a Heroku application, it automatically adds that Heroku remote and here we're posting it to the master branch. The master branch is the only branch Heroku is actually going to do anything with. The application is getting pushed up; it should be ready in just a few seconds. Once it's done, we can open up the URL in the browser and see exactly what we get.

Heroku logs

Another command I want to talk about for just a moment is a command called `heroku logs`. The `heroku logs` command shows you the server lives for your application. If anything goes wrong you usually get an error message inside of the Terminal:

```
[Gary:node-todo-api Gary$ heroku logs
2018-03-14T04:22:20.086147+00:00 heroku[web.1]: Starting process with command `npm start`
2018-03-14T04:22:22.265908+00:00 app[web.1]:
2018-03-14T04:22:22.265929+00:00 app[web.1]: > todo-api@1.0.0 start /app
2018-03-14T04:22:22.265931+00:00 app[web.1]: > node server/server.js
2018-03-14T04:22:22.265932+00:00 app[web.1]:
2018-03-14T04:22:22.804787+00:00 app[web.1]: Started on port 4765
2018-03-14T04:22:23.764741+00:00 heroku[web.1]: State changed from starting to up
Gary:node-todo-api Gary$ 
```

Now, as you can see, we have our **Started on port 4765** message printing at the bottom, which is great; your port is going to be different. As long as you have this message everything should be good to go. I am going to run `heroku open`.

This is going to open up the application in my browser. I'm going to choose to copy the URL. I'll move into Chrome, and I can visit it:

Now, visiting the root of the app should do nothing because we haven't set up a root URL, but if we go to /todos we should get our todos JSON coming back:

Here you can see we have an empty array, which is expected because we haven't added any Todo items, so let's go ahead and do that.

What I want to do is grab the URL and head over to Postman. Inside of Postman we're going to make a few calls. I'm going to create a POST /todos request; all I need to do is take the URL and swap it out with the one I just copied, then I can send off the request because the body data is already configured. I'm going to send that off. We get our Todo item and this is not coming from our local machine, this is coming from our Heroku application, which is talking to our Mongo Lab MongoDB database:

Now, all the other commands should also work. I'm going to go to GET /todos, paste in the URL, and we should be able to get all of our Todo items:

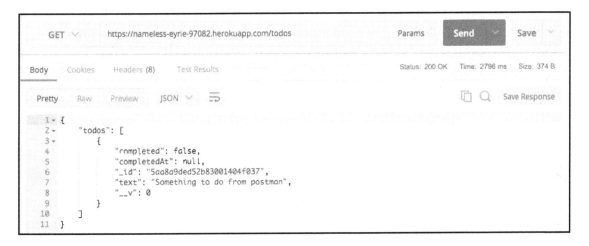

I'm also going to check what happens when we try to fetch an individual Todo. I'll copy the `_id`, add it on to the URL, and send off that request:

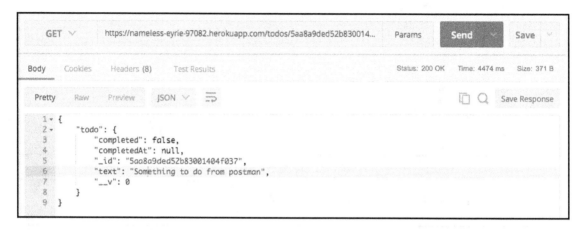

I get the individual Todo item. So, no matter which call we use, everything is working as expected and this is fantastic. Our application is now running on Heroku with a real production database, and that is it for this one. Now that we're clued up on Heroku, in the next section I'm going to show you a few tweaks and tricks we can use inside of Postman to make switching between our local environment and our Heroku environment much, much easier.

Postman environments

Before we get back to creating our express routes, we're going to take a quick moment to explore a feature of Postman that's going to make it a lot easier to switch between your local environment and the Heroku application. This is called Postman Environments.

Managing Postman environments

Now, in order to illustrate this I am going to start up my local server by running `node server/server.js` command, and over inside of Postman we're going to start making a few requests. Now, if you remember, in the last section we made a request to our Heroku application. I click **Send** on the `GET /todos` URL and I get the `todos` array back as expected. The problem is that the actual items saved in the **Collections** tab, they all use that localhost URL and there's no good way to switch between the two. To fix this issue we're going to create environments, one for our local machine, and one for Heroku. This is going to let us create a variable as the URL and we can change that variable by flicking a switch over in the **No environments** dropdown. To illustrate exactly how this is going to work I am going to be copying the Heroku URL right now, then I'm going to head over to the **No environment** dropdown, and click **Manage Environments**:

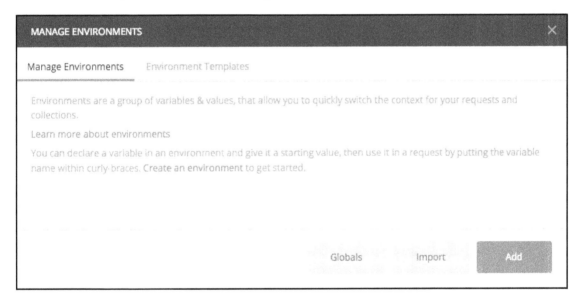

Here we currently have none, but we can go ahead and add in two.

Todo App Local environment

For the first environment I'm going to call `Todo App Local`. This is going to be the local Todo application and we can set up a set of key value pairs. Now, the only key we're going to set is url. We're going to set a localhost URL for the Todo App Local environment and we'll set the Heroku URL for the Todo App Heroku environment, which we'll create in just a second. We'll enter `url` as `localhost:3000`:

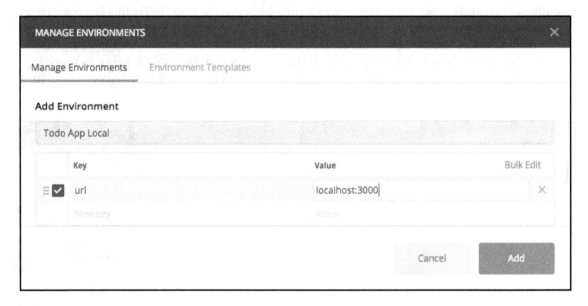

We're leaving off paths because that is going to depend on the individual route. I'm going to go ahead and add that environment.

Todo App Heroku environment

We can create a second one; this one will be called `Todo App Heroku` and we're going to set the `url` key once again. This time though we're setting it equal to the value I copied to the clipboard, the Heroku application URL:

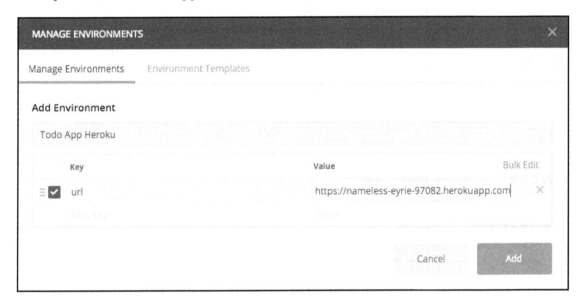

I'm going to add that, now we have our two environments and I can close that window manager.

I'm going to close all of my tabs and I'm not going to make any changes by saving, then I'm going to go to GET /todos. Now, currently, GET /todos automatically fetches from localhost. What we're going to do is replace the URL, everything before the slash, with the following syntax, which will look similar if you're familiar with any templating engines: two curly braces followed by the variable name, url, followed by two closing braces, {{url}}. This is going to inject the URL meaning that the GET /todos request is now dynamic. We can change which endpoint it requests from, localhost or Heroku, based on the environment. I'm going to save this request and fire it off, and you'll notice when you try to fire this request that we get an error:

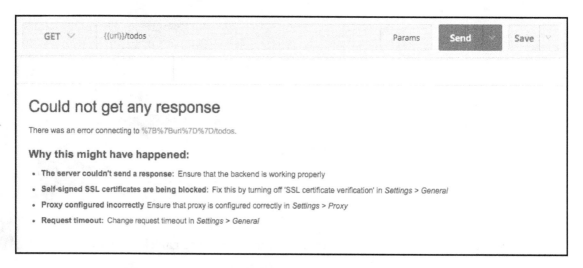

It's trying to make a request to a URL that starts with the curly braces; it is the encoded character, url, the closing curly braces, and todos. That's because the url variable is currently not defined. We need to switch to an environment. Over in the environments list we now have **Todo App Heroku** and **Todo App Local**. If I click **Todo App Local** and send that request off, I get my two items in the local database:

If I switch over to **Todo App Heroku**, this is going to make a request to the Heroku application. It's going to be updating the URL and when we fire it off we get a different set of data:

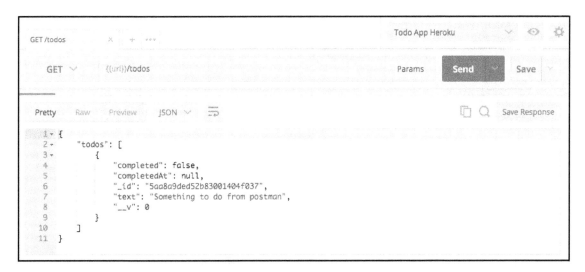

This time around all we have is our one Todo item, the one that's available on the Heroku application. With this in place, GET /todos can now easily be used to fetch localhost or Heroku items, and we can do the same thing with our POST /todos request. I'm going to replace the URL with curly braces, and inside of those curly braces we'll have the url variable. Now I can go ahead and save this request, fire it off, and it's going to make a new Todo on the Heroku application:

If I switch to the **Todo App Local**, we can fire that off and now we have a new Todo on the Local environment:

The last request to change is going to be the GET /todos/:id request. We're going to take that localhost:3000 once again, then we're going to go ahead and replace it with url just like this, {{url}}, and now we are done. We can save the request and we can go ahead and fire it off. Now, this one has a second variable:

This is the actual Todo ID; you could add this as a variable as well. For now though, since it's going to change as we add and delete Todos, I'm going to simply grab one from the local database, move into the GET /todos request, swap it out, and send it off, and we get our todo back:

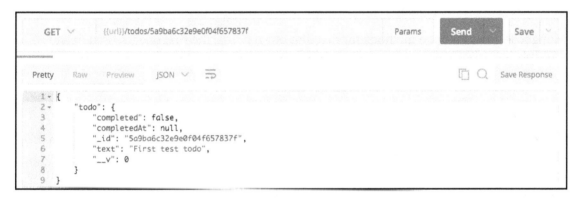

If I make it a Todo ObjectID that doesn't exist, by changing one of the numbers to 6, I get a 404 status code. Everything is still working as expected, and it's also going to work in the Heroku environment. I'm going to fetch all the todos from the Heroku environment, grab one of the _ids, move to the GET /todos/:id request, swap out the ID, send it off, and we get the todo item.

Hopefully you're starting to see why these Postman Environments are so convenient. You can easily switch between two environments, changing exactly what happens to the request. Now, in this case, we happen to only have one variable url; you could add others, and we will a little bit later. For now though, that is it, we have a way to swap between the two environments inside of Postman. Now that we have this in place, we're going to move back into the Atom editor and we're going to start adding new routes. There's two more to go. In the next section, you're going to learn how to delete Todos by ID.

Deleting a resource – DELETE /todos/:id

In this section, we're going to explore how to remove documents from our MongoDB collections using Mongoose. Then you're going to be responsible for filling out the `delete` route, which will let someone delete a Todo by the ID.

To get started we're going to duplicate that `mongoose-queries` file, calling the new file `mongoose-remove`. Inside of the file we can remove everything below our initial imports. I'm going to highlight everything in the file, including the uncommented-out code, remove it, and we end up with a file that looks like this:

```
const {ObjectID} = require('mongodb');

const {mongoose} = require('./../server/db/mongoose');
const {Todo} = require('./../server/models/todo');
const {User} = require('./../server/models/user');
```

Mongoose gives us three methods for deleting our records; the first one lets you delete multiple records.

Todo.remove method

This one is `Todo.remove`, and `Todo.remove` works kind of like `Todo.find`. You pass in a query and that query matches multiple records, removing all of them. If it matches none, none will get removed. Now, the difference between `Todo.find` and `Todo.remove`, other than the fact that remove removes the docs, is that you can't pass in an empty argument and expect all the documents to get removed. If you want to remove everything from your collection you need to run it like `Todo.remove({})`. If we run this we're going to have everything get removed. I'm going to tack `then`. We're going to get back our result and we can print that result to the screen using `console.log(result)`, just like this:

```
Todo.remove({}).then((result) => {
    console.log(result);
});
```

Now we can run the `mongoose-remove` file, which is going to remove all of the Todos from our database:

node playground/mongoose-remove.js

```
Gary:node-todo-api Gary$ node playground/mongoose-remove.js
{ n: 3, ok: 1 }
```

Now when we run the `remove` method, once again we get back a `result` object; a lot of this stuff is not useful to us but up at the very top there is a `result` property. We can see that the removal did work, we got a `1` back as opposed to `0`, and we have the number of records that were removed. In this case the number of records happens to be `3`.

Todo.findOneAndRemove method

There are two other ways to remove documents and these are going to be much more useful for us in this section. The first one is going to be `Todo.findOneAndRemove`. Now, `findOneAndRemove` is going to work kind of like `findOne`: it's going to match that very first document, only it's going to remove it. This will also return the document so you can do something with the removed data. The data will be removed from the database but you will get the object back so you can print it to the screen or send it back to the user. This is unlike the `remove` method. In the `remove` method we do not get the docs back that got removed, we just get a number saying how many were removed. With `findOneAndRemove` we do get that information back.

Todo.findByIdAndRemove method

Another method is `Todo.findByIdAndRemove`. The `findByIdAndRemove` method works just like `findById`: you pass in the ID as the argument and it removes it. Now, both of these are going to return the doc and that is exactly what we want. There's no need to run both of them, we can just run one. The `Todo.findByIdAndRemove` method, this is going to let us remove a `Todo` `ById`, some ID like `asdf`, and we're going to be able to attach a `then` method providing our callback, and the callback is going to get the doc back. You could call it doc, or in this case we can call it `todo` since it is a Todo item:

```
Todo.findByIdAndRemove('asdf').then((todo) => {
});
```

Now that we have this in place, we just need to create a Todo, since we deleted all of them, and include the ID. Over inside of Robomongo I can right-click that `todos` collection and insert a document. We're just going to set a `text` property and I'll set that `text` property equal to `Something to do`, and we can save that record. I'm going to make sure that when I click **View Documents** we do get our one document:

Now obviously it is missing some of the properties since I created it in Robomongo, but that is fine for our purposes. I'm now going to edit that document and grab the ID, and this is the ID we can add in to our playground file to make sure the document gets removed. Over inside of Atom, in the `findByIdAndRemove` method, we'll pass in our string. This is the string ID, and inside of our `then` callback we're going to use `console.log` to print the todo to the console. I am going to comment out this call to remove previous because otherwise it would remove the document we're trying to remove:

```
//Todo.remove({}).then((result) => {
// console.log(result);
//});
Todo.findByIdAndRemove('5aa8b74c3ceb31adb8043dbb').then((todo) => {
    console.log(todo);
});
```

With this in place, I can now save the file, head into the Terminal, and rerun the script. I'm going to shut it down and start it up again:

```
Gary:node-todo-api Gary$ node playground/mongoose-remove.js
{ completed: false,
  completedAt: null,
  _id: 5aa8b74c3ceb31adb8043dbb,
  text: 'Something to do' }
```

We get our documents, which is fantastic, and if I head into Robomongo and try to fetch the documents in todos, we're going to get an error that there are no documents; we had one but we deleted it. Now, inside of Atom we can also play around with `findOneAndRemove`. The `findOneAndRemove` method works exactly the same as `findByIdAndRemove`, only it takes that query object. This would be `Todo.findOneAndRemove`; we would pass in the query object like this, pasting in our ID, and we could attach our `then` callback, which would get called with the document:

```
Todo.findOneAndRemove({_id: '57c4670dbb35fcbf6fda1154'}).then((todo) => {

});
```

Both of these work very similarly, but the big difference is whether or not you need to query by more than just the ID. Now that you know how to use `findByIdAndRemove`, we're going to go into the `server` file and start filling out the actual route. This is going to be the route that lets us delete a Todo. I'll do the setup for the route for you, but you're going to be responsible for filling out everything inside of the callback function.

Creating a delete route

To create a delete route we're going to use `app.delete`. Then we're going to provide the URL, which will look identical to the one we have for getting an individual Todo by Id, `/todos/:id`. This will be the ID we can access inside of the callback function. The callback function will get the same request and response arguments, and inside I'll leave some comments to guide you in the right direction, but you're going to be responsible for filling every single thing out. First up, get the id. You're going to pull off the ID just like we do up above and we're going to do that because the next thing you're going to do is validate the id. If it's not valid, return `404`. If it's not valid you're going to send a 404 back just like we do above. Next up, you're going to remove todo by id and this is going to require you to use that function we just discussed over inside of the `mongoose-remove` file. You're going to remove it by ID and there's two ways that could go. We could have a success or we could have an error. If we do get an error you can respond in the usual way, sending back a `400` status code with empty body. Now, if it's a success we're going to need to make sure that a Todo was actually deleted by checking that the doc came back; if no doc, send `404`, so the person knows that the ID could not be found and it could not be removed, if `doc`, send `doc` back with `200`. Now, the reason we need to check if the doc exists is because this function, `findByIdAndRemove`, is still going to have its success case called even if no Todo gets deleted.

I can prove this by rerunning the file after having deleted the item with that ID. I'm going to comment out `findOneAndRemove`, head into the Terminal, and rerun the script:

```
Gary:node-todo-api Gary$ node playground/mongoose-remove.js
null
```

We get **null** as the value of Todo. That means you want to set up an `if` statement, to do something specific if no item was actually deleted. With this in place, you are ready to go. You know how to do all of this, most of it is done in the route up above and everything specific to removing an item was done over in this `playground` file.

The first thing we need to do is grab the ID off of the request object. I'm going to make a variable called `id`, setting it equal to `req.params`; this is where all of our URL parameters are stored, then we get it by value. We have id set up so we would get the `id` property. I'm going to remove the comment and down below we can validate the ID, `if(ObjectID.isValid)`. Now, we're checking if this ID is valid, and if it is valid, well we don't really want to do anything, all we care about is if it's not valid. So, I'm going to flip the Boolean value and inside of the `if` condition we can now run some code when the ID is not valid. That code is going to send back a `404` status code. I'm going to use `return` to prevent the rest of the function from being executed, then we're going to go ahead and respond, setting the status, `res.status`, equal to `404`, and we'll call `send` to initiate the response with no body data. Now that the ObjectID is valid, we can move on down below actually removing it.

We're going to kick things off by calling `Todo.findByIdAndRemove`. Now, `findByIdAndRemove` as you know takes just one argument, the actual `id` to remove, we can call `then`, passing in our success callback, which as we know will get called with the individual `todo` document. Now, inside of the success case we still have to make sure a Todo is actually deleted. If there was no Todo, we're going to send a 404 back; if there was no Todo, we are going to respond using `return` and set the status using `res.status` to `404`, and call `send` to initiate the response. Now, if this if statement doesn't run it means a Todo was actually deleted. In that case we want to respond with `200`, letting the user know that everything went well, and we're going to send the `todo` argument back, `res.send`, passing in `todo`. The only thing left to do for this Todo challenge is to call `catch`. We're going to call catch so we can do something with any potential errors. All we're going to do is respond using `res.status`, setting it equal to `400`, and we'll go ahead and call `send` with no arguments sending back an empty response:

```
app.delete('/todos/:id', (req, res) => {
    var id = req.params.id;
```

```
if(!ObjectID.isValid(id)) {
      return res.status(404).send();
}
Todo.findByIdAndRemove(id).then((todo) => {
      if(!todo) {
            return res.status(404).send();
      }
      res.send(todo);
}).catch((e) => {
      res.status(400).send();
});
});
```

With this in place, we are now good to go. We have everything set up just like we wanted to, which means we can remove the comments from down below, and you'll notice that the method we have down below looks really similar to the one we have up above, and this is going to be the case for a lot of our routes that manage an individual Todo item. We're always going to want to get that ID, we're always going to want to validate that the ObjectID is indeed a real ObjectID, and inside of our success and error cases, similar things are also going to happen. We want to make sure that a doc was actually deleted. If it wasn't we'll send back that 404, and with this in place we can now verify that this route works.

Now we can save the file and start up the server in the Terminal. I'll use the clear command to clear the Terminal output and then we can run the following command:

node server/server.js

Once the server is up, we can move into Postman and start firing off a couple of requests. First up, I'm going to create a few Todos. I'll send this POST /todos off, and then I'll change the text property and send it off again. I'll change the body text to Some other todo item, sending that off, and now we should have two todos. If I go to GET /todos and fetch them, we get our two todos:

```
 1 ▾ {
 2 ▾       "todos": [
 3 ▾             {
 4                   "completed": false,
 5                   "completedAt": null,
 6                   "_id": "5aa8ce41424f9507a211e7f8",
 7                   "text": "Something to do from postman",
 8                   "__v": 0
 9             },
10 ▾             {
11                   "completed": false,
12                   "completedAt": null,
13                   "_id": "5aa8ce8a424f9507a211e7f9",
14                   "text": "Some other todo item",
15                   "__v": 0
16             }
17       ]
```

Now, I am going to need one of these IDs; this is going to be the todo that we delete, so what I will do is copy this to the clipboard, then we can go ahead and create our new route. This new route is going to use the `delete` method so we're going to switch from **GET** to **DELETE**, then we can go ahead and provide the URL using the environment variable URL that we created in the last section. The route is `/todos/id`. I'm going to paste the ID in there:

Now I can go ahead and run the request. When we run it, we get a status code of **200 OK**; everything went well, and we have the document that we deleted:

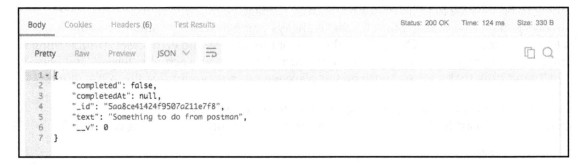

If I go back to GET `/todos` and rerun it, now we only have one document; the item that we passed in as the ID to delete did indeed get deleted. I'm going to save this request to our collection so we can fire it off without having to manually enter all of that information. Let's save as DELETE, followed by the route `/todos/:id`:

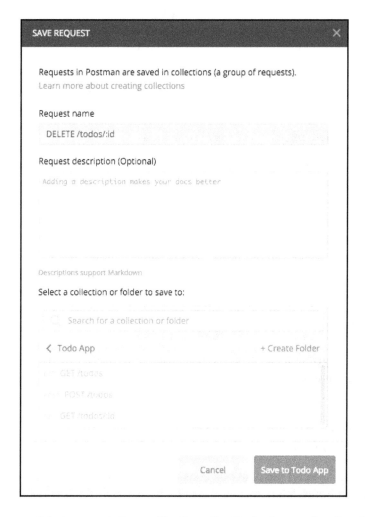

We are going to save this to an existing collection, the **Todo App** collection. Now we have a DELETE /todos/:id route sitting right in **Collections**, we can always go ahead and access it whenever we need to. Now, from here, we're going to go ahead and fire the request again, this is going to try and delete a Todo whose ID is valid but doesn't match one in the collection, and we get 404 back. Now if I make this ID invalid by deleting a bunch of characters and I send that off, we also get a 404 status code because the ID is invalid, which is fantastic.

With this in place, we can now make a commit. Over inside of the Terminal, I'm going to shut the server down, run `git status`, and you'll see we have two files.

We have a new file, the Mongoose playground file, and we have our modified `server` file. I'm going to use `git add .` to add all of those to the next commit, and we'll use `git commit` with the `-m` flag to make the commit, `Add DELETE/todos/:id route`:

```
git commit -m 'Add DELETE /todos/:id route'
```

I'm going to make the commit and push it up to GitHub. We can also go ahead and deploy our application using the following command:

```
git push heroku master
```

Now we'll be able to delete our Todos inside of the Heroku application. With this in place, we are now done. In the next section we're going to write some test cases for the route we just set up.

Testing DELETE /todos/:id

In this section, you're going to write some test cases that verify our `delete` route works as expected. Now, before we get into that, what we're going to do is make one quick change to the delete route to make it match our other routes. Our other routes return an object and on that object, the response body, we have a `todo` property, and we did the same thing for the `todos` call. On the response body we have the `todos` property and that stores the array. For the delete request, we never did that.

What I'm going to do is send back an object as the response body, where the `todo` property equals the `todo` that got deleted, although we'll just use that ES6 syntax to send that back:

```
Todo.findByIdAndRemove(id).then((todo) => {
    if (!todo) {
        return res.status(404).send();
    }
    res.send({todo});
}).catch((e) => {
    res.status(400).send();
});
```

With this in place, we can now go ahead and write some test cases that verify the `delete` route works as expected, and this is going to happen at the very bottom of our `server.test` file. I'm going to create a new `describe` block for the `DELETE /todos/:id` route. We'll provide our arrow function and we can go ahead and call it three times.

Test case 1 - should remove a todo

The first test case, `it('should remove a todo')`, this is going to be test case number one; it's going to verify that when we pass in an ID that does exist inside of the Todos collection, the item gets removed:

```
describe('DELETE /todos/:id', () => {
    it('should remove a todo', (done) => {

    });
});
```

Test case 2 - should return 404 if todo not found

Next up, `it('should return 404 if todo not found')`. If we try to delete the Todo but nothing was actually deleted, we're going to send a `404` status code back so the user knows that the call probably didn't work as expected. Yes, the call didn't necessarily fail, but you never deleted the item you wanted to delete, so we are going to consider that a failure, and that's what we did when we sent the `404` status code back:

```
describe('DELETE /todos/:id', () => {
    it('should remove a todo', (done) => {

    });
    it('should return 404 if todo not found', (done) => {

    });
});
```

Test case 3 - should return 404 if object id is invalid

The last test we're going to write is `it('should return 404 if object id is invalid')`. This test is going to verify that when we have an invalid ObjectID, we do get a `404` status code back which is the expected response status code:

```
describe('DELETE /todos/:id', () => {
    it('should remove a todo', (done) => {
    });
    it('should return 404 if todo not found', (done) => {

    });
    it('should return 404 if object id is invalid', (done) => {

    });
});
```

Now, these two tests we'll fill out a little bit later; we're going to go ahead and focus on the first one because this is where we're going to need to do a few complex things. Not only are we going to need to send off the request, but after the request comes back, we're going to want to assert some things about it, and we're going to want to query the database, making sure the Todo was actually removed from the `Todos` collection. The first thing I'm going to do is figure out which Todo I want to delete. We have two options up above. I'm going to go ahead and delete the second Todo item, though that choice is irrelevant; you could easily just do this with the first one. Down below, we'll create a `hexId` variable, like we did for our previous test case. We're going to set that equal to the second item from the `todos` array, then we're going to go ahead and grab its `_id` property, calling the `toHexString` method:

```
var hexId = todos[1]._id.toHexString();
```

Now that we have the `hexId` for the second Todo item, we can start worrying about making the request. I'm going to call `request`, passing in the `app` we want to make the request to, then we can call `delete`, which is going to trigger a delete HTTP request. The following URL is going to have some variables injected into it, so I will use template strings: it's `/todos/` followed by the ID. I'm going to inject the `hexId` variable. Now that we have our `delete` method all set up, we can move on and start making our expectations. We're going to `expect` that we get a `200` status code back; we should get a `200` status code because `hexId` is going to exist in the database. Next up, we can assert that the data comes back as the response body. I'm going to make a custom `expect` call, passing in our function, where we have the response argument sent in, and all we're going to do is assert that the ID is the ID right in the `hexId` variable. We're going to `expect` that the `res.body` property has a `todo` prop where the `_id` property equals the `hexId`, `toBe(hexId)`. If this is the case then we can verify the call pretty much worked as expected:

```
request(app)
.delete(`/todos/${hexId}`)
.expect(200)
.expect((res) => {
    expect(res.body.todo._id).toBe(hexId);
})
```

The last thing we need to do is query the database and make sure the item was actually removed. I'm going to call `end`, passing in a callback, so we can do a few asynchronous things before we wrap up the test case, and if you remember it gets called with an error and the response. If there is an error we're going to need to handle that because otherwise there's no need to query the database, `if (err)`. We're going to `return` to prevent the function execution, `done`, passing in that error so the error gets rendered by Mocha. Now we can go ahead and make the query, and this is actually going to be your challenge for this section.

What I want you to do is query database using `findById`. You're going to try to find the Todo item that has the ID stored in the `hexId` variable. When you try to find that ID it should fail, and you should get nothing back. You're going to create that `Todo` variable in your `then` call and make sure it does not exist. You can make sure something doesn't exist using the `toNotExist` assertion. That would look something like this, we `expect(null).toNotExist()`. Although, instead of `null`, you'll pass in the `Todo` argument which is going to be in your success handler. Now, this usually would contain the Todo item, but since we've just deleted it, it should not exist; this is going to get all of that done. Now, if there is an error you're going to do the exact same thing we did in our test case for `POST /todos`. We simply add a `catch` clause, passing the error through to `done`. Now that you know what to do, it's your job to get it done. What I'd like you to do is fill this out, fill out the query, make sure to handle the errors, make sure to call `done`, then you can go ahead and run the test suite, verifying that this test case passes. The last two test cases are going to fail, so for the moment I'm just going to comment them out; they're going to fail because we have a `done` argument specified, but we never called it so the test will timeout after two seconds.

The first thing to do is call `Todo.findById`, passing in that `hexId`. This is the item that should have gotten deleted. Now we can call then, passing in our callback, it is going to get called with the doc, the `todo` variable, and all we're going to do is verify that it does not exist. We just deleted it, so `findById` should return null for the doc. We're going to `expect` that the `todo` variable does not exist using the `toNotExist` method available on that expect library. Now, we do need to call `done` to wrap up the test case. From here, we can go ahead and call `catch`. I'm going to call `catch`, grabbing that error argument and passing it through to `done`. There's no need to provide curly braces here; we just have one statement so we can use the shortcut, which is available in ES6 for error functions. With our actual query in place, we can remove the comments that outlined what was supposed to happen and we can run the test case:

```
.end((err, res) => {
  if(err){
      return done(err);
  }

  Todo.findById(hexId).then((todo) => {
      expect(todo).toBeFalsy();
      done();
  }).catch((e) => done(e));
});
```

Over inside of the Terminal we can now run the test suite to verify that everything we set up worked as expected. Over inside of Terminal, I'm going to run the following command to start up our test suite with Nodemon:

```
npm run test-watch
```

And when it runs we see that we have our one test under the DELETE describe block and it is passing; it should remove a todo passed without any errors:

```
Started on port 3000
  POST /todos
    ✓ should create a new todo (237ms)
    ✓ should not create todo with invalid body data

  GET /todos
    ✓ should get all todos

  GET /todos/:id
    ✓ should return todo doc
    ✓ should return 404 if todo not found
    ✓ should return 404 for non-object ids

  DELETE /todos/:id
    ✓ should remove a todo


  7 passing (351ms)
```

Now that we have our one test case in place we can fill out the two other ones. These test cases are going to be basically identical to the test cases we have for the GET /todos/:id route. There's no shame in copying and pasting code when you:

- Know exactly what the code does; we know what it does because we wrote it
- Actually do need it—we can't reuse it, we need to tweak it just a little bit, so it does make sense to copy

Test case 4 - should return 404 if todo not found

I'm going to copy the `should return 404` test case for the `should return 404 if todo not found` test, and we're going to paste that into the exact same test for the `delete` route, and all we have to do is change `.get` to `.delete`, and save the file. This is going to rerun the test suite, and now we have two tests under delete; they are both passing:

```
POST /todos
  ✓ should create a new todo (79ms)
  ✓ should not create todo with invalid body data

GET /todos
  ✓ should get all todos

GET /todos/:id
  ✓ should return todo doc
  ✓ should return 404 if todo not found
  ✓ should return 404 for non-object ids

DELETE /todos/:id
  ✓ should remove a todo
  ✓ should return 404 if todo not found
  1) should return 404 if object id is invalid


8 passing (2s)
1 failing

1) DELETE /todos/:id
     should return 404 if object id is invalid:
   Error: Timeout of 2000ms exceeded. For async tests and hooks, ensure "done()" is called; if returning a
Promise, ensure it resolves.
```

You can see our last test still fails, so we can go ahead and do the same thing. I'm going to copy the code from `should return 404 for non-object ids`, which verifies that non-ObjectIDs cause a `404` status code. I'm going to paste it in the last test case, changing the `.get` method call to `.delete`. If I save the file it's going to rerun the test suite and this time around all 9 test cases are passing:

```
Started on port 3000
  POST /todos
    ✓ should create a new todo (205ms)
    ✓ should not create todo with invalid body data

  GET /todos
    ✓ should get all todos

  GET /todos/:id
    ✓ should return todo doc
    ✓ should return 404 if todo not found
    ✓ should return 404 for non-object ids

  DELETE /todos/:id
    ✓ should remove a todo
    ✓ should return 404 if todo not found
    ✓ should return 404 if object id is invalid


  9 passing (340ms)
```

With this in place, we now have `DELETE /todos` tested. Let's go ahead and wrap this one up by making a commit over inside of the Terminal.

I'm going to run `git status` to see what changes I have going on. We made one small change to the `server` file and we added our tests to the `server.test` file. I can use `git commit` with the `-am` flag to make it commit, and a good message for this one would be `Test the DELETE /todos/:id route`:

```
git commit -am 'Test the DELETE /todos/:id route'
```

I'm going to take that commit and push it up to GitHub, and there's no need to deploy to Heroku since we haven't created anything visually different. We did tweak the `server` code just a little bit, but we'll worry about that a little bit later. For now, everything is good; we can move on to the next section where you are going to create the final route for managing Todos. This is going to be a route that lets you update a Todo.

Updating a Resource - PATCH /todos/:id

The `delete` route is now set up and tested, so it's time to start on the final route for managing our Todo resources. This is going to be the route that lets you update a Todo item whether you want to change the text to something else or whether you want to toggle it as completed. Now this is going to be the most complex route we write; everything so far has been relatively straightforward. We're going to need to do a few extra things to get this updating route to work as expected.

The first thing I want to do before we go ahead and create the route down below is install that Lodash library we used in one of the previous sections for this course.

Installing Lodash library

If you remember, Lodash provides a few really great utility functions and we'll be taking advantage of a couple of those inside of our update route. Right in the Terminal, I'm going to use `npm i` with the `--save` flag to install it; the module name itself is called `lodash`, and we'll be using the most recent version `@4.15.0`:

```
npm i --save lodash@4.17.5
```

Now, once this is installed, we can `require` it up top and then we can go ahead and add our route. At the very top of the `server.js` file we can make a constant; we'll use underscore as the name for the variable that stores the Lodash library, then we'll go ahead and `require` it, `require('lodash')`. Now, I've used regular variables instead of constants for my other imports, so I can go ahead and switch these variables to constants as well:

```
const _ = require('lodash');

const express = require('express');
const bodyParser = require('body-parser');
const {ObjectID} = require('mongodb');
```

Now that we have this in place we are ready to move to the bottom of the file and start adding the new route. This route is going to use the HTTP `patch` method; `patch` is what you use when you want to update a resource. Now remember, none of this is really set in stone. I could have a `delete` route that creates new Todos and I could have a `post` route that deletes todos, but these are just the general guidelines and best practices for API development. We're going to set up a `patch` method route by calling `app.patch`. This is what is going to allow us to update Todo items. Now, the URL is going to be the exact same URL as it has been when we're managing an individual Todo item, `/todos/:id`. Then we can set up our callback with our request and response arguments. Inside of the callback, one of the first things that we're going to need to do is grab that id just like we do for all our other routes. I'm going to make a variable called `id` and set it equal to `req.params.id`. Now, on the next line we're going to go ahead and create a variable called `body` and this is the reason I loaded in Lodash. The body, the request body, that's where the updates are going to be stored. If I want to set a Todos text to something else, I would make a `patch` request. I would set the `text` property equal to whatever I wanted the Todo text to be. The problem here is that someone can send any property along; they could send along properties that aren't on the Todo items or they could send along properties we don't want them to update, for example, `completedAt`. The `completedAt` property is going to be a property that gets updated, but it's not going to be updated by the user, it's going to be updated by us when the user updates the completed property. `completedAt` is going to be generated by the program, which means we do not want a user to be able to update it.

In order to pull off just the properties we want users to update, we're going to be using the `pick` method, `_.pick`. The `pick` method is fantastic; it takes an object, we're going to pass in `req.body`, then it takes an array of properties that you want to pull off, if they exist. For example, if the `text` property exists, we want to pull that off of `req.body`, adding it to `body`. This is something that users should be able to update, and we'll do the same thing for completed. These are the only two properties a user is going to be able to update; we don't need users updating IDs or adding any other properties that aren't specified in the Mongoose model:

```
app.patch('/todos/:id',(req, res) => {
    var id = req.params.id;
    var body = _.pick(req.body, ['text', 'completed']);
});
```

Now that we have this in place, we can get started down the usual path, kicking things off by validating our ID. There's no need to rewrite the code since we've written it before and we know what it does; we can simply copy it from `app.delete` block and paste it in `app.patch`:

```
if(!ObjectID.isValid(id)){
```

```
            return res.status(404).send();
    }
```

And now we can go ahead and move onto the slightly complex part of `patch`, which is going to be checking the `completed` value and using that value to set `completedAt`. If a user is setting a Todos `completed` property to `true`, we want to set `completedAt` to a timestamp. If they're setting it to `false`, we want to clear that timestamp because the Todo won't be completed. We're going to add an `if` statement checking if the `completed` property is a Boolean, and it's on `body`. We're going to use the `_.isBoolean` utility method to get that done. We want to check if `body.completed` is a Boolean; if it is a Boolean and that Boolean is true, `body.completed`, then we're going to go ahead and run some code. This code is going to run if it's a Boolean and it's `true`, otherwise we're going to run some code if it's not a Boolean or it's not `true`.

If it is a Boolean and it is `true`, we're going to set `body.completedAt`. Everything we set on body is eventually going to be updated in the model. Now, we don't want the user to update everything, so we've picked off certain ones from the `req.body`, but we can make some modifications of our own. We're going to set `body.completedAt` equal to the current timestamp. We're going to create a new date, which we've done before, but instead of calling `toString`, which is the method we used in the previous section, we'll be using a method called `getTime`. The `getTime` method returns a JavaScript timestamp; this is the number of milliseconds since midnight on January 1st of the year 1970. It's just a regular number. Values greater than zero are milliseconds from that moment forward, and values less than zero are in the past, so if I had a number of -1000, it would be 1000 milliseconds before that Unix epoch, which is the name for that date, that January 1st at midnight on 1970:

```
if(_.isBoolean(body.completed) && body.completed) {
    body.completedAt = new Date().getTime();
} else {

}
```

Now that we have that in place we can go ahead and fill out the `else` clause. Inside of the `else` clause, if it is not a Boolean or it's not `true`, we're going to go ahead and set `body.completed = false` and we're also going to clear `completedAt`. `body.completedAt` is going to get set equal to `null`. When you want to remove a value from the database you can simply set it to null:

```
if(_.isBoolean(body.completed) && body.completed) {
    body.completedAt = new Date().getTime();
} else {
    body.completed = false;
```

```
        body.completedAt = null;
    }
```

Now we're going to go ahead and follow a usual pattern: we're going to be making a query to actually update the database. The query that we're going to be making is going to be really similar to the one we made in our `mongodb-update` file. Inside of `mongodb-update` we used a method called `findOneAndUpdate`. It took a query, the update object, and a set of options. We're going to be using a method called `findByIdAndUpdate` which takes a really similar set of arguments. Right here in `server`, we will call `Todo.findByIdAndUpdate`. The first argument for `findByIdAndUpdate` is going to be `id` itself; since we're using a `findById` method, we can simply pass in `id` as opposed to passing in a query. Now we can go ahead and set the values on our object, which is the second argument. Remember, you can't just set key value pairs—you have to use those MongoDB operators, things like increment or, in our case, `$set`. Now, `$set`, as we explored, takes a set of key value pairs, and these are going to get set. In this case, we've already generated the object, as shown in the following code:

```
$set: {
    completed:true
}
```

We just happen to generate it in the `app.patch` block and it happens to be called `body`. So I will set the `$set` operator equal to the `body` variable. Now we can go ahead and move onto the final options. These are just some options that let you tweak how the function works. If you remember, in `mongodb-update`, we set `returnOriginal` to `false`; this meant we got the new object back, the updated one. We're going to use a similar option with a different name; it's called `new`. It has similar functionality, it just has a different name because that's what the Mongoose developers chose. With a query in place though, we are done, and we can tack on a `then` callback and a `catch` callback, and add our success and error code. If things go well, we're going to get our `todo` doc back, and if things don't go well we are going to get an error argument, and we can go ahead and send back a `400` status code, `res.status(400).send()`:

```
    Todo.findByIdAndUpdate(id, {$set: body}, {new: true}).then((todo) => {

    }).catch((e) => {
        res.status(400).send();
    })
```

Now, we are going to need to check if the `todo` object exists. If it doesn't, if there is no `todo`, then we're going to go ahead and respond with a `404` status code, `return` `res.status(404).send()`. If `todo` does exist, that means we were able to find it and it was updated, so we can simply send it back, `res.send`, and we're going to send it back as the `todo` property where todo equals the `todo` variable using the ES6 syntax:

```
Todo.findByIdAndUpdate(id, {$set: body}, {new: true}).then((todo) => {

if(!todo)
{
    return res.status(404).send();
}
res.send({todo});
}).catch((e) => {
    res.status(400).send();
})
```

With this in place, we are now done. It's not too bad but it was a little more complex than any of the routes we've done before, so I wanted to walk you through it step by step. Let's take just a quick moment to recap what we did and why we did it. First up, the first unusual thing we did is we created the `body` variable; this has a subset of the things the user passed to us. We didn't want the user to be able to update anything they chose. Next up, we updated the `completedAt` property based off of the completed property, and finally we made our call to `findByIdAndUpdate`. With these three steps we were able to successfully update our Todos when we make the patch call.

Testing Todos for the patch call

Now, to test this out I'm going to save the `server` file and start up the server over in the Terminal. I'll use `clear` to clear the Terminal output and we can run `npm start` to start up the app. The app is up and running on port 3000, so over inside of Postman we can make some requests to see exactly how this works. I'm going to switch to the **Todo App Local** environment and make a `GET /todos` request so we can get a real ID for one of our Todo items, and you can see we have some old data from our tests right here:

```
1 ▾ {
2 ▾     "todos": [
3 ▾         {
4                "completed": false,
5                "completedAt": null,
6                "_id": "5aa8ee8725ee02097de810f7",
7                "text": "First test todo",
8                "__v": 0
9            },
10 ▾        {
11               "completed": false,
12               "completedAt": null,
13               "_id": "5aa8ee8725ee02097de810f8",
14               "text": "Second test todo",
15               "__v": 0
16           }
17       ]
18  }
```

I'm going to grab this second one with a `text` property equal to `Second test todo`, then I'm going to go ahead and create a new request, changing the method from **GET** to **PATCH**. We're going to provide our URL, it'll be `{{url}}`, then we'll have `/todos/` the ID we copied:

```
PATCH ∨    {{url}}/todos/5aa8ee8725ee02097de810f8                          Params
```

Now remember, the **PATCH** request is all about updating the data so we have to provide that data as the request body. I'm going to go to **Body | raw | JSON** in order to do just that. Let's go ahead and make some updates to the Todo. I'm going to set `"completed": true` and if you look in the **GET /todos** tab you can see that second Todo has a `completed` value of `false` so it should change and the `completedAt` property should get added. With the request set up I'm going go ahead and send it off:

```
1 ▾ {
2 ▾     "todo": {
3            "completed": true,
4            "completedAt": 1521023452135,
5            "_id": "5aa8ee8725ee02097de810f8",
6            "text": "Second test todo",
7            "__v": 0
8        }
9  }
```

We get our `todo`, completed is set to `true`, and `completedAt` is set to the timestamp. Now I can also go ahead and tweak this, changing `"completed": true` to `"completed": false` to send off the request; this now sets `"completed": false` and clears `completedAt`. Lastly, we could go ahead and do something like setting the `text` property. I'm going to set it back to `true` and add a second property, `text`, setting that equal to `Updates from postman`. I can fire off this request and down below we get our Todo, looking just as we had expected it to look:

```
1 ▾ {
2 ▾     "todo": {
3           "completed": true,
4           "completedAt": 1521023996759,
5           "_id": "5aa8ee8725ee02097de810f8",
6           "text": "Updates from postman",
7           "__v": 0
8       }
9   }
```

We have our `text` update; we also have our `completed` update and the timestamp showing up in the `completedAt` field. With this in place, we now have the ability to get, delete, update, and create Todo items—those are the four main CRUD actions.

The next thing we're going to do is write some tests that verify `patch` works as expected, so we can automatically run them and catch any regressions in our code. For now, that is it, we are going to go ahead and, in the Terminal, make a commit and push our changes. We'll push them up to Heroku and test that out as well. `git status` reveals that we have just those two changed files which means we can use `git commit` with the `-am` flag to make the commit. A good message for this one is, `Add PATCH /todos/:id`:

```
git commit -am 'Add PATCH /todos/:id'
```

I'm going to make the commit and push it up to GitHub, and once it's on GitHub we can push it up to Heroku using the following command:

```
git push heroku master
```

Remember, the master branch is the only branch Heroku has access to; we're not going to be using branching in this book, but in case you already know branching and you're running into any issues, you do need to push to the Heroku master branch to have your app redeploy. Like I said, that is not an issue if you're using all the commands as I use them.

Now that the app is deployed, we can go ahead and open it up; we're going to open it up by making requests inside of Postman. I'm going to switch to the **Todo App Heroku** environment, then I'm going to go ahead and inside of **GET /todos**, fire off the request:

```
1 ▼ {
2 ▼     "todos": [
3 ▼         {
4               "completed": false,
5               "completedAt": null,
6               "_id": "5aa8a9ded52b83001404f037",
7               "text": "Something to do from postman",
8               "__v": 0
9         },
10 ▼        {
11              "completed": false,
12              "completedAt": null,
13              "_id": "5aa8b188d52b83001404f038",
14              "text": "Something to do from postman",
15              "__v": 0
16        }
17     ]
18 }
```

These are all the Todos available on Heroku. I'm going to grab this first one. I'm going to go over to the **PATCH** request, swap out the ID, and keep the same body. I'm going to set `"completed": true` and `"text": "Updates from postman"`:

```
1 ▼ {
2 ▼     "todo": {
3           "completed": true,
4           "completedAt": 1521024494393,
5           "_id": "5aa8a9ded52b83001404f037",
6           "text": "Updates from postman",
7           "__v": 0
8     }
9 }
```

When we send that off, we get back the updated Todo. `completed` looks great, `completedAt` looks great, and `text` looks great as well. Now I'm going to go ahead and add this to my collections; the patch call is going to come in handy down the line, so I will click **Save As**, giving it the name we've used for all of ours, the HTTP method followed by the URL. I am going to save it to our existing collection, **Todo App**:

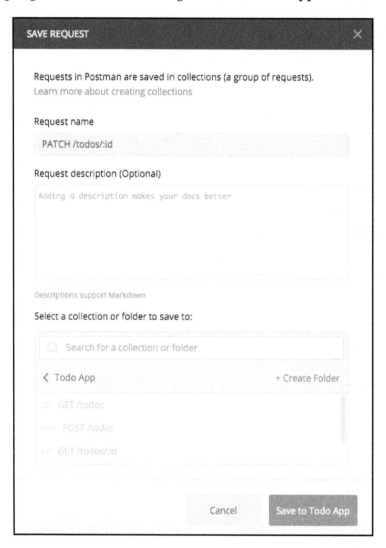

With this in place, we are done; we have our `patch` route working and it's time to move onto the next section where we will test this code.

Testing PATCH /todos/:id

In this section, we, well I guess more appropriately you, are going to be writing two test cases that verify `patch` works as expected. We're going to take one Todo that's not completed and make it complete, and we'll take a second one that is complete and make it incomplete.

Now, in order to do that, we are going to need to tweak the seed data we have in our `server.test` file. The seed data right in `server.test` file is two Todo items; neither of them have the `completed` property specified, which means it's going to default to `false`. For the second item, we're going to go ahead and set it. We're going to set `completed:` `true` and we're also going to set `completedAt` equal to whatever value we want. You can choose any number at all. I'm going to go ahead and use `333`:

```
const todos = [{
    _id: new ObjectID(),
    text: 'First test todo'
},{
    _id: new ObjectID(),
    text: 'Second test todo',
    completed: true,
    completedAt: 333
}];
```

Now we have two Todos that are going to let us toggle both ways. To get started down below I will help you create the describe an `It` block so we're on the same page, but you will be responsible for filling out the actual test cases. This section is basically going to be a challenge because we've done a lot of this stuff before. First up, the `describe` block. We're going to `describe` this group of tests; we'll use the method followed by the URL to do just that, then we can go ahead and add our function, and then we can define our two test cases:

```
describe('PATCH /todos/:id', () => {

});
```

The first test is going to take our first Todo and set its `text` equal to something else, and we'll change `completed` from `false` to `true`, `it('should update the todo')`. We can provide our function with the `done` argument, and I'll leave some comments inside in just a moment to give you an idea as to how I'd like you to accomplish this. The second test is going to be for toggling that second Todo where the `completed` value is already equal to `true`, and then `it('should clear completedAt when todo is not completed')`. This test case is going to make sure that when we go ahead and remove the `completed` status, setting it equal to `false`, `completedAt` gets cleared. Now, for the first test case what you're going to do is grab the ID of the first item, `grab id of first item`, then you're going to make our patch request; you're going to provide the proper URL with the ID inside of it, and you're going to use send to send some data along as the request body. For this one I want you to update text, set it equal to whatever you like, and you're going to `set completed equal` to `true`. Now, once you send that off you'll be ready to make your assertions and you're going to make one assertion using the basic system, assert that you get a `200` status code back, and you're going to make one custom assertion. The custom assertion is going to verify that the response body has a `text` property equal to the text you sent in, `text is changed`. You're going to verify that `completed` is `true`, and you're also going to verify that `completedAt` is a number, and you can use the `.toBeA` method available inside of `expect` to get that done. Now, for the second test we're going to do something similar but we're just going to go in the other direction; we're going to `grab id of second todo item`, you're going to update the `text` to something different, and you're going to set `completed` to `false`. Then you can make your assertions. Once again, we will be expecting `200` for this one and we will be expecting that the response body now represents those changes, that the text is changed to whatever you happen to pick. I also want you to check that `completed` is now `false` and to check that `completedAt` is `null`, and you can use the `.toNotExist` method available on expect to make that assertion. This is what you need to do to complete the test suite. Once you're done I want you to run `npm test` and make sure both test cases pass.

Test 1 - To complete the incomplete todo

Let's fill out the first test case first and I'll kick things off by grabbing the proper ID. Let's make a variable called `hexId`, setting it equal to the first todos, `_id` property, and we're going to call `toHexString` to get the string back we can pass in to the URL. Next up, I'm going to go ahead and create some dummy text; this will be the new updated text. Let's make a variable called `text` and set it equal to whatever you like. This should be the new text. Now we can go ahead and actually make our request using `request` to our express application. We will be using the `patch` method; hopefully you were able to figure that out on your own, and if you weren't maybe you used the documentation for super test since I did not explicitly tell you how to make that `patch` call. Next up, we are going to be using a template string as our URL, `/todos/`, then we're going to inject `hexId`. Now, before we can make our assertions we do need to send some data along as well, so I'll call `send`, passing in the data. This is going to be the things we want to change. For this test we did want to set `completed` equal to `true`. I'm going to set `completed: true`, and we do want to update the text, so I'll set `text` equal to the `text` variable up above, and I can always leave off this part using ES6:

```
it('should update the todo', (done) => {
    var hexId = todos[0]._id.toHexString();
    var text = 'This should be the new text';

    request(app)
    .patch(`/todos/${hexId}`)
    .send({
        completed: true,
        text
    })
});
```

Now that we have send in place, we can start making our assertions. The first one's easy, we're just expecting 200. I'm going to `expect(200)` to be the return status code, and before we add our custom assertion, we can call `end`, passing in `done`. Now, the last thing we need to do is make those assertions about the data coming back. I'm going to call `expect`, passing in a function; this function as we know by now gets called with the response and we can make our custom assertions. We're going to make an assertion about `text`, `completed`, and `completedAt`. First up, `text`. We use `expect(res.body.todo.text).toBe(text)`, the variable we defined up above. If this is equal to the data that came back, then we're good to go.

Next up, let's make some assertions about that `completed` property. We're going to use `expect(res.body.todo.completed)` and check that it's true using `.toBe(true)`. We set `completed` to `true` so it should have changed from `false` to `true`. Now the last assertion we're going to make inside of our custom expect call is going to be an assertion about `completedAt`, making sure it's a number. We're going to use `expect(res.body.todo.completedAt)` equals a number using `.toBeA`, inside of quotes the `number` type:

```
it('should update the todo', (done) => {
    var hexId = todos[0]._id.toHexString();
    var text = 'This should be the new text';

    request(app)
    .patch(`/todos/${hexId}`)
    .send({
        completed: true,
        text
    })
    .expect(200)
    .expect((res) => {
        expect(res.body.todo.text).toBe(text);
        expect(res.body.todo.completed).toBe(true);
        expect(res.body.todo.completedAt).toBeA('number');
    })
    .end(done);
});
```

With this in place, our first test is now complete. We can go ahead and remove those comments and actually verify it's working by running it over in the Terminal. Our second test is going to fail; that's fine, as long as the first one passes, we're good to continue on. I'm going to run `npm test`, and this is going to fire off the test suite. We can see our first PATCH test succeeds; this is the one we just filled out, and our second one fails. We're getting a timeout after two seconds, which is expected because we never call `done`:

```
DELETE /todos/:id
  ✓ should remove a todo
  ✓ should return 404 if todo not found
  ✓ should return 404 if object id is invalid

PATCH /todos/:id
  ✓ should update the todo
  1) should clear completedAt when todo is not completed


10 passing (2s)
1 failing

1) PATCH /todos/:id
    should clear completedAt when todo is not completed:
    Error: Timeout of 2000ms exceeded. For async tests and hooks, ensure "done()" is called; if returning a
Promise, ensure it resolves.
```

Now that the first one is in place though, we can go ahead and fill out the second one. Now, the code for these two tests is going to be really, really similar. Now, since we just wrote the code and we know exactly what it does, we can copy and paste it. I'm not a fan of copying and pasting code I don't understand, but I am a fan of being efficient. Since I know what that code does, I can paste it right in second test case, and now we can go ahead and make some changes.

Test 2 - to make complete todo incomplete

Instead of grabbing the `hexId` variable or the first Todo item, we want to grab the `hexId` variable for the second Todo item, and then the next thing we need to do is update the data we're sending. We don't want to set `completed` equal to `true`; we already did that manually up above. This one we're trying to set to `false`. We are also going to update the `text` so we can leave that in place. I'm going to go ahead and tweak the text value a little bit, adding a couple of exclamation marks on the end. Next up, the assertions. We're still expecting a `200` to be the status code that comes back. That part's great, and we are still expecting the `text` to equal `text`. For completed, though, we're expecting that to be `false` and we're not expecting `completedAt` to be a number; it was a number originally but after this update it should have been cleared since the Todo is no longer completed. We can use `toNotExist` to assert that `completedAt` doesn't exist:

```
it('should clear completedAt when todo is not completed', (done) => {
    var hexId = todos[1]._id.toHexString();
    var text = 'This should be the new text!!';

    request(app)
    .patch(`/todos/${hexId}`)
```

```
    .send({
        completed: false,
        text
    })
    .expect(200)
    .expect((res) => {
        expect(res.body.todo.text).toBe(text);
        expect(res.body.todo.completed).toBe(false);
        expect(res.body.todo.completedAt).toNotExist();
    })
    .end(done);
});
```

With this in place, our test case is done. We can now delete those comments, save the file, and rerun things from the Terminal. I'm going to rerun the test suite:

We get both of our PATCH tests passing. Now, as you've probably noticed, for patch we didn't write those test cases for invalid ObjectIDs or ObjectIDs not found; you could add those but we've done them so many times so far, I don't see that as a necessary exercise. These two test cases, though, they do validate that our patch method is working as expected, especially when it comes to the slightly more complex logic that patch requires to get everything done. With this in place though, we are done testing our last route.

We can go ahead and make a commit and move on to the final section of the chapter. Over in the Terminal I'm going to run git status. We'll see we have one modified file, server.test file, which looks great. We can use git commit with the -am flag to make the commit, Add tests for PATCH /todos/:id:

```
git commit -am 'Add tests for PATCH /todos/:id'
```

I'm going to go ahead and make that commit, then I'll take a moment to push it up to GitHub and with that in place we are done. In the next section, which is the last one for the chapter, you will learn how to use a separate test database locally, so you're not always wiping your data in the development database as you run your tests.

Creating a Test database

Now that all of our Todo routes are set up and tested, in this final section we're going to be exploring how to create a separate Test database for our application. That means when we run the test suite we're not going to be deleting all of the data inside of our `TodoApp` database. We will have a separate database alongside of `Test` and `TodoApp`, used for the testing DB.

Now, in order to set all that up we need a way to differentiate between running our app locally and running our test suite locally, and that's exactly where we're going to start. This whole issue stems from the fact that in our `mongoose.js` file we either use the `MONGODB_URI` environment variable or we use the URL string. This string is used for both testing and for development, and when I say testing I mean when we run our `test` script, and when I say development I mean when we run our app locally so we can use it inside of tools like Postman. What we really need is a way to set environment variables locally as well, so we always use the `MONGODB_URI` variable and we never have a default string like the one we have in the `mongoose.js` file. Now, in order to get that done we're going to look at an environment variable that's actually pretty special: it's `process.env.NODE_ENV` and you don't have to write this code. I'm going to be deleting it in just a moment. This `NODE_ENV` environment variable was made popular by the Express library but it now has been adopted by pretty much any Node-hosting company. For example, Heroku sets this value equal to the string `production` by default. That means that we're going to have three environments total. We already have a `production` environment. This is what we call our app on Heroku; we're going to have a `development` environment when we run our app locally, and we'll have a `test` environment when we run our app through Mocha. This means we'll be able to set up a different value for `MONGODB_URI` for all three of those, creating a separate test database.

To kick things off we're going to add some code in the `server.js` file up at the very top. We'll be moving this code out of `server.js` a little bit later, but for now we're going to tack it at the top. Let's make a variable called `env` and we're going to set it equal to `process.env.NODE_ENV`:

```
var env = process.env.NODE_ENV;
```

Now, this variable currently is only set on Heroku; we don't have this environment variable set locally. Environment variables in general are used for much more than just Node. Your machine has probably close to two dozen environment variables, telling the computer all sorts of things: where certain programs exist, what versions of libraries you want to use, that sort of stuff. The NODE_ENV variable, however, is something that we're going to need to configure inside of our `package.json` file for our development and test environments. Then, just down below, we'll be able to add some if else statements to configure our app depending on the environment. If we're in development we'll use one database, if we're in test we'll use a different one. Now to kick things off inside of `package.json` we are going to need to tweak the test script, setting the NODE_ENV environment variable. You can set environment variables by chaining together multiple commands. The code we're about to write is going to have a fallback for Windows as well, so you can write the exact same line if you're on macOS, Linux, or Windows. This is going to work everywhere, including Heroku. The goal here is to just set NODE_ENV equal to test before we run the test suite. In order to do that we're going to start by using the export command. The export command is available in macOS and Linux. This is the way to get it done, type this even if you're in Windows because when you deploy to Heroku you are going to be using Linux. We're going to export NODE_ENV, setting it equal to test:

```
"scripts": {
    "start": "node server/server.js",
    "test": "export NODE_ENV = test mocha server/**/*.test.js",
    "test-watch": "nodemon --exec 'npm test'"
}
```

Now, if you're on Windows, the export command is going to fail; export is going to trigger an error, something along the lines of export command not found. For Windows users, we're going to add this || block where we will call SET. SET is the same as export only it's the Windows version of the command. Right after it, we'll be providing the exact same argument, NODE_ENV=test. After the final test we're going to add two ampersands to chain these commands together:

```
"scripts": {
    "start": "node server/server.js",
    "test": "export NODE_ENV = test || SET NODE_ENV = test && mocha
server/**/*.test.js",
    "test-watch": "nodemon --exec 'npm test'"
}
```

So, let's go ahead and break down exactly what's going to happen. If you're on Linux, you're going to run the `export` command; the `SET` command is never going to run because the first one did. Then we're going to chain on a second command, running `mocha`. If you're on Windows, the `export` command is going to fail, which means you will run the second command; either way you get the `NODE_ENV` variable set, then finally you'll chain on a call to `mocha`. With this in place, we now have a way to set our `NODE_ENV` variable right inside a `package.json`.

> This is a quick cross-OS update; as you can see here, we have a modified version of that `test` script:
>
> `"test": "export NODE_ENV=test || SET \"NODE_ENV=test\" && mocha server/**/*.test.js"`
>
> The original test script had a problem on the Windows side of things: it would set the environment variable equal to the string test with a space at the end, as opposed to just the string `test`. In order to properly set the `env` variable to just `test`, and not `test`, we're going to be wrapping the entire set argument inside of quotes, and we're escaping those quotes since we use quotes inside of our JSON file. This command is going to work on Linux, macOS, and Windows.

Now I'm actually not going to add a `start` script for `scripts`. The `start` script, which is for the development environment, will just be the default. We'll have it set to production on Heroku, we'll have it set to `test` inside of our `test` script, and in the case of this script we'll just default it inside of `server.js` because we tend to run the file without actually going through the `start` script. Right in the `server.js` file, I'll set a default to `development`. If we're on production, `NODE_ENV` is going to be set, if we're on test, `development` is going to be set, and if we're on development, `NODE_ENV` won't be set and `development` will be used, which means we are ready to add some `if` statements. `if(env)` is `development` we want to do something. The thing we want to do is set up the MongoDB URL. `else if (env)` is the `test` environment. In that case we also want to set up a custom database URL:

```
if(env === 'development') {

} else if(env === 'test') {

}
```

Now we can go ahead and actually set up our environment variables. We have two environment variables being used throughout the app, both of which are set on Heroku, so there's no reason to worry about that environment, the production environment. We have our PORT environment variable, and we have our MONGODB_URI variable. Over inside of server.js, if we are in the development environment, we're going to go ahead and set process.env.PORT=3000. This means that we can actually remove the default from the port variable; there's no need to have a default because PORT is already going to be set. It'll be set on Heroku for production, it'll be set locally for development, and right in the else if block we'll set it for our final environment, the test environment, setting it equal to 3000. Inside mongoose.js, what we're going to do is set a MONGODB_URI environment variable for development and test, which is the exact same name for the variable we have on production. I'm going to remove our default, taking the string and cutting it out so it's in my clipboard, then I can remove all the excess code for setting that default, and what we're left with is just a reference to the environment variable:

```
mongoose.connect(process.env.MONGODB_URI);
```

Over inside of server.js we can now set that environment variable for both environments, process.env.MONGODB_URI, and we're going to set that equal to the string I just copied, mongodb://localhost:27017/TodoApp. We are using the TodoApp database.

Now, down below in the else if block, we can set process.env.MONGODB_URI equal to the string we just copied, but instead of setting it equal to the TodoApp database, we're going to set it equal to the TodoAppTest database:

```
if(env === 'development') {
  process.env.PORT = 3000;
  process.env.MONGODB_URI = 'mongodb://localhost:27017/TodoApp';
} else if(env === 'test') {
  process.env.PORT = 3000;
  process.env.MONGODB_URI = 'mongodb://localhost:27017/TodoAppTest';
}
```

When we run our application in test mode, we're going to be using a completely different database, so it's not going to wipe the database that we're using for development. To test that everything is working as expected, right below the env variable all I'm going to do is log out of the environment variable using console.log. I'm going to print the string env with a couple of asterisks so it's easy to spot in the Terminal output, and then I'll go ahead and pass the env variable in as the second argument:

```
console.log('env *****', env);
```

Now we can go ahead and test that everything is working as expected. Over inside of the Terminal I'm going to start up our app using the following command:

```
node server/server.js
```

We get an `env` equal to `development`, which is exactly what we'd expect:

```
[Gary:node-todo-api Gary$ node server/server.js
env ***** development
Started on port 3000
```

And now we can play around with it in Postman. Over inside of Postman I'm going to switch to my Local environment, **Todo App Local**, then I'm going to go ahead and fetch all of my Todos, and you can see we have some leftover test data:

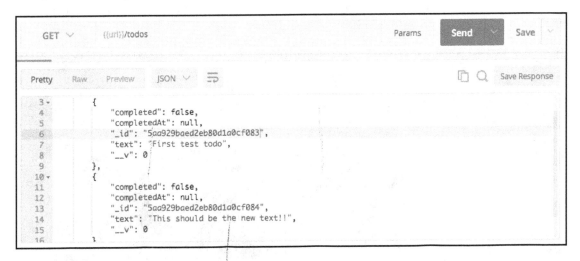

What I want to do is go ahead and tweak this first one so it's different. Then we'll run our tests and make sure that the tweaked Todo still shows up, because when we run the tests we shouldn't be accessing the same database, so none of this data should get changed. I'm going to copy the id for the first item, moving it into my PATCH call. I'm updating the `text` property and the `completed` property, so that's good, I don't need to change that. I'm going to go ahead and swap out the ID in the URL, send off the call, and now we have the updated Todo with the `text` property of `Updates from postman`:

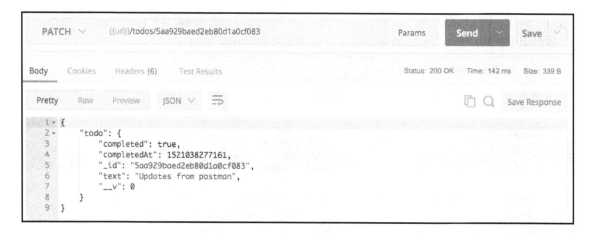

Next up, I'm going to go into the Terminal, shut down node server, and run our tests using
`npm test`:

```
POST /todos
  ✓ should create a new todo (232ms)
  ✓ should not create todo with invalid body data

GET /todos
  ✓ should get all todos

GET /todos/:id
  ✓ should return todo doc
  ✓ should return 404 if todo not found
  ✓ should return 404 for non-object ids

DELETE /todos/:id
  ✓ should remove a todo
  ✓ should return 404 if todo not found
  ✓ should return 404 if object id is invalid

PATCH /todos/:id
  ✓ should update the todo (39ms)
  ✓ should clear completedAt when todo is not completed


11 passing (1s)
```

We get our `env` variable set to `test`, then it runs through the test suite; all of our tests pass,
which is fantastic. The true test as to whether or not what we set up works is if we start up
the server again and we try to fetch our data from the `development` database.

Over inside of Postman I'm going to make that `GET /todos` request one last time and right there our Todo data still shows up as expected. Even though the test suite did run, it didn't matter because it's not wiping this database anymore, it's now wiping a brand new database you can view in Robomongo. If I click the connection and click **Refresh**, we now have two `TodoApp` databases: we have `TodoApp` and we have `TodoAppTest`. This is fantastic; everything is set up and we are ready to get rolling.

Now what I do want to do before we go is take all of this code out of `server.js` and move it somewhere else; it doesn't really belong here and it only makes the server file more complex than it needs to be. In the `server` folder, I'm going to make a brand new folder called `config`, and in the `config` folder I'll make a new file called `config.js`, and inside we can do all of that process environment variable configuration. I'm going to copy all of the code and replace it with a `require` call to that file. It's a relative file so we'll go to `/config/config`:

```
require('./config/config');
```

Inside of `config.js` we can now copy the code in and remove the line related to `console.log`. Let's wrap this section up by committing our changes and deploying to Heroku.

Over inside of the Terminal I'm going to clear the Terminal output, then we can go ahead and run `git status` to see what files we have changed, and we have quite a few:

```
[Gary:node-todo-api Gary$ git status
On branch master
Your branch is up-to-date with 'origin/master'.

Changes not staged for commit:
  (use "git add <file>..." to update what will be committed)
  (use "git checkout -- <file>..." to discard changes in working directory)

        modified:   package.json
        modified:   server/db/mongoose.js
        modified:   server/server.js

Untracked files:
  (use "git add <file>..." to include in what will be committed)
```

We also have some new files in the `server` directory. I'm going to use `git add .` to add all of that to the next commit and I'll use `git status` again to confirm everything looks good. Now we're ready for the commit and I can go ahead and do that, `git commit` with the `-m` flag providing our message, Setup separate test and development envs:

```
git commit -m 'Setup separate test and development envs'
```

And I'm also going to deploy it to Heroku so we can verify we haven't broken anything there:

```
git push heroku master
```

Once this is done we'll wrap the section up by heading into Postman and making a GET /todos request to our Heroku application. Over inside of Postman I'm going to switch environments from **Todo App Local** to **Todo App Heroku** and we can fire off the request:

```
 1 ▾ {
 2 ▾     "todos": [
 3 ▾         {
 4               "completed": true,
 5               "completedAt": 1521024494393,
 6               "_id": "5aa8a9ded52b83001404f037",
 7               "text": "Updates from postman",
 8               "__v": 0
 9           },
10 ▾         {
11               "completed": false,
12               "completedAt": null,
13               "_id": "5aa8b188d52b83001404f038",
14               "text": "Something to do from postman",
15               "__v": 0
16           }
17       ]
18   }
```

Now, as shown in the preceding screenshot, we get our two todo items coming from the real database, which means nothing was broken on the Heroku application, and it shouldn't be—technically we haven't changed anything. In Heroku, all we're doing is we're running the config file, but we don't use the default because it's already set, and it's not going to pass any of those statements because the env variable is going to be equal to the string production, so as far as Heroku is concerned, nothing has changed, and it's showing that because the data is still coming back as expected.

That is it for this section, and that is it for this chapter. In this section, we learned about MongoDB, Mongoose APIs, Postman, testing, routes, all sorts of great features. In the next chapter, we're going to wrap up the Todo application by adding authentication.

Summary

In this chapter, we worked on learning Mongoose queries and ID validation. Next, we looked into getting an individual resources and moved on to take a few challenges. After deploying the API to Heroku and exploring the Postman environments, we learnt about different methods of deleting a resource. Finally, we looked into creating a test database.

In the next chapter, we will learn about Real-Time Web Apps with Socket.io

5
Real-Time Web Apps with Socket.io

In this chapter, you're going to learn about Socket.io and WebSockets, which enable two-way communication between the server and the client. This means that we're not only going to be setting up a Node server, but also a client. This client could be a web app, an iPhone app, or an Android app. For this book, the client will be a web app. This means that we're going to be connecting the two, allowing data to flow seamlessly from the browser to the server and from the server to the browser.

Now, our todo app data can only flow in one direction, and the client has to initialize the request. With Socket.io, we're going to be able to send data back and forth instantly. This means that for real-time apps, such as an email app, a food ordering app, or a chat app, the server doesn't need to wait for the client to request information; the server can say, "*Hey, I just got something you probably want to show the user, so here it is!*" This is going to open up a world of possibilities, and we're going to get started by figuring out how to integrate Socket.io into a Node app. Let's dive in!

Creating a new web app project

Before you can add sockets to your web application, you need a web application to add them to, which is exactly what we'll create in this section. We'll make a basic Express app, which we'll get up on GitHub. Then, we'll deploy it to Heroku so we can view it live in the browser.

Now, the first step to that process is going to be to making a directory. We'll do a few things together to get us all going in the right direction. The first step in the process from the desktop is to run `mkdir` to make a new directory for this project; I'm going to call it `node-chat-app`.

Then, we can use `cd` to navigate into that directory and we can run a few commands:

```
mkdir node-chat-app
cd node-chat-app
```

First up, `npm init`. As with all of our projects in this book, we'll be taking advantage of npm, so we'll run the following command:

```
npm init
```

```
Gary:node-chat-app Gary$ npm init
This utility will walk you through creating a package.json file.
It only covers the most common items, and tries to guess sensible defaults.

See `npm help json` for definitive documentation on these fields
and exactly what they do.

Use `npm install <pkg>` afterwards to install a package and
save it as a dependency in the package.json file.

Press ^C at any time to quit.
package name: (chat-app)
```

Then, we'll use the *enter* key to use the default value for every option:

```
package name: (chat-app)
version: (1.0.0)
description:
entry point: (index.js)
test command:
git repository:
keywords:
author:
license: (ISC)
About to write to /Users/Gary/Desktop/node-chat-app/package.json:

{
  "name": "chat-app",
  "version": "1.0.0",
  "description": "",
  "main": "index.js",
  "scripts": {
    "test": "echo \"Error: no test specified\" && exit 1"
  },
  "author": "",
  "license": "ISC"
}

Is this ok? (yes)
```

When we're done, we can type `yes`, and now we have a `package.json` file. Before we move into Atom, we'll run the following command to initialize a new Git repository:

```
git init
```

We'll be putting this project under version control using Git, and we'll also use Git to push to GitHub and Heroku. With this in place, I can use the `clear` command to clear the Terminal output, and we can move into Atom. We'll start by opening up the folder and setting up our basic app structure.

Setting up our basic app structure

To set up the basic app structure, I'm going to open up the folder that we just created on the desktop, called `node-chat-app`:

In this folder, we'll get started by making a couple of directories. Now, unlike the other apps in the previous chapters, the chat app is going to have a frontend, which means we'll be writing some HTML.

We'll also add some styles and writing some JavaScript code that runs in the browser, as opposed to running on the server. For this to work, we'll have two folders:

- One will be called `server`, which will store our Node.js code
- The other one will be called `public`, which will store our styles, our HTML files, and our client-side JavaScript

Now, inside `server`, just like we did for the todo API, we'll have a `server.js` file, which is going to be the root of our Node application:

```
+  Enter the path for the new file.
server/server.js
```

This file will do stuff like create a new Express app, configure the public directory to be the static folder Express serves up, and call `app.listen` to start up the server.

Inside `public`, what we'll do for this section is create just one file, called `index.html`:

```
+  Enter the path for the new file.
public/index.html
```

The `index.html` file will be the markup page we serve when someone visits the app. For now, we'll make a really simple one that just prints a message to the screen so we can confirm it's getting served up properly. In the next section, we'll worry about integrating Socket.io on the client.

Setting up the index.html file for DOCTYPE

For now though, in our `index.html` file, we'll provide DOCTYPE so the browser knows which version of HTML we want to use. We tell it to use HTML which refers to HTML5. Next up, we'll open and close our `html` tag:

```
<!DOCTYPE html>
<html>

</html>
```

This tag is going to let us provide the head and body tags, which are exactly what we'll need to get things working:

- First up is head. Inside head, we can provide various configuration tags. We'll use just one for now, meta, so we can tell the browser which charset we want to use. In the meta tag, we'll provide the charset attribute, setting it equal to utf-8 inside quotes:

```
<!DOCTYPE html>
<html>
<head>
  <meta charset="utf-8">
</head>
</html>
```

- Next up, we'll provide the body tag inside html. This contains the HTML we want to actually render to the screen, and what we'll do for this one is render a p tag, which is for a paragraph, and we'll have some simple text like Welcome to the chat app:

```
<!DOCTYPE html>
<html>
<head>
  <meta charset="utf-8">
</head>
<body>
  <p>Welcome to the chat app</p>
</body>
</html>
```

This is all that's going to show up for the moment. Now, we can move outside the html file, going back into the server file.

Setting up the server.js file for the public directory

In our server file, we want to set up this server to serve up the public folder. Now, in this case, the server.js file is not in the root of the project, which means we have to go up a directory from server to node-chat-app. Then, we have to go into the public folder. This will make it a little hard to set up the Express middleware. What we'll do is take a look at a built-in Node module that makes it really easy to convert paths.

Now, in order to show you what I'm talking about, let's go ahead and use two `console.log` calls:

```
console.log();
console.log();
```

The first `console.log` call will show us how we used to do it, and the second one will show us the better way to do it.

Inside the first `console.log` call, we'll provide the same path we provided for our very first Express app. We use `__dirname` to reference the current directory, which in this case is the `server` directory because the file is inside the `server` folder. Then, we concatenate it, `/public`. Now, in this case, we do not have a `public` folder in the `server` folder; the `public` folder and the `server` folder are at the exact same level, which means we need to use `..` to go up a directory and then we need to go into `public`:

```
console.log(__dirname + '/../public');
console.log();
```

This is the old way of doing things, and if we run this from the Terminal, we can see why it looks a little weird. I'm going to run `server/server.js`:

nodemon server/server.js

What we get is this path, as shown in the following screenshot:

```
[Gary:node-chat-app Gary$ nodemon server/server.js
[nodemon] 1.14.10
[nodemon] to restart at any time, enter `rs`
[nodemon] watching: *.*
[nodemon] starting `node server/server.js`
/Users/Gary/Desktop/node-chat-app/server/../public

[nodemon] clean exit - waiting for changes before restart
```

We go into the `Users/Andrew/Desktop/` project folder, which is expected, then we go into `server`, out of `server`, and into `public`—this is absolutely unnecessary. What we'd like to do is just go from the `project` folder right into `public`, keeping a clean, cross-OS compatible path. In order to do that, we'll use a module that comes with Node called `path`.

The join method

Now, let's see the documentation of `path`, because `path` has plenty of methods that we won't be using in this section. We'll go to `nodejs.org`, where we can find the **Docs** tab. We'll go to the **Docs** page and then the API reference page:

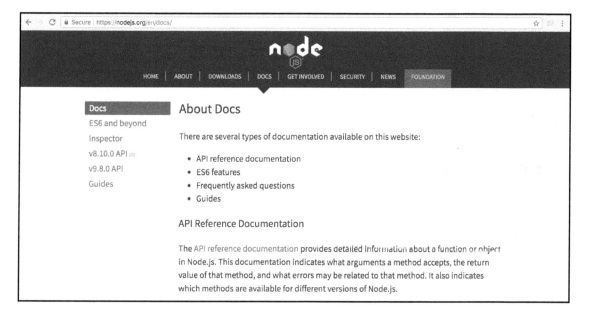

Here's a list of all the modules we have available to us. We're using the **Path** module:

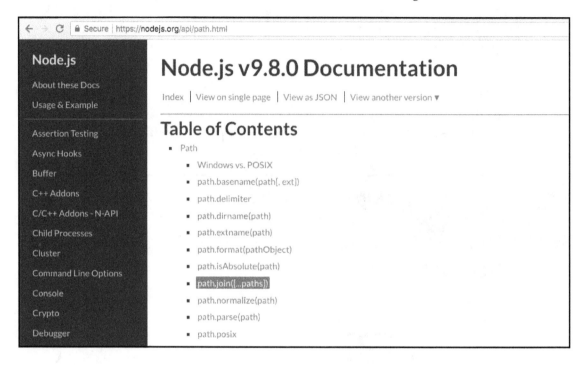

Inside **Path,** the method we'll use is `join`, which you can see in the preceding screenshot. If you click on this method, you can go to a little example of how `join` works:

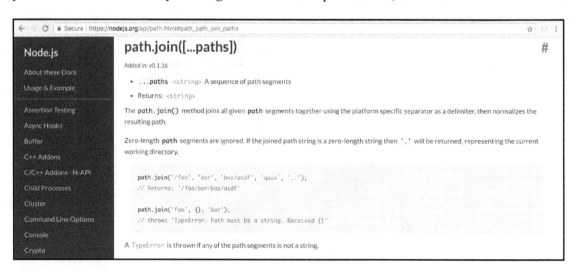

The `join` method takes your partial paths and joins them together, which means the example shown in the preceding screenshot results in the simpler path. In this example, we can see that we start with `foo`. We then go into `bar`, which also shows up; we then go into `baz/asdf`, which does indeed show up. The next part is the interesting part: we go into the `quux` directory, then we go out using `..`, and you can see the result path doesn't show us going into and out of, like our path does inside the Terminal; instead, it resolves that into the final path, where the `quux` directory is nowhere in sight.

We'll use this exact same method to clean up our path. Inside Atom, we can load in the `path` module by creating a constant called `path` and requiring it:

```
const path = require('path');
```

Remember, this one does not need to be installed: it is a built-in module, and you have access to it without using `npm`. Next up, we'll make a variable called `publicPath`. I'll make that a constant variable, since we'll be making any changes to it, and we'll call `path.join`:

```
const path = require('path');
const publicPath = path.join();
```

We'll pass some arguments into `path.join` in a moment. Before we do, though, I'm going to call `console.log(publicPath)`:

```
const path = require('path');
const publicPath = path.join();

console.log(__dirname + '/../public');
console.log(publicPath);
```

Now, inside `path.join`, what we want to do is take the two paths, `__dirname` and `'/../public'`, and pass them in as separate arguments. We do still want to start in the `server` folder of the `dirname` directory. Then, as the second argument, we'll specify the relative path inside quotes. We'll go out of the directory using `..` then use a forward slash to go into the `public` folder:

```
const path = require('path');
const publicPath = path.join(__dirname, '../public');
```

I'll save the `server` file, and we should now be able to go back to the Terminal and see our new path—and here it is:

```
[nodemon] restarting due to changes...
[nodemon] starting `node server/server.js`
/Users/Gary/Desktop/node-chat-app/server/../public
/Users/Gary/Desktop/node-chat-app/public
[nodemon] clean exit - waiting for changes before restart
```

Instead of going into `server` and then going out, we go right into the `public` directory, which is ideal. This is the path we want to provide to the Express static middleware.

Now that we have this `public` path variable in place, let's set up Express locally. Before we get into that, we will install it using `npm i`. The module name is `express`, and we'll use the most recent version, `@4.16.3`, with the `--save` flag:

```
npm i express@4.16.3 --save
```

We'll run the installer, and then we can go ahead and actually use it inside `server.js`. In `package.json`, we now have it sitting in the dependencies object.

Configuring basic server setup

With the Express installer in place, you'll create a brand new Express application and configure the Express static middleware, as we've done previously to serve up the `public` folder. Finally, you'll call `app.listen` on port `3000`. You'll provide one of those little callback functions to print a message to the Terminal, such as `server is up on port 3000`.

Once you have the server created, you'll start it up inside the Terminal and head to `localhost:3000` inside the browser. If we go there right now we'll get an error, because there is no server running on that port. You should be able to refresh this page and see the little message we typed in the paragraph tag over inside `index.html`.

The first thing I'll do is inside `server.js`, load in Express by creating a constant called `express` and requiring the library we just installed:

```
const path = require('path');
const express = require('express');
```

Next up, you need to make an `app` variable where we can configure our Express application. I'll make a variable called `app` and set it equal to a call to `express`:

```
const path = require('path');
const express = require('express');

const publicPath = path.join(_dirname, '../public');
var app = express();
```

 Remember, we don't configure Express by passing in arguments; instead, we configure Express by calling methods on `app` to create routes, add middleware, or start up the server.

First up, we'll call `app.use` to configure our Express static middleware. This will serve up that `public` folder:

```
const path = require('path');
const express = require('express');

const publicPath = path.join(_dirname, '../public');
var app = express();

app.use();
```

What you need to do is call `express.static` and pass in the path. We create a `publicPath` variable, which stores exactly the path we need:

```
app.use(express.static(publicPath));
```

The last thing to do is call `app.listen`. This will start up the server on port `3000`, and we'll provide a callback function as the second argument to print a little message to the Terminal once the server is up.

I'll use `console.log` to print `Server is up on port 3000`:

```
app.listen(3000, () => {
  console.log('Server is up on port 3000');
});
```

With this in place, we can now start up the server inside the Terminal and make sure our `index.html` file shows up in the browser. I'll go ahead and use the `clear` command to clear the Terminal output, then I'll use `nodemon` to run the server, using the following command:

nodemon server/server.js

```
[Gary:node-chat-app Gary$ nodemon server/server.js
[nodemon] 1.14.10
[nodemon] to restart at any time, enter `rs`
[nodemon] watching: *.*
[nodemon] starting `node server/server.js`
Server is up on port 3000
```

Here, we get our little message, `Server is up on port 3000`. In the browser, if I give things a refresh, we get our markup, `Welcome to the chat app`, as shown in the following screenshot:

We now have a basic server set up, which means in the next section, we can actually add Socket.io on both the client and the backend.

Setting up a gitignore file

Now, before we start getting things on GitHub and Heroku, we'll first set up a few things inside Atom. We need to set up a `.gitignore` file, which we'll provide in the root of the project.

 Inside `.gitignore`, the only thing we'll be ignoring is the node_modules folder. We do not want to commit any of this code to our repo, because it can be generated using `npm install` and it's subject to change. It's a real pain to manage that sort of thing, and it is not recommended that you commit it.

The next thing we'll do is configure a few things for Heroku. First up, we have to use the `process.env.PORT` environment variable. I'll create a constant called `port` next to the `publicPath` variable, setting it equal to `process.env.PORT` or 3000. We'll use it locally:

```
const publicPath = path.join(__dirname, '../public');
const port = process.env.PORT || 3000;
```

Now, we can provide `port` in `app.listen`, and we can provide it in the following message by changing our regular string to a template string to get `Server is up on`. I'll inject the `port` variable value:

```
app.listen(port, () => {
  console.log(`Server is up on ${port}`);
});
```

Now that we have that in place, the next thing we need to change in order to get our app set up for Heroku is update the `package.json` file, adding a `start` script and specifying the version of Node we want to use. Under `scripts`, I'll add a `start` script telling Heroku how to start the application. In order to start the app, you have to run the `node` command. You'll have to go into the `server` directory, and the file to start it up is `server.js`:

```
"scripts": {
  "start": "node server/server.js",
  "test": "echo \"Error: no test specified\" && exit 1"
},
```

We're also going to specify `engines`, which we've done before. `engines`, as you know, lets you tell Heroku which version of Node to use:

```
"engines": {

},
```

This will be important as we are taking advantage of some features only available in the latest versions of Node. Inside `engines`, I'll provide the exact same key-value pair I used previously, setting `node` equal to `9.3.0`:

```
"engines": {
  "node": "9.3.0"
},
```

If you're using a different version of Node, you can provide that instead of the version I have added here.

Making a commit with the current uncommitted files

Now that we have this in place, you are ready to make a commit with all of the current uncommitted files. You'll then go into GitHub and create a GitHub repository, where you'll push your local code up. Make sure the code actually gets on GitHub; you can do that by refreshing the GitHub repo page. You should see your directory structure right there on the repo.

The next thing you need to do is create a Heroku application and deploy to it. Once your application is deployed, you should be able to visit the app URL on the browser. You should see the exact same message as the one we have in our `localhost:3000`. The `Welcome to the chat app` message should print, but instead of being on `localhost:3000`, you should be on the actual Heroku app.

Now we have made all the changes necessary inside the project. We have configured the `port` variable and we have set up our `scripts` and `engines`, so you don't have to make any more code changes; you just need to work your wizardry in the browser and the Terminal to get this done.

The first step is to make a new GitHub repository. We need a place to push up our code. We can head over to `github.com`, click on that big green **New repository** button, and make a new one. I'll call my repository `node-course-2-chat-app`. I will leave this public and create it:

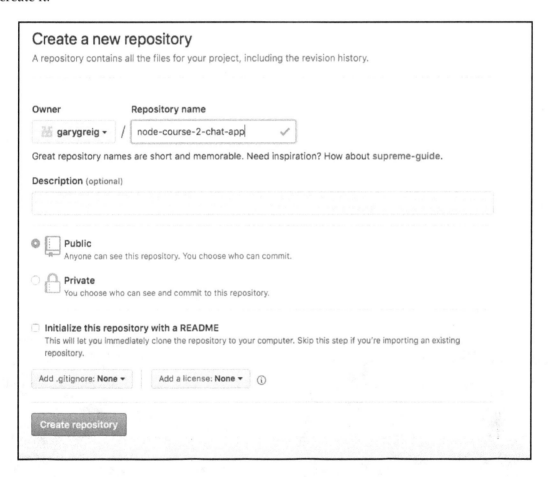

Now that we've created the repository, we have a list of commands we can use. We have an existing repository we want to push, so we can copy these lines:

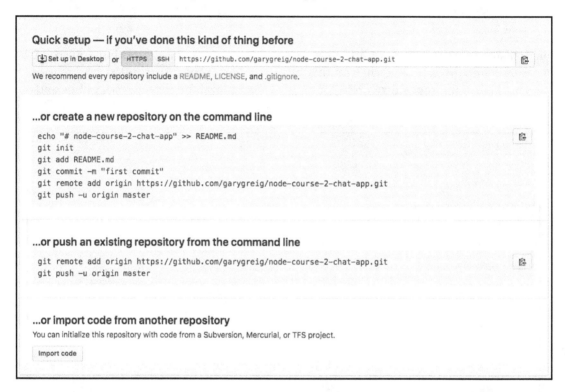

In the Terminal, before we can actually push anything, we need to make a commit. I'll shut down `nodemon` and run the `git status` command:

```
[Gary:node-chat-app Gary$ git status
On branch master

No commits yet

Untracked files:
  (use "git add <file>..." to include in what will be committed)

        .DS_Store
        .gitignore
        package-lock.json
        package.json
        public/
        server/

nothing added to commit but untracked files present (use "git add" to track)
```

Here, you see we have our expected files, we have the `public` and `server` folders, we have `.gitignore`, and we have `package.json`. However, `node_modules` is nowhere in sight. Then, you need to use `git add .` to add these untracked files to the next commit.

If you run the `git status` command again, you can see everything does look good:

```
[Gary:node-chat-app Gary$ git add .
[Gary:node-chat-app Gary$ git status
On branch master

No commits yet

Changes to be committed:
  (use "git rm --cached <file>..." to unstage)

        new file:   .DS_Store
        new file:   .gitignore
        new file:   package-lock.json
        new file:   package.json
        new file:   public/index.html
        new file:   server/server.js
```

We have four changes to be committed: four new files. I'll run `git commit` with the -m flag to specify a message. The -a flag is not required, since all of the files are already added. In the quotes, `Init commit` will get the job done:

```
git commit -m 'Init commit'
```

Once you have that commit in place, you can actually push it up to GitHub by running the two lines they gave you. I'll run both of those:

```
git remote add origin
https://github.com/garygreig/node-course-2-chat-app.git

git push -u origin master
```

As shown here, it's now up on GitHub. We can confirm that by refreshing the page, and instead of seeing the instructions, we see the files we created:

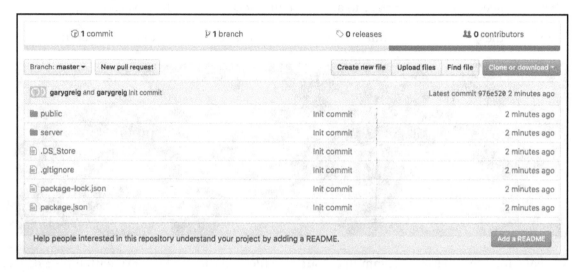

The next and last thing to do is get the app on Heroku. You don't actually have to go to the Heroku web app to get that done; we can run `heroku create` inside the Terminal:

```
Gary:node-chat-app Gary$ heroku create
Creating app... done, ● rocky-sierra-37964
https://rocky-sierra-37964.herokuapp.com/ | https://git.heroku.com/rocky-sierra-37964.git
```

Let's go ahead and create the application. We can use the following command to deploy the app. I'm going to go ahead and run that:

```
git push heroku master
```

This will take my local code and push it up to Heroku. Heroku will see that new code was pushed, so it will then go ahead and deploy it:

```
remote: -----> Pruning devDependencies
remote:         Skipping because npm 5.5.1 sometimes fails when running 'npm prune' due to a known issue
remote:         https://github.com/npm/npm/issues/19356
remote:
remote:         You can silence this warning by updating to at least npm 5.7.1 in your package.json
remote:         https://devcenter.heroku.com/articles/nodejs-support#specifying-an-npm-version
remote:
remote: -----> Build succeeded!
remote: -----> Discovering process types
remote:         Procfile declares types      -> (none)
remote:         Default types for buildpack -> web
remote:
remote: -----> Compressing...
remote:         Done: 17.6M
remote: -----> Launching...
remote:         Released v3
remote:         https://rocky-sierra-37964.herokuapp.com/ deployed to Heroku
remote:
remote: Verifying deploy... done.
To https://git.heroku.com/rocky-sierra-37964.git
 * [new branch]      master -> master
Gary:node-chat-app Gary$ 
```

Once it's up, we can use the `heroku open` command to open up the app URL on the browser. Alternatively, you can always grab the URL from the Terminal. I'll copy the URL, shown in the preceding screenshot, head into the browser, and paste it:

As shown in the preceding screenshot, we should see our app. **Welcome to the chat app** shows up on the screen, and with this in place, we are done! We have a basic Express server, we have a backend and a frontend, it's up on GitHub, and it's up on Heroku!

We are ready to move on to the next section, where we are actually going to start integrating Socket.io.

Adding Socket.io to an app

Now that you have a basic Express application up and running, in this section, you'll configure your server to allow for incoming WebSocket connections. This means the server will be able to accept connections and we'll be setting up the client to make the connections. Then, we'll have a persistent connection and we can send data back and forth, whether it's data from the server to the client, or data from the client to the server. That is the beauty of WebSockets—you can send data in either direction.

Now, in order to set up WebSockets, we'll be using a library called Socket.io. Just like Express makes it really easy to set up an HTTP server, Socket.io makes it dead simple to set up a server that supports WebSockets and to create a frontend that communicates with the server. Socket.io has a backend and frontend library; we'll be using both to set up WebSockets.

Setting up Socket.io

To get started, inside the Terminal, let's go ahead and install the most recent version of Socket.io using `npm i`. The module name is `socket.io`, and the most recent version at time of writing is `@2.0.4`. We'll use the `--save` dev flag to update the `package.json` file:

```
npm i socket.io@2.0.4 --save
```

Once this is in place, we can go ahead and make a few changes to our `server` file. First up, we'll load in the library. I'll make a constant called `socketIO` and set it equal to the `require` statement for the `socket.io` library:

```
const path = require('path');
const express = require('express');
const socketIO = require('socket.io');
```

With this in place, we now need to integrate Socket.io into our existing web server. Currently, we use Express to make our web server. We create a new Express app, we configure our middleware, and we call `app.listen`:

```
var app = express();

app.use(express.static(publicPath));

app.listen(port, () => {
  console.log(`Server is up on ${port}`);
});
```

Now, behind the scenes, Express is actually using a built-in Node module called `http` to create this server. We'll need to use `http` ourselves. We need to configure Express to work with `http`. Then, and only then, will we also be able to add Socket.io support.

Creating a server using the http library

First up, we'll load in the `http` module. So, let's make a constant called `http`, which is a built-in Node module so there's no need to install it. We can simply enter `require('http')`, just like this:

```
const path = require('path');
const http = require('http');
const express = require('express');
const socketIO = require('socket.io');
```

From here, we'll create a server using this `http` library. Just below our `app` variable, let's make a variable called `server`. We'll call `http.createServer`:

```
const path = require('path');
const http = require('http');
const express = require('express');
const socketIO = require('socket.io');

const publicPath = path.join(_dirname, '../public');
const port = process.env.PORT || 3000;
var app = express();
var server = http.createServer()
```

Now, you might not know it but you're actually already using the `createServer` method behind the scenes. When you call `app.listen` on your Express app, it literally calls this exact same method, passing in the app as the argument for `createServer`. The `createServer` method takes a function. This function looks really similar to one of our Express callbacks, and it gets called with a request and a response:

```
var server = http.createServer((req, res) => {

})
```

Now, as I mentioned, `http` is actually used behind the scenes for Express. It's integrated so much so that you can actually just provide `app` as the argument, and we are done:

```
var server = http.createServer(app);
```

Before we integrate Socket.io, let's go ahead and wrap up this change. We'll use the HTTP server as opposed to the Express server, so instead of calling `app.listen`, we'll call `server.listen`:

```
server.listen(port, () => {
  console.log(`Server is up on ${port}`);
});
```

Once again, there's no need to change the arguments passed in the `server.listen` method—they're exactly the same and built really closely to each other, so the `server.listen` arguments are the same as the Express `app.listen` arguments.

Now that we have this in place, we haven't actually changed any app functionality. Our server is still going to work on port 3000, but we're still not going to have access to Socket.io. In the Terminal, I can prove this by clearing the Terminal output and starting up our server using `nodemon` command:

```
nodemon server/server.js
```

Then, I'll load `localhost:3000` in the browser URL and see what I get back:

As shown in the preceding screenshot, we get our HTML, and **Welcome to the chat app** shows up. This means that our app is still working even though we're now using the HTTP server.

Configuring the server to use Socket.io

The next thing that we'll do is configure the server to use Socket.io—that's the entire reason we made this change. Next to the `server` variable, we'll make a variable called `io`.

We'll set it equal to a call to `socket.io` and pass in `server`, which we want to use with our WebSockets:

```
var server = http.createServer(app);
var io = socketIO(server);
```

Now we have access to that server via the `server` variable, so we'll pass it in as the first and only argument. Now, what we get back is our WebSockets server. On here, we can do anything we want in terms of emitting or listening to events. This is how we're going to communicate between the server and the client, and we'll talk more about that later in this section.

With this in place, our server is ready to go; we are ready to accept new connections. The problem is that we don't have any connections to accept. When we load our web page, we're not doing anything. We're not actually connecting to the server. We are going to need to manually run some JavaScript code to initiate that connection process.

Now, when we integrated Socket.io with our server, we actually got access to a few cool things. First up, we got access to a route that accepts incoming connections, which means that we can now accept WebSocket connections. Plus, we got access to a JavaScript library, which makes it really easy to work with Socket.io on the client. This library is available at the following path: `localhost:3000/socket.io/socket.io.js`. If you load this JavaScript file in the browser, you can see it's just a really long JavaScript library:

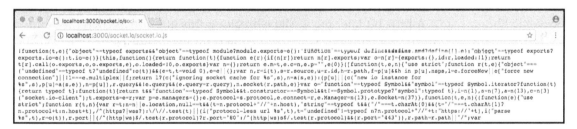

This contains all of the code we'll need on the client to make the connection and to transfer data, whether it's from server to client or client to server.

What we'll do in order to make the connection from our HTML file is load this in. I'll go back to `localhost:3000`. Now, we can go ahead and move into Atom, opening up `index.html`, and near the bottom of the `body` tag, we'll add a `script` tag to load in the file we just pulled up in the browser.

First up, we'll make the `script` tag itself, opening and closing it, and in order to load in an external file, we'll use the `src` attribute to provide the path:

```
<body>
  <p>Welcome to the chat app</p>

  <script src=""></script>
</body>
```

Now, this path is relative to our server. It's going to be `/socket.io/socket.io.js`, which is exactly as we typed it in the browser earlier:

```
<script src="/socket.io/socket.io.js"></script>
```

By adding the `script` tag, we're now loading in the library. On the browser, we have access to all sorts of methods available, thanks to the `socket` library. One of those methods is going to let us initiate a connection request, and that's exactly what we're going to do in the next line. Let's add a second `script` tag. This time, instead of loading an external script, we'll write some JavaScript right in the line:

```
<script src="/socket.io/socket.io.js"></script>
<script>

</script>
```

We can add any JavaScript we like, and this JavaScript is going to run right after the Socket.io library loads. A little bit later on, we'll be breaking this out into its own file—but for the moment, we can simply have our JavaScript code right inside our HTML file. We're going to call `io`:

```
<script src="/socket.io/socket.io.js"></script>
<script>
  io();
</script>
```

`io` is a method available to us because we loaded in this library. It's not native to the browser, and when we call it, we're actually initiating the request. We're making a request from the client to the server to open up a WebSocket and keep that connection open. Now, what we get back from `io` is really important; we'll save that in a variable called `socket`, just like this:

```
<script src="/socket.io/socket.io.js"></script>
<script>
  var socket = io();
</script>
```

This creates our connection and stores the socket in a variable. This variable is critical to communicating; it's exactly what we need in order to listen for data from the server and send data to the server. Now that we have this in place, let's go ahead and save our HTML file. We'll move into the browser and open up Chrome Developer Tools.

 Now regardless of what browser you use, whether it's IE, Safari, Firefox, or Chrome, you'll have access to a set of developer tools, which makes it really easy to debug and see what's going on behind the scenes in your web page. We'll be using the Chrome Developer Tools here to do a little debugging, I'd highly recommend using Chrome for the course just so you can follow along exactly.

To open up **Developer tools**, we go to **Settings** | **More tools** | **Developer tools**. You can also use the keyboard shortcut particular to your operating system. When you open **Developer tools**, you're going to be greeted with an overwhelming set of options, as shown here:

You're most likely brought to the **Elements** panel if you've never used Chrome Developer Tools before. The panel we're going to be using right now is the **Network** panel.

The **Network** panel keeps track of all of the requests made by your web page. So, if I make a request for a JavaScript file, I'm going to see that in a nice list, as shown in the preceding screenshot.

We're going to have to refresh the page in order to see the list of network requests; right here, we have five:

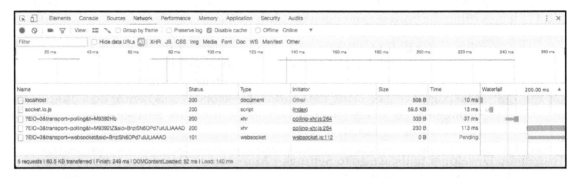

The network request at the very top is the first one that was made, and the one at the very bottom is the last one that was made. The first one was for the `localhost:3000` page, which was for the HTML file that loads `Welcome to the chat app`. The second one is for that JavaScript file that we saw on the browser, which gives us the library and gives us access to calling that `io` method that starts the connection process. The next four are all related to starting up and maintaining that connection. With this in place, we now have that live connection between the client and the server, and we can start communicating whatever we want to communicate.

Communication between the client and server

Now, the communication could be anything at all. In this case, it comes in the form of an event. Events can be emitted from both the client and the server, and both the client and the server can listen for events. Let's talk about an event that might happen in an email app.

In an email app, the server might emit an event called `newEmail` when a new email comes in. The client is then going to listen for that event. When it fires, it will get the `newEmail` data and render the email to the screen below the other ones. The same thing could happen the other way: maybe the client wants to create a new email and send it to someone else. It will ask for the email address of the person and the contents of the message, and it's then going to emit an event on the client that the server is going to listen for. So, this whole server/client relationship is entirely run via these events.

Now, we'll create custom events for our specific application throughout this chapter; but for now, we're going to look at a couple of default built-in ones that let you keep track of new users and disconnecting users. This means we'll be able to do something like greet a user when they join our application.

The io.on method

In order to play around with this inside Atom, in `server.js`, we are going to call a method on `io` called `io.on`:

```
app.use(express.static(publicPath));

io.on();
```

The `io.on` method lets you register an event listener. We can listen for a specific event and do something when that event happens. One built-in event that we're going to use—the most popular one—is called `connection`. This lets you listen for a new connection of a client to the server, and lets you do something when that connection comes in. In order to do something, you provide a callback function as the second argument, and this callback function is going to get called with a `socket`:

```
io.on('connection', (socket) => {

});
```

This `socket` argument is really similar to the `socket` argument we have access to inside the `index.html` file. This represents the individual socket, as opposed to all of the users connected to the server. Now, with this in place, we can do whatever we like. For example, I could use `console.log` to print a little message, such as `New user connected`:

```
io.on('connection', (socket) => {
  console.log('New user connected');
});
```

Every time a user connects to our app, we'll print a message to the console. I'll go ahead and save the `server.js` file, move into the Terminal, and you'll see that the message actually already exists:

```
[nodemon] restarting due to changes...
[nodemon] starting `node server/server.js`
Server is up on 3000
New user connected
```

To explain why, we need to understand one thing about WebSockets. WebSockets, as I mentioned, are a persistent technology, meaning that the client and server both keep the communication channel open for as long as either of them want to. If the server shuts down, the client doesn't really have a choice, and vice versa. If I close a browser tab, the server cannot force me to keep the connection open.

Now, when a connection drops the client, it's still going to try to reconnect. When we restart the server using `nodemon`, there's about a quarter of a second where the server is down, and the client notices that. It says, "woah, woah, woah! Server went down! Let's try to reconnect!" Eventually it reconnects, and that's why we're seeing the message, `New user connected`.

Go ahead and shut down the server, and over inside the client, you'll see that network requests are being made in Chrome Developer Tools:

They're trying to reconnect to the server, and you can see they're failing because the server is not up. Now, go back into the Terminal and restart the server like this:

```
[^CGary:node-chat-app Gary$ nodemon server/server.js
[nodemon] 1.14.10
[nodemon] to restart at any time, enter `rs`
[nodemon] watching: *.*
[nodemon] starting `node server/server.js`
Server is up on 3000
```

Inside the client, we'll try to reconnect again. We'll get a success result from the server—and boom—we are back! Just like this:

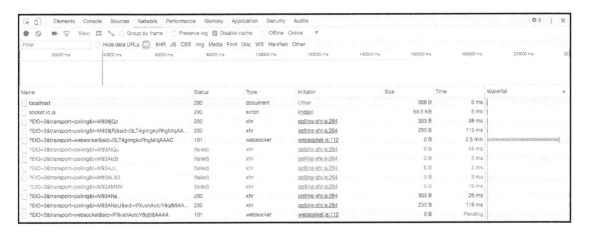

Now, when we reconnect, you can see that we get the message again, and that's why we saw it when we first added it to the `server.js` file.

Adding a connection event in the client

Now, the connection event also exists in the client. This means that in the client, we can do something when we successfully connect to the server. It may not happen right away; it may take a little time. Over inside Atom, we can add this event inside `index.html`, right below our call to `io`. As shown, we'll call `socket.on`:

```
var socket = io();

socket.on
```

We want to listen for an event, and this event is a little different to the one we have in our `server.js` file. It's not `on('connection')`, but `on('connect')`:

```
var socket = io();

socket.on('connect');
```

The `on` method here is exactly the same as the one we used in `server.js`. The first argument is the event name and the second argument is the callback function. In this case, we don't get access to a `socket` argument, since we already have it as a `socket` variable.

In this case, all I'll do is use `console.log` to print a little message to the console, `Connected to server`:

```
socket.on('connect', () => {
  console.log('Connected to server');
});
```

Now that we have this in place, we can go into the browser and go to a new tab in **Developer tools**. We'll load the **Console** tab. The **Console** tab is kind of like the Terminal inside Node. If we use `console.log` in our client-side JavaScript code, those messages are going to show up there. As you can see in the preceding screenshot, we also have some errors. These errors occurred when our server was down as I was showing you how it reconnects; but if we refresh the page, as you're going to see, `Connected to server` shows up, as shown here:

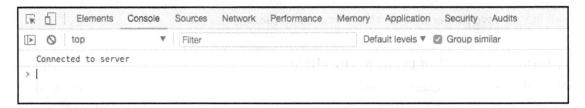

As soon as the connection happens, the client and the server both have that event fired. The client prints `Connected to server` and the server prints `New user connected`.

With this in place, we've now used the event system in Socket.io. We haven't set our own custom events, but we have taken advantage of some built-in ones.

The disconnect event

The last thing we're going to talk about in this section is the `disconnect` event, which lets you do something on both the server and the client when the connection drops. We'll add an event listener on the client, and do the same thing on the server.

On the client, next to our `connect` event, we can call `socket.on` again to listen to a new event. Once again, the name of the event here is the name of a built-in event, so it's only going to work if you type it correctly. This one is called `disconnect`:

```
socket.on('disconnect');
```

The `disconnect` event is going to fire whenever the connection drops. If the server goes down, the client is going to be able to do something. For now, that something is just going to be log a message, `console.log('Disconnected from server')`:

```
socket.on('disconnect', () => {
  console.log('Disconnected from server');
});
```

Now that we have this message in place, we can actually save our `index.html` file. Go over to the browser and give it a refresh to load in our new JavaScript file. Go ahead and make your browser screen just a little bit smaller so we can see it in the background of the Terminal.

I'll go to the Terminal, shut down the connection by shutting down the server, and over inside the browser, we get `Disconnected from server` printing to the screen:

If I restart my server inside the Terminal, you can see we've automatically connected, as `Connected to server` prints to the screen:

Now, the exact same event exists on the server. We can listen for a disconnecting client and we can do something when they leave. In order to register this event, you are going to go into `server.js`, and inside our callback, you're going to call `socket.on` in `server.js`, just like we did in the `index.html` file. It's the exact same signature. The first argument is the event name, `disconnect`. The callback function should do something simple, like print `client disconnected`.

Once you have that in place, what I want you to do is open up the browser and open up the Terminal, then close the browser tab. You should see the message print in the server—whatever message you happened to type here. Open up another browser tab, close it, and make sure you get the same message. This message should print every time one of your browser tabs closes, assuming that browser tab had an open connection.

Now, to do this, all you need to do is copy the exact same signature as we used in the `io.on` method. `socket.on` takes two arguments: the first one is the name of the event we're trying to listen to, `disconnect`; and the second argument is the function to run when the event fires:

```
socket.on('disconnect', () => {

});
```

In this case, all we're going to do is use `console.log` to print `User was disconnected`, just like this:

```
socket.on('disconnect', () => {
  console.log('User was disconnected');
});
```

Then, we'll save the file, which is automatically going to restart our application. Switch to the Terminal and then to the browser, so you can see the Terminal in the background. I'm going to open up a new tab, so when I close this currently open tab, the Chrome browser doesn't close completely. Close the tab with the open connection and, as shown in the following screenshot, inside the Terminal, we get `User was disconnected`:

```
[nodemon] restarting due to changes...
[nodemon] starting `node server/server.js`
Server is up on 3000
New user connected
User was disconnected
```

If I open up a new tab and go to `localhost:3000`, then `New user connected` prints. As soon as I close it, `User was disconnected` prints to the screen on the server. Hopefully, you're starting to see why WebSockets are so awesome—that instant two-way communication makes any sort of real-time application effortless to build.

Now, let's wrap this one up with a commit. I'll shut down our server and run `git status`. We can see that we only have modified files:

```
[^CGary:node-chat-app Gary$ git status
On branch master
Your branch is up-to-date with 'origin/master'.

Changes not staged for commit:
  (use "git add <file>..." to update what will be committed)
  (use "git checkout -- <file>..." to discard changes in working directory)

        modified:   package-lock.json
        modified:   package.json
        modified:   public/index.html
        modified:   server/server.js

no changes added to commit (use "git add" and/or "git commit -a")
```

So, `git commit` with the `-am` flag is going to get the job done. We can add our message, `Add connect and disconnect event handlers`:

```
git commit -am 'Add connect and disconnect event handlers'
```

I'll make the commit and push it up to GitHub by using the `git push` command.

With that in place, we are done. In the next section, we're going to get into the very interesting stuff—you're going to learn how to emit and listen to custom events. This means you can send any data you like from the server to the client, and vice versa.

Emitting and listening to custom events

In the previous section, you learned how to listen to those built-in events—things such as connection events and disconnection events. Those are fine, and they're a great starting place, but in this section, what we want to talk about is emitting and listening to custom events, and this is where Socket.io gets really interesting.

When you're able to emit and listen to custom events, you can send anything you want from the server to the client or from the client to the server. Now, to go through a quick example of how that'll look, we're going to use an example app, which will be an email application:

On the left, we have our server, which is starting up a Socket.io web server. On the right, we have our email app, which is showing a list of all our current emails. Now, one custom event that our app might require is a `newEmail` event:

The `newEmail` event is going to be emitted by the server when an email comes in. For example, if I sign up to a new service, that service sends me an email to confirm my email. Then, the server eventually gets that email and it emits an event that the client listens to. The client is going to listen for the `newEmail` event and will be able to re-render the list of emails in the browser using jQuery, React, Ember, or whatever library it happens to be using, showing the new email to me, the user.

Now, aside from just sending a message that an event happened, the most important piece to the puzzle is sending data, and we can actually do that. When you create and emit a custom event, you can send whatever information you like from the server to the client or from the client to the server. Usually, this takes the form of an object with various properties. In the case of getting a new email, I might want to know who the email is from. I definitely need to know the text of the email, and I also want to know when the email arrived at my server so I can render what I need to inside the browser for whoever happens to be using the email app.

Now, this is data flowing from the server to the client, which is something we were not able to accomplish with HTTP requests, but it is something we can accomplish using Socket.io. Now, another event, the `createEmail` event, is going to flow from the client to the server:

When I create a new email inside my web browser, I'll need to emit that event from the client, and the server is going to listen for that event. Once again, we will be sending some data across. Although the data will be a little different, we want to know who the email needs to be sent to, we need the text of the email, and maybe we want to schedule it for down the line, so a `scheduleTimestamp` field could be used.

Obviously, these are all just example fields; your fields for a real email app would probably be a little different. With this in place, though, we are ready to go ahead and actually create these two events inside our application.

Creating custom events inside an application

Let's dive in to creating custom events inside our application, starting with creating `newEmail` and `createEmail` events. Before we start emitting or listening to custom events, let's go ahead and make a few tweaks to our client-side JavaScript.

Moving the JavaScript into a separate file

As you might have noticed in the last section, I accidentally used ES6 arrow functions inside our client-side JavaScript code. As I mentioned, we want to avoid this; the project is going to work correctly in Chrome, but if you tried to load it up on your mobile phone, Internet Explorer, Safari, or some versions of Firefox, the program would crash. So, instead of using arrow functions, we'll use regular functions by removing the arrow and adding the `function` keyword before our arguments. I'll do this for the `on('connect'` listener and for the `on('disconnect'` listener, adding the `function` keyword and removing the arrow:

```
socket.on('connect', function () {
  console.log('Connected to server');
});

socket.on('disconnect', function () {
  console.log('Disconnected from server');
});
```

I'll also take our JavaScript and move it into a separate file. Instead of editing the client-side JavaScript right inside our HTML file, we'll have a separate file where that code lives. This is a better method to get things done.

In the `public` folder, we can make a new folder for this JavaScript file. I'll make one called `js` (we'll have multiple JavaScript files by the time this app is over, so it's a good idea to create a folder to house all of those). For now, though, we just need one, `index.js`. The `index.js` file will load when we load `index.html`, and it will contain all the JavaScript required to get this page to work, starting with the JavaScript we wrote in the last section. Cut out all of the code in the `script` tag and paste it into `index.js`:

```
var socket = io();

socket.on('connect', function () {
  console.log('Connected to server');
});

socket.on('disconnect', function () {
  console.log('Disconnected from server');
});
```

We can save the file and update our `script` tag. Instead of having the code in line, we'll load it in by providing the `src` attribute, with the path to the file as `/js/index.js`:

```
    <script src="/socket.io/socket.io.js"></script>
    <script src="/js/index.js"></script>
</body>
```

Now that we have this in place, we have the exact same functionality that we had before—only this time around, the JavaScript has been broken out into its own file. Start up the server using `nodemon server/server.js`. Once it's up, we can go ahead and load the app by going to the browser and opening up `localhost:3000`. I'll open up **Developer tools** as well, so we can make sure everything is working as expected. Inside the console, we see `Connected to server` is still printing:

This is code that exists in `index.js`, and the very fact that it's showing up here proves that the file was loaded. With this in place, we can now move on to our custom events.

Now, we have two events that we talked about for our example email application: we have `newEmail`, which is from the server to the client; and we have `createEmail`, which is an event emitted by the client and listened to by the server. We're going to get started with `newEmail`, and to kick things off, we're going to head into our client-side JavaScript and listen for that event.

When that event fires, we want to do something: we want to take the data and use jQuery, React, or some other frontend framework to render it to the browser so the user can see the email as soon as it comes in.

Adding a newEmail custom event

Now, in order to listen to a custom event, we are still going to use `socket.on`; although, instead of specifying the name of one of the built-in events, we'll provide the first argument inside quotes as the name of our custom event. In this case, that name is going to be newEmail:

```
socket.on('newEmail');
```

Now, the second argument for `socket.on` is the same as the second argument for the built-in event listeners. We'll provide a function, and this function is going to get called when the event fires:

```
socket.on('newEmail', function () {

});
```

For now, all we're going to do inside the function is use `console.log` to print a little message, New email:

```
socket.on('newEmail', function () {
  console.log('New email');
});
```

This will print inside of the web developer console every time the client hears this event coming across the pipeline. Now that we have the listener in place for newEmail, let's go ahead and emit this event inside server.js.

The emit method

Inside server.js, what we want to do is call a method on socket. The socket method has a method called emit, which we'll use on both the client and the server to emit events:

```
io.on('connection', (socket) => {
  console.log('New user connected');
  socket.emit('');
});
```

The `emit` method is really similar to the listeners; although, instead of listening to an event, we are creating the event. The first argument is the same. It's going to be the name of the event you want to emit. In this case, we have to match it exactly as we specified in `index.js`, `newEmail`. Now, as shown in the following code, we'll provide `newEmail`:

```
io.on('connection', (socket) => {
  console.log('New user connected');
  socket.emit('newEmail');
});
```

Now, this is not a listener, so we'll not provide a callback function. What we want to do is specify the data. Now, by default, we don't have to specify any data; maybe we just want to emit `newEmail` without anything, letting the browser know that something happened. If we do this, over inside the browser we can refresh the app, and we get `New email`, as shown in the following screenshot:

The event is still happening even though we're not sending across any custom data. If you do want to send custom data, which is most likely the case, that's super easy. All you have to do is provide a second argument for `newEmail`. Now, you could provide an argument of three, or true, or anything else, but you usually want to send multiple pieces of data across, so an object is going to be your second argument:

```
socket.emit('newEmail', {

});
```

This is going to let you specify anything you like. In our case, we might specify who the email is from by specifying a `from` attribute; for instance, it's from `mike@example.com`. Maybe we also have the `text` attribute for the email, `Hey. What is going on`, and we might have other attributes as well. For example, `createdAt` could be a timestamp of when the server got the email, as shown here:

```
socket.emit('newEmail', {
  from: 'mike@example.com',
  text: 'Hey. What is going on.',
  createdAt: 123
});
```

The data shown in the preceding code block will get sent along with the `newEmail` event from the server to the client. Now, go ahead and save `server.js`, and inside our client-side JavaScript `index.js` file, we can go ahead and do something with that data. The data that's emitted with your event is provided as the first argument to your callback function. As shown in the following code, we have our callback function for `newEmail`, which means we can name the first argument `email` and do whatever we want with it:

```
socket.on('newEmail', function (email) {
  console.log('New email');
});
```

We might be appending it to a list of emails in a real web app, but for our purposes, all we'll do right now is provide it as the second argument to `console.log`, rendering it to the screen:

```
socket.on('newEmail', function (email) {
  console.log('New email', email);
});
```

With this in place, we can now test that everything is working as expected.

Testing the newEmail event

If I go to the browser and give things a refresh using *command + R*, we see over inside the console that we have `New email`, and below this we have `Object`. We can click on `Object` to expand it and we see all of the properties we specified:

We have our `from` property, the `text` property, and our `createdAt` property. All of it is showing up as expected, which is fantastic! In real time, we were able to pass not only an event, but event data from the server to the client, which is something we could never do with an HTTP API.

Adding a createEmail custom event

Now, on the other side of things, we have a situation where we want to emit an event from the client trying to send some data to the server. This is for our createEmail event. Now, in this case, we will add our event listener inside server.js using socket.on, just as we do for any other event listener, such as we have in server.js.

The io.on method we used for the connection event is a very special event; you will usually not be attaching anything to io, or be making calls to io.on or io.emit, other than the one we have mentioned in this function. Our custom event listeners are going to happen in the following statement by calling socket.on as we do for disconnect, passing in the name of the event you want to listen to—in this case, it is the createEmail event:

```
socket.emit('newEmail', {
  from: 'mike@example.com',
  text: 'Hey. What is going on.',
  createdAt: 123
});

socket.on('createEmail');
```

Now, for createEmail, we do want to add a listener. We are in our Node code, so we can use an arrow function:

```
socket.on('createEmail', () => {

});
```

We're probably going to expect some data, such as the email to create, so we can name that first argument. We name it after the data sent along with the event, so I'm going to call this newEmail. For this example, all we're going to do is print it to the console so we can make sure the event is properly going from client to server. I'll add console.log and log out the event name, createEmail. As the second argument, I'll log out the data so I can view it in the Terminal and make sure everything works as expected:

```
socket.on('createEmail', (newEmail) => {
  console.log('createEmail', newEmail);
});
```

Now we have our listener in place and our server did restart; however, we're never actually emitting the event on the client. We can go ahead and fix this by calling socket.emit in index.js. Now, call it inside our connect callback function. We don't want to emit the event until we are connected, and socket.emit is going to let us do just that. We can call socket.emit to emit the event.

The event name is `createEmail`:

```
socket.on('connect', function () {
  console.log('Connected to server');

  socket.emit('createEmail');
});
```

Then, we can pass any data we like in as the second argument. In the case of an email app, we're probably going to need to send it to someone, so we'll have an address for that—something like `jen@example.com`. We're obviously going to need some text—something like `Hey. This is Andrew`. Also, we might have other properties, such as subject, but for now we're going to stick with just these two:

```
socket.emit('createEmail', {
  to: 'jen@example.com',
  text: 'Hey. This is Andrew.'
})
```

So, what we've done here is we've created a client-side script that connects it to the server, and as soon as it connects, it emits this `createEmail` event.

 Now, this is not a realistic example. In a real-world app, a user is most likely going to fill out a form. You'll grab the previously mentioned pieces of data from the form, and then you'll emit the event. We will be working with HTML forms a little later; for now, though, we're just calling `socket.emit` to play around with these custom events.

Save `index.js`, and inside the browser, we can now give the page a refresh. As soon as it connects, it's going to emit that event:

```
   Elements   Console   Sources   Network   Performance   Memory   Application   Security   Audits

   top              ▼  Filter                       Default levels ▼  ✅ Group similar

   Connected to server
   New email ▼ {from: "mike@example.com", text: "Hey. What is going on.", createdAt: 123}
                createdAt: 123
                from: "mike@example.com"
                text: "Hey. What is going on."
             ▶ __proto__: Object
   >
```

In the Terminal, you see `createEmail` printing:

```
[nodemon] restarting due to changes...
[nodemon] starting `node server/server.js`
Server is up on 3000
New user connected
User was disconnected
New user connected
createEmail { to: 'jen@example.com', text: 'Hey. This is Andrew.' }
```

The event was emitted from the client to the server. The server got the data and all is well.

socket.emit in the developer console

Now, another cool thing about the console is that we have access to the variables created by our application; most notably the socket variable. This means that inside Google Chrome, in the developer console, we can call `socket.emit` and we emit whatever we like.

I can emit an action, `createEmail`, and I can pass in some data as the second argument, an object where I have a to attribute equal to `julie@example.com`. I have my other attributes too—something like `text`, which I can set equal to `Hey`:

```
socket.emit('createEmail', {to: 'julie@example.com', text: 'Hey'});
```

This is an example of how we can use the developer console to make debugging our app even easier. We can type a statement, hit *enter*, and it's going to go ahead and emit the event:

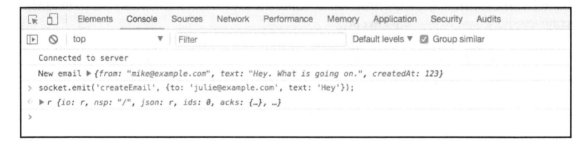

Inside the Terminal, we'll get that event and do something with it—whether it's creating the email or doing anything else we might require. Inside the Terminal, you can see `createEmail` showed up. We'll send that one to Julie, and then there's the text, `Hey`. It all got to the server from the client:

```
[nodemon] restarting due to changes...
[nodemon] starting `node server/server.js`
Server is up on 3000
New user connected
User was disconnected
New user connected
createEmail { to: 'jen@example.com', text: 'Hey. This is Andrew.' }
createEmail { to: 'julie@example.com', text: 'Hey' }
```

Now that we have this in place and we've played around with how we can use these custom events, it's time to move from the email application to the actual app we're going to be building: *the chat app.*

The custom events in the chat app

Now that you know how to emit and listen to custom events, we're going to move on to creating two events that we'll actually use in the chat app. These are going to be newMessage and createMessage:

Now, for the chat app, we once again have our server, which is going to be the server we build; and we have our client, which is going to be a user who is in the chat app. There are most likely going to be multiple users who all want to communicate with each other.

Now, the first event we'll have is a newMessage event. This is going to be emitted by the server and listened to on the client:

When a new message comes in, the server will send it to everyone connected to the chat room, so they can display it to the screen and a user can go ahead and respond to it. The newMessage event is going to require some data. We're going to need to know who the message was from; a string of someone's name, such as Andrew, the text of the message, something like, hey, can you meet up at six, and a createdAt timestamp.

All of this data is going to get rendered inside our chat application in the browser. We'll be doing that for real in a little bit, but for now we'll just print it to the console. So, this is the first event I want you to create. You'll make this newMessage event, emit it from the server—for now, you can simply emit it when a user connects—and you'll listen to it on the client. For now, on the client, you can just print with console.log a little message when you get the data. You can say something like got new message, printing the object that was passed with this data.

Next up, the second event we'll work with is createMessage. This will come from the client to the server. So if I'm user 1, I'll fire a createMessage event from my browser. This will go to the server, and the server will fire newMessage events to everyone else so they can see my message, which means the createMessage event is going to get emitted from the client and the server is going to be the one who's listening for the event:

Now, this event will require some data. We'll need to know who the message was from and also the text: what did they want to say? We need both of these pieces of information.

Now, notice a discrepancy here: we're sending the from, text, and createdAt properties to the client, but we're not asking for a createdAt property from the client when they create a message. This createdAt property is actually going to get created on the server. This is going to prevent the user from being able to spoof the time a message was created at. There are certain properties we're going to trust the user to provide us with; there's others that we will not trust them to provide us with, and one of those is going to be createdAt.

Now, for createMessage, all you have to do is set up an event listener on the server that waits for this to fire, and once again, you can simply print a message, for example, create message, and then you can provide the data that was passed along to console.log, printing it to the Terminal. Now, once you have that listener in place, you'll want to emit it.

You can emit it when you user first connects, and you can also fire a couple of `socket.emit` calls from Chrome Developer Tools, making sure that all of the messages show up in the Terminal, listening for the `createMessage` event.

We're going to get started inside `server.js` by listening for that `createMessage` event, and this is going to happen down below the `socket.emit` function in `server.js`. Now, we have an old event listener from `createEmail`; we can remove that, and we can call `socket.on` to listen to our brand new event, `createMessage`:

```
socket.on('createMessage');
```

The `createMessage` event is going to require a function to call when the event actually happens. We'll want to do something with the message data:

```
socket.on('createMessage', () => {

});
```

For the moment, all you need to do is use `console.log` to print it to the Terminal so we can verify that everything works as expected. We'll get our message data, which will include `from` property and a `text` property, and we'll print it to the screen. You don't have to specify the exact message I used; I'll just say `createMessage`, and the second argument will be the data that was passed from the client to the server:

```
socket.on('createMessage', (message) => {
  console.log('createMessage', message);
});
```

Now that we have our listener in place, we can go ahead and emit this inside the client in `index.js`. Now, we currently have an emit call for the `createEmail` event. I'll remove this emit call. We'll call `socket.emit` first and then `emit('createMessage')`:

```
socket.on('connect', function () {
  console.log('Connected to server');

  socket.emit('createMessage');
});
```

Next, we'll emit `createMessage` with the necessary data.

> Remember when you're emitting a custom event that the first argument is the event name and the second is the data.

For the data, we'll provide an object with two properties: `from`, this one's from `Andrew`; and `text`, which is the actual text of the message, which could be something like `Yup, that works for me`:

```
socket.emit('createMessage', {
  from: 'Andrew',
  text: 'Yup, that works for me.'
});
```

This is going to be the event we emit. I'm going to save `index.js`, head over to the browser, and we should be able to refresh the app and see the data in the Terminal:

```
[nodemon] restarting due to changes...
[nodemon] starting `node server/server.js`
Server is up on 3000
New user connected
createEmail { to: 'jen@example.com', text: 'Hey. This is Andrew.' }
User was disconnected
New user connected
createMessage { from: 'Andrew', text: 'Yup, that works for me.' }
```

As shown in the preceding screenshot, inside the Terminal we have `createMessage` with the `from` property that we specified, and the text, `Yup, that works for me`.

Now, we can also emit events from Chrome Developer Tools to play around with Socket.io. We can add `socket.emit`, and we can emit any event we like, passing in some data:

```
socket.emit('createMessage', {from: 'Jen', text: 'Nope'});
```

The event we'll emit is `createMessage`, and the data is a `from` attribute; this one's from `Jen` and a text attribute, `Nope`:

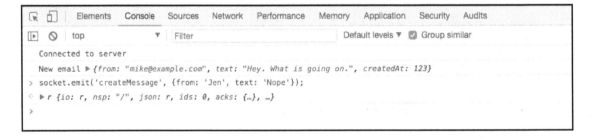

When I send this off, the message shows up on the server in real time, and as shown in the following screenshot, you can see it's from `Jen`, the text is `Nope`, and everything is working as expected:

```
[nodemon] restarting due to changes...
[nodemon] starting `node server/server.js`
Server is up on 3000
New user connected
createEmail { to: 'jen@example.com', text: 'Hey. This is Andrew.' }
User was disconnected
New user connected
createMessage { from: 'Andrew', text: 'Yup, that works for me.' }
createMessage { from: 'Jen', text: 'Nope' }
```

Now, that's the first event; the other one is the `newMessage` event, which is going to be emitted by the server and listened to by the client.

The newMessage event

To get started with this one, we'll add our event listener inside `index.js`. We have the old event listener for `newEmail`. I'm going to go ahead and remove that, and we'll call `socket.on` to listen to the new event, `newMessage`. The `newMessage` event is going to require a callback:

```
socket.on('newMessage', function () {

});
```

For the moment, we'll use `console.log` to print the message to the console, but later, we'll be taking this message and adding it to the browser so a user can actually see it on the screen. Now, we are going to get the message data. I'll create an argument called `message` for the moment, and we can go ahead and simply log it to the screen using `console.log`, printing the name of the event so it's easy to track in the Terminal, and the actual data that was passed from server to client:

```
socket.on('newMessage', function (message) {
  console.log('newMessage', message);
});
```

Now, the last thing we need to do is simply emit `newMessage` from the server, making sure it shows up in the client. Inside `server.js`, instead of emitting `newEmail`, we will call `socket.emit`, emitting our custom event, `newMessage`:

```
io.on('connection', (socket) => {
  console.log('New user connected');

  socket.emit('newMessage');
});
```

Now, we will need some data—that message data. We'll also provide that as the second argument. It'll be an object with a `from` property. It could be from whoever you like; I'll go with `John`:

```
socket.emit('newMessage', {
  from: 'John',
});
```

Next up, we'll provide the `text` property. This can be anything as well, such as `See you then`, and finally we'll provide the `createdAt` property. This will be generated by the server later so a user can't spoof the time a message was created at, but for now, we'll just use some sort of random number, such as `123123`:

```
socket.emit('newMessage', {
  from: 'John',
  text: 'See you then',
  createdAt: 123123
});
```

Now, as soon as a user connects to the server, we'll be emitting that event. Inside the browser, I can go ahead and refresh things. We have our `newMessage` event showing up and the data is exactly as we specified it in our `server.js` file:

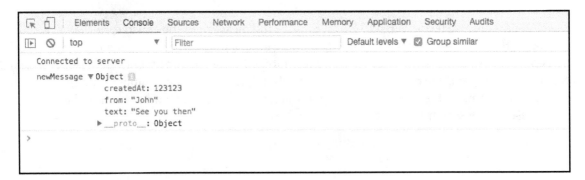

We have our `createdAt` timestamp, our `from` property, and our `text` property. In future, we'll be literally taking this data and rendering it into the browser so it shows up and someone can read it and respond to it, but for now we are done. We have our event listener on the server for `createMessage`, and our event listener on the client for `newMessage`.

That is it for this section! Since we are done, we will be making a quick commit. I'll shut down the server and run the `git status` command:

```
[Gary:node-chat-app Gary$ git status
On branch master
Your branch is up-to-date with 'origin/master'.

Changes not staged for commit:
  (use "git add <file>..." to update what will be committed)
  (use "git checkout -- <file>..." to discard changes in working directory)

        modified:   public/index.html
        modified:   server/server.js

Untracked files:
  (use "git add <file>..." to include in what will be committed)

        public/js/
```

As shown in the preceding screenshot, we have quite a few changes here. We have our new js file in the `public.js` folder, and we've also changed `server.js` and `index.html`. I'll run the `git add .` command to add all of that to the next commit, and then I'll create a commit using `git commit` with the `-m` flag. A good message for this one is `Add newMessage and createMessage events`:

```
git commit -m 'Add newMessage and createMessage events'
```

With this in place, we can now push our code up to GitHub. There's no need to do anything with Heroku since we don't have anything visual just yet; we'll hold off on that until later.

In the next section, we're going to wire up messages, so when tab 1 emits a message, it's visible by tab 2. This is going to bring us one step closer to actually communicating in real time between different browser tabs.

Broadcasting events

Now that we have our custom event listeners and emitters in place, it's time to actually wire up the message system so when one user sends a message to the server, it actually gets sent to every connected user. If I have two tabs open and I emit a `createMessage` event from one tab, I should see the message arrive in the second one.

To test things locally, we'll be using separate tabs, but the same would work on Heroku with separate browsers on separate networks; as long as everyone has the same URL on their browser, they will be connected, regardless of which machine they're on. Now, for localhost, we obviously don't have the right privilege, but as we deploy to Heroku, which we will be doing in this section, we'll be able to test this out between, say, your phone and the browser running on your machine.

Wiring up the createMessage listener for all users

To get started, we'll update the `createMessage` listener. Currently, all we do is log the data to the screen. But here, instead of just logging it, we actually want to emit a new event, a `newMessage` event, to everybody, so each connected user gets the message that was sent from a specific user. In order to get that done, we'll call a method on `io`, which will be `io.emit`:

```
socket.on('createMessage', (message) => {
  console.log('createMessage', message);
  io.emit
});
```

`Socket.emit` emits an event to a single connection, whereas `io.emit` emits an event to every single connection. Here, we are going to emit the `newMessage` event, specifying it as our first argument. The second argument, as with `socket.emit`, is the data you want to send:

```
socket.on('createMessage', (message) => {
  console.log('createMessage', message);
  io.emit('newMessage', {
  })
});
```

Now, we know we'll get a `from` property and a `text` property from the client—those appear in `socket.emit` for the `createMessage` event in `index.js`—which means what we need to do is pass those along, setting `from` equal to `message.from`, and setting `text` equal to `message.text`:

```
io.emit('newMessage', {
  from: message.from,
  text: message.text
})
```

Now, along with `from` and `text`, we'll also specify a `createdAt` property, which will be generated by the server to prevent a specific client from spoofing the time a message was created. The `createdAt` property is set equal to `new Date`, and we'll call the `getTime` method to get that timestamp back, which we've done before:

```
io.emit('newMessage', {
  from: message.from,
  text: message.text,
  createdAt: new Date().getTime()
});
```

Now that we have this in place, we actually have messaging wired up. We can go ahead and remove our emit calls—the `newMessage` emit call and the `createMessage` emit call—from `server.js` and `index.js`, respectively, making sure to save both files. With this in place, we can go ahead and test this by opening up two connections to the server and emitting some events.

Testing the messaging events

I'm going to start up the server inside the Terminal using the `nodemon server/server.js` command:

```
[Gary:node-chat-app Gary$ nodemon server/server.js
[nodemon] 1.14.10
[nodemon] to restart at any time, enter `rs`
[nodemon] watching: *.*
[nodemon] starting `node server/server.js`
Server is up on 3000
```

Inside the browser, we can now open up two tabs, both at `localhost:3000`. For both tabs, I am going to open up **Developer tools,** since that's currently the graphic user interface for our application. We don't have any forms just yet, which means we need to use the **Console** tab to run some statements. We'll do the same thing for a second tab:

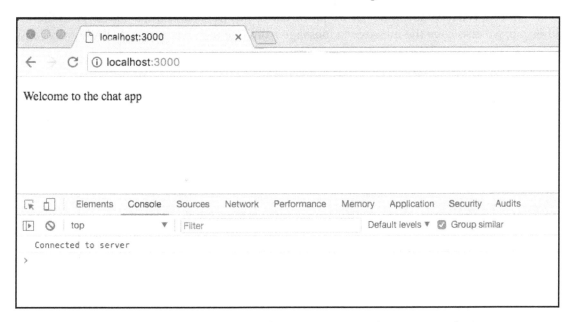

Notice that as soon as we open the tabs, we'll get `New user connected` messages in the Terminal:

```
Gary:node-chat-app Gary$ nodemon server/server.js
[nodemon] 1.14.10
[nodemon] to restart at any time, enter `rs`
[nodemon] watching: *.*
[nodemon] starting `node server/server.js`
Server is up on 3000
New user connected
New user connected
```

Now that we have our two tabs open, we can go ahead and emit a `createMessage` event from either one. I'll emit it from the second tab by calling `socket.emit`, emitting a custom event. The event name is `createMessage`, and it takes those two properties we just discussed—the `from` property and the `text` property—both of which I'll specify in the `socket.emit` object. The `from` property will be set equal to the first name, `Andrew`, and the `text` property will get set equal to `'This should work'`:

```
socket.emit('createMessage', {from: 'Andrew', text: 'This should work!'});
```

With this in place, we can now emit my event from the browser. It will go to the server, which will send the message to every connected user, including the currently connected user who sent the message. We're going to hit *enter*, it fires it off, and we see that we get `newMessage`. We have the message we just created, but the cool thing is that over in the other tab, we also have the message: a message from one user has reached another user in a separate tab:

With this in place, we now have a very basic messaging system set up: a user emits an event, it goes to the server, and the server sends it to everyone else who is connected. With this in place, I'd like to make a commit and deploy to Heroku so we can test it out.

Committing and deploying messaging to Heroku

If I run the `git status` command in the Terminal, I see I have my two changed files as expected:

```
[^CGary:node-chat-app Gary$ git status
On branch master
Your branch is up-to-date with 'origin/master'.

Changes not staged for commit:
  (use "git add <file>..." to update what will be committed)
  (use "git checkout -- <file>..." to discard changes in working directory)

        modified:   public/js/index.js
        modified:   server/server.js

no changes added to commit (use "git add" and/or "git commit -a")
```

I can then run the `git commit` command with the `-am` flag to specify a message for this commit—something like `Emit newMessage on createMessage` will get the job done:

```
git commit -am 'Emit newMessage on createMessage'
```

I can then go ahead and actually make the commit, pushing it up to both GitHub and Heroku. The `git push` command is going to get it on GitHub.

The `git push heroku master` command is going to deploy it live to the web.

We'll be able to open up our chat application and make sure it works regardless of the browser, computer, or any other variable:

```
remote: -----> Pruning devDependencies
remote:        Skipping because npm 5.5.1 sometimes fails when running 'npm prune' due to a known issue
remote:        https://github.com/npm/npm/issues/19356
remote:
remote:        You can silence this warning by updating to at least npm 5.7.1 in your package.json
remote:        https://devcenter.heroku.com/articles/nodejs-support#specifying-an-npm-version
remote:
remote: -----> Build succeeded!
remote: -----> Discovering process types
remote:        Procfile declares types      -> (none)
remote:        Default types for buildpack -> web
remote:
remote: -----> Compressing...
remote:        Done: 22.4M
remote: -----> Launching...
remote:        Released v4
remote:        https://rocky-sierra-37964.herokuapp.com/ deployed to Heroku
remote:
remote: Verifying deploy... done.
To https://git.heroku.com/rocky-sierra-37964.git
   b514226..77a5b8e  master -> master
```

As shown in the preceding screenshot, we are compressing and launching the app. It looks like everything is done. I'll use the `heroku open` command to open it up. This will open it up in my default browser, and as shown in the following screenshot, you'll see that we have `Welcome to the chat app`:

Testing messaging in a Firefox browser using Heroku

Now, to demonstrate this, what I'll open up a separate browser. I'll open up Firefox and type in the exact same URL. Then, I'll copy this URL and grab the Firefox browser, making it smaller so we can quickly switch between the two, opening up the Heroku app here:

Now, Firefox also has Developer Tools available via the menu in the top-right corner. There, we have a **Web Developer** section; we're looking for **Web Console**:

Now that we have this open, we can go into **Developer tools** for our Chrome tab connected to the Heroku application, and what we'll do is emit an event using `socket.emit`. We'll emit a `createMessage` event. We'll specify our custom properties inside of the object, then we can go ahead and have `from` set to `Mike`, and we can set the `text` property equal to `Heroku`:

```
socket.emit('createMessage', {from: 'Mike', text: 'Heroku'});
```

Now, when I go ahead and emit this event, everything should work as expected. We're calling `socket.emit` and emitting `createMessage`. We have our data, which means it will go to the Heroku server, which will send it over to Firefox. We'll send this off, which should mean we get `newMessage` in Chrome Developer tools. Then, inside Firefox, we also have the message. It's from `Mike`, the text is `Heroku`, and we have the `createdAt` timestamp added by our server:

With this in place, we have a messaging system—not only working locally, but also on Heroku—which means anybody in the world can visit this URL; they can emit the event, and everyone else connected is going to see that event in the console.

Now that we've tested it out across browsers, I will close Firefox, and we'll move on to the second part of this section.

Broadcasting events to other users

In this part of the section, we'll talk about a different way to emit events. Some events you want to send to everybody: a new message should go to every single user, including the one who sent it so it can show up inside the list of messages. Other events, on the other hand, should only go to other people, so if user one emits an event, it shouldn't go back to user one, but instead go only to users two and three.

A good example of this is when a user joins a chatroom. I want to print a little message, like `Andrew joined`, when someone joins, and I want to print a message, like `welcome Andrew`, for the actual user who joined. So, in the first tab I would see `welcome Andrew`, and in the second tab I would see `Andrew joined`. In order to get that done, we'll look at a different way to emit events in the server. This will be done via broadcasting. Broadcasting is the term for emitting an event to all but one specific user.

I'll start up the server once again using the `nodemon server/server.js` command, and inside Atom, we can now tweak how we emit the event in the `io.emit` method in `server.js`. Now, this is going to be the final way we do things, but we'll play around with broadcasting as well, which means I'll comment this out as opposed to removing it:

```
socket.on('createMessage', (message) => {
  console.log('createMessage', message);
  //io.emit('newMessage', {
  //  from: message.from,
  //  text: message.text,
  //  createdAt: new Date().getTime()
  //});
});
```

To broadcast, we have to specify the individual socket. This lets the Socket.io library know which users shouldn't get the event. In this case, the user that we call here is not going to get the event, but everyone else will. Now, we need to call `socket.broadcast`:

```
socket.on('createMessage', (message) => {
  console.log('createMessage', message);
  //io.emit('newMessage', {
  //  from: message.from,
  //  text: message.text,
  //  createdAt: new Date().getTime()
  //});
  socket.broadcast
});
```

Broadcast is an object that has its own emit function, and it's the exact same syntax as `io.emit` or `socket.emit`. The big difference is who it gets sent to. This will send the event to everybody but the mentioned socket, which means if I fire a `createMessage` event, the `newMessage` event will fire to everybody but myself, and that's exactly what we can do here.

It's going to be identical, which means we can go ahead and pass in the message event name. The arguments will be identical: the first one will be `newMessage`, and the other one will be the object with our properties, `from: message.from` and `text: message.text`. Last up, we have `createdAt` equal to a new timestamp, `new Date().getTime`:

```
socket.broadcast.emit('newMessage', {
  from: message.from,
  text: message.text,
  createdAt: new Date().getTime()
});
```

With this in place, we will not see the messages we send, but everybody else will. We can prove this by heading over to Google Chrome. I'll give both tabs a refresh, and from the second tab, once again, we will emit an event. We can actually use the up arrow key inside the web developer console to rerun one of our previous commands, and that's exactly what we'll do:

```
socket.emit('createMessage', {from: 'Andrew', text: 'This should work'});
```

Here, we're emitting a `createMessage` event with a `from` property set to `Andrew` and a `text` property equal to `This should work`. If I hit *enter* to send this off, you'll notice that this tab no longer receives the message:

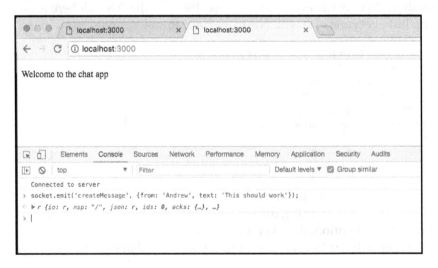

However, if I go to `localhost:3000`, we will get `newMessage` showing up with the message data:

This is because tab two broadcasts the event, which means it was only received by other connections, such as tab one or any other connected user.

Emitting two events when a user connects

With broadcasting in place, let's get into the final way we emit messages. We'll emit two events in `socket.io`, right when a user connects. Now, we'll not actually use broadcasting in this context, so we'll comment the broadcast object out and uncomment our old code. It should look like this:

```
socket.on('createMessage', (message) => {
  console.log('createMessage', message);
  io.emit('newMessage', {
    from: message.from,
    text: message.text,
    createdAt: new Date().getTime()
  });
  // socket.broadcast.emit('newMessage', {
  // from: message.from,
  // text: message.text,
  // createdAt: new Date().getTime()
  //});
});
```

You'll first call `socket.emit` to emit a message to the user who joins. Your message should come from the admin, `from Admin`, and the text should say something like `Welcome to the chat app`.

Now, along with `socket.emit`, you'll also call `socket.broadcast.emit`, which will get sent to everybody but the user who joined, which means you can go ahead and set `from` equal to `Admin` once again, and you can set `text` equal to `New user joined`:

```
// socket.emit from Admin text Welcome to the chat app
// socket.broadcast.emit from Admin text New user joined
```

This means that when we join a chatroom, we'll see a message greeting us, and everyone else is going to see a message letting them know that someone else has joined. Both of these events are going to be `newMessage` events. We'll have to specify `from` (which is `Admin`), the `text` (which is whatever we said it should be), and `createdAt`.

Greeting an individual user

To kick things off, we'll fill out the first call. This is a call to `socket.emit`, and this call will be responsible for greeting the individual users:

```
// socket.emit from Admin text Welcome to the chat app
socket.emit
```

We will still send an event of `newMessage` type and the exact same data from `text` and `createdAt`. The only difference here is that we'll be generating all the properties as opposed to getting some of them from the user as we did earlier. Let's get started with `from`. This one will be from `Admin`. Any time we send a message via the server, we'll call `Admin` and the text will be our little message, `Welcome to the chat app`. Next, we'll add `createdAt`, which will be set equal to `new Date` by calling the `Date().getTime` method:

```
socket.emit('newMessage', {
  from: 'Admin',
  text: 'Welcome to the chat app',
  createdAt: new Date().getTime()
});
```

Later on, we'll greet them by name. We don't have that information for the moment, so we'll stick with a generic greeting. With this call in place, we can remove the comment and we can move on to the second one. This is the broadcast call that's going to alert every other user, except for the one who joined, that someone new is here.

Broadcasting a new user in the chat

To broadcast a new user in the chat, we'll use `socket.broadcast.emit` and we'll emit a `newMessage` event, providing our props. The `from` property, once again, will be set equal to the `Admin` string; `text` is going to be set equal to our little message, `New user joined`; and last up is `createdAt`, which is going to be set equal to `new Date` by calling the `Date().getTime` method:

```
// socket.broadcast.emit from Admin text New user joined
socket.broadcast.emit('newMessage', {
  from: 'Admin',
  text: 'New user joined',
  createdAt: new Date().getTime()
})
```

Now we can remove our comment for the second call and everything should work as expected. The next thing you need to do is test out that all of this is working as expected by heading into the browser. There's a couple ways you could have done it; as long as you got it done, it doesn't really matter.

Testing the user connection

I'll close both of my old tabs and open up **Developer tools** before ever visiting the page. Then, we can go to `localhost:3000` and we should see a little message in **Developer tools**:

Here we see a new message, `Welcome to the chat app`, printing, which is fantastic!

Next up, we want to test that the broadcast is working as expected. For the second tab, I'll also open up **Developer tools** and go to `localhost:3000` once again. Once again, we get our little message, `Welcome to the chat app`:

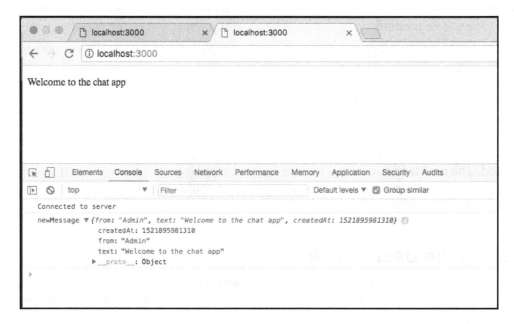

If we go to the first tab, we also see that a new user joined, and this is fantastic too!

Now, I will make a commit to save these changes. Let's go ahead and shut down the server and use `git status` command:

```
Gary:node-chat-app Gary$ git status
On branch master
Your branch is up-to-date with 'origin/master'.

Changes not staged for commit:
  (use "git add <file>..." to update what will be committed)
  (use "git checkout -- <file>..." to discard changes in working directory)

        modified:   server/server.js

no changes added to commit (use "git add" and/or "git commit -a")
```

Then, we can go ahead and run the `git commit` command with the `-am` flag and specify a message, `Greet new user and alert others`:

```
git commit -am 'Greet new user, and alert others'
```

Once the commit is in place, we can use the `git push` command to push it up to GitHub.

There's no need to deploy to Heroku right now, although you could easily deploy and test if you feel so inclined. With this in place, we are now done!

Summary

In this chapter, we looked into Socket.io and WebSockets to enable two-way communication between the server and client. We worked on setting up a basic Express server, a backend and a frontend, and we committed it up on GitHub and on Heroku. Next, we looked into adding `socket.io` to the app to set up communication between the server and client.

Then, we looked into emitting and listening to custom events inside our application. Lastly, we wired up the message system by broadcasting the events such that when one user sends a message to the server, it actually gets sent to every connected user excluding the user who sends the message.

With all this in place, we now have a rudimentary—but working—messaging system, which is a great place to start! We're going to continue on in the next chapter by adding more features and building out the UI.

6
Generating newMessage and newLocationMessage

In the previous chapter, we looked into Socket.io and WebSockets, to enable two-way communication between the server and the client. In this chapter, we'll discuss how to generate text and geolocation messages. We looked into generating `newMessage` and `newLocationMessage` objects and then writing test case for both type of messages.

Message generator and tests

In this section you are going to break out some functionality currently in `server.js` into a separate file, and we're also going to set up our test suite so that we can verify if those utility functions are working as expected.

For the moment, our goal is going to be to create a function that helps us generate the `newMessage` object. Instead of having to define the object every single time, we'll simply pass in two arguments to a function, the name and the text, and it'll generate the object so we don't have to do that work.

Generating the newMessage object using the utility function

To generate `newMessage`, we are going to make a separate file that we load into `server.js` with a method we call instead of defining the object. Inside the `server` folder, we'll make a new directory called `utils`.

Inside `utils` we'll make a file called `message.js`. This will store our utility functions related to messaging, and in our case, we'll make a new one called `generateMessage`. Let's make a variable called `generateMessage`. This is going to be a function and will take the two arguments I talked about earlier, `from` and `text`:

```
var generateMessage = (from, text) => {

};
```

It will then return an object just like the objects we pass in as the second argument to emit in `server.js`. Now all we need to do is `return` an object, specifying `from` as the from argument, `text` as the text argument, and `createdAt`, which is going to get generated by calling a `new Date` and calling its `getTime` method:

```
var generateMessage = (from, text) => {
  return {
    from,
    text,
    createdAt: new Date().getTime()
  };
};
```

With this in place our utility function is now done. All we need to do is export it down below, `module.exports`. We'll set that equal to an object that has a `generateMessage` property equal to the `generateMessage` variable we have defined:

```
var generateMessage = (from, text) => {
  return {
    from,
    text,
    createdAt: new Date().getTime()
  };
};

module.exports = {generateMessage};
```

We'll eventually be able to integrate this into `server.js`, but before we do that let's go ahead and write some test cases to make sure it works as expected. This means we will need to install Mocha, and we'll also need to install the Expect assertion library. Then we'll set up our `package.json` scripts and write the test case.

Writing test cases

First up, inside the Terminal, we're going to install, using `npm install`, two modules. We need Expect, which is our assertion library, `@1.20.2`, and `mocha` to run our test suite at version `5.0.5`. We'll then use the `--save-dev` flag to add these as development dependencies:

```
npm install expect@1.20.2 mocha@5.0.5 --save-dev
```

Let's go ahead and run this command, and once it's done we can move into `package.json` and set up those test scripts.

 They're going to be identical to the ones we used in the last project in the previous chapter.

Inside `package.json` we now have our two `dev` dependencies, and inside the scripts we can get started by removing the old test script. We'll add those two scripts, `test` and `test-watch`:

```
"scripts": {
  "start": "node server/server.js",
  "test": "echo "Error: no test specified" && exit 1",
  "test-watch": ""
},
```

Adding the test-watch script

Let's go ahead and fill out the basics first. We'll set `test` equal to an empty string for the moment, and `test-watch`. The `test-watch` script, as we know, simply calls `nodemon`, calling the `npm test` script, `nodemom --exec`, then `npm test` inside single quotes:

```
"scripts": {
  "start": "node server/server.js",
  "test": "",
  "test-watch": "nodemon --exec 'npm test'"
},
```

This will get the job done. Now when we run `nodemon` here, we're actually running the globally-installed `nodemon`; we can also install it locally to fix that.

To get that done, all we're going to do is run `npm install nodemon`, add the most recent version, which is version `1.17.2`, and use the `--save-dev` flag to install it:

```
npm install nodemon@1.17.2 --save-dev
```

Now when we install `nodemon` like this, our application no longer relies on that global `nodemon` installation. So if someone else grabs this from GitHub, they're going to be able to get started without needing to install anything globally.

Adding the test script

Next up is the `test` script. It first has to set up those environment variables that we're going to be configuring; we'll do that later. For now, all we're going to do is run `mocha`, passing in the pattern for the files we want to test.

The files we want to test are in that `server` directory. They could be in any subdirectory, so we'll use `**`, and the files, regardless of their name, are going to end in `test.js`:

```
"scripts": {
  "start": "node server/server.js",
  "test": "mocha server/**/*.test.js",
  "test-watch": "nodemon --exec 'npm test'"
},
```

With this in place, we are done. We can now run our test suite.

Running the test suite for the message utility

Over in the Terminal, if I run `npm test`, all we're going to see is that we have zero tests in place:

```
Gary:node-chat-app Gary$ npm test

> chat-app@1.0.0 test /Users/Gary/Desktop/node-chat-app
> mocha server/**/*.test.js

Warning: Could not find any test files matching pattern: server/**/*.test.js
No test files found
npm ERR! Test failed.  See above for more details.
```

Here we have the `server-test` file globbing pattern; it could not resolve any files. We can fix this issue by simply adding a test file. I'm going to add a test file for the message utility, `message.test.js`. Now we can go ahead and rerun the `npm test` command. This time around it does indeed find a file and we see we have zero passing tests, which is a great starting point:

```
Gary:node-chat-app Gary$ npm test

> chat-app@1.0.0 test /Users/Gary/Desktop/node-chat-app
> mocha server/**/*.test.js



  0 passing (2ms)
```

Inside `message.test.js`, we'll need to add a test for the message function we just defined. Now this test is going to verify that the object we get back is what we would expect given the parameters we passed in. We'll set up the basic structure of the test file together, and you'll write the individual test case.

First up we need to load in Expect using `var expect = require('expect')`. This will let us make our assertions about the return value from our `generateMessage` function:

```
var expect = require('expect');
```

The next thing we're going to do is add a `describe` block. Here, we're going to add a `describe` block for the function `generateMessage`, and inside the callback function we'll have all of the test cases for that function:

```
describe('generateMessage', () => {

});
```

Before we can actually create a test case and fill it out, we do need to load in the module we're testing. I'll make a variable and using ES6 destructuring. We're going to pull off `generateMessage`, and then we can go ahead and require it using `require`, specifying the local path, `./message`:

```
var expect = require('expect');
var {generateMessage} = require('./message');

describe('generateMessage', () => {

});
```

It's in the same directory as the test file where we currently are, so there's no reason to do any directory moving. With this in place we can now add the individual test case, it ('should generate the correct message object'). This is going to be a synchronous test, so there is no need to provide done. All you need to do is call generateMessage with two values, from and text. You're going to get the response back, and store the response in variable:

```
describe('generateMessage', () => {
  it('should generate correct message object', () => {
    //store res in variable
  });
});
```

Then you're going to make some assertions about the response. First up, assert that from is correct, assert from matches the value you passed in. You're also going to assert that the text matches up, and lastly you're going to assert that the createdAt value is a number:

```
var expect = require('expect');
var {generateMessage} = require('./message');

describe('generateMessage', () => {
  it('should generate correct message object', () => {
    // store res in variable
    // assert from match
    // assert text match
    // assert createdAt is number
  });
});
```

It doesn't matter what number it is; you're going to use the toBeA method to check the type and assert createdAt is number. To get this done, the first thing I'll do is define some variables.

To get started I'll make a from variable to store the from value. I'll go ahead and use Jen. I'll also make a text variable to store the text value, Some message. Now what I want to do is make my final variable, which is going to store the response, the message that comes back from the generateMessage function, which is exactly what I'm going to call. I'm going to call generateMessage passing in the two necessary arguments, the from argument and the text argument:

```
describe('generateMessage', () => {
  it('should generate correct message object', () => {
    var from = 'Jen';
    var text = 'Some message';
    var message = generateMessage(from, text);
```

Next up, and the final thing, we need to do is make assertions about this object that comes back. I'm going to expect that `message.createdAt` is a number using `toBeA` and passing in the type `number`:

```
describe('generateMessage', () => {
    it('should generate correct message object', () => {
        var from = 'Jen';
        var text = 'Some message';
        var message = generateMessage(from, text);

        expect(message.createdAt).toBeA('number');
```

This was the first assertion you needed to make to verify the property is correct. Next up we're going to `expect` that message has certain properties inside it. We're going to do this using the `toInclude` assertion, though you could have created two separate statements: one for `message.from` and a separate one for `message.text`. All of those are valid solutions. I'll just use `toInclude` and specify some things that message should include:

```
expect(message.createdAt).toBeA('number');
expect(message).toInclude({

});
```

First up, it should have a `from` property equal to the `from` variable. We can go ahead and use ES6 to define that; and the same thing is going to happen for `text`, `text` should equal `text` and we're going to use ES6 to set that up. We can even simplify this further using `from, text`:

```
expect(message.createdAt).toBeA('number');
expect(message).toInclude({from, text});
```

With this in place our test case is now done and we can go ahead and remove these commented outlines, and the final thing you needed to do was run the test suite from the Terminal by running `npm test`. When we do it what do we get? We get our one test under `generateMessage`, should generate correct message object, and it is indeed passing, which is fantastic:

```
[Gary:node-chat-app Gary$ npm test

> chat-app@1.0.0 test /Users/Gary/Desktop/node-chat-app
> mocha server/**/*.test.js


  generateMessage
    ✓ should generate correct message object


  1 passing (9ms)
```

Now that we have some tests verifying our function works as expected, let's go ahead and integrate it into our application by moving into `server.js` and replacing all of the objects we pass to the emit function with calls to our new function.

Integrate the utility function into our application

The first step in this process will be to import the function we just created. I'm going to do that creating a constant in `server.js`. We'll use ES6 destructuring to grab `generateMessage`, and we're going to grab it off of a call to `require`. Now we're requiring a local file in a different directory. We're going to start with `./`, go into the `utils` directory since we're currently in the `server` directory, and then grab the file message by specifying it:

```
const socketIO = require('socket.io');

const {generateMessage} = require('./utils/message');
```

Now we have access to `generateMessage`, and instead of creating these objects we can call `generateMessage`. In `socket.emit`, we're going to replace `Welcome to the chat app` and the `Admin` variables with arguments `generateMessage ('Admin', 'Welcome to the chat app')`:

```
socket.emit('newMessage', generateMessage('Admin', 'Welcome to the chat
app'));
```

We have the exact same functionality but now we're using a function to generate that object for us, which is going to make scaling that out a lot easier. It's also going to make updating what is inside a message much easier as well. Next up, we can change the one we have down below for *New user joined*. We're going to go ahead and replace this with the call to `generateMessage` as well.

Once again this one's from the `Admin` so the first argument will be the string `Admin`, the second argument is the text `New user joined`:

```
socket.emit('newMessage', generateMessage('Admin', 'Welcome to the chat
app'));
```

This one is done too, and the final one is the one that actually gets sent to the user from a user, which means we have `message.from` and `message.text`; those are going to be our arguments. We're going to call `generateMessage` with those two arguments, `message.from`, and `message.text` as the second argument:

```
socket.on('createMessage', (message) => {
  console.log('createMessage', message);
  io.emit('newMessage', generateMessage('Admin', 'New user joined'));
```

With this in place we are done. The last thing left to do for this section is test that this is working as expected. I'm going to start up the server using `nodemon`, without a space between `node` and `mon`, `server/server.js`:

`nodemon server/server.js`

Once the server is up, we can go ahead and test things out by opening up a couple of tabs with the **Developer Tools** open.

For the first tab I'm going to visit `localhost:3000`. Inside the console we should see our new message printing, the object looks the same even though it's now generated by the function, and we can test that everything else is working as expected too by opening up a second tab and opening up its **Developer Tools**:

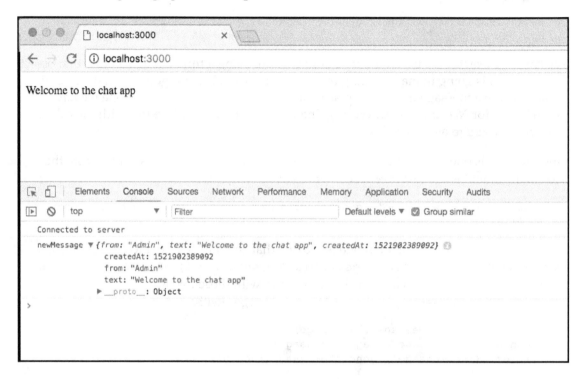

This time around the first tab should see a new message, here we have a `New user joined` text, that's still working. If we emit a custom message from this second tab, it should show up in the first. I'm going to use the up arrow key to run one of our previous `createMessage` event emitters.

I'm going to fire off the function, and if I go to the first tab we do indeed get the message, which is fantastic:

This should work, prints in the first tab and it also prints in the second since we're calling `io.emit` as opposed to the broadcast method.

Now that everything is working, we are done; we can make a commit and wrap this section. I'm going to call `git status` from the Terminal. Here we have new files as well as modified ones, which means we're going to want to call `git add ..` Next up, we can call `git commit` with a message flag, create `generateMessage` utility:

```
git commit -m 'create generateMessage utility'
```

I'm going to push this up to GitHub and that is it for this one. In the next section, we're going to take a look at `Socket.io` acknowledgments.

Event acknowledgements

In this section you're going to learn how to use event acknowledgments. That's a fantastic feature inside `Socket.io`. In order to illustrate exactly what they are and why you'd ever want to use them, we're going to quickly run through the diagram for the chat app. These are the two events that we actually have in our application, if you remember the first one is the **newMessage Event**, it gets emitted by the server and it gets listened to by the client, it sends across the **from**, **text**, and **createdAt** properties, all of which are required to render the message to the screen:

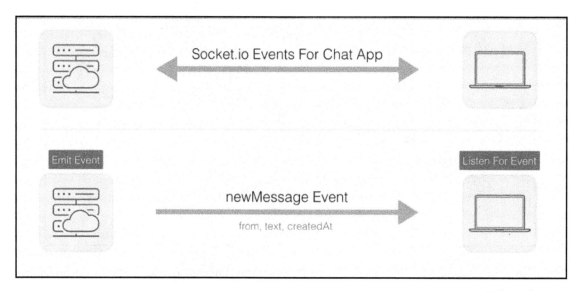

Now the event that we're going to be updating is the **createMessage Event**. This one gets emitted by the client and listened to by the server:

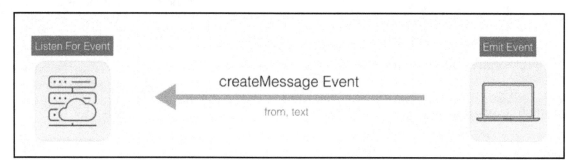

Once again we are sending some data across from and text. Now the problem with our **createMessage Event** is that the data flows in one direction. The data comes from a form inside the browser. It then gets sent over to the server and the server is kind of stuck. Sure, the data might be valid, the **from** and **text** fields might be correctly set up. In that case, we can emit a **newMessage Event**, rendering it to every browser who's connected to the server, but if the server receives invalid data it has no way to let the client know that something went wrong.

What we need is a way to acknowledge we got a request and have the option to send some data back. In this case we're going to add an acknowledgment for **createMessage**. If the client emits a valid request with valid from and text properties, we're going to acknowledge it, sending back no error message. If the data sent from client to server is invalid we're going to acknowledge it sending back the errors, so the client knows exactly what it needs to do to send a valid request. Now the result is going to look a little bit like this, and the data flow from server to client is going to be done via a callback:

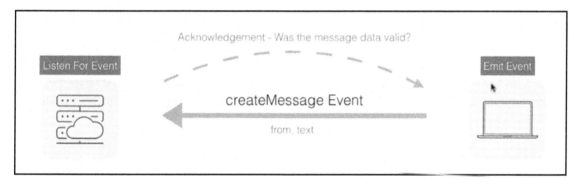

Your acknowledgment could be anything you like. In our case it could be was the message data valid? If you're creating an email application, you might only send the acknowledgement back to the client when the email was successfully sent. You don't need to send data, which is what we're going to do when valid data is sent across the pipeline. We're simply going to say, hey we got that message, everything's good to go, and the client can respond to that.

Now that we've gone through this, let's go ahead and implement it into our application.

Setting up acknowledgements

Setting up acknowledgments really isn't that bad if you already have a listener in place. All you have to do is make a quick change to the listener and a quick change to the emitter, and everything will work as expected.

Now in this case, the listener happens to be on the server and the emitter is going to be on the client, but acknowledgments also work in the other direction. I can emit an event from the server and I can acknowledge it from the client.

In order to set this up we are going to emit a `createMessage` event over inside `index.js` using `socket.emit`, and we're going to pass in the same arguments we would otherwise. The first one is the event name, `createMessage`, and we're going to pass in some valid data, an object with those two properties. We can set `from` equal to something like `Frank`, and we can set a `text` property equal to something like `Hi`:

```
socket.emit('createMessage', {
  from: 'Frank',
  text: 'Hi'
});
```

Now with this in place we have a standard event emitter and a standard event listener. I can go ahead and start up the app using `nodemon` and we can make sure everything is working as expected, `nodemon server/server.js`:

nodemon server/server.js

Once the server is up we can visit it in the browser, I'm going to open up the **Developer Tools** as well. Then we're going to go to `localhost:3000`, and you can see over inside of the Terminal we have `createMessage` showing up, and we also have `newMessage` showing up here. We have the `newMessage` for our little `Welcome to the chat app` greeting, and we have the `newMessage` from `Frank`, which we emitted:

Now the goal here is to send an acknowledgement from the server back to the client that we got the data.

Sending an acknowledgement from server to the client

In order to get this done we have to make a change to both the listener and the emitter. If you only make a change to one it is not going to work as expected. We're going to start with the event emitter. We want a way to run some code when the acknowledgement has been sent from the server back to the client.

Updating the event emitter

To send acknowledgement d=from server to client, we're going to add a third argument which is going to be a callback function. This function is going to fire when the acknowledgement arrives at the client, and we can do anything we like. For now we'll just print using `console.log('Got it')`:

```
socket.emit('createMessage', {
  from: 'Frank',
  text: 'Hi'
}, function () {
  console.log('Got it');
});
```

Now this is all we need to do bare-bones style to add an acknowledgement to the client.

Updating the event listener

It's also pretty simple on the server; we're going to add a second argument to our `callback` argument list. The first one is still going to be the data that was emitted, the second one though is going to be a function that we're going to refer to as `callback`. And we can call it anywhere in `socket.on` to acknowledge that we got the request:

```
socket.on('createMessage', (message, callback) => {
  console.log('createMessage', message);
  io.emit('newMessage', generateMessage(message.from, message.text));
  callback();
```

When we call this function, like we're going to call it right here, it is in turn going to send an event back to the frontend and it is going to call the function as we have it in event emitter in `index.js`.

This means that if I save both files we can play around with acknowledgments over in the browser. I'm going to refresh the app, and what do we get? We get **Got it**:

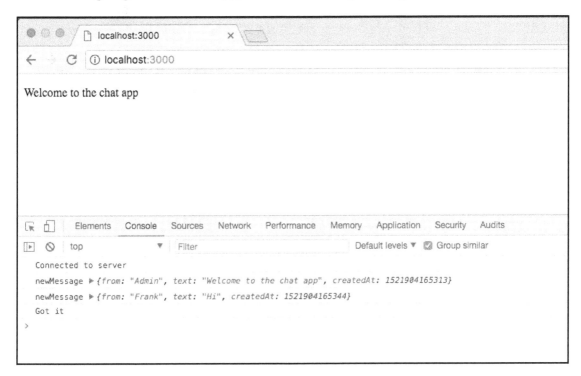

That means our data successfully went to the server; we can prove that by seeing the `console.log` statement in the Terminal, the server acknowledged it got the data by calling callback:

```
Gary:node-chat-app Gary$ nodemon server/server.js
[nodemon] 1.14.10
[nodemon] to restart at any time, enter `rs`
[nodemon] watching: *.*
[nodemon] starting `node server/server.js`
Server is up on 3000
New user connected
createMessage { from: 'Frank', text: 'Hi' }
```

And in the **Developers Tool**, **Got it** prints.

Now acknowledgments are pretty useful, but they're even more useful when you send data back. If the data for the message is invalid, for example, we're probably going to want to send some errors back, something we will be doing a little later. For now though, we can play around with an acknowledgment by sending anything we want back.

We send data back by providing one argument to callback, if you want to add multiple things simply specify an object adding as many properties as you like. In our case, though, we can send a string as the only argument to `callback`. I'm going to set my string to `This is from the server`:

```
socket.on('createMessage', (message, callback) => {
  console.log('createMessage', message);
  io.emit('newMessage', generateMessage(message.from, message.text));
  callback('This is from the server.');
});
```

This string is going to be passed into the callback and it's going to end up inside of our callback in `index.js`. This means I can create a variable for that value, we can call it `data` or anything else you like, and we can print it to the screen or do something with it. For now we're just going to print it to the screen:

```
socket.emit('createMessage', {
  from: 'Frank',
  text: 'Hi'
}, function (data) {
  console.log('Got it', data);
});
```

If I save `index.js`, we can test that everything is working as expected. I'm going to go ahead and give the app a refresh, and what do we see?

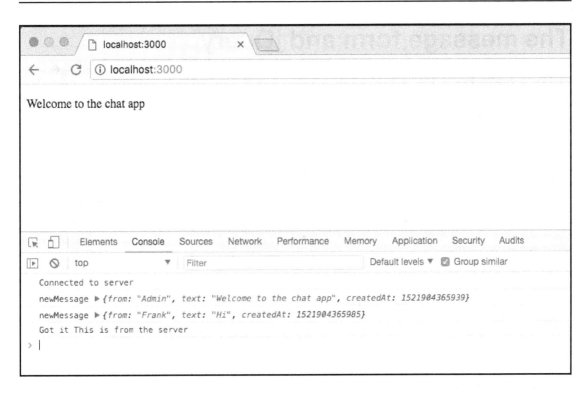

We see **Got it**, meaning we got the acknowledgment, and we see the data, the data that was sent from the server to the client.

Acknowledgments play an important role in real-time applications. Let's go back to that email app example for a second, imagine I type in some values like a to value and a text value when I send the e-mail. I want to get an acknowledgement back that either email sent successfully, or email was not sent, in which case I want to know why; maybe it was a form error where I can show some error messages to the user or maybe the server was down for maintenance or something like that.

Either way, acknowledgments allow the request listener to send something back to the request emitter. Now that we know how to use acknowledgments we're going to integrate them into our application. That is coming up in the next section, as we add an actual form field to our `index.html` file where users can submit new messages and view them.

The message form and jQuery

In this section you're going to add a form field to your `index.html` file. This is going to render an input field and a button to the screen, and the user is going to be able to interact with that as opposed to having to call `socket.emit` from the **Developer Tools**, which is not a sustainable option for real users. This only works for us developers.

Now in order to get started we're going to be editing `index.html`, then we're going to move into `index.js`. We're going to add a listener that's going to wait for the form to be submitted, and inside of that listener callback, we are going to fire `socket.emit` with the data typed in the field. We're also going to take a moment to render all incoming messages to the screen. At the end of this section, we'll have a ugly, yet working, chat application.

Using the jQuery library

Now before we do any of that, we are going to be using a library called jQuery to do DOM manipulation, which means that we want to be able to do stuff with our rendered HTML, but we want to be able to do that from our JavaScript file. We're going to use jQuery to make that a lot easier in terms of cross-browser compatibility. To grab this library, we're going to head over to Google Chrome, go to `jquery.com`, and you can grab the most recent version. The version is not going to matter for here, as we're using very basic features available in all versions:

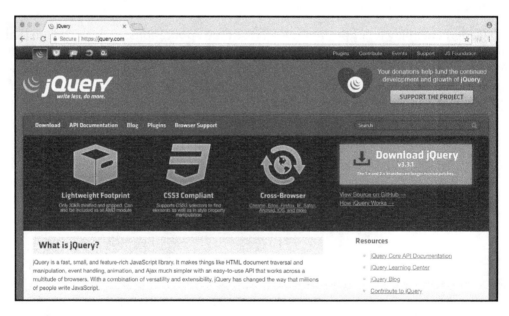

I'll grab the most recent version **3.3.1**. Then I'll go ahead and download the compressed production version by right-clicking and opening it in a new tab:

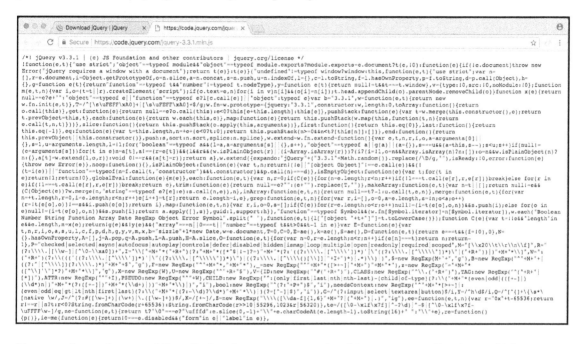

Here we have the actual JavaScript that we want to load in to our application, which means we can right-click some sort of empty area, click on **Save As**, and go into our projects folder, Desktop | node-chat-app | public | js. Inside of js, I'm going to create a new directory called libs, where we'll store third-party JavaScript. We're going to be working with a few more client-side JavaScript libraries throughout the section, so it's nice to create a folder to stay organized. I'm going to save that in there, close the tab as well as the downloads area, and now we can go ahead and load it in to index.html and add our form.

Adding the form field in index.html

Down here just between socket.io and index.js we're going to add a new script tag to load in jQuery. We've got to specify that src attribute with the path to the file /js/libs, followed by a forward slash and the file name, jquery-3.3.1.min.js:

```
<script src="/socket.io/socket.io.js"></script>
<script src="/js/libs/jquery-3.3.1.min.js"></script>
<script src="/js/index.js"></script>
```

Now let's go ahead and set up our `form` tag; this is going to render our form fields to the browser. If you're not familiar with these tags that is perfectly fine, simply follow along and I'll explain as we go.

Setting up the form tag

First step, we need a `form` tag; this creates a form that's submittable by the user. This is exactly what we're going to use to submit our messages. And on this `form` tag we're going to add one attribute; it's the `id` attribute which lets us give this element a unique identifier, making it really easy to target with our JavaScript a bit later on:

```
<form id>

</form>
```

 Remember, we're going to want to add a listener to this element. When the form gets submitted, we're going to want to do something in our JavaScript file. Notably what we're going to want to do is call `socket.emit`.

I'm going to set `id` equal to, inside quotes, `message-form`:

```
<form id="message-form">

</form>
```

Now that we have our form tag complete we can add some tags inside of it. To get started we're going to add a `button` which is going to appear at the `bottom` of the `form`. This `button` on click is going to submit the `form`. I'm opening and closing my tag, and just inside I can type whatever text I want to appear on the `button`. I'm going to go with `Send`:

```
<form id="message-form">
  <button>Send</button>
</form>
```

Adding the text field

Now that we have our `button` in place, the only thing we need to do is add the little text field. This is going to be the text field where a user types their message. This is going to require us to use an `input` tag, and instead of opening and closing an `input` tag, we're going to use the self-closing syntax:

```
<form id="message-form">
  <input/>
  <button>Send</button>
</form>
```

Because we don't need to actually put anything inside it like we do for `button`, or for `form`, we are going to be adding quite a few attributes onto input, first up, name, we want to give this field a unique name, something like `message` is going to get the job done. We also want to go ahead and set the type. There are a lot of different types for `input` tags. Types could include something like a checkbox, or in our case the type we're going to use inside quotes is `text`:

```
<input name="message" type="text"/>
```

The last attribute we're going to add to `input` is called `placeholder`. We're going to set this value equal to, inside quotes, a string. This string is going to get rendered in the field in a light gray before the user actually enters a value. I'm going to tell the user that this is where their `Message` goes:

```
<form id="message-form">
  <input name="message" type="text" placeholder="Message"/>
  <button>Send</button>
</form>
```

With this in place we can actually test out our form's rendering.

Testing the form's rendering

We can do the testing by starting at the server using `nodemon`:

```
nodemon server/server.js
```

The server is up, I'm going to visit Google Chrome, and go to `localhost:3000`. You'll notice something kind of cool, I haven't actually visited the URL yet but you can see that the connection has already occurred. Chrome does some lazy loading, if it thinks you're going to go to a URL it's actually going to make the request; so when I do visit it, it loads even faster. Now if I visit `localhost:3000` what do we get?

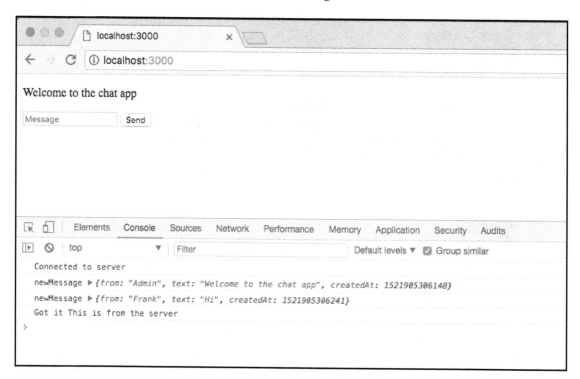

We get our little form, we can type in a message like `Test` and we can send it off. Now by default forms are very old school. If I try to submit this form, it's actually going to go through a full page refresh, and then it's going to add the data, like our message text, as a query string on the URL. This is not what we want to do, we want to run some custom JavaScript on form submit. So we're going to attach a custom event listener and override the default behavior. To get that done we are going to have to use jQuery, and we're going to need to select this `form` field.

Using jQuery to select element

Before we dive into `index.js` let's take a quick moment to talk about how we can use jQuery to select elements. jQuery, which is accessible via the `jQuery` variable, takes your selector as its argument. Then, we're going to add a string and we can select our elements. For example, if we want to select all the paragraph tags on the screen we would type p in the quotes:

```
jQuery('p');
```

These are really similar to CSS selectors if you're familiar with them, and as shown, we've selected our paragraph tag.

I could also go ahead and select all of the `div` inside my program, or I could select elements by ID or class, and that's what we're going to do. In order to select an element by ID we first start with the pound sign (#), then we type the name. In our case we have a `form` called `message-form`, and if I fire this off we do indeed get that back:

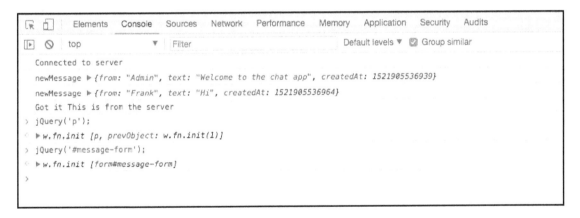

This is going to allow us to add an event listener.

Adding the selector element to index.js

Inside `index.js` we're going to add that exact same selector near the bottom, `jQuery`, calling it with our selector `#message-form`. Now we're going to add an event listener, and the event listener is going to look pretty similar to our `Socket.io` event listeners. We are going to be calling on, and we are going to be providing, those two arguments, the event name inside quotes, `submit`, and a `function`, which is going to fire when a user tries to submit the `form`:

```
jQuery('#message-form').on('submit', function(){
});
```

Now unlike our `Socket.io` event listeners, we are going to get one argument in the `function`, an e event argument, and we are going to need to access this. We're going to need to access this event argument in order to override that default behavior that causes the page refresh. Right here we're going to call `e.preventDefault`:

```
jQuery('#message-form').on('submit', function(){
  e.preventDefault();
});
```

The `preventDefault` method prevents the default behavior for the event, and by default a submit event goes through that page refresh process.

We can go ahead and test that everything is working by going into Google Chrome, giving the page a refresh. I'm also going to remove the query string from the URL. Now we can type in some sort of message like `test`, hit **Send**, and you can see that nothing happens. Nothing happens because we overrode the default behavior, all we need to do to make something happen is call `socket.emit` in `index.js`. We're going to emit the `createMessage`:

```
jQuery('#message-form').on('submit', function(){
  e.preventDefault();

  socket.emit('createMessage', {

  });
});
```

Then, we're going to go ahead and provide our data. Now the name `from` field for now is just going to be `User` in uppercase. We're going to leave this as anonymous for the moment, although we will be updating that a bit later. Now for the text field, this is going to come from the `form`. We're going to want to add a selector and get the value back. Let's go ahead and do that using `jQuery`:

```
socket.emit('createMessage', {
  from: 'User',
  text: jQuery('')
})
});
```

We're going to call `jQuery` once again, and we're going to select the input in the `index.html` file. We can go ahead and select it by its name, `name="message"`:

```
<input name="message" type="text" placeholder="Message"/>
```

In order to get that done we're going to open up brackets in `socket.emit` in `index.js`, setting `name` equal to `message`. This is going to select any element that has a `name` attribute equal to `message`, which is just our one, and we can go ahead and get its value using the `.val` method:

```
socket.emit('createMessage', {
  from: 'User',
  text: jQuery('[name=message]').val();
})
});
```

No semicolon required since we're inside object creation. With this in place we can now go ahead and add our callback function for our acknowledgment. For the moment it doesn't really do anything, but that's perfectly fine. We have to add it in order to fulfill the acknowledgement set up we currently have in place:

```
jQuery('#message-form').on('submit', function (e) {
  e.preventDefault();
  socket.emit('createMessage', {
    from: 'User',
   text: jQuery('[name=message]').val()
  }, function () {
  })
});
```

Now that we have our event listener set up, let's go ahead and test this out.

Testing the update event listener

I'm going to head back into Chrome, give the page a refresh, type in some message like `This should work,` and when we submit the form we should see it show up over here as a new message:

I'm going to send it off and you can see that right inside the Terminal, we have a user sending `This should work,` and it also shows up in Chrome:

```
[nodemon] restarting due to changes...
[nodemon] starting `node server/server.js`
Server is up on 3000
New user connected
Disconnected from server
New user connected
createMessage { from: 'Frank', text: 'Hi' }
createMessage { from: 'User', text: 'This should work' }
```

The same thing is true if I open up a second connection, I'm going to open up the **Developer Tools** so we can see exactly what's happening behind the scenes. I'm going to type some message like `From tab 2`, **Send** it off:

We should see it over in tab 1, and we do:

Perfect, everything is working as expected. Now obviously the setup is not complete; we want to wipe that form value after we send the message, and we want to take care of a few other UI-related things, but for now it is working pretty well.

With a basic form in place, the second thing we're going to do is render incoming messages to the screen. Now once again it is going to look pretty ugly, but it will get the job done.

Rendering incoming messages to the screen

To get this done we have to create a place inside our DOM, inside our `index.html` file, where we can render the messages. Once again we're going to give this element an ID that we can easily access over inside `index.js`, so we can render those messages.

Creating an ordered list to render messages

First up, what we're going to do is create an ordered list by creating an `ol` tag just like this:

```
<body>
  <p>Welcome to the chat app</p>
  <ol></ol>
```

This list is going to let us add items to it, and those items are going to be the individual messages. Now we are going to be giving this an `id` attribute. I'm going to call `id`, in this case, `messages`:

```
<ol id="messages"></ol>
```

Now this is all we need to do in `index.html`, all of the heavy lifting is going to happen over inside `index.js`. When a new message comes in we want to add something inside of the ordered list so that gets rendered to the screen.

Over inside `index.js` we can get this done by modifying our callback function when a new message arrives.

Using jQuery to create element in index.js

The first thing we're going to do is create a list item, and we're going to do this once again using jQuery. We're going to make a variable, this variable is going to be called `li`, and we're going to go ahead and use jQuery slightly differently:

```
socket.on('newMessage', function (message) {
  console.log('newMessage', message);
  var li = jQuery();
});
```

Rather than using `jQuery` to select an element, we're going to use `jQuery` to create an element, then we can modify that element and add it into the markup, making it visible. Inside quotes, we're going to open and close an `li` tag, just like we would inside `index.html`:

```
socket.on('newMessage', function (message) {
  console.log('newMessage', message);
  var li = jQuery('<li></li>');
});
```

Now that we have this in place we have to go ahead and set its text property, I'm going to set `li.text`, by calling `li.text` with the value I want to use.

In this case the text is going to require us to set up a little template string, inside the template string we are going to go ahead and use the data that comes back. For now we're going to use the `from` attribute and the `text` attribute. Let's get started with who it's `from`, then we'll add a little colon and a space to separate that from the actual `message`, and finally, we'll inject `message.text` at the end:

```
var li = jQuery('<li></li>');
li.text(`${message.from}: ${message.text}`);
```

Now at this point we've created an element but we haven't rendered it to the DOM. What we're going to do is use `jQuery` to select that brand new element we created, we gave it an ID of `messages`, and we're going to `append` something to it by calling the `append` method:

```
var li = jQuery('<li></li>');
li.text(`${message.from}: ${message.text}`);

jQuery('#messeges').append
```

This is going to add it as its last child, so there's already three items in the list; the newest one will show up below those three as the fourth item in our ordered list. All we have to do is call append as a function, passing in our list item:

```
var li = jQuery('<li></li>');
li.text(`${message.from}: ${message.text}`);

jQuery('#messeges').append(li);
});
```

And with this in place we are done. Now if you're not familiar with jQuery this can be a bit overwhelming, but I promise the techniques we use here we'll be using throughout the book. By the end, you'll be much more comfortable selecting and creating elements.

Testing the incoming messages

Let's go ahead and test things out over inside Google Chrome. I'm going to refresh tab 1, and when I do you can see our two messages, **Welcome to the chat app** shows up and **Frank** says **Hi**:

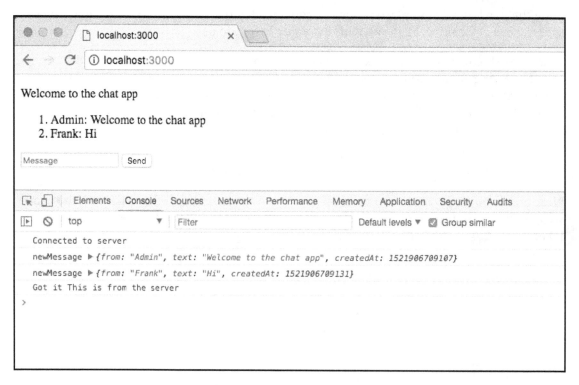

Now **Welcome to the chat app** should show up. The **Frank Hi** message is coming from `socket.emit` inside `index.js`:

```
socket.emit('createMessage', {
  from: 'Frank',
  text: 'Hi'
}, function (data) {
  console.log('Got it', data);
});
```

We can actually go ahead and remove that, we no longer need to automatically emit messages since we have a `form` set up to get that done for us. Once again we can save the file, refresh the browser and this time around we have a nice little setup, **Welcome to the chat app**:

I'm going to do the same thing for our second tab. This time around we get **Welcome to the chat app** and in the first tab we get **New user joined**; this is fantastic:

Now the true test is going to be to send a message from one tab to the other, `This should go to tab 2`. I'm going to **Send** this off, and when I click on this button, it's going to emit the event that's going to go to the server, and the server is going to send it to everyone connected:

Here, I can see **This should go to tab 2** renders, and over inside my second tab we get the message as well:

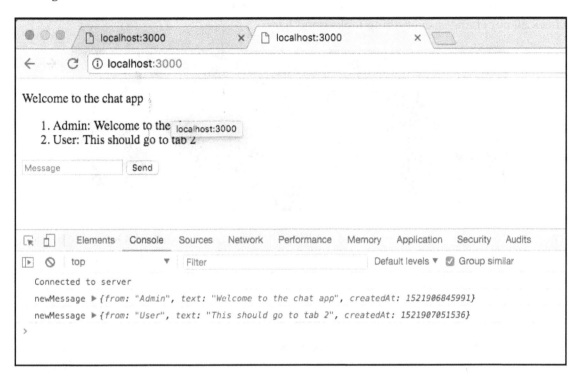

Now we're not quite done with the UI or the actual user experience; custom names and timestamps are coming up, but we do have a fantastic start. We now have a form where we can submit messages and we can see all the incoming messages inside the browser, which means we do not need to do anything in the **Developer Tools** anymore in terms of emitting or reading our messages. That is it for this one, let's go ahead and wrap things up by making a commit now that we have some working changes.

Making a commit for the message form

I'm going to shut down the server, clear the output, and run `git status` so we can double-check all our changes; everything looks good here:

```
Gary:node-chat-app Gary$ git status
On branch master
Your branch is up-to-date with 'origin/master'.

Changes not staged for commit:
  (use "git add <file>..." to update what will be committed)
  (use "git checkout -- <file>..." to discard changes in working directory)

        modified:   public/index.html
        modified:   public/js/index.js
        modified:   server/server.js

Untracked files:
  (use "git add <file>..." to include in what will be committed)

        public/js/libs/

no changes added to commit (use "git add" and/or "git commit -a")
```

I'm going to use `git add` to add all of the files, including my untracked jQuery file to the repo. Then I use `git commit` to make the `commit`. I'm going to use the `-m` flag here, and a good message for this one would be `Add form for messages and show incoming messages in browser`:

```
git commit -m 'Add form for messages and show incoming messages in browser'
```

Once we have this in place, we can go ahead and `push` this up to GitHub. I am going to take a moment to deploy to Heroku now that we have something real, visible, and tangible to use; `git push heroku master` is going to get that done:

```
remote:
remote: -----> Node.js app detected
remote:
remote: -----> Creating runtime environment
remote:
remote:        NPM_CONFIG_LOGLEVEL=error
remote:        NODE_VERBOSE=false
remote:        NODE_ENV=production
remote:        NODE_MODULES_CACHE=true
remote:
remote: -----> Installing binaries
remote:        engines.node (package.json):  9.3.0
remote:        engines.npm (package.json):   unspecified (use default)
remote:
remote:        Resolving node version 9.3.0...
remote:        Downloading and installing node 9.3.0...
remote:        Using default npm version: 5.5.1
remote:
remote: -----> Restoring cache
remote: Verifying deploy........ done.
To https://git.heroku.com/rocky-sierra-37964.git
   77a5b8e..faf6cad  master -> master
```

Once this is up, we'll be able to visit it in the browser. As you can see over inside my console, `Socket.io` is trying to reconnect to the server. Unfortunately, we're not going to be bringing it back up so it's going to try a little longer.

Here we are, we're verifying the deploy and everything is up and running. You can either run `heroku open` or copy the URL directly. I'm going to go ahead and close my two localhost tabs and open up the actual Heroku app.

Right here, we do get our **Welcome to the chat app** message and we do get our form; everything looks good so far. I'm going to go ahead and open up a different browser like Safari. I'm going to go to the chat app as well, and we're going to bring these windows side by side. Over inside Safari I'm going to type a little message, `This is live on Heroku`, click on **Send** or hit the *enter* key, and instantly it shows up in the other browser in the other tab. This is because our live socket server is transmitting this data:

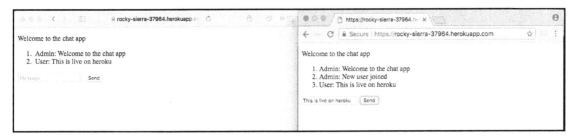

This could happen between any computer in the world, you do not need to be on my machine since we're using a real Heroku URL. Now that everything is working on Heroku, we are done.

Geolocation

In this section, you're going to start part one of a two-part series on geolocation. Instead of just sending text back and forth, we're also going to set it up so I can beam my actual coordinates, my longitude and latitude, to everyone else connected to the chat app. Then we can render a link and that link could go wherever we like; in our case, we're going to set it up to pull up a Google Maps page where the actual location of the user who sent their location is marked.

Now to actually fetch a user's location we're going to use the geolocation API, which is available in your client-side JavaScript, and it's actually a pretty well-supported API. It's available on all modern browsers, whether that's mobile or desktop, and the documentation can be found by Googling `geolocation api`, and looking for the MDN documentation page.

The MDN Docs, or the Mozilla Developer Network, are my favorite docs for client-side technologies, such as your web APIs, your CSS and your HTML guidelines:

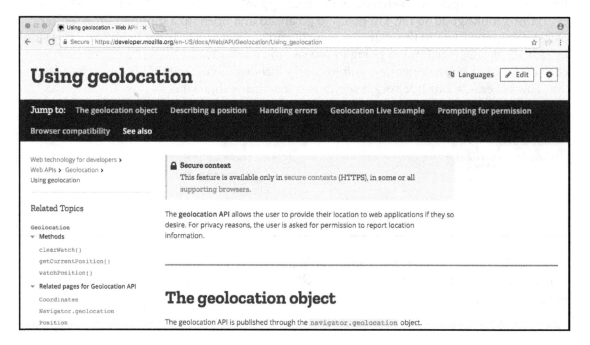

Now as I mentioned this is a well supported feature, you can pretty much use it everywhere except for older versions of Internet Explorer and the Opera Mini browser. But all your major desktop and mobile browsers are going to support this, and if the browser is old, we will set up a little message to let them know their browser does not support geolocation. If you ever want to learn more about geolocation or explore features that we do not cover in this section, you can refer to this page, though we will be using most of the features geolocation has to offer.

Adding the Send Location button to the application

To get started what we're going to do is add a new button to our application. It's going to sit alongside of **Send** and it's going to say something like **Send Location**. When the user clicks that **Send Location** button we're going to use the geolocation API. Usually, this is going to require the user to confirm they want to share their location with this tab in the browser, that pop-up box is going to happen, it's going to be triggered by the browser, there's no way around that.

You're going to need to make sure the user actually wants to share their location. Once you have the coordinates you're going to emit an event, that's going to go to the server, the server is going to send it to all the other connected users and we're going to be able to render that information in a nice link.

To kick things off we're going to add that button, this is going to be the button that starts the entire process. Over inside Atom, inside `index.html`, we're going to add a button just below our `form` tag. It's going to be outside our existing form. We're going to add the `button` tag, and we're going to go ahead and give this an ID of `send-location`. Now as for the visible `button` text we can go ahead and use `SendLocation` as our string, and save the file:

```
<form id="message-form">
  <input name="message" type="text" placeholder="Message"/>
  <button>Send</button>
</form>
<button id="send-location">Send Location</button>
```

If we go ahead and refresh our app in the browser, we should now see we have our **Send Location** button showing up:

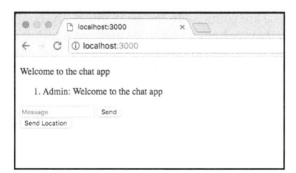

We're going to fix all this later when we add the default styles, but for now this does get the job done.

Now clicking this button currently is not going to do anything, it's not tied to a `form` so it's not going to do any weird `form` submissions or page reloads. All we need to do is add a `click` listener to this button and we'll be able to run whatever code we like. In our case, we're going to run that geolocation code.

Adding a click listener to the Send Location button

We are going to add a `click` listener, inside Atom, inside `index.js`, and we're going to add some code down near the bottom.

Now the first thing I want to do is create a variable, and I'm going to call this variable `locationButton`; this is going to store our selector. This is the jQuery selector that targets the button we just created, because we're going to need to reference it multiple times and storing it in a variable saves the need to make those calls again. We're going to call `jQuery` like we've done for our other selectors, passing in one argument, a string, and we're selecting something by ID, which means we got to start with that hash sign (#), and the actual ID is `send-location`:

```
var locationButton = jQuery('#send-location');
```

Now that we have this in place we can go ahead and do whatever we like. In our case, what we're going to be doing is add a click event, and we want to do something when someone clicks that button. To get that done we're going to go to `locationButton.on`:

```
var locationButton = jQuery('#send-location');
locationButton.on
```

 This is identical to doing the `jQuery`, selecting the ID `send-location`, both of these are going to do the same thing. The benefit of the first solution is that we have a reusable variable,, which we are going to reference later on. Making two jQuery calls to the same selector, wastes time because it is going to require jQuery to manipulate the DOM, fetching that information, and that's expensive.

`locationButton.on` is going to be our event listener. We're listening for the `click` event, inside quotes for the first argument, and the second argument as always is going to be our function:

```
var locationButton = jQuery('#send-location');
locationButton.on('click', function () {

});
```

This function is going to get called when someone clicks the button.

Checking access to the geolocation API

For now all we're going to do is check if the user has access to that geolocation API. If they don't we want to go ahead and print a message.

We're going to create an `if` statement. The geolocation API exists on `navigator.geolocation`, and we want to run some code if it doesn't exist:

```
var locationButton = jQuery('#send-location');
locationButton.on('click', function () {
  if(navigator.geolocation){

  }
});
```

So we're going to flip it. If there is no geolocation object on navigator we want to do something. We're going to use `return` to prevent the rest of the function from executing, and we're going to call the `alert` function available in all browsers that pops up one of those default alert boxes that makes you click on **OK**:

```
if(navigator.geolocation){
  return.alert()
}
```

We're going to use this as opposed to a fancier modal. If you are using something like Bootstrap or Foundation, you can implement one of their built-in tools.

For now, though, we're going to use `alert`, which takes just one argument (a string, your message) `Geolocation not supported by your browser`:

```
var locationButton = jQuery('#send-location');
locationButton.on('click', function ()
  if (!navigator.geolocation) {
    return alert('Geolocation not supported by your browser.');
  }
```

Now users who don't have support for this are going to see a little message, as opposed to wondering whether or not anything actually happened.

Fetching a user's position

To actually fetch a user's position we're going to use a function available on geolocation. To access it we'll add `navigator.geolocation.getCurrentPosition` inside the `locationButton.on` function next to the `if` statement. The `getCurrentPosition` function is a function that starts the process. It's going to actively get the coordinates for the user. In this case, it's going to find the coordinates based off of the browser, and this takes two functions. The first one is your `success` function, right here we can add our first callback. This is going to get called with the location information, we're going to name this argument `position`:

```
navigator.geolocation.getCurrentPosition(function (position) {
  }
});
```

The second argument to `getCurrentPosition` is going to be our error handler if something goes wrong. We're going to create a `function` and we'll be alerting a message to the user when we're not able to fetch the location using `alert`. Let's go ahead and call `alert` a second time, printing a message like `Unable to fetch location`:

```
navigator.geolocation.getCurrentPosition(function (position) {

}, function() {
    alert('Unable to fetch location.');
  });
});
```

This is going to print `if` someone gets prompted to share their location with the browser but they click on **Deny**. We're going to say `Hey, we can't fetch the location if you don't give us that permission`.

Now the only case left is the success case. This is where we're going to `emit` the event. But before we do that, let's go ahead and simply log it to the screen so we can take a peek at what is happening inside the `position` argument:

```
navigator.geolocation.getCurrentPosition(function (position) {
    console.log(position);
        }, function () {
    alert('Unable to fetch location.');
    });
});
```

I'm going to log this to the screen, our server is going to restart, and over inside Google Chrome we can open up the **Developer Tools**, refresh the page, and click on that **Send Location** button. Now this is going to work on desktop and mobile. Some mobile browsers are going to require you to be on HTTPS, which is something that we're going to have set up for Heroku, as you know the Heroku URL is secure which means it's not going to work on localhost. You can always test your mobile browsers by deploying the app to Heroku and running it there. For now, though, I will be able to click on **Send Location**. This is going to go ahead and start that process; the process can take up to a second:

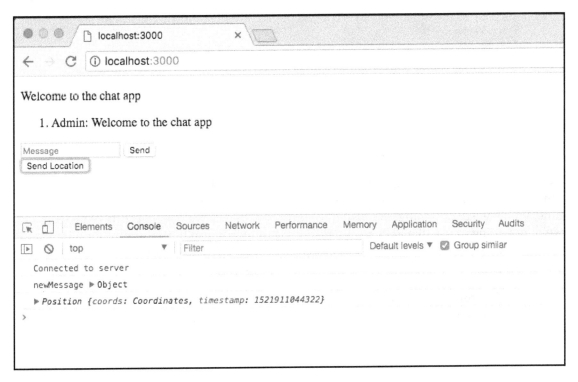

Now as you can see I did get my geolocation position. But I was never prompted as to whether or not I wanted to share my location; that's because I've already given it permission. Over the top-right corner, I can go ahead and click on **Clear these settings for future visits**, this means that I'm going to need to reauthorize. If I refresh the page and click on **Send Location** again, you're going to see this little box, which is probably going to show up for you. You can either block it, if I block it it's going to print **Unable to fetch location**; or you can accept it.

I'm going to clear those settings one more time, give the page a refresh, and this time I am going to accept the location sharing, And we're going to get the geolocation printing out in the console:

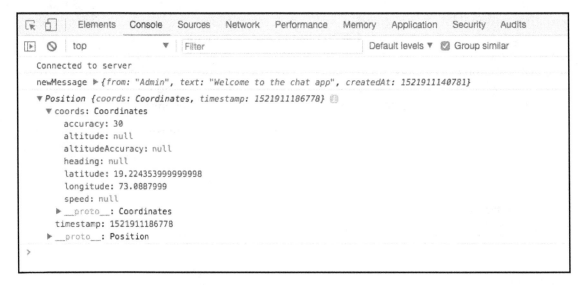

Now once we get it we can go ahead and dive in, the object itself is pretty simple, we have a timestamp of exactly when we fetched the data, this is useful if you're tracking a user over time, which we're not doing. We also have our coordinates, we have all sorts of properties we're not going to use like `accuracy`, `altitude`, which doesn't exist, and other related ones. We also have `speed` which is `null`. The only two we're ever going to use off this object is `latitude` and `longitude`, which do indeed exist.

This is the information we want to pass to the server so the server can send it to everybody else. This means we're going to go into the `position` object, go into the `coords` object, and grab those two.

Adding the coordinates object in the users position

Let's go ahead and do that over inside Atom, we are going to call `socket.emit` and `emit` a brand new event, one we do not have registered yet. We're going to call this one `createLocationMessage`:

```
navigator.geolocation.getCurrentPosition(function (position) {
  socket.emit('createLocationMessage', {
  });
});
```

The `createLocationMessage` event is not going to take the standard text; instead, it's going to take those `longitude` and `latitude` coordinates. We're going to specify both of them starting with `latitude`; we want to set `latitude` equal to `position.coords.latitude`. This is the variable that we explored over inside of the console, and we're going to do the same thing for `longitude`, setting it equal to `position.coords.longitude`:

```
navigator.geolocation.getCurrentPosition(function (position) {
  socket.emit('createLocationMessage', {
    latitude: position.coords.latitude,
    longitude: position.coords.longitude
  });
```

Now that we have this in place we can actually go ahead and listen for this event over in the server, and when we get it what we're going to do is pass the above data along to all the connected users.

Passing coordinates data with the connected users

Let's go ahead and do just that over inside `server.js`, registering a new event listener. I'm going to remove the old commented out broadcast call that's no longer needed in `createMessage`. Just below `createMessage`, we're going to call `socket.on` again, specifying a listener for this event, `createLocationMessage`, just as we defined it over inside `index.js`. Now we are using ES6 since we're in Node, which means we can go ahead and set up our arrow function. We're going to have one argument, this is going to be the `coords`, and we can go ahead and finish off the arrow function.

```
socket.on('createMessage', (message, callback) => {
  console.log('createMessage', message);
  io.emit('newMessage', generateMessage(message.from, message.text));
  callback('This is from the server.');
});
```

```
socket.on('createLocationMessage', (coords) => {

});
```

In here we're going to be able to run whatever code we like. For the moment all we're going to do is `emit` a `newMessage` event passing along the coordinates, although later in the chapter, we'll be making this a lot nicer, setting up that URL for Google Maps. Right now, though, we're going to call `io.emit`, `emit` a `newMessage` event, and provide the necessary data by calling `generateMessage`:

```
socket.on('createLocationMessage', (coords) => {
  io.emit('newMessage', generateMessage)
});
```

For the moment `generateMessage` is going to take some bogus username, I'm going to go ahead and type in `Admin`, and we are going to set the text, for now we're simply going to set it equal to the coordinates. Let's go ahead and use a template string to set that up. We're going to first inject the `latitude`, which is available on `coords.latitude`, then we're going to go ahead and add a comma, a space, and we'll inject the `longitude`, `coords.longitude`:

```
socket.on('createLocationMessage', (coords) => {
  io.emit('newMessage', generateMessage('Admin', `${coords.latitude},
${coords.longitude}`));
});
```

Now that we have this call in place the location information is going to get passed back and forth between the users, and we can go ahead and actually prove this.

Over inside the browser I'm going to give this page a refresh, and I'm also going to open up a second tab. In this second tab I'm going to click on **Send Location**. It's not going to prompt me if I want to share my location since I've already told it I do want to share my location with this tab. You can see we have our **Admin** message and we have our `latitude`, and the `longitude`:

We also have it over inside the second tab. If I take this information we can actually Google it and prove that it is working as expected. Later in the chapter, we're going to be setting up a nice link so this information isn't visible; it'll be there but the user doesn't really need to know the coordinates, what they really want is a link to a map. That's what we're going to set up, but for now we can put this in Google, Google is going to show us exactly where it is and the coordinates are indeed correct. I am in Philadelphia, which means the location was correctly fetched for these localhost tabs.

Rendering clickable link in place of text coordinates

So far, we got the data flowing, and now we're going to make it a little more useful. Instead of rendering `latitude` and `longitude` information as text, we're going to render a clickable link. A user will be able to click that link; when they receive the location from someone else, it's going to bring them over to Google Maps and they'll be able to view exactly where the other user is. This is going to be much more useful than spitting out the text `latitude` and `longitude`.

Now in order to get that done we are going to need to tweak how we transmit the coordinate data. The way we send the data is still fine over inside `index.js`, we are still going to emit, `createLocationMessage`. But inside `server.js` instead of emitting a new message, we need to `emit` something else entirely. We're going to set up a new event called `newLocationMessage`, we're going to emit that, and then over inside `index.js` we'll write a handler for `newLocationMessage` similar to `newMessage` but distinctly different. Instead of rendering some text, it's going to help us render a link.

Sorting out the URL structure

Now in order to get started before we can do any of this we have to figure out exactly what sort of URL structure we're going to use to get that data, the `latitude` and `longitude` information, showing up correctly in Google Maps. And there's actually a pretty uniform way to set up the URL, which is going to make this really easy.

To show you exactly what URL we're going to be using, let's go ahead and open up a new tab. The URL is going to go to `https://www.google.com/maps`. Now from here we are going to be providing a query parameter, and the query parameter will be specifying; it's called `q`:

And it is going to expect the `latitude` and `longitude` to be the value separated by a comma. Now we actually have that here in the `localhost:3000` tab. Although there will be a little space between the comma, either way we can copy that value, head back over into the other tab, paste it in, and just remove the space.

With this in place we now have a URL that we can use inside our application. Now when I hit *enter*, we are going to view a map at the correct location, but you'll notice the URL changes. That's perfectly fine; as long as we send the user to this URL, it doesn't really matter what it ends up becoming. I'm going to hit *enter*; you can see right away we are getting a Google Map, and as the page loads the URL is indeed going to change.

Now we're looking at something completely different from what we typed in, but the actual pin, the red pin, it is correct within a couple of houses. Now with that knowledge we can generate a URL that follows that same format, spit that out inside the website, and we'll have that clickable link where someone can view the location of someone else.

Emitting newLoactionMessage

To get started, let's go ahead and move into Atom into `server.js`, and instead of emitting a `newMessage` event we're going to emit `newLocationMessage`:

```
socket.on('createLocationMessage', (coords) => {
  io.emit('newLocationMessage', generateMessage('Admin',
`${coords.latitude}, ${coords.longitude}`));
});
```

Now we don't have a handler for that over in `index.js`, but that's perfectly fine, we'll set that up later in the section. Now we are going to need to change the data we send across too. Currently, we're sending the plain text data; what we want to do is generate a URL. We're actually going to create a completely separate function for generating a location message, and we'll call it `generateLocationMessage`.

```
io.emit('newLocationMessage', generateLocationMessage('Admin',
`${coords.latitude}, ${coords.longitude}`));
```

Now this function is going to take some arguments to generate the data; Just like we have for the `generateMessage` function, we're going to start with the from name and then move on to the data specific to this function, that's going to be the `latitude` and `longitude`.

I'm going to remove our template string and we're going to pass in the raw values. The first value will be `coords.latitude` and the second one will be `coords.longitude`. Now it's the second coordinate value but it is indeed the third argument:

```
io.emit('newLocationMessage', generateLocationMessage('Admin',
coords.latitude, coords.longitude));
```

With this arguments list set up, we can actually go ahead and define `generateLocation`. We'll be able to export it, require it in this file and then everything is going to work as expected. Let's go ahead and load it in up top before we actually add it to the message file. We are going to load `generateLocationMessage` alongside `generateMessage`:

```
const {generateMessage, generateLocationMessage} =
require('./utils/message');
```

Let's save `server.js` and move into our `message` file.

Adding generateLocationMessage in the message.js file

Now the function that we're about to create is going to look really similar to this, we're going to take some data in and we're going to return an object. The big difference is that we'll be generating that URL as well. Instead of `from`, `text`, and `createdAt`, we're going to have `from`, URL, and `createdAt`.

We can make a new variable, we can call this variable `generateLocationMessage`, and we can go ahead and set it equal to a function that takes those three arguments `from`, `latitude`, and `longitude`:

```
var generateLocationMessage = (from, latitude, longitude)
```

Now we can finish off the arrow function (=>) adding the arrow and our curly braces, and inside of here we can get started by returning the empty object:

```
var generateLocationMessage = (from, latitude, longitude) => {
  return {

  };
};
```

Now we're going to set up those three properties from property, the URL property and `createdAt`. Here `from` is going to be easy; just like we do for `generateMessage`, we're simply going to reference the argument. The URL one is going to be a little trickier; for now we'll set that equal to an empty template string, we'll come back to it in a moment. And finally, `createdAt`, we've done that before; we're going to set it equal to a timestamp by getting a `new Date` and calling `getTime`:

```
var generateLocationMessage = (from, latitude, longitude) => {
  return {
    from,
    from,
    url: ``,
    createdAt: new Date().getTime()
  };
};
```

Now for the URL we're going to need to use that exact same format that we just typed into the browser, `https://www.google.com/maps`. Then we've got to set up our query parameter, adding our question mark and our `q` param, setting it equal to the `latitude` followed by a comma, and followed by the `longitude`. We're going to inject the `latitude`, add a comma, and then inject the `longitude`:

```
var generateLocationMessage = (from, latitude, longitude) => {
  return {
    from,
    url: `https://www.google.com/maps?q=${latitude},${longitude}`,
    createdAt: new Date().getTime()
  };
};
```

Now we're done! `generateLocationMessage` is going to work as expected, although you will be writing a test case a little later on. For now we can simply export it. I'm going to export `generateLocationMessage`, like this:

```
var generateLocationMessage = (from, latitude, longitude) => {
  return {
    from,
    url: `https://www.google.com/maps?q=${latitude},${longitude}`,
    createdAt: new Date().getTime()
  };
};

module.exports = {generateMessage, generateLocationMessage};
```

Now the data is going to flow from the client by calling `emit`, passing in `generateLocationMessage`. We're going to get the `latitude` and `longitude`. Over inside the `server.js`, we are then going to `emit` the `newLocationMessage` event with the object that we just defined over inside `generateLocationMessage`:

```
socket.on('createLocationMessage', (coords) => {
  io.emit('newLocationMessage', generateLocationMessage('Admin',
coords.latitude, coords.longitude));
});
```

Adding an event listener for newLocationMessage

The last piece to the puzzle to really get all this working is to add an event listener for the `newLocationMessage` event. In `index.js` we can call `socket.on` to do just that. We're going to pass in our two arguments. First up is the event name we want to listen for, `newLocationMessage`, and the second and final argument is our `function`. This is going to get called with the `message` information once the event occurs:

```
socket.on('newLocationMessage', function (message) {

});
```

Now that we have this, we can go ahead and start generating the DOM elements that we want to spit out to the user, and just like we did above, we're going to make a list item and we're going to add our anchor tag, our link inside of it.

We're going to make a variable called `list item` and we're going to make a new element using `jQuery`. As that first argument we're going to pass in our string and we are going to go ahead and set it equal to the list item:

```
socket.on('newLocationMessage', function (message) {
  var li = jQuery('<li></li>');
});
```

Next up we can go ahead and create the second element we're going to need. I'm going to make a variable, call this variable a for the anchor tag, and set it equal to the return value once again to a call to `jQuery`. This time around we're going to create the anchor tag. Now the anchor tag uses the a tag, and the contents inside of the tag, that's the link text; in our case, we're going to go with `My current location`:

```
socket.on('newLocationMessage', function (message) {
  var li = jQuery('<li></li>');
  var a = jQuery('<a>My current location</a>');
});
```

Now we are going to be specifying one attribute on the anchor tag. This is going to be a non-dynamic attribute, meaning it's not going to come from the message object, this one is going to be called `target`, and we're going to set `target` equal to " `_blank`":

```
var a = jQuery('<a target="_blank">My current location</a>');
```

When you set target equal to `_blank`, it tells the browser to open up the URL in a new tab as opposed to redirecting the current tab. If we redirected the current tab, I'd get kicked out of the chatroom. If I clicked one of the links with the target set to `blank`, we'll simply open up a new tab to view the Google Maps information:

```
socket.on('newLocationMessage', function (message) {
  var li = jQuery('<li></li>');
  var a = jQuery('<a target="_blank">My current location</a>');

});
```

Next up, we're going to go ahead and set some properties on these attributes. We're going to set the text using `li.text`. This is going to let us set the person's name as well as that colon. Right inside template strings, we are going to inject the value `message.from`. After that value, we're going to add a colon and a space:

```
var a = jQuery('<a target="_blank">My current location</a>');

li.text(`${message.from}: `);
```

Next up, we're going to go ahead and update our anchor tag, `a.attr`. You can set and fetch attributes on your jQuery-selected elements using this method. If you provide one argument, like `target`, it fetches the value, in which case it would return the string `_blank`. If you specify two arguments, it actually sets the value. Here, we can set the `href` value equal to our URL, which we have under `message.url`:

```
li.text(`${message.from}: `);
a.attr('href', message.url)
```

Now you'll notice for all these dynamic values, I'm not simply adding them in template strings. Instead, I'm using these safe methods like `li.text` and `a.attribute`. This prevents any malicious behavior; if someone tries to inject HTML, they shouldn't be injecting using this code.

With this in place we can now go ahead and append the anchor tag to the end of the list item, which is going to add it after the text we just set using `li.append`, and we're going to append the anchor tag. And now we can go ahead and add all of this to the DOM using the exact same statement in case of `newMessage` event listener. I'm going to copy and paste it in the `newLocagtionMesaage` event listener:

```
socket.on('newLocationMessage', function (message) {
  var li = jQuery('<li></li>');
  var a = jQuery('<a target="_blank">My current location'</a>);

  li.text(`${message.from}: `);
  a.attr('href', message.url);
  li.append(a);
  jQuery('#messages').append(li);
});
```

With this in place we are done. Now I'm going to save `index.js` and restart things over in the browser. We made quite a few changes so it's alright if you had a few typos; as long as you're able to track them down it's no big deal.

I'm going to refresh both of my tabs over inside Chrome; this is going to get the new connections up and running using the latest client-side code, and to kick things off I'm going to send a simple message from the second tab to the first tab. It's showing up here in the second tab, and if I go over to the first tab we see **User: test**. Now I can click on **Send Location**, this is going to take about one to three seconds to actually get the location. Then it's going to go through the `Socket.io` chain and what do we get? We get the link **My current location** showing up for user one:

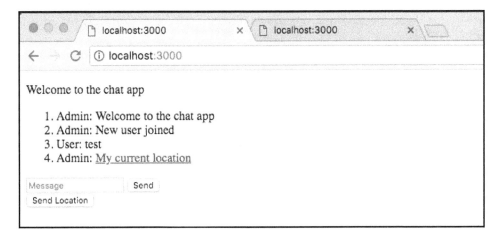

And for user two as well. Now if I click on that link, it should open up a brand new tab with the proper URL, `latitude`, and `longitude` information rendered in it.

Right here, we have the location for the user who clicked that **Send Location** button. With this in place, we have a fantastic geolocation feature. All you do is you click on the button; it fetches your current location no matter where you are, and it renders a clickable link so anyone else can view it inside Google Maps. Now before we go, I would like you to add a single test case for that brand new `generateLocationMessage` function.

Adding test case for generateLocationMessage

Over inside the Terminal, I can shut down the server and use `clear` to clear the output. If I run our test suite using `npm test`, we see that we have our one test and it's passing:

```
Gary:node-chat-app Gary$ npm test

> chat-app@1.0.0 test /Users/Gary/Desktop/node-chat-app
> mocha server/**/*.test.js


  generateMessage
    ✓ should generate correct message object


  1 passing (19ms)
```

Your job is going to be to add a second test case over inside of `message.test.js`.

We'll get started together. Right here, we're going to add a `describe` block, describe the `generateLocationMessage` function, and you're going to be responsible for adding a test case inside of the callback:

```
describe('generateLocationMessage', () => {

});
```

In here, you're going to call `it ('should generate correct location object')`. Next up, we can go ahead and add our function, this is going to be a synchronous test so there is no need to add the done argument:

```
describe('generateLocationMessage', () => {
  it('should generate correct location object', () => {

  });
});
```

Now, we are going to write a test case pretty similar to one for `generateMessage` event, although instead of passing in `from` and `text`, you're going to pass in `from`, `latitude`, and `longitude`. Then you're going to make some assertions about the values you get back. Then we're going to run the test case and make sure everything passes over inside the Terminal.

Adding variables for the test case

To get started I'm going to make two variables. I'm going to make a `from` variable and I'll set that equal to something like `Deb`. Then we can go ahead and create a `latitude` variable, I'm going to set that equal to `15`. And we can go ahead and create a variable `longitude` setting that equal to something like `19`:

```
describe('generateLocationMessage', () => {
  it('should generate correct location object', () => {
    var from = 'Deb';
    var latitude = 15;
    var longitude = 19;
  });
});
```

Then I can go ahead and finally create a `url` variable. The `url` variable is going to be the final result, the URL I would expect to get back. Now that URL is going to be inside of quotes `https://www.google.com/maps`, and then we're going to add the appropriate query parameter given the information we're going to pass in. If the latitude is `15`, we would expect `15` after the equal sign, and if the longitude is `19` after the comma, we would expect `19`:

```
describe('generateLocationMessage', () => {
  it('should generate correct location object', () => {
    var from = 'Deb';
    var latitude = 15;
    var longitude = 19;
    var url = 'https://www.google.com/maps?q=15,19';
  });
});
```

Now that we have that in place we can actually go ahead and call our function storing the response. I'm going to make a variable called `message`, then we're going to go ahead and call `generateLocationMessage`, which currently isn't required, we can do that in just a second. And we're going to pass in our three arguments `from`, `latitude`, and `longitude`:

```
describe('generateLocationMessage', () => {
  it('should generate correct location object', () => {
    var from = 'Deb';
    var latitude = 15;
    var longitude = 19;
    var url = 'https://www.google.com/maps?q=15,19';
    var message = generateLocationMessage(from, latitude, longitude);
  });
});
```

Now let's go ahead and also pull off `generateLocationMessage` along with `generateMessage`:

```
var expect = require('expect');

var {generateMessage, generateLocationMessage} = require('./message');
```

Now the only thing left to do is make our assertions.

Making assertion for generateLocationMessage

We're going to start much the same way. I'm actually going to copy these two lines from `generateMessage` to the `generateLocationMessage` test case:

```
expect(message.createdAt).toBeA('number');
expect(message).toInclude({from, text});
```

We're expecting the `message.createdAt` property to be a number which it should be, then we're expecting message to include a `from` property equal to `Deb`, and we're going to expect it to have a `url` property equal to the `url` string we defined:

```
describe('generateLocationMessage', () => {
  it('should generate correct location object', () => {
    var from = 'Deb';
    var latitude = 15;
    var longitude = 19;
    var url = 'https://www.google.com/maps?q=15,19';
    var message = generateLocationMessage(from, latitude, longitude);

    expect(message.createdAt).toBeA('number');
    expect(message).toInclude({from, url});
```

```
        });
    });
```

If both of these assertions pass then we know the object returned from
`generateLocationMessage` is correct.

Running the test case for generateLocationMessage

I'm going to rerun the test suite over inside the Terminal, and everything should work as
expected:

```
[Gary:node-chat-app Gary$ npm test

> chat-app@1.0.0 test /Users/Gary/Desktop/node-chat-app
> mocha server/**/*.test.js


  generateMessage
    ✓ should generate correct message object

  generateLocationMessage
    ✓ should generate correct location object


  2 passing (13ms)
```

And that's it for this one! We have geolocation all set up, we have our link rendered, we are
in great shape to continue on. I'm going to go ahead and add a `commit` over inside the
Terminal. I'm going to run the `clear` command to clear the `Terminal` output, then we'll
run `git status` to see all our changed files and we can use `git commit` with the `am` flag
to add a message for this one, `Add geolocation support via geolocation api`:

```
git commit -am 'Add geolocation support via geolocation api'
```

I'm going to go ahead and commit this and push it up to GitHub, and we can also take a
quick moment to deploy this to Heroku as well using `git push heroku master`.

This is going to deploy our latest code which has geolocation stuff built in. We'll be able to run this, and this code is going to run on things like the Chrome mobile browser because we'll be on HTTPS. Google Chrome's browser on mobile and other mobile browsers have pretty strict security guidelines as to when they'll send geolocation information. It is going to need to be over an HTTPS connection, which is exactly what we have here. I'm going to open up our Heroku app in a few tabs. We'll open it up in tab one and we'll also open it up in a second tab. I'm going to click on that **Send Location** button. I do need to approve this since it's a different URL, yes I do want them to be able to use my location. It's going to grab the location, send it off, and the first tab gets the link. I click on the link and hopefully we get the same spot.

Summary

In this chapter, we worked on generating text and location messages. We looked into generating the newMessage object and then writing a test case for it. Then, we learned about how to use event acknowledgments. Then we added the message form field and rendered an input field and a button to the screen. We also discussed the concept of jQuery and used that to select and create incoming message elements.

In the geoloaction section, we gave a new button to the user. This new button allow the users to send their location. We set up a click listener for that **Send Location** button, which means every time a user clicks it, we do something as per their access to geoloaction API. If they do not have access to the geolocation API, we simply print a message. If they do have access we try to fetch the location.

In the next chapter, we'll look into styling our chat page and make it look more like a real web app.

7
Styling Our Chat Page as a Web App

In the previous chapter, you learned about Socket.io and WebSockets, which enable two-way communication between the server and the client. In this chapter, we'll continue our discussion on styling our chat page and make it look more like a real web app. We'll look into timestamps and formatting time and date using Moment methods. We'll create and render templates for `newMessage` and `newLocation` messages. We'll also look into auto scrolling, making the chat a little less annoying.

Styling the chat page

In this section you're going to get some styles in place so our app looks a little less like an unstyled HTML page, and a little more like a real web app. Now in the following screenshot, on the left we have **People** panel, we're not going to be wiring that up yet although we are giving it a place inside of our page. Eventually this is going to store a list of all the people connected to the individual chatroom, that's going to come a bit later.

Over right side, in the main area is going to be the messages panel:

Now the individual messages are still unstyled, that's going to come later, but we do have a place to put all of that stuff. We have our footer, this includes our form for sending a message, the textbox, and the button, and it also includes our **Send Location** button.

Now to get all of this done we're going to add a CSS template that I've created for this project. We're also going to be adding some classes to our HTML; this is going to let us apply the various styles. Finally we'll be making a few small tweaks to our JavaScript to improve the user experience. Let's go ahead and dive in.

Storing the template styles

The first thing we're going to do is make a new folder and a new file to store our styles. This is going to be the template styles we'll be grabbing in just a moment, then we're going to go ahead and load it into `index.html` so those styles are used when we render the chat app.

Now the first thing we're going to do is create a new folder inside of `public`, and call this folder `css`. We're going to add just one file to it, a new file called `styles.css`.

Now before we go off and grab any styles, let's go ahead and import this file into our application, and in order to test and make sure that it's working what we're going to do is write a very simple selector, we're going to select everything using the *, then inside of curly braces we're going to add a style, setting the `color` for everything equal to `red`:

```
* {
    color: red;
}
```

Go ahead and make your file just like this one, we're going to save it and then we'll import it over inside of `index.html`. Right at the bottom of the `head` tag following our `meta` tag, we're going to add a `link` tag, this is going to let us link a style sheet. We have to provide two attributes to get that done, first off we have to tell HTML exactly what we're linking to by specifying the `rel`, or relation attribute. In this case we're trying to link a `style sheet`, so we're going to provide that as the value. Now the next thing we need to do is provide the `href` attribute. This is similar to the `src` attribute for the `script` tag, it's the path to the file you want to link. In this case we have that at `/css` and we just created the file `style.css`, `/styles.css`:

```
<head>
    <meta charset="utf-8">
    <link rel="stylesheet" href="/css/styles.css">
</head>
```

With this in place we can save `index.html` and give our page a refresh over inside of the browser or load it up for the very first time, and what we see is a hideously ugly page:

We've managed to make it even uglier than it was previously, but this is great because it means our style sheet file is getting imported correctly.

Now in order to grab the actual template we're going to be using for the chat app, we're going to visit a URL, `http://links.mead.io/chat-css`. This is just a bitly link that's going to redirect you over to a Gist, and here we have two options, we can grab either the minified style template or the unminified one:

I'm going to go ahead and grab minified one by either highlighting it or clicking **Raw** link which brings us to the file. We're going to grab the entire contents we see there, head over into Atom and paste it inside of our `styles.css` file, removing obviously the previous selector.

Now that we have this in place we can give our page a refresh, although we're not really going to see much improvement. Over inside of `localhost:3000` I'll give the browser a refresh and clearly things are different:

That is because we need to apply some classes to our HTML in order to get everything to work correctly.

Tweaking the structure for alignment

We're going to need to tweak the structure, adding a few container elements to help with alignment. Over inside of Atom we can get this done in just a few moments. This template was built around a few key classes. The first one needs to get applied to the `body` tag by setting the `class` attribute equal to, inside of quotes, `chat`:

```
<body class="chat">
```

This tells the style sheet load these styles for this chat page, and we're going to go ahead and remove `Welcome to the chat app`, this is no longer necessary. Now the next thing we're going to do is create a `div` tag and this `div` is going to house that `People` list we saw on the left-hand side. It's going to be empty for the moment but that's fine we can still go ahead and create it.

We're going to make `div` and we're going to give this div class, and that `class` is going to get set equal to the following, `chat__sidebar`:

```
<body class ="chat">

    <div class="chat">

    </div>
```

This is a naming convention used in some style sheet templates, it's really a matter of preference, you could call this whatever you want when you create the style sheet, I happen to call it `chat__sidebar`. It's a sub-element inside of the greater chat app.

Now inside the `div` tag, we're going to add a little title using the `h3` tag, we're going to give this a title of `People`, or whatever you want to call that sidebar list, and we're also going to provide a `div` which will eventually house the individual users, although as I mentioned we're not going to be wiring that up yet. Now we can go ahead and give this an `id` setting it equal to `users` so we can target it a bit later. And that's all we need for the chat sidebar at the moment:

```
<div class ="chat__sidebar">
  <h3>People</h3>
  <div id="user"></div>
</div>
```

Now the next thing that we're going to do is create a `div` tag, and this `div` is going to house that main area which means it's going to contain not only our chat messages, but also the little form at the bottom, everything on the right-hand side of the sidebar.

This also is going to require a custom class for some styles, this one is called `chat__ main`, and inside of here we're going to add not only our unordered list, but also our `form` and `button`. Let's go ahead and take all of our current markup, the unordered list, down to the Send Location button, cut it out and paste it inside of `chat__main`:

```
<div class="chat__main">
  <ol id="messages"></ol>

  <form id="message-form">
    <input name="message" type="text" placeholder="Message"/>
    <button>Send</button>
  </form>
  <button id="send-location">Send Location</button>
</div>
```

Now we're not quite done yet there are a few more things to tweak. First up we have to add a class to our ordered list, we'll set `class` equal to `chat__messages`, this is going to provide the necessary styles, and the last `div` we need to create is going to be for that footer. This is going to be the gray bar at the bottom that contains both your `form` as well as the `Send Location` button. We're going to make `div` which is going to help with alignment, and we're going to add the `form` and the `button` tag inside of it by cutting it out and pasting it inside `div` of ordered list:

```
<div class="chat__main">
  <ol id="messages" class="chat__messages"></ol>

  <form id="message-form">
    <input name="message" type="text" placeholder="Message"/>
```

```
    <button>Send</button>
  </form>
  <button id="send-location">Send Location</button>
</div>
```

Now we are going to need a class here too as you might have guessed, setting the `class` attribute equal to the string `chat__footer`:

```
<div class="chat__footer">
  <form id="message-form">
    <input name="message" type="text" placeholder="Message"/>
    <button>Send</button>
  </form>
  <button id="send-location">Send Location</button>
</div>
```

Now we have all of our classes in place and we can head over to the browser and see what we get when we give the page a refresh:

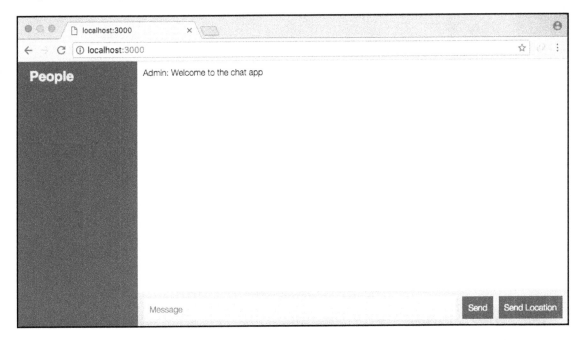

We have our styled chat application and we can still do whatever we were able to do before. I can send off a message, `Hey this should still work`, hit *enter* and `Hey this should still work` shows up to the screen:

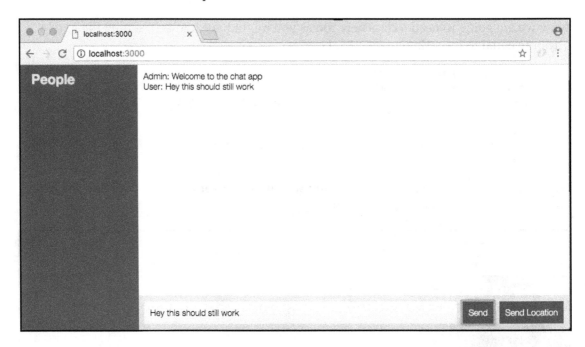

The same thing is true for **Send Location**, I can send off my location, this is going to send it to the server, it's going to send it to all the clients, and I can click the **My current location** link and the location is going to show up inside of Google Maps. We've maintained all of the old functionality while adding a nice set of styles:

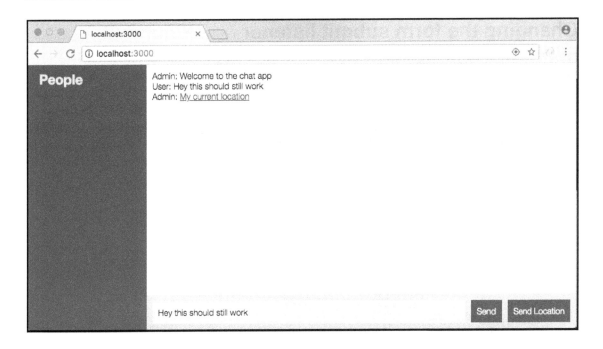

Making user experience improvements

Now for the second half of this section I want to make some user experience improvements to the form next.

One improvement we're going to make is wiping the text value once a message was successfully sent. We're also going to do something similar with **Send Location**. As you might have noticed it can take up to a second or two for the **Send Location** geolocation call to actually complete, we're going to set this button to be disabled so someone doesn't spam it wondering what's happened. We're also going to update the text to say `Sending Location` so someone knows that something is happening in the background.

In order to get both those things done all we need to do is modify a few lines over inside of `index.js`. Near the bottom of the file we have our two jQuery event listeners, both of these are going to get changed.

Changing the form submit listener

Now the first thing we're going to change is going to be the form submit listener. In `socket.emit` we fetch the value from the field, and that's what we pass along. What we want to do next inside of the acknowledgment callback is clear the value. Once the request has been received by the server there's no reason to keep it around, so what we can do is add the same `jQuery` selector, targeting the field where the `name` attribute equals `message`. We're going to go ahead and clear its value by calling `val` once again, but instead of getting a value by providing no arguments, we're going to set the value to an empty string by passing in an empty string as the first argument:

```
jQuery('#message-form').on('submit', function (e) {
  e.prevenDefault();

  var messageTextbox =

  socket.emit('createMessage', {
    from: 'User',
    text: jQuery('[name=message]').val()
  }, function () {
    jQuery('[name=message]').val('')
  });
});
```

You could set the value to anything you like, but in this case we just want to clear it so we're going to use the following method call.

We have the same selector twice to speed things up, we're going to make a variable, we'll call that variable `messageTextbox`, and then we can go ahead and set it equal to the selector we just created, and now we can refer to `messageTextbox` anywhere we need access to that input. We can reference it, `messageTextbox` and next, `messageTextbox` like this:

```
var messageTextbox = jQuery('[name=message]');

socket.emit('createMessage', {
  from: 'User',
  text: messageTextbox.val()
}, function() {
  messageTextbox.val('')
});
```

Now the listener for `createMessage`, which is over inside of `server.js`, and we do indeed call the callback with a string. For now, we're going to just remove that bogus value passing in zero arguments, like this:

```
socket.broadcast.emit('newMessage', generateMessage('Admin, 'New user
joined'));

socket.on('createMessage', (message, callback) => {
  console.log('createMessage', message);
  io.emit('newMessage', generateMessage(message.form, message.text));
  callback();
});
```

This means that the acknowledgement function will still get called but we don't actually need any data we just need to know when the server responded. Now that we have this in place we can go ahead and refresh things over inside `localhost:3000`, type a message, `Here is a message` and hit the *enter* key and we get the value cleared and it was indeed sent:

The same thing is going to hold true if I type in a message, `Andrew` and click the **Send** button.

Updating the input tag

Now one thing we're going to do real quick is update the `input` tag for the textbox. If I refresh the page we're currently not brought right into the message field, it would be really nice to do that. It would also be really nice to turn off autocomplete, as you can see autocomplete isn't really a useful feature and the values inside of it are usually trash.

So what we're going to do over inside of Atom is add two attributes to customize the input. The first one is going to be `autofocus` which doesn't require a value, `autofocus` is going to autofocus on the input when the HTML gets rendered, and the second one we're going to add is `autocomplete`, and we're going to set that equal to the string `off`:

```
<div class="chat__footer">
<form id="message-form">
  <input name="message" type="text" placeholder="Message" autofocus
autocomplete="off"/>
  <button>Send</button>
<form>
<button id="send-location">Send Location</button>
```

With this in place we can save `index.html`, head back over to Chrome, refresh the page and test things out. I'm going to type in `test`, I have no autocomplete which is good we turned that off, and if I click the **Send** button I am indeed still sending the message. I was also brought right into the textbox when I reloaded the page, I didn't need to do anything in order to start typing.

Customizing the Send Location

The next thing we're going to do is customize that **Send Location** button using a bit more jQuery. Now we're new to jQuery and this isn't really a jQuery course. The goal here is to change the button text and disable it while the process is occurring. When the process is complete, meaning that the location was either sent or not sent, we can return the button to its normal state, but while the geolocation call is happening we don't want someone spamming away.

To get that done we're going to make some tweaks to the final on listener we have inside of `index.js`, just next our on submit listener we have our on click listener. Here we're going to need to make some changes to the button, the `locationButton` variable we have defined. We're going to set an attribute that's going to disable the button.

To get that done we will reference the selector, `locationButton`, and we're going to call a jQuery method.

Now we're only going to disable it after we've confirmed they even have support for it, if they don't have support for the feature there's no reason to go ahead and disable it. Here `locationButton.attr` is going to let us set an attribute, we're going to set the `disabled` attribute equal to the value `disabled`. Now this disabled needs to be in quotes as well:

```
var locationButton = jQuery('#send-location');
locationButton.on('click', function () {
  if (!navigator.geolocation) {
    return alert('Geolocation not supported by your browser.');
  }

  locationButton.attr('disabled', 'disabled');
```

Now that we have disabled the button we can actually test this out, we never undisable it so it's going to be broken after clicking it once, but we can confirm that this line works. Over in the browser I'm going to give things a refresh, click **Send Location** and you can see right away that the button it does get disabled:

Now it is going to send off the location once but if I try to click it again the button is disabled and it's never going to refire the `click` event. The goal here is to only disable it while the process is actually occurring, once it's sent like it is here we want to re-enable it so someone can send an updated location.

To get that done over inside of Atom we're going to add a line of jQuery into both the success handler and the error handler. If things go well we're going to reference `locationButton` and we're going to remove the disabled attribute by using `removeAttr`. This takes just one argument, the name of the attribute, in this case we have that, it's a string, `disabled`:

```
locationButton.attr('disabled', 'disabled');

navigator.geolocation.getCurrentPosition(function (position) {
  locationButton.removeAttr('disabled');
  socket.emit('createLocationMessage', {
    latitude: position.coords.latitude,
    longitude: position.coords.longitude
  });
```

This is going to remove the `disabled` attribute we defined previously re-enabling the button. And we can do the exact same thing, literally copying and pasting the line next inside `function`. If for some reason we're not able to fetch the location, maybe the user denied the request for `geolocation`, we still want to disable that button so they can try again:

```
navigator.geolocation.getCurrentPosition(function (position){
  locationButton.removeAttr('disabled');
  socket.emit('createLocationMessage', {
    latitude: position.coords.latitude,
    longitude: position.coords.longitude
  });
}, function (){
  locationButton.removeAttr('disabled');
  alert('Unable to fetch location');
});
```

Now that we have this set up we can test out that code by refreshing the browser and trying to send off our location. We should see the button is disabled for a little bit and then it gets re-enabled. We can click it to prove that it is working as expected, and the button was re-enabled, which means we can go ahead and click it at a later time sending our location once again.

Updating the button text

Now the last thing we're going to do is update the button text while the process is occurring. To get that done over inside of Atom we're going to use that `text` method we've used in the past.

In the `locationButton.attr` line, we're going to set the `text` property equal to, by calling text, `Sending location...`. Now, in the `index.js` file, the real button text is `Send Location`, I'm going to go ahead and lowercase `location` that to keep things uniform:

```
var locationButton = jQuery('#send-location');
locationButton.on('click', function (){
  if (!navigator.geolocation){
    return alert('Geolocation not supported by your browser.');
  }
  locationButton.attr('disabled', 'disabled').text('Sending location...');
```

Now that we have this set up we are updating the text while the process occurs, the only thing left to do is tweak it back to its original value next by setting `text` equal to the string `Send location`, and we're going to do the exact same thing in error handler, calling `text` passing in the string `Send location`:

```
locationButton.attr('disabled', 'disabled').text('Sending location...');

navigator.geolocation.getCurrentPosition(function (position){
  locationButton.removeAttr('disabled').text('Send location');
  socket.emit('createLocationMessage', {
    latitude: position.coords.latitude,
    longitude: position.coords.longitude
  });
}, function(){
  locationButton.removeAttr('disabled').text('Send location');
  alert('Unable to fetch location');
});
```

Now we can go ahead and test that this is working as expected, both of these lines (in success as well as error handler) are identical, regardless of whether it succeeds or fails we're going to do the same thing.

Over inside of Chrome I'm going to give my page a refresh one more time, we're going to click that **Send Location** button and you can see the button is disabled and the text was changed, **Sending location...** shows up:

And as soon as the process is complete and the location was actually sent, the button returns to its default state.

With this in place we now have a much nicer user experience than we had previously. Not only do we have a nice set of styles, we also have a better UI for our form and the Send location button. That is where we are going to stop for this section.

Let's go ahead and make a quick commit by shutting down the server, running `git status`, running `git add .` to add all of those files, and finally we're going to go ahead and run `git commit` with the -m flag providing a message, Add css for chat page:

```
git commit -m 'Add css for chat page'
```

We can go ahead and push this up to GitHub using `git push` and I'm going to avoid deploying for Heroku as of now, although you are welcome to deploy and test your application live.

Timestamps and formatting with Moment

Throughout the course we have used timestamps quite a bit, we've generated them in the to-do app and we also have them generated for all of our messages in the chat app, but we've never gone as far as formatting them to something human-readable. That's going to be the topic in this section, and in the next section we'll put that into action.

By the end of the next section we'll have a formatted message area with the name, timestamp and message, and we'll have some better styles for it as well. Now in this section, it's going to be all about time and timestamp, we're not going to make any changes to the frontend of our app, we're simply going to learn how time works inside of Node.

Timestamps in Node

To explore this we're going to create a new `playground` file, over inside of Atom we're going to make a `playground` folder to store this file, and inside of the `playground` folder we can make a new file calling it `time.js`. In here it will play around with time, and we'll take what we learn here into the frontend of the application in the next section.

We are no strangers to timestamps, we know they're nothing more than just integers whether positive or negative, something like `781` is a perfectly valid timestamp, so is something like minus a couple of billion or whatever any number happens to be, all valid, even `0` is a perfectly valid timestamp. Now all of these numbers, they're all relative to a certain moment in history referred to as the Unix epoch, which is January 1, 1970 at midnight 0 hours 0 minutes and 0 seconds am. This is stored in UTC which means it's timezone independent:

```
// Jan 1st 1970 00:00:00 am

0
```

Now my time stamp `0` actually represents this moment in history perfectly, and positive numbers like 1000 head into the future, while negative numbers like -1000 head into the past. -1000 as a timestamp would represent December 31, 1969 at 11:59 and 59 seconds, we've gone one second into the past from January 1, `1970`.

Now these timestamps inside of JavaScript, they're stored in milliseconds since the Unix epoch inside of regular Unix timestamps, they're actually stored in seconds. Since we are using JavaScript in this course, we will always be using milliseconds as our timestamp values, which means at a timestamp like this, 1000, represents one second into January 1st, since there's 1000 milliseconds in a second.

A value like 10000 would be ten seconds into this day and so on and so forth. Now the problem for us was never getting the timestamp, getting the timestamp was really easy, all we had to do was call `new Date` calling its `getTime` method. Things are going to get a lot harder though and we want to format a human-readable value like the one we have earlier.

We're going to want to print something to the screen inside of our web app that's not just the timestamp, we're going to want to print something like maybe five minutes ago, letting a user know the message was sent five minutes ago, or maybe you want to print the actual date with the month, day, hour, minute and A.M or P.M value. Regardless of what you want to print we are going to need to talk a bit about formatting, and this is where the default `Date` object falls short.

Yes there are methods that allow you to get the specific values out of a date, like the year, the month, or the day of month, but they are very limited and it is a huge burden to customize.

The Date object

To talk about exactly the problem let's go ahead and pull up the documentation for date by Googling `mdn date`, this is going to bring us to the Mozilla Developer Network documentation page for *Date*, which is a really great set of documentation:

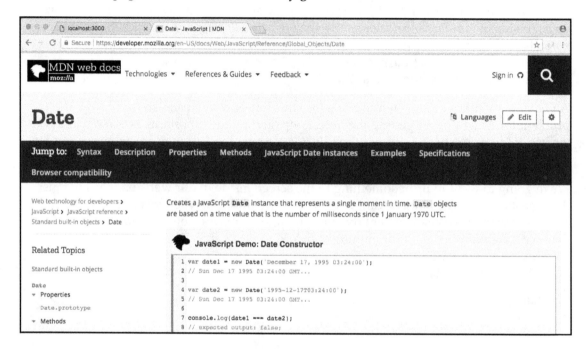

On this page, we have access to all of the methods available, these are all methods kind of like `getTime` that return something specific about the date:

Methods

Getter

`Date.prototype.getDate()`
 Returns the day of the month (1-31) for the specified date according to local time.

`Date.prototype.getDay()`
 Returns the day of the week (0-6) for the specified date according to local time.

`Date.prototype.getFullYear()`
 Returns the year (4 digits for 4-digit years) of the specified date according to local time.

`Date.prototype.getHours()`
 Returns the hour (0-23) in the specified date according to local time.

`Date.prototype.getMilliseconds()`
 Returns the milliseconds (0-999) in the specified date according to local time.

`Date.prototype.getMinutes()`
 Returns the minutes (0-59) in the specified date according to local time.

`Date.prototype.getMonth()`
 Returns the month (0-11) in the specified date according to local time.

For example, as shown in the previous screenshot, we have a `getDate` method that returns the day of the month, a value from 1 to 31. We have something like `getMinutes`, which returns the current minutes for the timestamp. All of these exist inside of `Date`.

Now the problem is that these are really unflexible. For example, inside Atom we have this little date, `Jan 1st 1970 00:00:10 am`. It's a shorthand version for January. Now we can get the actual month to show you how we'll create a variable called `date`. We'll go ahead and create `new Date` and then we're going to go ahead and call a method. I'm going to use `console.log` to print the value to the screen, and we're going to call `date.getMonth`:

```
// Jan 1st 1970 00:00:10 am

var date = new Date();
console.log(date.getMonth());
```

The getMonth method, as defined over inside of the documentation, is going to return a 0-based month value from 0 to 11, where 0 is January and 11 is December. Over inside the Terminal, I'm going to kick off our app using nodemon, since we're going to be restarting it quite a bit. Nodemon is in the playground folder not the server folder, and the file itself is called time.js:

```
nodemon playground/time.js
```

Once it's up and running we see we get 2 back which is expected:

```
Gary:node-chat-app Gary$ nodemon playground/time.js
[nodemon] 1.14.10
[nodemon] to restart at any time, enter `rs`
[nodemon] watching: *.*
[nodemon] starting `node playground/time.js`
2
[nodemon] clean exit - waiting for changes before restart
```

It's currently March 25th 2018 and a 0 index value for March would be 2, even though you commonly think of it as 3.

Now the previous result is fine. We have the number 2 to represent the month, but getting an actual string Jan or January is going to be much more difficult. There is no built-in way to get this value. This means if you do want to get that value you're going to have to create an array, maybe you call the array months, and you store all of the values like this:

```
var date = new Date();
var months = ['Jan', 'Feb']
console.log(date.getMonth());
```

This is going to be fine and it might not seem like that big of a deal for month, but things get just as confusing for the day of the month, like the 1st we have. All we can really get back is the number 1. Actually formatting it to 1st, 2nd, or 3rd is going to be much more difficult. There just are not a good set of methods for formatting your date.

Things get even more complex when you want to have a relative time string, something like three minutes ago. It would be nice to print that inside the web app alongside the message, printing the actual month, the day and the year is not particularly useful. It would be cool if we could say hey this message was sent three hours ago, three minutes ago, or three years ago like a lot of chat applications do.

Using Moment for timestamps

Now when you get into formatting like this, your first instinct is usually to create some utility methods that help with formatting a date. But there is no need to do that because what we're going to look at in this section is a fantastic time library called **Moment**. Moment is pretty much the only library of its kind. It is universally accepted as the go-to library for working with time and JavaScript, I've never worked on a Node or frontend project that didn't have Moment used, it is truly essential when you're working with dates in any capacity.

Now in order to show off why Moment is so great we are going to first install it over inside of the Terminal. Then we're going to play around with all of its capabilities, it has a lot. We can install it by running npm i, I'm going to go ahead and use the current version moment@ version 2.21.0, and I will also use the --save flag to add it as a dependency, a dependency that we're going to need on Heroku as well as locally:

```
npm i moment@2.21.0 --save
```

Now once it's installed I can use clear to clear the Terminal output, and we can go ahead and restart nodemon. Over inside the playground folder it's time to require Moment and take a look at exactly what it can do for us.

To kick things off, let's go ahead and try to fix the problem we tried to solve with date. We want to print the shorthand version of a month like Jan, Feb, and so on. The first step is going to be to comment the previous code out and load in Moment previous at the top, requiring it. I'm going to make a variable called moment and require it by requiring the moment library:

```
var moment = require('moment');

// Jan 1st 1970 00:00:10 am

//var date = new Date();
//var months = ['Jan', 'Feb']
//console.log(date.getMonth());
```

Then next to this code, we'll kick things off by making a new moment. Now just like we create a new date to get a specific date object, we're going to do the same thing with moment. I'm going to call this variable `date` and we're going to set it equal to a call to `moment`, the function we loaded in previous, without any arguments:

```
var moment = require('moment');

// Jan 1st 1970 00:00:10 am

//var date = new Date();
//var months = ['Jan', 'Feb']
//console.log(date.getMonth());

var date = moment();
```

This creates a new moment object that represents the current point in time. From here we can go ahead and try to format things using its really useful format method. The format method is one of the main reasons I just love Moment, it makes it dead simple to print whatever you want as a string. Now in this case, we have access to our `date` and we're going to go ahead and call that method I just talked about, `format`:

```
var moment = require('moment');
var date = moment();
console.log(date.format());
```

Before we get into what we pass to format let's go ahead and run it just like this. When we do that over inside the Terminal, nodemon is going to go ahead and restart itself, and right here we have our formatted date:

```
[nodemon] starting `node playground/time.js`
2018-03-25T15:56:53+05:30
[nodemon] clean exit - waiting for changes before restart
```

We have the year, the month, the day, and other values. It's not still really user-friendly but it is a step in the right direction. The real power of the `format` method comes when you pass a string inside of it.

Now what we pass inside the format method is patterns, which means that we have access to a specific set of values we can use to output certain things. We're going to explore all of the patterns available to you in just a second. For now, let's go ahead and just use one; it's the triple uppercase M pattern:

```
var date = moment();
console.log(date.format('MMM'));
```

When Moment sees this pattern inside, format it's going to go ahead and grab the shorthand version of the month, which means if I save this file and restart it over inside the Terminal once again. We should now see the shorthand version for the current month September, which would be Mar:

```
[nodemon] starting `node playground/time.js`
Mar
[nodemon] clean exit - waiting for changes before restart
```

Right here we have Sep just as expected and we were able to do that super simply by using the format method. Now format returns a string that has just the things you specify. Here we only specified that we want the shorthand version of the month, so all we got back was the shorthand version of the month. We can also add on another pattern, four Ys, which prints out the full year; in the current case, it would print out 2016 in numbers:

```
console.log(date.format('MMM YYYY'));
```

I'm going to go ahead and save time again and right here we get Mar 2018:

```
[nodemon] starting `node playground/time.js`
Mar 2018
[nodemon] clean exit - waiting for changes before restart
```

Now Moment has a fantastic set of documentation so you can use whatever patterns you like.

The Moment documentation

Over inside the browser we can pull it up by going to momentjs.com. The documentation for Moment is fantastic. It's available on the **Docs** page, and to get started in order to figure out how to use format we're going to go to the **Display** section:

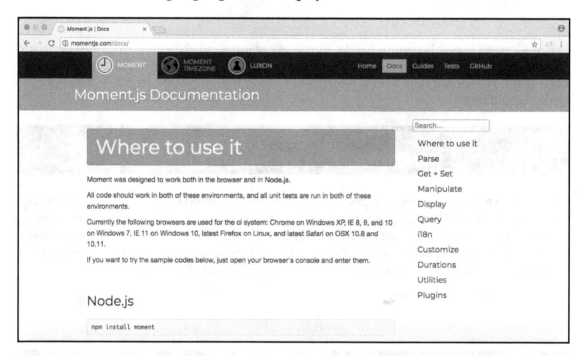

The first item in **Display** is format. There are a few examples about how to use format, but the really useful information is what we have here:

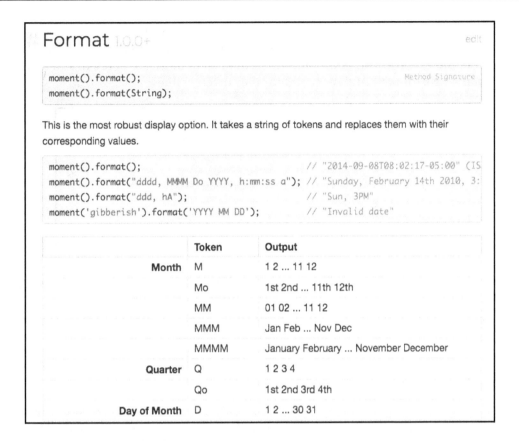

```
Format 1.0.0+                                                        edit
```

```
moment().format();                                          Method Signature
moment().format(String);
```

This is the most robust display option. It takes a string of tokens and replaces them with their corresponding values.

```
moment().format();                            // "2014-09-08T08:02:17-05:00" (IS
moment().format("dddd, MMMM Do YYYY, h:mm:ss a"); // "Sunday, February 14th 2010, 3:
moment().format("ddd, hA");                   // "Sun, 3PM"
moment('gibberish').format('YYYY MM DD');     // "Invalid date"
```

	Token	Output
Month	M	1 2 ... 11 12
	Mo	1st 2nd ... 11th 12th
	MM	01 02 ... 11 12
	MMM	Jan Feb ... Nov Dec
	MMMM	January February ... November December
Quarter	Q	1 2 3 4
	Qo	1st 2nd 3rd 4th
Day of Month	D	1 2 ... 30 31

Here we have all the tokens that we can put inside the string to format our day as we like. Up previous you can see you can use as many of these tokens as you like to create really complex date outputs. Now we already explored two. We explored MMM, which is defined right under the **Month** header, as you can see there are five different ways to represent the month.

The `YYYY` pattern which we used for a year is also defined here. There are three ways to use year. We just explored one of them. And there are sections for everything, year, day of week, day of month, **AM/PM**, hour, minute, second, all of those are defined, and all of them can be put inside a format just like we did for the current values:

Year	YY	70 71 ... 29 30
	YYYY	1970 1971 ... 2029 2030
	Y	1970 1971 ... 9999 +10000 +10001 **Note:** This complies with the ISO 8601 standard for dates past the year 9999
Week Year	gg	70 71 ... 29 30
	gggg	1970 1971 ... 2029 2030
Week Year (ISO)	GG	70 71 ... 29 30

Now in order to explore this just a little more, let's head back into Atom and take advantage of some of these. What we're going to try to do is print the date like this: `Jan 1st 1970`, the shorthand month and the year which we already have, but now we also need the day of the month formatted like 1st, 2nd, 3rd, as opposed to 1, 2, 3.

Formatting date using Moment

In order to do that what I would do if I had not used Moment before is I would look in the docs for the **Day of Month** section, and I look at the available options. I have the **D** pattern that prints 1 through 31, **Do **that prints what we want, 1st, 2nd, 3rd, so on and so forth, and **DD** that prints the number with a 0 in front of it for the values less than 10.

Now in this case we want to use **Do** pattern so all we have to do is type it over inside format. I'm going to open up the Terminal and Atom so we can see it refresh in the background, and we're going to type:

```
console.log(date.format('MMM Do YYYY'));
```

Saving the file, when it starts, we get `March 25th 2018`, which is indeed correct:

```
[nodemon] starting `node playground/time.js`
Mar 25th 2018
[nodemon] clean exit - waiting for changes before restart
```

Now we can also add other characters like a comma:

```
console.log(date.format('MMM Do, YYYY'));
```

A comma is not part of the patterns that format expects so it's simply going to pass it through, which means the comma gets shown just as we typed it in `March 25th, 2018`:

```
[nodemon] starting `node playground/time.js`
Mar 25th, 2018
[nodemon] clean exit - waiting for changes before restart
```

Using format in this way gives us a lot of flexibility as to how we want to print the date. Now format is just one of the many methods. There are a ton of methods on Moment for doing just about anything, although I find I use pretty much the same six in most of my projects. There really isn't a lot of need for most of them although they do exist because they are useful in certain situations.

The Manipulate section in Moment

To take a quick peek at some other things Moment can do, let's head back into the docs and go to the **Manipulate** section:

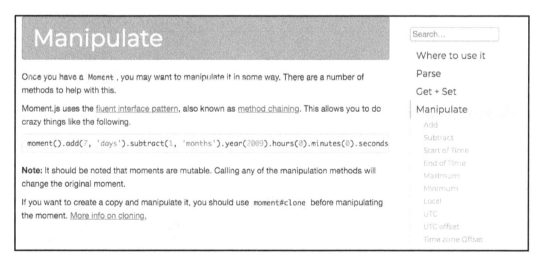

The first two methods defined under **Manipulate** are `add` and `subtract`. This lets you easily add and subtract time. We can call `add` adding seven days and we can call `subtract` subtracting seven months as shown in this example:

```
moment().add(7, 'days').subtract(1, 'months').year(2009).hours(0).minutes(0).seconds
```

To this example, you can get a quick idea about what you can add and subtract, years, quarters, months, weeks, pretty much any unit of time can be added or subtracted:

Key	Shorthand
years	y
quarters	Q
months	M
weeks	w
days	d
hours	h
minutes	m
seconds	s
milliseconds	ms

Now to take a look at what exactly that does to the timestamp, we can go ahead and add and subtract some values. I'm going to call `date.add` and we're going to go ahead and add a year by putting `1` in as the value and `year` in as the unit:

```
var date = moment();
date.add(1, 'years')
console.log(date.format('MMM Do, YYYY'));
```

Now it doesn't matter if you use the single or plural version, both are going to work the same. Here you can see we get `2019` in the Terminal:

```
[nodemon] starting `node playground/time.js`
Mar 25th, 2019
[nodemon] clean exit - waiting for changes before restart
```

If I change it to year singular, I also get that same value. We can add as many years as we like, I'm going to go ahead and add `100` years:

```
var date = moment();
date.add(100, 'year')
console.log(date.format('MMM Do, YYY'))
```

And now we're at `2118`:

```
[nodemon] starting `node playground/time.js`
Mar 25th, 2118
[nodemon] clean exit - waiting for changes before restart
```

The same thing is true with `subtract`. We can chain on the call or we can add it as a separate statement. I'm going to subtract just like this:

```
date.add(100, 'year').subtract(9, 'months');
```

And we are currently in September, and when we subtract 9 months we go back to June:

```
[nodemon] starting `node playground/time.js`
Jun 25th, 2117
[nodemon] clean exit - waiting for changes before restart
```

Now you notice we went from 2118 to 2117 because subtracting those 9 months required us to change years. Moment is really great at handling just about anything you throw at it. Now we're going to be to play around with format a little more. I'm going add an output I would like and we'll need to figure out which patterns to use over inside of the documentation to get that output.

Now the current time at the writing, this is 10:35, and it is in the am, so I have a lowercase am. Your goal is to print a format like this. Now obviously if it's 12:15 when you run the code you're going to see 12:15 as opposed to 10:35; it's just the format that matters, the actual values aren't that important. Now as you'll see when you try to print hours and minutes, you're going to have a lot of options. For both of them you're going to have a padded version like 01 or an unpadded version like 1.

I want you to use the padded version for minutes and the unpadded version for hours, which would be 6, like this, and 01. If you padded the hour it looks kind of weird, and if you don't pad the minute it looks just terrible. So we would want to print something like this if it happened to be 6:01 am. Now for hour, you're also going to have the option to do either 1 to 12 or 1 to 24, I usually use a 12-hour clock so I'm going to do that using am.

Before we start, I am going to comment out the previous code, I would like you to write everything from scratch. I am going to make a new variable date by calling moment with no arguments, and we're also going to go ahead and call format inside console.log so we can print that formatted value to the screen, date.format:

```
var date = moment();
console.log(date.format(''))
```

Inside the quotes, we're going to provide our pattern and start with the unpadded hour and the padded minute. We can grab both of those patterns by heading over to the docs, going back to **Display**, and taking a peek. If we scroll next, the first one we're going to run into is **Hour** and we have quite a few options:

Hour	H	0 1 ... 22 23
	HH	00 01 ... 22 23
	h	1 2 ... 11 12
	hh	01 02 ... 11 12
	k	1 2 ... 23 24
	kk	01 02 ... 23 24
Minute	m	0 1 ... 58 59
	mm	00 01 ... 58 59

We have 24-hour options, we have 1 through 12; what we want is lowercase **h** which is 1 through 12 unpadded. The padded version, which is **hh**, exists right next that is not what we want for this one. We're going to kick things off by adding an **h**:

```
var date = moment();
console.log(date.format('h'));
```

I'm also going to save the file, check it out in the Terminal:

```
[nodemon] starting `node playground/time.js`
4
[nodemon] clean exit - waiting for changes before restart
```

We have 4, which looks great. Next up is that padded minute, we're going to go ahead and find that pattern just next. For minute we have a lot fewer options, either padded or unpadded, we want to use **mm**. Now before I add **mm**, I am going to add a colon. This is going to get passed through in plain text, meaning it's not going to get changed. We're going to add our two lowercase **m**s:

```
console.log(date.format('h:mm'));
```

We can then save `time.js` and make sure the correct thing prints in the Terminal, and it does, `4:22` shows up:

```
[nodemon] starting `node playground/time.js`
4:22
[nodemon] clean exit - waiting for changes before restart
```

Next up is going to be grabbing that lowercase am and pm values. We can find that pattern over inside Google Chrome just previous to **Hour**:

AM/PM	A	AM PM
	a	am pm

Here we can either use uppercase **A** for uppercase AM and PM, or lowercase **a** for the lowercase version. I'm going to go ahead and use a lowercase a after a space to use that lowercase version:

```
var date = moment();
console.log(date.format('h:mm a'))
```

I can save the file and over inside the Terminal, I do indeed have `4:24` printing to the screen, and we have the pm after it:

```
[nodemon] starting `node playground/time.js`
4:24 pm
[nodemon] clean exit - waiting for changes before restart
```

Everything looks great. That is it for this section! In the next one, we're going to actually integrate Moment into our server and our client rather than just having it in a `playground` file.

Printing message timestamps

In this section, you're going to be formatting your timestamps, and you're going to be displaying them to the screen along with the chat message. Currently, we show who it's from and the text, but the `createdAt` timestamp is not used anywhere.

Now the first thing we need to figure out is how we can take that timestamp and get a Moment object back, because at the end of the day we want to call the `format` method to format it as we like. In order to do that, all you have to do is take your timestamp. We'll make a variable called `createdAt` to represent that value, and pass it in as the first argument to `moment`, which means I simply pass in `createdAt`, just like this:

```
var createdAt = 1234;
var date = moment(createdAt);
```

When I do this, we're creating a moment with the same methods like format, add, and subtract, but it's representing a different point in time. By default, it uses the current time. If you pass in a timestamp, it uses that time. Now this number, `1234`, is barely a second past the Unix epoch, but if we go ahead and run the file, we should see the correct thing printing. Using the `nodemon` command, in the `playground` folder, we're going to run `time.js`, and we get `5:30 am` as shown in the following screenshot:

```
[nodemon] starting `node playground/time.js`
5:30 am
[nodemon] clean exit - waiting for changes before restart
```

This would be expected since it's taking into account our local timezone.

Getting the formatted values back from timestamps

Now that we have this in place, we have everything we need to actually take those timestamps and get back formatted values. The other thing we can do is we can create timestamps with Moment, it has the exact same effect as the `new Date().getTime` method we've used.

In order to do this, all we do is we call `moment.valueOf`. For example, we can make a variable called `someTimestamp`, setting it equal to a call to `moment`. We're going to generate a new moment and we're going to call its `valueOf` method.

This is going to go ahead and return a timestamp in milliseconds since the Unix epoch, `console.log`. We're going to log out the `someTimestamp` variable just to make sure it looks correct, and here we have our timestamp value:

```
var someTimestamp = moment().valueOf();
console.log(someTimestamp);
```

Updating the message.js file

The first thing we're going to do is tweak our `message.js` file. Currently inside `message.js`, we generate timestamps using `new Date().getTime`. We're going to switch over to Moment, not because it changes anything, I just want to be consistent with using Moment everywhere we use time. This is going to make it a lot easier to maintain and figure out what's going on. At the top of the `message.js`, I'm going to make a variable called `moment` setting it equal to `require('moment')`:

```
var moment = require('moment');

var generateMessage = (from, text) => {
  return {
    from,
    text,
    createAt: new Date().getTime()
  };
};
```

And we're going to go ahead and replace the `createdAt` property with calls to `valueOf`. What I would like you to do is go ahead and do just that, call `moment`, call the `valueOf` method in `generateMessage` and in `generateLocationMessage`, and then go ahead and run the test suite and make sure both tests pass.

The first thing we need to do is tweak the `createdAt` property for `generateMessage`. We're going to call `moment`, call `valueOf` getting back the timestamp, and we're going to do the same thing for `generateLocationMessage`:

```
var moment = require('moment');

var generateMessage = (from, text) => {
  return {
    from,
    text,
    createdAt: moment().valueOf()
  };
};
```

```
var generateLocationMessage = (from, latitude, longitude) => {
  return {
    from,
    url: `https://www.google.com/maps?q=${latitude},${longitude}`,
    createdAt: moment().valueOf()
  }
};
```

Now we can go ahead and save `message.js`. Head over into the Terminal and run our test suite using the following command:

```
npm test
```

We get two tests and they both still pass, which means the value we're getting back is indeed a number as our tests assert:

```
Gary:node-chat-app Gary$ npm test

> chat-app@1.0.0 test /Users/Gary/Desktop/node-chat-app
> mocha server/**/*.test.js


  generateMessage
    ✓ should generate correct message object

  generateLocationMessage
    ✓ should generate correct location object


  2 passing (26ms)
```

Now that we have Moment integrated on the server, we're going to go ahead and do the same thing on the client.

Integrating Moment on client

The first thing we need to do is load in Moment. Currently, the only library we load in on the frontend is jQuery. We can do this a few different ways; I'm going to go ahead and actually grab a file out of the `node_modules` folder. We've installed Moment, version 2.15.1, and we can actually grab the file we need for the frontend, which is sitting inside the `node_modules` folder.

We're going to go into `node_modules`, we have a really long list of alphabetical folders, I'm looking for the one called `moment`. We're going to go into `moment` and grab `moment.js`. I'm going to right-click to copy it, then I'm going to scroll up to the very top, close `node_modules`, and I'm going to paste it right inside of our `js | libs` directory. We now have `moment.js` and if you open it, it's a really long library file. There's no need to make any changes to that file, all we have to do is load in `index.js`. Just next to our jQuery import, we're going to add a brand new `script` tag, we'll then provide that `src` attribute setting it equal to `/js/js/moment.js`, just like this:

```
<script src="/socket.io/socket.io.js"></script>
<script src="/js/libs/jquery-3.1.0.min.js"></script>
<script src="/js/libs/moment.js"></script>
<script src="/js/index.js"></script>
```

Now that we have this in place, we have access to all those Moment functions only on the client side, which means that over inside `index.js` we can properly format the timestamp that comes back inside the message. Now before we make any changes, let's go ahead and start up our server using the following command:

nodemon server/server.js

We can go ahead and move into the browser, going to `localhost:3000` and giving it a refresh, and our app is working as expected. If I open up the **Developer Tools**, inside the **Console** tab we can actually use Moment. We have it accessible via moment just like we did over inside Node. I can use moment, calling `format:moment().format()`.

We get back our string:

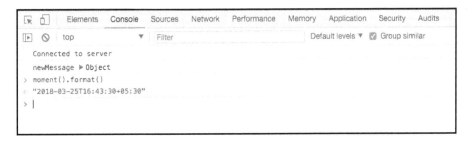

You should be able to make this call if you've successfully imported Moment. If you are seeing this, then you are ready to move on to the actual updating of `index.js`.

Updating the newMessage property

If you remember, on message we have a `createdAt` property for both `newMessage` and `newLocationMessage`. All we need to do is get that value, pass it in to `moment`, and then generate our formatted string.

We can make a new variable called `formattedTime`, and we can set this equal to a call to `moment` passing in the timestamp, `message.createdAt`:

```
socket.on('newMessage', function (message) {
    var formattedTime = moment(message.createAt)
```

Now we can go ahead and do whatever we like. We could call format passing in the exact same string we use over in `time.js`, the hour, the minutes and the am/pm; `h:`, two lowercase `m`s, followed by a space and a lowercase `a`:

```
var formattedTime = moment(message.createdAt).format('h:mm a');
```

With this in place we now have that formatted time and we can go ahead and add it inside `li.text`. Now I know I'm using template strings inside of our client-side code. We'll be removing this pretty soon so there's no need to make that tweak yet since I'm not testing in Internet Explorer or any other browser, although the final version of the app will not include template strings. Right after the `from` statement, we're going to go ahead and inject another value, the `formattedTime` which we just created previous. So our message should read name like Admin, the time followed by the text:

```
socket.on('newMessage', function (message) {
    var formattedTime = moment(message.createAt).format('h:mm a');
    var li = jQuery('<li></li>');
    li.text('${message.from} ${formattedTime}: ${message.text}');
```

I'm going to go ahead and save `index.js`, and give the browser a refresh to load that client-side code:

As shown in the preceding screenshot, we see **Admin 4:49 pm: Welcome to the chat app,** and that is the correct time. I can go ahead and send a message, `This is from a user,` send it off, and we can see it's now **4:50 pm**:

This is from a user shows up, everything is working great.

Updating the newLocationMessage property

Now for **Send Location**, we currently don't use Moment; we only updated the `newMessage` event listener. This means that when we print that location message, we don't have the timestamp. We're going to modify `newLocationMessage`, you can go ahead and use the same techniques we used previously to get the job done. Now in terms of where to actually render the formatted time, you can simply put it in `li.text` just like we did earlier in case of `newMessage` property.

Step one in the process is going to be to make that variable called `formattedTime`. We can actually go ahead and copy the following line:

```
var formattedTime = moment(message.createdAt).format('h:mm a');
```

And pasting it right above the `var li = jQuery('<li></li>');` line like this:

```
socket.on('newLocationMessage', function(message) {
    var formattedTime = moment(message.createAt).format('h:mm a');
```

We want to do the exact same thing, we want to take that `createdAt` field, get a moment object, and call `format`.

Next up, we do have to modify what gets displayed, show this `formattedTime` variable, and put it right in the `li.text` statement:

```
socket.on('newLocationMessage', function(message) {
    var formattedTime = moment(message.createAt).format('h:mm a');
    var li = jquery('<li></li>');
    var a = jQuery('<a target="_blank">My current location</a>');

    li.text(`${message.from} ${formattedTime}: `);
```

Now we can go ahead and refresh the app, and we should see our timestamp for regular messages. We can send off a regular message and everything still works:

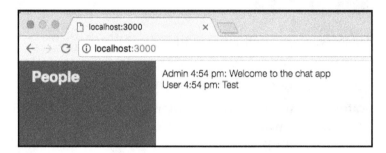

Then we can send off a location message, which we just changed. It should take just a second to get going and we have our current location link. We have our name and we have the timestamp, which is fantastic:

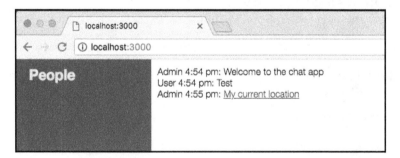

That is it for this section. Let's go ahead and actually make a commit to save our changes.

Even though we're not quite done with the message area, we have all the data correctly showing up. It's just showing up in a way that's not really pleasing to the eye. For now though, we will head into the Terminal and shut down the server. I'm going to run `git status`, and we have new files as well as some modified files:

```
Changes not staged for commit:
  (use "git add <file>..." to update what will be committed)
  (use "git checkout -- <file>..." to discard changes in working directory)

        modified:   .DS_Store
        modified:   package-lock.json
        modified:   package.json
        modified:   public/.DS_Store
        modified:   public/index.html
        modified:   public/js/index.js
        modified:   server/.DS_Store
        modified:   server/utils/message.js

Untracked files:
  (use "git add <file>..." to include in what will be committed)

        playground/
        public/js/libs/moment.js

no changes added to commit (use "git add" and/or "git commit -a")
```

Then, `git add .` is going to take care of all of that. Then we can make our commit, `git commit` with the -m flag, and a good message for this one is Format with an timestamps using momentjs:

```
git commit -m 'Format timestamp using momentjs'
```

I am going to go ahead and push this up to GitHub using the `git push` command, and we are done.

In the next section, we'll talk about a templating engine Mustache.js.

Mustache.js

Now that we have our timestamps rendering correctly to the screen. We're going to go ahead and talk about a templating engine called **Mustache.js**. This is going to make it much easier to define some markup and render it multiple times. In our case, our messages are going to have the same set of elements in order to render properly. We're going to have a header tag for the user's name, we're going to add the text into a paragraph, all that sort of stuff.

Now instead of doing that inside `index.js`, like we currently are, we're going to create some templates, some markup in `index.html`, and we're going to render those, which means we're not going to need to manually create and manipulate these elements. This can be a huge burden.

Adding mustache.js to the directory

Now in order to get started before we actually create any templates or render them, we do need to download the library. We can get this by going to Google Chrome and Googling `mustache.js`, and we're looking for the GitHub repository, which in this case happens to be the first link. You can also go to `mustache.github.io` and click on the JavaScript link to get to the same location:

Now once you're here, we do want to grab a specific version of the library. We can go to the **Branch** drop-down and switch from **Branches** to **Tags**. This is going to show us all the versions that were released; the version I'm going to be using here is the most recent one **2.3.0**. I'm going to grab that, it's going to refresh the repository next, and we're looking for a file called `mustache.js`. This is the library file we're going to need to download and add in to `index.html`:

I can click on **Raw** to grab the raw JavaScript file, and I can go ahead and save it into the project by right-clicking and clicking on **Save As...**. I'm going to go into the project on the desktop, the `public | js | libs` directory, and right there we're going to add the file.

Now once you have the file in place, we can kick things off by importing it inside `index.html`. Near the bottom, we currently have `script` tags for `jquery` and `moment`. This one is going to look pretty similar. It's going to be a `script` tag, then we'll add that `src` attribute so we can load in the new file, `/js/libs`, and finally it's `/mustache.js`:

```
<script src="/js/libs/moment.js"></script>
<script src="/js/libs/mustache.js"></script>
```

Now with this in place, we can go ahead and create a template and render it.

Creating and rendering template for newMessage

Creating a template and rendering it, is going to give you a pretty good idea about exactly what Mustache can do, then we'll go ahead and actually wire it up with our `newMessage` and `newLocationMessage` callbacks. To kick things off over inside `index.html` we are going to make a new template by defining a `script` tag just next the `chat__footer` div.

Now inside of the `script` tag, we're going to add our markup, but before we can do that we have to provide a couple of attributes on `script`. First up this is going to be a reusable template and we're going to need a way to access it, so we'll give it an `id`, I'm going to call this one `message-template`, and the other property we're going to define is something called the `type`. The `type` property lets your editor and the browser know what's stored inside the `script` tag. We're going to set the type equal to, inside quotes, `text/template`:

```
<script id = "message-template" type="text/template">

</script>
```

Now we can write some markup and it's going to work as expected. To kick things off let's just go ahead and make a really simple paragraph tag. We're going to make a p tag inside of the `script` tag, and we'll add some text inside of it, `This is a template`, and we're going to go ahead and close the paragraph tag, and that is it, this is where we're going to start:

```
<script id="message-template" type="text/template">
  <p>This is a template</p>
</script>
```

We have a message-template `script` tag. We can go ahead and now render this over inside `index.js` by commenting out all the code inside the `newMessage` listener. I'm going to comment out all of that code and now we can implement the Mustache.js rendering method.

Implementing the Mustache.js rendering method

First up, we have to grab the template, make a variable called `template` to do just this, and all we're going to do is select it with `jQuery` using the ID we just provided, `#message-template`. Now we need to call the `html` method, which is going to return the markup inside `message-template`, which is the template code, our paragraph tag in this case:

```
socket.on('newMessage', function (message) {
    var template = jquery('#message-template').html();
```

Once we have that we can go ahead and actually call a method on Mustache, which was available to us because we added that `script` tag. Let's make a variable called `html`; this is the thing we're eventually going to add it to the browser and we're going to set it equal to a call to `Mustache.render`.

Now `Mustache.render` takes the `template` you want to render:

```
socket.on('newMessage', function (message) {
  var template = jquery('#message-template').html();
  var html = Mustache.render(template);
```

We're going to go ahead and render it and now we can spit it out in the browser by adding it to the `messages` ID just like we do earlier. We're going to select the element with an ID of messages, call `append`, and append the template we just rendered which we have access to inside of HTML:

```
socket.on('newMessage', function (message) {
  var template = jQuery('#message-template').html();
  var html = Mustache.render(template);

  jQuery('#messages').append(html);
```

Now with this in place our server restarted and we can actually play around with this by refreshing the browser. I'm going to give the browser a refresh:

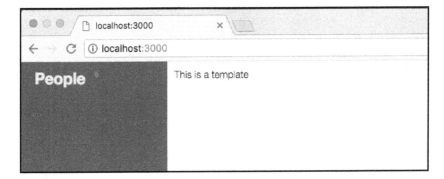

We get **This is a template** for our welcome message, and if I type anything else we also get **This is a template**. Not super interesting, not super useful, what is cool though is that Mustache lets you inject values, which means we can set up places in our template where we expect a value to get passed in.

For example, we have that `text` property. In order to reference a value, you can use the double curly braces syntax like this:

```
<script id="message-template" type="text/template">
  <p>{{text}}</p>
</script>
```

Then you can go ahead and type the name, like `text`. Now in order to actually provide this value, we have to send in a second argument to the render method. Instead of just passing in the template, we're going to pass in the template and an object:

```
socket.on('newMessage', function (message) {
    var template = jquery('#message-template').html();
    var html = Mustache.render(template, {

    });
```

This object is going to have all the properties that you're going to be allowed to render. Now we're currently expecting the `text` property, so we should probably go ahead and provide it. I'm going to set `text` equal to the value that comes back on `message.text`:

```
var html = Mustache.render(template, {
    text: message.text
});
```

Now we're rendering the template in a dynamic way. The template serves as the reusable structure but the data is always going to change because it gets passed in when we call render:

With this in place we can go ahead and refresh Chrome, and right here we see **Welcome to the chat app**, and if I go ahead and type a message, that is going to show to the screen, which is fantastic:

Getting all the data showing up

Now the next step in the process is going to be to get all the data showing, we have a `from` property and a `createdAt` property too. We actually have access to that `createdAt` property via `formattedTime`.

We're going to go ahead and uncomment the `formattedTime` line, and this is the only one we're actually going to carry over to the new system. I'm going to add it up inside `newMessage` callback:

```
socket.on('newMessage', function (message) {
  var formattedTime = moment(message.createAt).format('h:mm a');
  var template = jQuery('#message-template').html();
  var html = Mustache.render(template, {

  });
```

Because we do still want to use `formattedTime` when we render. Now before we do anything else with the template, let's go ahead and simply pass in the values. We already passed the `text` value in. Next up, we can pass in `from`, it's accessible via `message.from`, and we can also pass in a timestamp. You can call that property whatever you like, I'm going to continue to call it `createdAt` and set it equal to the `formattedTime`:

```
var html = Mustache.render(template, {
  text: message.text,
  from: message.from,
  createdAt: formattedTime
});
```

Providing a custom structure

Now with this in place all the data is indeed getting passed in. We just need to actually go ahead and use it. In `index.html` we can use all of it, and we're also going to provide a custom structure. Just like we did when we set up the code previously, we're going to be using some classes I've defined inside the template for this project.

Adding the list item tag

We're going to start off with a list item using the `li` tag. We're going to go ahead and add a class, and we're going to call this class `message`. In there, we can add two `div`s. The first `div` is going to be the title area where we add the `from` and `createdAt` values, and the second `div` is going to be the body of the message:

```
<script id="message-template" type="text/template">
  <li class="message">
    <div></div>
    <div></div>
  </li>
</script>
```

Now for the first `div` we are going to provide a class, the class will equal `message__title`. This is where the message title information is going to go. We're going to kick things off in here by providing an `h4` tag, which is going to render a nice header to the screen, and all we're going to put inside `h4` is the `from` data, which we can do by using those double curly braces, `{{from}}`:

```
<script id="message-template" type="text/template">
  <li class="message">
    <div class="message__title">
      <h4>{{from}}</h4>
    </div>
```

The same exact thing holds true for `span`, that's going to happen next. We'll add a `span` tag, and inside the `span` tag, we're going to inject `createdAt`, adding our double curly braces, and specifying the property name:

```
<script id="message-template" type="text/template">
  <li class="message">
    <div class="message__title">
      <h4>{{from}}</h4>
      <span>{{createAt}}</span>
    </div>
```

Adding the message body tag

Now we can go ahead and move on to the actual message body itself. That's going to happen next inside our second `div`, which we will be giving a class. The second `div` is going to have a class equal to `message__body`, and for a basic message, a non location-based message. All we're going to do is add a paragraph tag, and we're going to render our text inside by providing it two curly braces followed by `text`:

```
<script id="message-template" type="text/template">
  <li class="message">
    <div class="message__title">
      <h4>{{from}}</h4>
      <span>{{createdAt}}</span>
    </div>
    <div class="message__body">
      <p>{{text}}</p>
    </div>
  </li>
</script>
```

With this in place we actually have a really great system for rendering our message template. The code, the markup, it's defined over inside `message-template`, which means that it's reusable and inside `index.js`. We just have a little bit of code to get everything wired up. This is a much more scalable solution, and it's a lot easier than managing the elements like we did next for `newLocationMessage`. I'm going to go ahead and save `index.js`, move into the browser, and give things a refresh.

When we do we can see we now have a nice set of styles for the message, `This is some message`. I'm going to send that off; we get the name, the timestamp, and the text all printing. It looks a lot better than it did earlier:

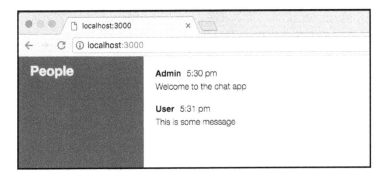

Creating template for the newLocation message

Now our send location message is still going to look like trash. If I click on **Send Location**, it's going to take a few seconds to get the job done and here it is! It's unstyled because it is not using a template. What we're going to do is add a template for the `newLocationMessage`. We're going to set up the markup for the template, and then we'll be to render it and pass in the necessary values.

Over inside `index.html` we can get started doing this by creating a second template. Now the second template is going to be pretty similar to the first. We can actually go ahead and duplicate this template by copying and pasting it next. All we need to do is change the `id` attribute from `message-template` to `location-message-template`:

```
<script id="location-message-template" type="text/template">
  <li class="message">
    <div class="message__title">
    <h4>{{from}}</h4>
    <span>{{createAt}}</span>
  </div>
```

```
        <div class="message__body">
          <p>{{text}}</p>
        </div>
      </li>
    </script>
```

Now the title area is going to be the same. We're going to have our `from` property as well as `createdAt`; it's the body that's going to change.

Instead of rendering a paragraph with the text. We're going to render a paragraph that has the link using an anchor tag. Now to add that anchor tag, we're going to add the a tag. Then inside the `href` attribute, we're going to be injecting the value. This is going to be the URL that gets passed from server to client. We're going to add our equal signs, our curly braces, and the value we want to add is `url`:

```
    <div class="message__body">
      <p>
        <a href="{{url}}"
      </p>
    </div>
```

Next up, we are going to carry over that `target` property, setting an equal to _blank, which will open up the link in a new tab. And finally, we can go ahead and close the anchor tag, adding the text for the link inside. Some good text for this link would be My current location, just like we have right now:

```
    <script id="location-message-template" type="text/template">
      <li class="message">
        <div class="message__title">
          <h4>{{from}}</h4>
          <span>{{createdAt}}</span>
        </div>
        <div class="message__body">
          <p>
            <a href="{{url}}" target="_blank">My current location</a>
          </p>
        </div>
      </li>
    </script>
```

This is all we need to do for the template. Next, we are going to wire up all of this inside of `index.js`, which means inside `newLocationMessage`, you want to do something pretty similar to what we have previous in `newMessage`. Instead of rendering everything with jQuery, you're going to render the template, passing in the necessary data, text, URL, and the formatted timestamp.

Rendering the newLocation template

The first thing we're going to do is comment out the code we no longer need; that's everything but the variable `formattedTime`:

```
socket.on('newLocationMessage', function (message) {
  var formattedTime = moment(message.createAt).format('h:mm a');
  // var li = jQuery('<li></li>');
  // var a = jQuery('<a target="_blank">My current location</a>');
  //
  // li.text(`${message.from} ${formattedTime}: `);
  // a.attr('href', message.url);
  // li.append(a);
  // jQuery('#message').append(li);
});
```

Next up we're going to go ahead and grab the template from the HTML by making a variable called `template`, and we're going to use `jQuery` to select it by ID. Right inside the quotes, we'll add our selector. We want to select by ID so we'll add that. `#location-message-template` is the ID we provided, and now we want to go ahead and call `html` to get its inner HTML back:

```
socket.on('newLocationMessage', function (message) {
  var formattedTime = moment(message.createAt).format('h:mm a');
  var template = jQuery('#location-message-template').html();
```

Next up, we're going to go ahead and actually render the template by creating a variable called `html` to store the return value. We're going to call `mustache.render`. This takes those two arguments, the template you want to render and data you want to render into that template. Now the data is optional, but we do indeed need to pass some data through so we will be providing that as well. `template` is our first argument and the second one is going to be an object:

```
socket.on('newLocationMessage', function (message) {
  var formattedTime = moment(message.createAt).format('h:mm a');
  var template = jQuery('#location-message-template').html();
  var html = Mustache.render(template, {

  });
```

I'm going to start by setting `from` equal to `message.from`, and we can do the same thing with `url`, setting it equal to `message.url`. For `createdAt`, we're going to use the `formattedTime` variable instead, `createdAt` gets set equal to `formattedTime`, which is defined in case of `newMessage` template:

```
socket.on('newLocationMessage', function (message) {
  var formattedTime = moment(message.createAt).format('h:mm a');
  var template = jQuery('#location-message-template').html();
  var html = Mustache.render(template, {
    from: message.from,
    url: message.url,
    createdAt: formattedTime
  });
```

Now that we have access to the HTML we need to render. We can use a jQuery selector to select the element with an ID of messages, and we're going to call append to add a new message. The new message we want to add is available via the `html` variable:

```
socket.on('newLocationMessage', function(message) {
  var formattedTime = moment(message.createdAt).format('h:mm a');
  var template = jQuery('#location-message-template').html();
  var html = Mustache.render(template, {
    from: message.from,
    url: message.url,
    createdAt: formattedTime
  });
  jQuery('#messages').append(html);
});
```

Now that we have our function completely converted over. We can remove the old commented out code, save the file, and test things out over inside Chrome. I'm going to give the page a refresh to load that latest code, I'll send a text message to make sure that still works, and now we can go ahead and send a location message. We should see in just a second the new data rendering and it is indeed working as expected:

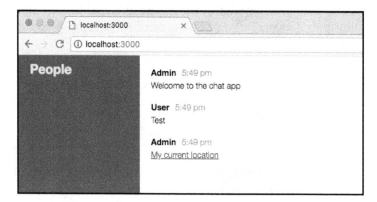

We have the name, the timestamp, and the link. I can go ahead and click on the link to make sure it is still working.

With this in place we now have a much better setup for creating these frontend templates. Instead of having to do the heavy lifting inside `index.js`, we can do the template inside of `index.html`, simply passing the data in, it's a much more scalable solution.

Now that we have this in place we are done, and we can go ahead and commit our changes by shutting down the server and running `git status`. We have a new file as well as a couple of modified ones, `git add .` is going to take care of all of that for us, and we can make our commits, `git commit` with the `-am` flag. Actually, we already added it so we can just use the `-m` flag, `Add mustache.js for message templates`:

```
git commit -m 'Add mustache.js for message templates'
```

I'm going to push this up to GitHub and we can go ahead and take a quick moment to deploy to Heroku too using `git push heroku master`. I'm going to push this up just to make sure all the templates are rendering properly on Heroku just like they are locally. It should take just a second to deploy. Once it's up, we can open it up by either running `heroku open` or grabbing that URL as we've done before. Here it's launching the app:

```
remote: -----> Pruning devDependencies
remote:        Skipping because npm 5.5.1 sometimes fails when running 'npm prune' due to a known issue
remote:        https://github.com/npm/npm/issues/19356
remote:
remote:        You can silence this warning by updating to at least npm 5.7.1 in your package.json
remote:        https://devcenter.heroku.com/articles/nodejs-support#specifying-an-npm-version
remote:
remote: -----> Build succeeded!
remote: -----> Discovering process types
remote:        Procfile declares types      -> (none)
remote:        Default types for buildpack -> web
remote:
remote: -----> Compressing...
remote:        Done: 24.9M
remote: -----> Launching...
remote:        Released v7
remote:        https://rocky-sierra-37964.herokuapp.com/ deployed to Heroku
remote:
remote: Verifying deploy... done.
To https://git.heroku.com/rocky-sierra-37964.git
   df657f9..de0a811  master -> master
```

It looks like everything did go as expected. I'm going to grab the app URL, move into Chrome, and open it up:

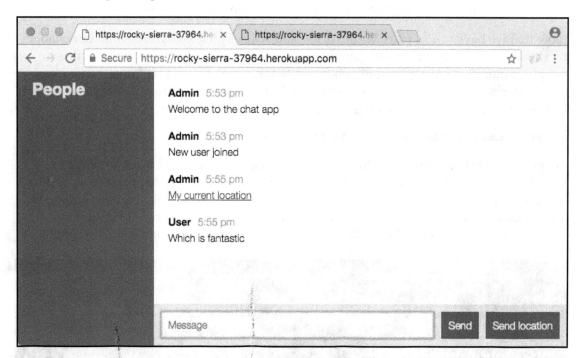

And now we're viewing our application live inside of Heroku, and the message data is showing up as expected. The same thing should hold true for sending the location, the send location message should use the new setup, and it is indeed working as expected.

Autoscrolling

If we're going to build a frontend we might as well do it right. In this section, we're going to add an autoscrolling feature. So if a new message comes in, it is visible inside of the messages panel. Now right away this is not a problem. I type an a, I hit *enter*, and it shows up. However, as we get further down the list, you'll see the messages start to disappear down the bottom of the bar:

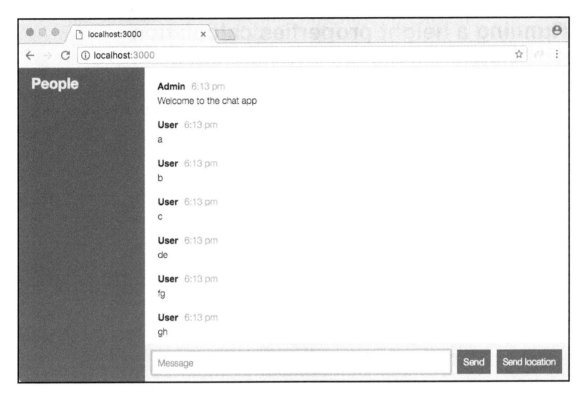

Now I can indeed scroll down to see the most recent messages, but it would be nice if I'm automatically scrolled to the most recent message. So if a new message comes in like 123, I'm automatically brought to the bottom.

Now, obviously, if someone does scroll up to read an old message, we're going to want to keep them there; we're not going to want to scroll them to the bottom, that would be just as annoying as not being able to see the new messages in the first place. This means that we're going to go ahead and calculate a threshold. If someone can see that last message, we're going to go ahead and scroll them to the bottom when a new message comes in. If I'm previous that message, we're going to go ahead and leave them alone, there's no reason to scroll them to the bottom if they're digging through the archives.

Running a height properties calculation

Now in order to do that we are going to have to run a calculation, grabbing a few properties, mostly the height properties, of various things. Now to talk about those height properties and figure out exactly how we're going to run this calculation, I've put together a really short section. Let's go ahead and dive right in. To illustrate exactly how we're going to run this calculation, let's take a look at the following example:

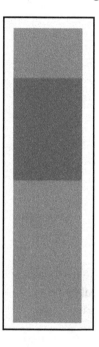

We have this light purple box, it's taller than the dark purple one. This is the entire messages container. It's probably going to contain way more messages than we can actually see in the browser. The dark purple area is what we actually see. As we scroll down the dark purple area is going to move down to the bottom, and as we scroll up it's going to shift up to the top.

Now we have access to three height properties that are going to let us make the calculations necessary to determine whether or not we should scroll down a user. These are the following:

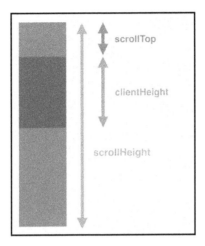

- First up `scrollHeight`. This is the entire height of our messages container regardless of how much is actually visible inside of the browser. This means that if we have messages before and after what we can see. They are still going to be accounted for in `scrollHeight`.
- Next up, we have `clientHeight`. This is the visible height container.
- Finally, we have `scrollTop`. This is the number of pixels we've scrolled down into the purple container.

Now in the current situation what do we want to do? We want to do nothing, the user really isn't scrolled that far down. It would be a burden to them if they got brought to the bottom every time a new message came in.

In the next scenario we scroll down just a little bit more:

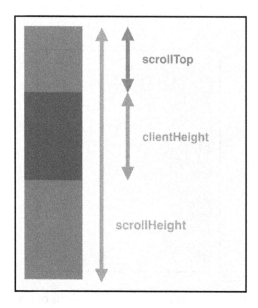

The `scrollTop` has increased, the `clientHeight` has stayed the same, and so has the `scrollHeight`. Now if we keep going down the list, eventually we're going to get to the very bottom. Currently, we should do nothing, but when we get to the bottom the calculations look a little different:

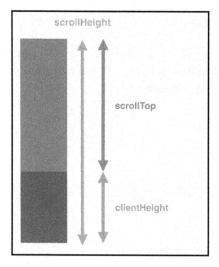

Here you can see the `scrollTop` value, which is the space previous what we can see, plus the `clientHeight` value is identical to `scrollHeight`. This is going to be the basics of our equation. If the `scrollTop` plus the `clientHeight` equals the `scrollHeight`, we do want to scroll the user down when a new message comes in, because we know they're at the very bottom of the panel. So in this situation what should we do? We should scroll to the bottom when a new message comes in. Now there is one slight little quirk:

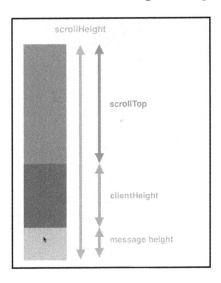

We are going to have that message already added so we're going to take into account the new `messageHeight` in our calculation, adding up `scrollTop`, `clientHeight`, and `messageHeight`, comparing that value to the `scrollHeight`. Using this we will once again be able to scroll the user to the bottom.

Let's go ahead and wire this up in Atom. Now that we know how we're going to run that calculation, let's go ahead and actually do it over inside `index.js`. We're going to make a new function that's going to do all this heavy lifting for us. It's going to determine whether or not we should scroll the user to the bottom depending on their position. Let's make a function inside at the top `index.js`. It's not going to take any arguments and we're going to go ahead and call this function `scrollToBottom`:

```
var socket = io();

function scrollToBottom () {

}
```

We're going to call `scrollToBottom` every time we add a new message to the chat area, which means we need to do it twice once inside of `newMessage` and `newLocationMessage`. Right inside the `newLocationMessage` callback, I can call `scrollToBottom` passing in no arguments:

```
socket.on('newMessage', function (message) {
  var formattedTime = moment(message.createAt).format('h:mm a');
  var template = jQuery('#message-template').html();
  var html = Mustache.render(template, {
    text: message.text,
    from: message.from,
    createdAt: formattedTime
  });

  jQuery('#message').append(html);
  scrollToBottom();
});
```

I'll do the same thing next when we append `scrollToBottom`:

```
socket.on('newLocationMessage', function (message) {
  var formattedTime = moment(message.createAt).format('h:mm a');
  var template = jQuery('#message-template').html();
  var html = Mustache.render(template, {
    from: message.from,
    url: message.url,
    createdAt: formattedTime
  });

  jQuery('#message').append(html);
  scrollToBottom();
});
```

Now all we need to do is wire up this function to:

- Determine if we should scroll them to the bottom, and
- Scroll them to the bottom if it's necessary.

Creating a new variable to scroll messages to the bottom

To get started, we are going to select the messages container creating a new variable to store that in. We're going to actually be creating quite a few variables to run our calculation, so I'm going to add two comments, `Selectors` and `Heights`. This is going to help us just break up the long list of variables.

We can make a variable, we'll call this variable `messages`, and we're going to set `messages` equal to a `jQuery` selector call. We're going to select all elements with an ID equal to `messages`, which is just our one:

```
function scrollToBottom () {
  // Selectors
  var message = jQuery('#message');
```

Now that we have messages in place we can focus on getting those heights. We are going to go ahead and fetch `clientHeight`, `scrollHeight`, and `scrollTop`. First up, we can make a variable called `clientHeight` setting that equal to `messages`, and then we're going to call a `prop` method, which gives us a cross-browser way to fetch a property. This is a jQuery alternative to doing it without jQuery. This makes sure it works across all browsers regardless of what they call the `prop`. We're going to go ahead and provide, inside quotes, `clientHeight` to fetch that `clientHeight` prop:

```
function scrollToBottom () {
  // Selectors
  var message = jQuery('#message');
  // Heights
  var clientHeight = message.prop('clientHeight');
}
```

We're going to do the exact same thing two more times for the other two values. `scrollTop` is going to get set equal to `messages.prop` fetching the prop `scrollTop`, and last but not least `scrollHeight`. A new variable called `scrollHeight` will store that value and we're going to set it equal to `messages.prop`, passing in the prop we want to fetch `scrollHeight`:

```
function scrollToBottom() {
  //selectors
  var messages = jQuery('#messages');
  //Heights
  var clientHeight = messages.prop('clientHeight');
  var scrollTop = messages.prop('scrollTop');
  var scrollHeight = messages.prop('scrollHeight');
```

```
   }
```

Now that we have this in place we can get started with our calculation.

Determining the calculation

We want to figure out if the `scrollTop` plus the `clientHeight` is greater than or equal to the `scrollHeight`. If it is, then we want to go ahead and scroll the user to the bottom because we know they're already near the bottom, if (clientHeight + scrollTop is >= scrollHeight):

```
var scrollHeight = message.prop('scrollHeight');

if (clientHeight + scrollTop >= scrollHeight) {

}
```

Now if this is the case then, we are going to go ahead and do something. For now, we'll just use `console.log` to print a little message to the screen. We'll just print Should scroll:

```
if (clientHeight + scrollTop >= scrollHeight) {
  console.log('Should scroll');
}
```

Now our calculation is not quite complete, since we are running this function. After we append the new message, we do need to take that into account also. As we saw over inside Atom, if we can see that last message, we do want to scroll them to the bottom; if I'm further up the list we won't scroll them. But if I'm pretty close to the bottom, a few pixels up previous, we should scroll them to the bottom because that's most likely what they want.

Taking into account the height of new message

In order to get this done, we have to take into account the height of that new message and the height of the previous message. Inside Atom, we're going to go ahead and get that done, by first up adding a selector.

We're going to make a variable called newMessage, and this is going to store the selector for the last list item, the one that was just added before the call to scroll to bottom. I'm going to use jQuery to get this done, but instead of creating a new selector, we can actually build off of our previous one, messages, and we're going to call its children method:

```
function scrollToBottom () {
  // Selectors
```

```
var message = jQuery('#message');
var newMessage = message.children();
```

This lets you write a selector specific to the children of the message, which means that we have all our list items so we could select our list items in another context, maybe we want to select all the children that are paragraphs. In our case, though, we're going to select the list items that are the last child using this last-child modifier:

```
var newMessage = messages.children('li:last-child');
```

Now we have just one item, the last list item in the list, and we can go ahead and get its height by making a variable called newMessageHeight, just next to the scrollHeight variable. We're going to set that equal to newMessage, and we're going to call its innerHeight method:

```
var scrollHeight = messages.prop('scrollHeight');
var newMessageHeight = newMessage.innerHeight();
```

This is going to calculate the height of the message taking into account the padding that we've also applied via CSS.

Now we need to take into account the height of the second-to-last message as well. To do that, we're going to create a variable lastMessageHeight, and we'll set it equal to newMessage, and we're going to call the prev method. This moves us to the previous child, so if we were at the last list item we are now at the second-to-last list item, and we can get its height by once again calling innerHeight:

```
var newMessageHeight = newMessage.innerHeight();
var lastMessageHeight = newMessage.prev().innerHeight();
```

Now we can account for both of these values inside our if statement as well. We're going to add them up, newMessageHeight, and we're also going to add lastMessageHeight taking that into account as we make our calculation:

```
function scrollToBottom() {
  //selectors
  var messages = jQuery('#messages');
  //Heights
  var clientHeight = messages.prop('clientHeight');
  var scrollTop = messages.prop('scrollTop');
  var scrollHeight = messages.prop('scrollHeight');
  var newMessageHeight = newMessage.innerHeight();
  var lastMessageHeight = newMessage.prev().innerHeight();
  if(clientHeight + scrollTop + newMessageHeight + lastMessageHeight >=
scrollHeight) {
```

```
        console.log('Should scroll');
    }
  }
```

Now that our calculation is complete we can actually test out that things are working as expected. We should see `Should scroll` when we should scroll.

Testing the calculations

Over inside the browser, I'm going to go ahead and give things a refresh, and I'm also going to open up the **Developer Tools** so we can view our `console.log` statement. You'll notice on smaller screens the styles remove the sidebar. Now I'm going to hit *enter* a few times. Obviously, we shouldn't be able to send empty messages but we can for the moment, and you can see that `Should scroll` is printing:

It's not actually going to scroll because the height of our messages container doesn't actually exceed the height of the browser space given to it, but it does indeed pass the condition. Now as we get down further and messages start to drop off the bottom of the screen, you'll notice the count in front of the message stops going up. The count incremented every time **Should scroll** printed, but now it stays at 2 even though I'm adding new messages further.

In this case, we can scroll back down to the bottom and add a new message, abc. This should cause the browser to scroll, we're kind of near the bottom. When I do it **Should scroll** increments to 3, which is fantastic.

If I scroll up to the top of the list and type 123 and hit *enter,* **Should scroll** does not increment to 4, which would be correct. We do not want to scroll a user to the bottom if they're up at the very top.

Scrolling a user when necessary

Now the only thing left to do is actually scroll a user when necessary. That's going to happen over inside our if statement, we can remove our console.log('Should scroll') call and we're going to replace it with a call to messages.scrollTop, which is the jQuery method for setting that scrollTop value, and we're going to set it to the scrollHeight, which is the total height of the container. This means that we're going to be moving to the bottom of the messages area:

```
if(clientHeight + scrollTop + newMessageHeight + lastMessageHeight >=
scrollHeight) {
  messages.scrollTop(scrollHeight);
}
```

Over inside Google Chrome, we can now refresh the page to grab that latest index.js file, and I'm just going to hold the *enter* key for a little bit. As you can see we are scrolling down the list automatically. If I add a new message, it'll show up correctly.

If I'm up near the top and a new message comes in, like 123, I am not going to scroll down the list, which is correct. Now if I'm not quite at the bottom but I'm pretty close, and a new message comes in, I am scrolled to the bottom. But if I'm a little past that last message, we're not going to get scrolled to the bottom which is exactly what we wanted. This is all happening because of our calculations.

Committing the calculation-related changes

Let's wrap this up with a commit over inside the Terminal. If we run `git status`, you'll see we just have one changed file. I can use `git commit -am` to make a commit, `Scroll to bottom if user is close to bottom`:

```
git commit -am 'Scroll to bottom if user is close to bottom'
```

I'm going to go ahead and push that up to GitHub using the `git push` command, and this is considered a wrap on the first part of this project.

Summary

In this chapter, we looked into styling the basic chat application in the HTML format. We also discussed timestamps and formatting the page using the Moment method. After that, we went through the concept of the Mustache.js, creating and rendering templates for the messages. At last, we learned about autoscrolling and running calculations with message height properties. With this, we have a basic chat application in place.

In the next chapter, the goal is going to be to add chat rooms and names, so I go to a signup page. I enter the room, I'd like to join and the name I'd like to use. Then I get brought to a chat page, but only for that specific room. So if there are two rooms, users in room 1 are not going to be able to talk to users in room 2, and vice versa.

8
The Join Page and Passing Room Data

In the previous chapter, we looked into styling our chat page more like a real web application and less like an unstyled HTML page. In this chapter, we'll continue our discussion about the chat page and look into join page and passing room data. We are going to update our HTML file and add form-fields for the chat page.

We'll take the name and room values and pass them from the client to the server so the server can keep track of who's in which room and we can set up a private communication. We'll also create test cases for the validation of the data.

Adding a join page

The goal for this section is to add a join page like the one you see in the following screenshot, where you provide a name and you provide the room name you want to join.

You'll then be able to join a given room, talk to anybody else in that room and you won't be able to communicate with other people in other rooms:

This means that when you click on this form, you're going to click on **Join** and we're going to have some custom information passed into the URL into the chat application as we know it, the one that looks like this:

Updating the HTML file

Now in order to get that done, the first thing we're going to do is tweak the current HTML file. Right now, index.html is going to load first. We actually don't want that to be the case, when we go to localhost:3000 we want to show our new join page. So what I'm going to do instead is move this page by renaming it. We're going to rename index.html to chat.html. I'm going to do the exact same thing with index.js, renaming it to chat.js.

Last but not least, I'm going to update the reference in the script where we load in index.js; instead, we'll load in chat.js. Now that we have this in place; we no longer have an HTML page that's going to load when you visit the site. If I try to go to localhost:3000, we're going to get an error saying we cannot get that route, nothing's coming back from the server:

To fix this, we're going to create our brand new page as index.html. This is going to be the one that loads when a user visits the app. Now we'll start off with a very basic template specifying things we've done before like DOCTYPE, setting it equal to HTML5, and then we're going to add our html tag. Inside here, we can then add our head and body tags:

```
<!DOCTYPE html>
<html>
  <head>
  </head>
  <body>
  </body>
</html>
```

Adding the head tag in the HTML file

I'm going to add my head tag first, and then I can go ahead and add my body tag. We'll then kick things off by adding a few tags into the head such as meta, so we can set our charset, and it is going to have a value of utf-8. We're also going to set a few other properties:

```
<head>
  <meta charset="utf-8">

</head>
```

I'm going to set a title tag, this is going to show up inside of the tab as the tab's title, we can set ours to Join then we can add a space, a vertical line by using |, and the name of our app, something like ChatApp: This will show up any tab title. Then we can go ahead and link in our style sheet just like we did for chat.html. I'm going to grab that style sheet reference from chat.html, copy it into the head:

```
<head>
  <meta charset="utf-8">
  <title>Join | ChatApp</title>
  <link rel="stylesheet" href="/css/styles.css">
</head>
```

I'm going to add a title tag to chat.html. In chat.html we can specify title, just like we did over inside index.html. We can give this one a page of Chat, with a bar surrounded by spaces, and we're also going to give it the same app name, ChatApp:

```
<!DOCTYPE html>

<html>

<head>
  <meta charset="utf-8">
  <title>Chat | ChatApp</title>
  <link rel="stylesheet" href="/css/styles.css">
</head>
```

Now that we have this in place there is one more thing I want to do before we start updating body, this is set a viewport tag. The viewport tags let you specify certain things about how your site should be rendered. The viewport tag I'm about to add is going to make our website display much better on mobile. Instead of being really zoomed out, it's going to fit to the width of your phone, tablet, or any other device.

We're going to copy this tag from index.html to chat.html when we're done, but for now we'll kick things off by adding a meta tag.

This time around instead of specifying charset like we've done in the past, we're going to give it a name equal to viewport:

```
<head>
  <meta charset="utf-8">
  <title>Join | ChatApp</title>
  <meta name="viewport" content="">
  <link rel="stylesheet" href="/css/style.css">
</head>
```

Now we can go ahead and add a few options about what we want to do to that viewport. All of this is going to happen inside content. This is going to be a comma-separated list of key-value pairs, for example is width will be device-width. This tells your browser to use the device's width as the web page's width, and then we can add a comma, a space, and specify our next key-value pair. I'm going to use initial-scale and set that equal to 1. This is going to scale the website appropriately so it doesn't look all zoomed out, and finally user-scalable will be set equal to no:

```
<head>
  <meta charset="utf-8">
  <title>Join | ChatApp</title>
  <meta name="viewport" content="width=device-width, initial-scale=1, user-scalable=no">
  <link rel="stylesheet" href="/css/styles.css">
</head>
```

We have styles in place to make the text bigger and to make sure that a user can always see everything, so there's no reason to give users the ability to scale. Now as mentioned, we're going to take this meta tag, copy it to the clipboard, and add it for chat.html as well. Now that we have our head tags, set up for index.html we can move on to the body.

Adding the body tag in the HTML file

We're going to be using a similar set of classes designed to work with this page. To kick things off on, the body tags, we're going to add a class of centered-form:

```
<body class="centered-form">
</body>
</html>
```

This is going to center that form in the screen and give the entire website that blue background with the gradient. Next up, we can go ahead and provide the little box. This is going to be the centered white box that has our form in it. That's going to be via `div` and we're going to give this `div` a class. We're going to set that class equal to, inside quotes, `centered-form__form`:

```
<!DOCTYPE html>
<html>

<head>
  <meta charset="utf-8">
  <title>Join | ChatApp</title>
  <meta name="viewport" content="width=device-width, initial-scale=1, user-
scalable=no">
  <link rel="stylesheet" href="/css/styles.css">
</head>

<body class="centered-form">
  <div class="centered-form__form">
  </div>
</body>

</html>
```

Now that we have these two classes in place we are ready to move on actually adding some of the fields that are going to go in that white box, starting with that title, `Chat`.

Adding the form-fields for the chat page

To do this, we're going to create a few divs. They're all going to look identical so we'll make them once and duplicate them. We're going to add a class equal to `form-field`. Now we'll use this four times: title, name, room name, and button. In order to get that done, what we're going to do is simply copy the line and paste it four times:

```
<body class="centered-form">
  <div class="centered-form__form">
    <div class="form-field"></div>
    <div class="form-field"></div>
    <div class="form-field"></div>
    <div class="form-field"></div>
  </div>
```

Now all of this needs to go inside a `form` tag. The whole goal of this page is to take that data and submit it, redirecting the user to the chat page where we can then bring them into a specific chat room using the name they provided. That means we want to wrap these `form` fields inside a `form` tag, by opening it just above the `div` tags and closing it down below, just like this:

```
<body class="centered-form">
  <div class="centered-form__form">
    <form>
      <div class="form-field"></div>
      <div class="form-field"></div>
      <div class="form-field"></div>
      <div class="form-field"></div>
    </form>
  </div>
</body>
```

Now previously we saw the default behavior for a `form` tag is to reload the current page, posting the data as a query string. What we're going to do instead is specify an `action` attribute which, lets us customize which page to go to. In this case, we're going to go to `/chat.html`, the page that we set up just now. This means that when someone's done filling out the form field, they're going to get redirected to the `chat` page and the data down below will get passed along too.

Now the title `div` is easy, what we're going to do is add an `h3` tag with whatever title you want; you could say `Chat` or `Join a Chat`. And then, I can go ahead and close my `h3`:

```
<form action="/chat.html">
  <div class="form-field">
    <h3>Join a Chat</h3>
  </div>
```

Then, I can move on to the next form field which is going to be the display name. I am going to use a label, a label is going to describe a field, this one will be `Display name` so we'll open and close the `label` tag like this:

```
<div class="form-field">
  <label>Display name</label>
</div>
```

Next up, we can add an `input`. We're going to add an `input` just like we did for the `input` on our message `form`. We're going to specify `type` equal to `text`. We want the user to be able to enter some text. We're also going to give it a `name` equal to `name`. We are going to use `autofocus`; once again, this is going to make sure that when a user first visits the app, their cursor is placed inside the **Name** field:

```
<div class="form-field">
  <label>Display name</label>
  <input type="text" name="name" autofocus/>
</div>
```

Next up is the field for the room name, which is going to look pretty similar to the one above, we are going to start with `label` once again. This `label` is going to be a string, something like `Room name`, and we're also going to add an input so the user can specify the room name, `type="text"`, and the `name` will equal `room`:

```
<div class="form-field">
  <label>Room name</label>
  <input type="text" name="room"/>
</div>
```

There is no need for `autofocus` on this one since we already have an `autofocus` input in the preceding code.

Now that we have this in place, we can go ahead and fill out the final `form` field, which is going to be the **Submit** button for our form by simply creating the `button` tag, and giving it a text value. We can have ours set to `Join`:

```
<div class="form-field">
  <button>Join</button>
</div>
```

With this in place our `index.html` file is actually done. We can load it over inside the browser. Our server had automatically restarted, so a quick refresh should show our page **Join a Chat** app:

The goal is to set this up to take a name like Andrew, and a room name like Node Course Students:

You click **Join** and it joins you into this room with this name. Now currently, all it's going to do is redirect us to chat.html, but as you'll see it does indeed pass the data along:

Here we have `name` equal to `Andrew` and we have `room` name equal to `Node Course Students`, just like we specified over inside of `index.html`. With this in place, we are now ready to start talking about how we can join specific rooms inside `Socket.io`, making sure the events we emit only go to other people connected to that room. We have the stuff in place to get this done, so we're going to get started with all of that in the next section.

For now we have a pretty great-looking join page, this is where we can join a room. Let's wrap this up with a commit, committing our changes.

Committing the changes in index.html

If I run `git status` you're going to see that we have a modified file `index.html`, and it also thinks we deleted `index.js`, although we add something down below, when we run `git add .` and rerun `git status` it's going to understand exactly what happened:

```
Gary:node-chat-app Gary$ git add .
Gary:node-chat-app Gary$ git status
On branch master
Your branch is up-to-date with 'origin/master'.

Changes to be committed:
  (use "git reset HEAD <file>..." to unstage)

        copied:      public/index.html -> public/chat.html
        modified:    public/index.html
        renamed:     public/js/index.js -> public/js/chat.js
```

Here, you can see we copied `index.html` to `chat.html`, we then modified `index.html` and renamed `index.js` to `chat.js`, which is exactly what we did. I'm going to go ahead and actually make the commit using `git commit` with the `-m` flag, `Add join page that submits to chat.html`:

```
git commit -m 'Add join page that submits to chat.html'
```

We can then make the commit, push it up to GitHub, and that is it for this one.

Passing room data

In the last section, we created a little chat page. We can type in a name like `Andrew` and a room like `Node Course`, and we can go ahead and join that room:

Now when we do, we're brought to the chat page, but nothing is actually happening behind the scenes to use any of these values, they're showing up in the URL but that's about it. The goal in this section is to take these values and pass them from the client to the server so the server can keep track of who's in which room, and we can set up that private communication. Currently, if user one is in the Node course and user two is in the React course, both of them are going to be able to talk to each other because this data is not used.

Getting data to the server

Now the first step in getting this data to the server is figuring out where it lives; this actually lives in the `location` object. We're going to use the console to just play around with it.

The `location` is a global object that's provided by your browser, and on it we have a whole bunch of really interesting things like `host`, `hostname`, `href`, `origin`, and `pathname`. What we're going to be using is `search`.

As you can see in the following screenshot, `search` is the query string, everything from the question mark to the end of the word course, what I have highlighted here:

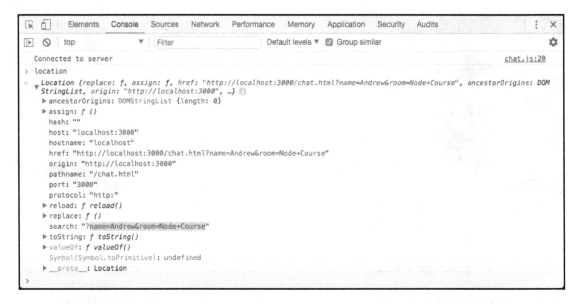

The goal is to get this into a more useful format. Right now we have just the string, we're going to need to parse this. We're actually going to use a library to do that now that we know where it lives. We can access `window.location.search` to get this value:

```
> window.location.search
< "?name=Andrew&room=Node+Course"
```

I'm adding window upfront the `location.search` just to make sure we're accessing the global location property as opposed to a local variable, which may or may not exist called location. This is going to be the most foolproof way to fetch the query string.

The params and deparams

Now the next thing we're going to do is talk about params and deparams. Inside jQuery, we actually have access to a function, we can access it by calling `jQuery.param`, and we can pass in an object. We'll set `name` equal to your first name, I'm going to set it equal to `Andrew`, and we'll set `age` equal to something like `25`. Now when I run this statement, jQuery is going to take that object and convert it into a set of parameters that could be added on to a URL:

```
> window.location.search
< "?name=Andrew&room=Node+Course"
> jQuery.param({name: 'Andrew', age: 25});
< "name=Andrew&age=25"
> |
```

Here you can see we have `name=Andrew` and `age=25`. This is similar to the format we had up in the URL, minus the question mark. All we'd have to do is add one at to the beginning and we would have a complete search string. Now the problem with jQuery is that it cannot do it in the other direction; meaning it cannot take the string and convert it back into an object, which is kind of what we want.

We want to be able to access this data easily, currently that is just not possible. There are also quirks like encoding and + characters. This was originally a space but it got converted to a + by the form. We're going to want to decode all of that too. Luckily, there is a simple library we can include and we can grab it by going to `links.mead.io/deparam`:

The `param` takes your object and returns the string, `deparam` takes the string, and returns an object. Here in the preceding screenshot, we have a simple Gist. It's a really short function that we're going to be adding to our project. Let's go to the **Raw** version of this page. We're going to save it using right-click, **Save as**, and we're going to add it right into a project. We have our `public`, `js`, and `libs` folder. Right in the `libs` folder, we'll simply save it as `deparam.js`:

Now once we have that file saved, we can actually include it. This is going to make it much easier to work with the search data. Inside Atom, I'm going to head over to `chat.html`. We're not going to need this in `index.html` but inside, `chat.html` we are going to load it in down below the `mustache.js` script. We'll make a new `script` tag, and we're going to go ahead and set the `src` equal to, inside quotes, `/js/libs/deparam.js`:

```
<script src="/socket.io/socket.io.js"></script>
<script src="/js/libs/jquery-3.3.1.min.js"></script>
<script src="/js/libs/moment.js"></script>
<script src="/js/libs/mustache.js"></script>
<script src="/js/libs/deparam.js"></script>
<script src="/js/chat.js"></script>
```

Now when we save `chat.html` and head back into the browser, we can actually refresh the page and play around with this in the console before ever adding it to our code. We now have access to `jQuery.deparam`. If I run this statement, we're going to get our function back, confirming that it does exist, and all we need to do is pass in the string, this is the search string, `window.location.search`:

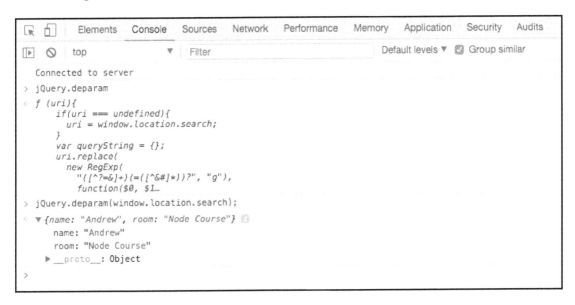

So we're taking that search string, passing it into `deparam`, and the resulting object is exactly what we want. We have a `name` property equal to `Andrew` and we have a `room` property equal to `Node Course`. All those special characters like the & symbol, the question mark, and the + character, have all been removed and replaced with this nicely formatted object. This is what we're going to use inside of our client-side code to get the values and pass them to the server, which is what we're going to do right now.

Inside Atom this is all going to happen in `chat.js`. In this file, we have our `connect` callback function. This happens when we first connect and right away when we connect, we're going to emit an event that's going to start the process of joining a room:

```
socket.on('connect', function () {
  console.log('Connected to server');
});
```

Now `Socket.io` has built-in support for the idea of rooms, creating the little isolated areas where only certain people can emit and listen to events. All of that gets set up on the server though, which means right in this function. When we connect to the server, all we're going to do is emit an event called join; this is going to start the process.

First up, let's go ahead and grab our parameters, the ones that we just learned how to `deparam` over inside the console, `var params = jQuery.deparam`, and we're going to pass in `window.location.search`, just like we did before in the **Developers Console**. Now we have our object and we can go ahead and emit an event. Next, we're going to call `socket.emit` and the event that we're going to emit will be a custom event we'll be creating, it's going to be called `join`:

```
socket.on('connect', function () {
  var params = jQuery.deparam(window.location.search);

  socket.emit('join')
});
```

This is going to get emitted from the client and it's going to get listened to by the server. When the server hears this `join` event, it's going to go through the process of setting up the room. Now not all of that's going to happen in this section, but we can get started. The data that we're going to send across is just going to be the `params` object:

```
socket.emit('join', params)
```

It may or may not include everything we need. We'll be doing a little validation on the server, and last but not least, we are going to set up acknowledgments for this one.

If someone does join the room we want to know that. We also want to if someone doesn't. This is because if they don't join the room, it's most likely because they provided invalid data, which means that we want to kick them back to that join form forcing them to provide both a name and a room name. We can go ahead and set up our `function`, and this `function` could take an argument. We're going to be setting it up ourselves, so we can decide if it takes an argument, and it definitely does make sense for it to take one. In this case, we're going to go ahead and provide any errors. If there is an error, that's fine we'll be able to handle it. If there is no error, that's great too; we'll go ahead and do something else:

```
socket.on('connect', function () {
  var params = jQuery.deparam(window.location.search);
  socket.emit('join', params, function (err) {
  });
});
```

In the function, we can do something if an error exists using `if (err)`. We can go ahead and add an `else` clause too; if there is no error we want to do a different thing:

```
socket.on('connect', function () {
  var params = jQuery.deparam(window.location.search);

  socket.emit('join', params, function (err) {
    if(err) {

    } else {

  });
});
```

Now we're not going to fill this out at the moment, what we're going to do at this point in time is go ahead and actually set up the listener inside `server.js` for join.

Setting up listener in server.js

That is going to happen over in `server.js`. We can make that the very first event just above `createMessage`, `socket.on('join')`:

```
socket.on('join');
```

Now as we already know we are going to be taking some arguments in the callback function. We're going to get our parameters. We can call these `params`, and get that `callback` function since we are setting up acknowledgments:

```
socket.on('join', (params, callback) => {

});
```

Inside the `join` function, the first thing that we want to do is actually validate the data that came through, both the name and the room. These are both potential properties on `params`. All we really care is that they are non-empty strings; meaning that it's not just a space, not just an empty string, and not a non-string type like a number or an object.

Defining the isRealString function

In order to set up this validation, which we're going to be doing in other places too like `createMessage`, we're going to create a separate `utils` file. In here, I'm going to call this `validation.js` and this is where we can put some validators that we're going to need throughout the project.

In this section we're going to create one called `isRealString`. This is going to verify that a value is of a type string and that it's not just a bunch of spaces; it actually has real characters inside it. We're going to set this equal to a function that takes a string. This is going to be the string we validate, and it's actually not going to be terribly difficult. We're going to `return` and we're going to `return` the following conditions. It'll return `true` if it is a real string and `false` if it's not. First up, we'll use `typeof`. This is going to get the type of the string variable, this needs to equal, in quotes, `string`:

```
var isRealString = (str) => {
   return typeof str === 'string';
};
```

Now currently, this is going to return `true` for any string and `false` for any non-string value, but it does not take into account the spaces. What we're going to do is use the `trim` method available on strings which takes a string like this:

```
' '
```

and converts it into a string like this, trimming all whitespace:

```
'     '
```

If you pass in a string like, this it's going to convert it into a string like this:

```
'  f  '
```

trimming leading and trailing whitespace only:

```
'f'
```

It's not going to trim any interior spacing, so if I have `f` space `r` like this:

```
'  f r  '
```

I am still going to get that space between `f` and `r`, but all of the leading and trailing spaces are removed:

```
'f r'
```

We're going to use that like this:

```
var isRealString = (str) => {
   return typeof str === 'string' && str.trim().length > 0;
};
```

After we call `trim`, we do need a length greater than 0, otherwise we have an empty string.

This is going to be our `isRealString` function, and we're going to go ahead and export it real quickly, `module.exports`, setting it equal to an object where we set `isRealString` equal to the `isRealString` function:

```
var isRealString = (str) => {
   return typeof str === 'string' && str.trim().length > 0;
};

module.exports = {isRealString};
```

Now I can go ahead and save this file. I'm also going to go ahead and inside `server.js` call the function.

Calling the isRealString function in server.js

We need to import the `isRealString` function first before we can actually validate those two properties. We can make a `const` just below the `generateMessage` constant and use ES6 destructuring to grab `isRealString`, and we're going to grab it using `require`. We require a local file `./`. It's in that `utils` directory and the file name is `validation`, just like this:

```
const {generateMessage, generateLocationMessage} =
require('./utils/message');
const {isRealString} = require('./utils/validation');
```

Now we can call `isRealString` inside `join`; that's exactly what we're going to do. We're going to check if either of them are not real strings. If one or more are not real strings, we're going to call the callback passing in the error. We'll add `if (params.name)` as the first one and pass that into `isRealString(params.name)`:

```
socket.on('join', (params, callback) => {
   if(isRealString(params.name))
});
```

Now we want to check if it's not a real string. So we're going to flip that, or (`||`), and then we're going to check if the other property, the room name, is not a real string. Now inside the query string, the room name property is called `room`. So if it's not `isRealString` passing in the correct value `params.room`, then that's going to be an error too:

```
socket.on('join', (params, callback) => {
   if(!isRealString(params.name) || !isRealString(params.room))
});
```

Next, we can handle that error by adding error handler function. For this, I'm going to do is call the `callback` with a little string message, `Name and room name are required`:

```
socket.on('join', (params, callback) => {
  if(!isRealString(params.name) || !isRealString(params.room)) {
    callback('Name and room name are required.');
  }
});
```

Now if that's not the case we do still want to call the `callback` but we don't want to pass any arguments in:

```
socket.on('join', (params, callback) => {
  if(!isRealString(params.name) || !isRealString(params.room)) {
    callback('Name and room name are required.');
  }

  callback();
});
```

Because remember that first argument we set that up to be the error argument in `chat.js`, and if both things are valid, we do not want to pass any errors back. Over inside `server.js`, we now have some pretty basic validation set up, and before we actually do anything in here, which is going to be in the upcoming section.

Adding error handler case in chat.js

We're going to do is add a few cases right here, in `chat.js`:

```
socket.on('connect', function () {
  var params = jQuery.deparam(window.location.search);

  socket.emit('join', params, function (err) {
    if(err) {

    } else {

    }
  });
});
```

If it is an error that's a pretty big problem, and we're going to want to send the user back to the root of the application by changing one of the properties under location, `window.location.href`. Here we can manipulate which page the user's on, essentially we're going to be redirecting them back to that root page by having the forward slash (/) value set to the `href` property:

```
socket.on('connect', function () {
  var params = jQuery.deparam(window.location.search);
  socket.emit('join', params, function (err) {
    if(err) {
      window.location.href = '/';
    } else {


    }
  });
});
```

Now before we do that we can do whatever we like, maybe we want to display a modal using our framework of choice, whether it's Foundation, Bootstrap, or anything else. To keep things simple here, all we're going to do is call `alert` passing in the error, just like this:

```
if(err) {
  alert(err);
    window.location.href = '/';
  } else {
```

So a user will see a little alert box, they'll then click on **OK**, and they'll be redirected back to the home page. Now if there is no error, all we're going to do for the moment is use `console.log` to print `No error`:

```
socket.on('connect', function () {
  var params = jQuery.deparam(window.location.search);

  socket.emit('join', params, function (err) {
    if(err) {
      alert(err);
      window.location.href = '/';
    } else {
      console.log('No error');
    }
  });
});
```

With this in place, let's go ahead and test that things are working as expected. Over inside the browser I'm going to give my current page a refresh. Now here, we do have a valid name and a valid room, so when I click on the Refresh button, we should see **No error** printing in the console, and that's exactly what we get:

The data that we passed through was indeed valid. Now we can go ahead and go to the root of the page and try some invalid data.

To demonstrate this, all I'm going to do is click on **Join** without providing either value. This is going to bring us to the chat app and you can see we get our little alert box, **Name and room name are required**. We click on **OK** which is all we can do, and we're immediately redirected back to **Join a Chat**:

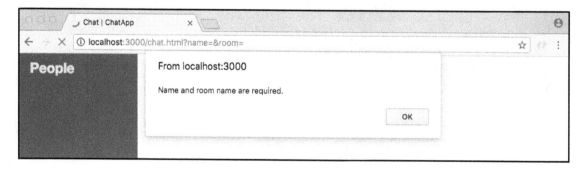

If I do provide some valid data, like a display name of `Mike` and a room name of `Developers`, we are going to be brought to the chat page and we'll see no error shows up, which is fantastic:

Now one last test real quick! If we have just spaces, I'm going to change the room name to a bunch of spaces. Now we click on **Join**, we are going to still get the error even though we do have a bunch of plus signs for spaces up above in the URL space:

Those are going to be swapped out for spaces when we run our code through `deparam` and the error is still going to occur. Now that we have this in place, we are in a pretty good spot to actually integrate rooms in the next section.

Adding test cases for the new validation function

The first thing to do would be to write some test cases for the brand new validation function we just created, which means we're going to make a new test file called `validation.test.js`.

Inside there, we're going to load in an expect making a variable called `expect`. We could also make it a constant. We're going to set that equal to `require` and we're going to require the `expect` library:

```
const expect = require('expect');
```

Next up, we're going to load in `RealString`, import `isRealString`, and we're going to add three test cases. The `describe` blocks should be something like `isRealString`, and the three test cases will be as follows:

- The first one, `should reject non-string` values, in this case I want you to pass a number object or anything else into the `isRealString` function, you should get false back.
- Next up, `should reject strings with only spaces`. If I have a string that's just a bunch of spaces that should not pass the `isRealString` function validation. That's also going to fail; trim is going to remove all of those spaces and the length will be 0.
- Last up, `should allow strings with non-space characters`. In this case you can pass in whatever you like, some sort of valid value. You could have space space LOTR for Lord of the Rings, the beginning spaces are going to get trimmed out so it's not important. You could add the letter a, any valid string is going to pass this one.

Go ahead and set up those three test cases, making sure the right Boolean value comes back from `isRealString`. When you're done run `npm test` from the Terminal, make sure all of your three tests passed.

The first thing we're going to do is import `isRealString` by making a variable. We can make this a constant or a variable, I'm going to go with a constant, and we're going to use ES6 destructuring to grab `isRealString`, and we're going to grab it off of the require call to our local file, `./validation`, which is just alongside the current file `validation.test.js`:

```
const expect = require('expect');

// import isRealString
const {isRealString} = require('./validation');
```

Now we can add the things we have down below starting with our `describe` block.

Test case 1 – should reject non-string values

We're going to `describe` the `isRealString` function. Then we can add our arrow function (`=>`), and inside there, we can go ahead and provide our individual test cases, `it`, and I'm going to copy it directly, `should reject non-string values`:

```
describe('isRealString', () => {
  it('should reject non-string values')
});
```

This is going to be a synchronous test, so there's no reason to add the `done` argument. Inside here, we're going to pass in a non-string value. I'll make a variable called response, which will store the return result from `isRealString`. We're going to call it passing in some sort of non-string value. Anything would work, I'm going to use a number, `98`:

```
describe('isRealString', () => {
  it('should reject non-string values', () => {
    var res = isRealString(98);
```

Now down below we can use expect to assert that the response variable equals false, which should be the case. We're expecting response `toBe(false)`:

```
describe('isRealString', () => {
  it('should reject non-string values', () => {
    var res = isRealString(98);
    expect(res).toBe(false);
  });
});
```

Test case 2 – should reject string with only spaces

Next up, `it('should reject string with only spaces')`. I'm going to copy that text exactly, pasting it inside of our `it` name. Then we can go ahead and add our arrow function (=>), and for this case what we're going to do is create a variable called response, passing in some sort of string with just spaces. We're still going to be calling `isRealString`, and we'll pass in a bunch of spaces. Now we're going to assert that response is `false`, `expect(res).toBe(false)`, which it should be because we do not have a valid string:

```
it('should reject string with only spaces', () => {
  var res = isRealString(' ');
  expect(res).toBe(false);
});
```

Test case 3 – should allow strings with non-space characters

Next up, last test case, `it ('should allow strings with non-space characters')`. I'm going to paste that in the `it` function and then we can actually set up the test case. You could have provided a bunch of different values as the argument to `isRealString`. We're still going to make that response variable. We're still going to call `isRealString`, but right here, I'm going to choose to pass in `(' Andrew ')`, which is valid. The `trim` function is going to remove those spaces in the validation process:

```
it('should allow string with non-space characters', () => {
  var res = isRealString('  Andrew  ');
});
```

Down below we can `expect` that response is true, `toBe(true)`. That's all you needed to do, we can go ahead and remove the comments since we have the actual code in place, and the last thing to do is run the test case to make sure our code actually works:

```
const expect = require('expect');

const {isRealString} = require('./validation');

describe('isRealString', () => {
  it('should reject non-string values', () => {
    var res = isRealString(98);
    expect(res).toBe(false);
  });

  it('should reject string with only spaces', () => {
    var res = isRealString('    ');
    expect(res).toBe(false);
```

```
  });

  it('should allow string with non-space characters', () => {
    var res = isRealString('D');
    expect(res).toBe(true);
  });
});
```

The `npm test` is going to get that done. This is going to run our test suite and right here we have our three test cases for `isRealString`, and all of them are passing, which is fantastic:

```
[Gary:node-chat-app Gary$ npm test

> chat-app@1.0.0 test /Users/Gary/Desktop/node-chat-app
> mocha server/**/*.test.js


  generateMessage
    ✓ should generate correct message object

  generateLocationMessage
    ✓ should generate correct location object

  isRealString
    ✓ should reject non-string values
    ✓ should reject string with only spaces
    ✓ should allow string with non-space characters


  5 passing (45ms)
```

Now as I mentioned you could pretty much pass anything in here. The letter n would work as a valid room name or username. If I rerun the test suite with D as my string, the test case still passes. It doesn't really matter what you passed into here as long as it had a real non-space character. Now that we have this in place we are done. We're not going to make a commit just yet we're kind of halfway through a feature, we'll commit once we have a little more in place.

Socket.io rooms

In the last section, we set up an event listener on the server listening for that join event, and we did some validation. This at least makes sure we have the `name` and the `room` name, both of which are going to be required.

The real next step is to actually use the `Socket.io` library to join rooms, and this is not going to let us just join rooms but it's also going to give us a different set of methods. We can choose to `emit` to everybody connected to the server or just to people in specific rooms, and that's exactly what we're going to be doing. We want to `emit` chat messages just to other people who are also in the `room`.

Now in order to join, what you do is you call `socket.join`. The `socket.join` takes a string `name`, and we have that `name` under `params.room`, just like we used in the previous section:

```
socket.on('join', (params, callback) => {
  if(!isRealString(params.name) || !isRealString(params.room)) {
    callback('Name and room name are required.');
  }

  socket.join(params.room);
  callback();
});
```

We now have a special place for people to talk who are in the same `room`. Now this is a string so it would be something like `The Office Fans`, or anything else, and you have to join by the string value. Right now, though, `params.room` will get the job done.

Now you can also choose to leave a room using `socket.leave`. The `socket.leave`, leaving the room by its name, `The Office Fans` for example, is going to kick you out of that group and you're not going to get those private messages, the messages sent specifically to the group. Now the next step in the process is to figure out how to actually take advantage of this:

```
socket.on('join', (params, callback) => {
  if(isRealString(params.name) || !isRealString(params.room)) {
    callback('Name and room name are required.');
  }
  socket.join(params.room);
  // socket.leave('The Office Fans');
  callback();
});
```

Targeting the specific user

Adding the user to the room is great, but if we can't target them specifically and others in that room, it's not very useful. Well it turns out we have a couple of ways to do just that. In order to illustrate how we're going to target specific users, let's look at all the ways we've emitted events on the server.

We've used `io.emit`. This emits it to every single connected user, and that's currently what we're doing for things like `createMessage`. A new message comes in and we emit it to everyone connected. Next up, we have used `socket.broadcast.emit`. We use that with `newMessage` and as we know this sends the message to everyone connected to the socket server except for the current user. The last one we used inside `server.js` is `socket.emit`. This emits an event specifically to one user. Now we can take these events and we can convert them over to their room counterpart. In order to send it to a specific room, we're going to be chaining on the to method.

This is going to look a little something like this. Let's say we want to emit an event to every single person connected to a room, and let's just call this room `The Office Fans` for the moment. To do that, we're going to call `io.to`. The `.to` is a method and it takes the room name exactly as it was provided in the call to join. In our case, that is going to be `The Office Fans`, just like this:

```
socket.join(params.room);
// socket.leave('The Office Fans');

// io.emit ->io.to('The Office Fans')
```

Then we would chain on a call to `emit`. This is going to send an event to everybody connected to a room, `The Office Fans`:

```
socket.join(params.room);
// socket.leave('The Office Fans');

// io.emit ->io.to('The Office Fans').emit
```

Now we can also do the same thing with broadcast, meaning that we want to send an event to everybody in a room except for the current user. In order to do that we would use `socket.broadcast.to`. This works just like the to the method defined previously, `The Office Fans` would get passed in, and on here we would call `emit`:

```
socket.join(params.room);
// socket.leave('The Office Fans');
// io.emit ->io.to('The Office Fans').emit
// socket.broadcast.emit -> socket.broadcast.to('The Office Fans')
```

This is going to send an event to everybody in `The Office Fans` room except for the current user, the one who's actually calling `socket.broadcast`.

Now the last way we've used `emit` is `socket.emit`. We're still going to use that when we want to send something to a specific user. There is no reason to target them by rooms since we just want to target them:

```
socket.join(params.room);
    // socket.leave('The Office Fans');
    // io.emit ->io.to('The Office Fans').emit
    // socket.broadcast.emit -> socket.broadcast.to('The Office Fans').emit
    // socket.emit
```

This are the two ways we're going to emit to specific rooms. Now in order to actually start wiring some of that up what we can do is take the following two calls and we can move them down inside `join`, meaning that we're not going to tell someone that someone joined a room until they've actually joined the room by calling `join`:

```
socket.emit('newMessage', generateMessage('Admin', 'Welcome to the chat app'));

socket.broadcast.emit('newMessage', generateMessage('Admin', 'New user joined'));
```

We're also not going to tell a user that they have joined a room until the call has actually gone through. It might not go through if the data, like the name or the room name, are invalid. Let's take both of these calls and cut them out, and we're just going to take them as they are and move them down into join. For the moment we can move them down below our comments; I'm going to leave the comments in place so you have these as a reference down the line. Now right below the `socket.join` line, we call `socket.emit` and we `emit` a new message, `Welcome to the chat app`:

```
socket.emit('newMessage', generateMessage('Admin', 'Welcome to the chat app'));
```

And this line it is actually going to stay the same, we still just want to target any specific user.

The next line is going to change though. Instead of broadcasting to every connected user, we're going to broadcast to just users inside the room we just joined, using `socket.broadcast.to`, passing in `params.room`. We're going to emit a new message and this is going to let everyone know that a new user has joined.

```
socket.broadcast.to(params.room).emit('newMessage',
generateMessage('Admin', 'New user joined'`));
```

Instead of new user, we can actually specify the name. We have access to that. Right here, I'm going to use a template string injecting the name first, `params.name`, followed by `has joined`:

```
socket.broadcast.to(params.room).emit('newMessage',
generateMessage('Admin', `${params.name} has joined.`));
```

Testing the specific user set up

Now that we have this in place we can actually test things out. What we're going to do is join a room, then we're going to have a second user join, and we should see the message right there: **Their name has joined**. We're also going to add a third user into the mix to make sure it's actually sending the message to just one room.

Over inside the browser, let's get started by creating a user called `User One`. This user is going to join a room called uppercase `A`:

Now we're going to go ahead and create a second user by going to `localhost:3000`. This one can be called `User Two` and we're going to join room `B`:

And if I go between room `A` and room `B` you can see that no join message printed because we haven't joined the same room. We're on completely separate rooms so we should not be getting those messages.

Next up we're going to add a third user, this user is also going to join room `A`, `User Three`, room name, room `A`, and we are going to hit **Join**. When we hit **Join**, we can go through the tabs and see what data we get back:

Here we get **Welcome to the chat** app as expected. This is only happening because we've successfully joined the room:

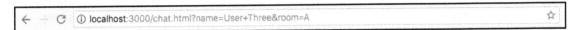

Then in the second tab we get **Welcome to the chat** app too. There is no message greeting that other user because the other user joined room A, and the first tab has our **User Three has joined** message. This is fantastic:

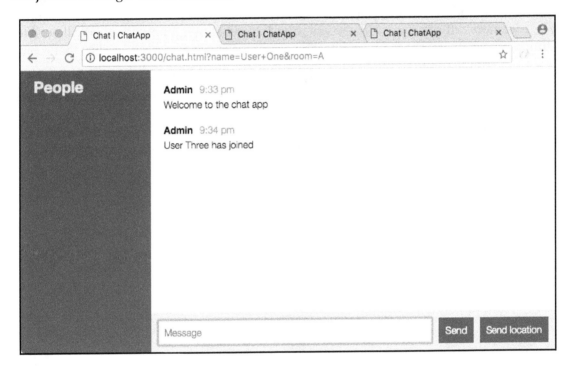

Both users are in room A so this user should get a message when a new user joins, and we've injected the name right here as expected.

Summary

In this chapter, we looked into adding a chat page. We'll built an HTML file and defined `head` and `body` tags as per our requirements. Then, we go ahead with passing the room data. We looked into the concept of `params` and `deparams` and created test cases for validating the data. In the last section, we discussed the `socket.io` rooms. We targeting a specific user for the chat room and tested the set up.

Things were relatively easy for our `join` event listener because we had access to both the name variable and the room variable. They were actually passed in as arguments. It's going to be a lot more difficult for `createMessage` and `createLocationMessage`. We'll need to figure out a way to get the room back for the given socket so we can `emit` to just that room.

We also need to set up that **People** list on the left-hand sidebar. We'll need to figure out how to use that `io` object to get a list of all the people by room and their names. All of that is going to be super important because currently the messages we `emit`, some message(s), for example, will show up to all users regardless of what room they're in. To get this working, to get those private rooms in place, we'll be persisting that data, which we are going to discuss in the next chapter.

9
ES7 classes

As we discussed in the last chapter, we have our socket `join` listener but the problem is that the information inside the listener. It gets lost once the callback is complete, things like the username and the room name, they are not persisted anywhere. We're going to need that information to complete our event listeners. `createMessage` is going to need to know the user's name as well as the room name to send that message to the specific room, and same is the case with `createLocationMessage`. We'll discuss that in this chapter.

We'll start with learning the ES6 class syntax and using it in creating `users` class and some other methods. We'll also see wiring up the users list, updating the people list when any user joins or leaves the chat. We'll also look into sending messages to a specific room and not to all the users.

Storing users with ES6 classes – Part I

We don't have access to the data (username and room name) that is inside `join`, but we do have access to one common thing, and that is the socket ID. We have access to the socket variable, `socket.id`, and we also have access to it inside our other event listeners. And this is going to be what we use inside of a data structure we're about to create. We're going to create an array of users where we can store this information, when we want to look up a user like we might want to do in `createMessage` and `createLocationMessage`. We'll simply pass the ID to some function, get back the name and the room name, and emit the event as we want.

Now in order to get that done, we are going to make a brand new file in `utils`. We're going to call this file `users.js`, and this is where we're going to store everything related to that user's data structure.

It's going to be an array of objects, and on each object, we're going to have the ID, which will be the socket ID, some sort of really long string:

```
[{
    id: '/#12hjwjhwfcydg',

}]
```

We'll also have our name. This is the display name for the user, mine might be `Andrew`; and finally the room the user joined, this could be something like `The Office Fans`:

```
[{
    id: '/#12hjwjhwfcydg',
    name: 'Andrew',
    room: 'The Office Fans'
}]
```

This is all the information we need to store in our data structure for a user to be able to wire everything up.

Now the real work is going to come inside the methods that we'll be creating to manipulate the array. We're going to have four methods:

- We want to be able to add a user via an `addUser` method; this is going to take three pieces of information, the ID, the name, and the room name.
- We're also going to want to have a method for removing a user when they leave a room; remember we want to update that **People** list in the left-hand sidebar in the chatroom. We're going to need a way to remove them as well as add them, `removeUser`, and we're going to be removing users by the socket ID.
- Next up, we're going to have a way to fetch a user, this is going to come in handy when we're trying to send a message like we do inside the `createMessage` listener. We're going to want access to the user's name as well as the room in order to fire off the `newMessage` event. That is going to happen via a `getUser` method, which is going to take an ID and it will return the object we have defined up above.
- The last one we're going to be adding is `getUserList`. The `getUserList` method is going to take the room name, figure out exactly which users are in that room, and return an array of names and will print those names to the client.

These four methods are all we need to get this done. Now there are a couple of ways we could do this. We might make an array called `users`, setting it equal to an empty array and then we might define our functions. We'll add `var addUser` and we'll set that equal to a function that takes `id`, `name` and `room`:

```
var users = [];

var addUser = (id, name, room) => {

}
```

Then inside the function, we'll do something like manipulate `users` array with `users.push`, pushing on some object. Then we'll export it using `modules.export`, exporting the `addUser` function as the `addUsers` property:

```
var users = [];

var addUser = (id, name, room) => {
  users.push({});
}

modules.export = {addUsers};
```

Then we would call `addUser` over in `server.js`. This approach works fine, but we're not going to be using this approach. Here, we have a `users` array and we can manipulate the array. It does get the job done but what we're going to do instead is use the ES6 class syntax. This is going to let us create a `users` class. We'll be able to make a new instance of that class and fire all of our methods, which we'll be defining.

I'm going to do this as opposed to creating ad hoc functions that all work with one piece of information. Now to get this done we are going to have to learn something new; we're going to be learning about ES6 classes.

The ES6 class syntax

In order to talk about ES6 classes, let's go ahead and simply create one. Now the syntax for creating a new class is going to look a little strange at first, it is unique to what we're about to do. But I promise that once you make one or two classes and add a few methods, you'll get really used to defining the methods and the classes themselves.

Creating the ES6 class for a person

To kick things off, we're going to create a simple class for a person. This means that we're making a set of data and a set of methods that are useful to manipulate Person. Now in order to get started, we are going to use the class keyword followed by the class name, Person. We're going to use an uppercase first letter for our class definition since we are going to be creating new instances of them with the new keyword. You do not need to use an uppercase P; this is just common convention across JavaScript. If a function is meant to be used with new, like new Person, new Object, or anything else, it should have an uppercase first letter; this is just a styling convention.

Now right after our name we can simply open and close some curly braces and there we have it:

```
class Person {

}
```

We have a brand new class and we can even make an instance of it. We can make a variable called me and set it equal to new Person calling it as a function just like this:

```
class Person {

}
var me = new Person();
```

Now we have a new instance of the class and we can do whatever we like with it. Currently, it doesn't do anything but we do have an instance created.

The constructor function

Now one of the first things about a class that's really great is the ability to add a constructor function. A constructor function is a special function, it is specific to the class, automatically fires, and lets you initialize the instance of your class. In this case, we want to do something to customize an individual person when a new Person is created.

To define a constructor function we start with the name, constructor, but instead of adding a colon or anything else, we simply go right to our function arguments and right into the curly braces:

```
class Person {
  constructor () {

  }
}
```

This is our function, it's just like a regular function. The code inside is going to get executed and the brackets are our arguments, but the syntax for setting it up does look pretty different than what we would do on an object or on anything else.

Now this constructor function gets called by default. You do not need to manually call it, and that actually gets called with the arguments that you specify right in Person, which means that we could have our Person constructor function take two arguments; maybe we want to initialize a new person with name and age. That means we would pass in name and age, I can say that name is a string, I'm going to set it as my name and age is a number like 25:

```
class Person {
    constructor (name, age){

    }
}

var me = new Person('Andrew', 25);
```

The constructor function is now going to get called with this data, and we can prove this by using console.log to print out the name, and as the second argument the age:

```
class Person {
  constructor (name, age){
    console.log(name, age);
  }
}

var me = new Person('Andrew', 25);
```

Now let's go ahead and run this file and see what we get; it's sitting in server/utils. I'm going to shut down nodemon and run it using following command:

node server/utiles/users.js

When I run the file, we get `Andrew 25` because the arguments were properly passed into the constructor:

```
[Gary:node-chat-app Gary$ node server/utils/users.js
Andrew 25
Gary:node-chat-app Gary$ █
```

Now passing data in really isn't useful, what we want to do is modify the specific instance. We want to set this person's name and age not the name and age for all people. In order to do that, we're going to use the `this` keyword. In class methods and in the constructor function, `this` refers to the instance as opposed to the class, which means we can set a property on this individual person, `this.name = name`, just like this:

```
class Person {
  constructor (name, age) {
    this.name = name;
  }
}
```

And we can do the exact same thing for age, `this.age = age`:

```
class Person {
  constructor (name, age) {
    this.name = name;
    this.age = age;
  }
}
```

Using this is how we customize the individual instance. Now what we have is an object, and we can actually access those properties. The `me` variable we defined is identical to the `this` variable, which means that we can actually access those properties. We'll add `console.log`, I'm going to print the string `this.name` for formatting only, and then I'm going to reference the actual `me.name` property. And we can do the exact same thing for age; we're going to print what we had put in as `this.age`, only we're going to access it via `me.age`:

```
var me = new Person('Andrew', 25);
  console.log('this.name', me.name);
  console.log('this.age', me.age);
```

We can now rerun the file using, `nodemon server/utils/users.js`, and we get exactly what we'd expect:

```
Gary:node-chat-app Gary$ nodemon server/utils/users.js
[nodemon] 1.14.10
[nodemon] to restart at any time, enter `rs`
[nodemon] watching: *.*
[nodemon] starting `node server/utils/users.js`
this.name Andrew
this.age 25
[nodemon] clean exit - waiting for changes before restart
```

The individual person was updated; `this.name` was set to `Andrew` and it is indeed showing. Now that we have a basic idea as to how we can initialize a class, let's go ahead and talk about methods.

The method function

Methods can be any function, they could take arguments, maybe they won't take arguments, and to define them all we do is the following. Without adding a comma, another quirk of the class syntax, we specify our method name. I'm going to create one called `getUserDescription`:

```
getUserDescription () {

}
```

This one is not going to take any arguments so we can leave that arguments list empty. Inside the function itself, we're going to go ahead and return a description, since the method after all is called `getUserDescription`. We're going to `return` a template string injecting some values inside there, the general flow is going to be `Jen is 1 year(s) old`:

```
getUserDescription () {
    return `Jen is 1 year(s) old`;
}
```

This is what we want to print, but we want to use those specific values for this individual person, and to do that we're going to access those properties once again. Instead a static name, we're going to inject `this.name`; and instead of a static age, we're going to inject the age, `this.age`:

```
getUserDescription () {
    return `${this.name} is ${this.age} year(s) old`;
}
```

Now we can go ahead and actually test out `getUserDescription` by calling it down below. We can make a variable called `description`, set it equal to `me.getUserDescription`, and can go ahead and do something with the return value, like print it to the screen using `console.log`. Inside the log argument list, I'm just going to pass in `description`:

```
class Person {
  constructor (name, age){
    this.name = name;
    this.age = age;
  }
  getUserDescription() {
    return `${this.name} is ${this.age} year(s) old`;
  }
}

var me = new Person('Andrew', 25);
var description = me.getUserDescription();
console.log(description);
```

Now we can save the file and we should see over inside the Terminal our `description`; in this case, `Andrew` and `25`, `Andrew is 25` years old. When I save the file `nodemon` is going to restart, and right here we get just that `Andrew is 25 year(s) old` printed to the screen:

```
[nodemon] starting `node server/utils/users.js`
Andrew is 25 year(s) old.
[nodemon] clean exit - waiting for changes before restart
```

This is the very basics of classes, there's a ton of class-related features we won't be exploring just yet, but for now this gives us everything we need in order to get started. Instead of a `Person` class, we're going to create a `users` class, and instead of methods like `getUserDescription`, we're going to create the custom methods. We're also going to be adding test cases as we go to make sure they work as expected.

Adding the users class

First, we're going to get started adding the `users` class and `then`. We'll finish it up adding all the methods. For now though, we can start defining the class, I am going to comment out the `Person` class we just added, since we do want it in place as documentation. But we're not going to exactly use it inside the app. We'll delete it a bit later once we are more comfortable with classes.

Now, we're going to start by creating our `users` class using the `class` keyword, `class Users`. We're then going to go ahead and open up and close our curly braces, and inside here we can specify any methods we like, such as the `constructor` function. We are going to define a `constructor` function, although they are completely optional when creating classes. We're going to set up our `constructor` function by name, then we'll have our arguments list followed by the opening and closing curly braces:

```
class Users {
  constructor () {
  }
}
```

Now the constructor function for users, unlike person, is not going to take any arguments. When we make a new `users` instance, we just want to start with an empty array of users. We're going to be making this new instance over inside `server.js` when we first start the app, that is going to happen up top of the code. And down below, we'll actually be using the methods when someone joins a room, leaves a room, or manipulates a room in whatever way they want. That means that all we need to do is set `this.users`, the `users` property, equal to an empty array:

```
class Users {
  constructor () {
    this.users = [];
  }
}
```

This is going to be the array we've defined at the top of the `users.js` file. The next thing we're going to do, now that we have our `constructor` function in place, is create the `addUser` method. We're going to create that just below the `constructor` function by defining it like we did for `getUserDescription`. We're going to set up the arguments list, this one is going to take some arguments we'll specify those in a moment, and we're going to open and close our curly braces for the actual function code:

```
class Users {
  constructor () {
    this.users = [];
  }
  addUser () {
  }
}
```

The three arguments we're going to require is `id`, `name`, and `room`. In order to add a user to the `users` array, we need those three pieces of information. Once we have them actually adding them to the list is going to be really easy.

I'm going to get started by creating a variable `user` so we can make an object to push on to the array. In `users`, we'll set an `id` property equal to the `id` argument, and we'll do the same thing for `name` and finally for `room`:

```
addUser (id, name, room) {
  var user = {id, name, room};
  }
}
```

Now we have a `user` object with those three properties we can go ahead and push it on the array, `this.users.push`, to add an object on to the end, and the thing we're going to be adding on to our array is the `user` variable:

```
addUser (id, name, room) {
  var user = {id, name, room};
  this.users.push(user);
}
```

Now that we have this in place, we are basically done. The last thing I'm going to do is go ahead and return the successfully created user, `return user just like this`:

```
addUser (id, name, room) {
  var user = {id, name, room};
  this.users.push(user);
  return user;
}
```

And there we go, `addUser` is complete. We're not going to wire it up just yet but we can add a test case for `addUser`.

Adding the test case for addUser

We'll add the test case over inside a brand new file called `users.test.js`. In here, we'll be able to load in users, test it, and do whatever else we might need to do. Now, the first step is going to be to actually export users.

Currently, inside the `user.js` file we have defined the class, but we do not export it. Exporting it is going to be the same as exporting anything else, there's nothing special there.

We'll add `module.exports`, and we're going to go ahead and export, inside of curly braces, an object where the users property equals the `Users` class definition we have, making sure to match the case:

```
addUser (id, name, room) {
    var user = {id, name, room};
    this.users.push(user);
    return user;
  }
}
module.exports = {Users};
```

Now that we have this in place, we can actually require our class and make new instances of it over inside the `users.test` file.

Adding new instances in the users.test file

Let's get started by loading in `expect`, `const expect = require('expect')`, and we can also go ahead and load in our users file, `const`. Using ES6 destructuring we're going to grab `Users`, and we're going to get that via the local file `./users`:

```
const expect = require('expect');

const {Users} = require('./users');
```

Now for the moment, we're just going to add a test case for adding a user. We'll make a quick `describe` block, most of the heavy lifting is going to happen later in the section. We'll `describe` our `Users` class, we can then add our arrow function and we can go ahead and add a test case, `it`, inside quotes, `should add new user`. I'm going to go ahead and set up the function for this one. It's going to be a synchronous function so there's no need for the `done` argument, and we can create a new instance of users, `var users`, equals a new `Users`:

```
describe('Users', () => {
  it('should add new user', ()=> {
    var users = new Users();
  });
});
```

Now since we don't take any arguments in the `constructor` function, we're not going to pass any in when we actually create our instance.

The next thing we're going to do is make a user, then we'll be passing its properties to addUser making sure the appropriate thing shows up in the end. Let's go ahead and make a variable user and we'll set that equal to an object:

```
it('should add new user', ()=> {
  var users = new Users();
  var user = {

  }
});
```

I'm going to go ahead and set on this object three properties, an id equal to something like 123, a name property equal to some name like Andrew, and you can go ahead and use your first name for example, Andrew, and a room name. I'm going to use The Office Fans:

```
describe('Users', () => {
  it('should add new user', ()=> {
    var users = new Users();
    var user = {
      id: '123',
      name: 'Andrew',
      room: 'The office fans'
    };
  });
});
```

Now we have the user in place and we can go ahead and call that method that we just created, the addUser method with the three necessary arguments, id, name, and room. I'm going to store the response in a variable called resUser, and we'll set it equal to users.addUser passing in those three pieces of information, user.id, user.name, and user.room as the third argument:

```
describe('Users', () => {
  it('should add new user', ()=> {
    var users = new Users();
    var user = {
      id: '123',
      name: 'Andrew',
      room: 'The office fans'
    };
    var resUser = users.addUser(user.id, user.name, user.room);
  });
});
```

With the call in place we can now start making our assertions.

Making the assertions for the users call

One assertion we want to make is that the actual `users` array was updated, it should have been updated when we called `this.users.push`. I'm going to expect that by calling `expect`. We're going to expect something about `users.users`: the first user refers to the `users` variable and the second one actually accesses the `users` array as defined in `users` file. Then we're going to call `toEqual`. Remember for arrays and objects, you have to use `toEqual` as opposed to `toBe`. We're going to `expect` it to be an array with just one item. The item should look just like the `user` object we have defined in the code:

```
var resUser = users.addUser(user.id, user.name, user.room);

expect(users.users).toEqual([user]);
```

If this passes, then we know our user was indeed added to the `users` array. I'm going to go ahead and save the file and shut down `nodemon`.

Running the addUser test case

I'm going to clear the Terminal output and run `npm test` to make sure our brand new test case is passing:

```
[Gary:node-chat-app Gary$ npm test

> chat-app@1.0.0 test /Users/Gary/Desktop/node-chat-app
> mocha server/**/*.test.js



  generateMessage
    ✓ should generate correct message object

  generateLocationMessage
    ✓ should generate correct location object

  Users
    ✓ should add new user

  isRealString
    ✓ should reject non-string values
    ✓ should reject string with only spaces
    ✓ should allow string with non-space characters


  6 passing (15ms)
```

When I run it, it does indeed pass. We have our `Users` block and `should add new user` is working as expected.

Adding the removeUser, getUser, and getUserList methods

Before we can integrate users into our application, let's go ahead and finish building it out. We have three more methods to add and test. The first one is `removeUser`, which is going to take an argument, the ID of the user you want to remove. This is also going to return the user that was just removed, so if I remove the user with an ID of 3, I want to get rid of it from the list but I do want to return the object.

We'll leave a little note about that, `return user that was removed`:

```
removeUser (id) {
  //return user that was removed
}
```

Now the next method that we're going to be filling out is `getUser`. The `getUser` method is going to take the exact same arguments as `removeUser`. We're going to find a user by ID returning the user object, but we're not going to be removing it from the array:

```
getUser (id) {

}
```

The final one that we're going to create, as specified up above, is a method called `getUserList`. This is going to get a list of all the users, just their names by the room name:

```
getUserList (room){
}
```

This means that we're going to iterate through the `users` array looking for all the users whose room matches the room specified. This is going to return an array, something like: `'Mike'`, `'Jen'`, `'Caleb'`, assuming those are the people inside of the room:

```
getUserList (room) {
  ['Mike', 'Jen', 'Caleb']
}
```

Now, notice here that we're not specifying the room or the ID property; we're just returning an array of strings.

Adding seed data for the test file

Now let's go ahead and add one thing to our test file. In order to get these methods to work, we're going to need seed data, we're going to need users that already exist otherwise we can't remove one or get one, and we definitely can't get a list of the rooms these non-existent users are in.

In order to fix that over inside user.test.js, we're going to add a beforeEach call, which we've used in the past. The beforeEach call, as we know, is going to get called before every single test case. It's going to help us initialize some data. Now the data we're going to initialize is going to be defined just above the beforeEach call, in a variable called users:

```
describe('Users', () => {
    var users;

    beforeEach(() => {

    });
```

The reason I'm defining it outside of beforeEach is so it's accessible inside of beforeEach and it's accessible inside of the test cases, we have defined down below.

Inside of beforeEach we're going to set users equal to new Users, and we're also going to set the users.users array. Here we can specify an array of objects, and this is going to let us add some initializing data:

```
beforeEach(() => {
    users = new Users();
    users.users = [{

    }]
});
```

Let's go ahead and provide three objects. The first one will have an `id` property equal to 2, we'll set the `name` property equal to something like `Mike`, and we can go ahead and set the `room` property equal to whatever we like, I'm going to go ahead and use a room name of `Node Course`:

```
var users;
beforeEach(() => {
  users = new Users();
  users.users = [{
    id: '1',
    name: 'Mike',
    room: 'Node Course'
  }]
});
```

We can take this object and copy it two more times. I'm going to add a comma, paste in what I just copied and do the same thing again, comma followed by a paste. I'm going to change it to an id of 2 for the second user, we'll change the name to something like `Jen` and we'll change the room name to `React Course`. Now for the last user, we are going to change `id` and `name`, we'll make `id` equals 3, and we'll make the name something like `Julie`, but we're going to leave the room as `Node Course` so we can test that our `getUserList` function does indeed return the correct results:

```
beforeEach(() => {
  users = new Users();
  users.users = [{
    id: '1',
    name: 'Mike',
    room: 'Node Course'
  },{
    id: '2',
    name: 'Jen',
    room: 'React Course'
  },{
    id: '3',
    name: 'Julie',
    room: 'Node Course'
  }]
});
```

The test cases aren't going to be required to use our `users` variable as defined here. We can still define a custom one as we defined in case of adding new user. If I run the `test-watch` script, `npm run test-watch`, we're going to see that our one test case is still passing:

```
> mocha server/**/*.test.js


  generateMessage
    ✓ should generate correct message object

  generateLocationMessage
    ✓ should generate correct location object

  Users
    ✓ should add new user

  isRealString
    ✓ should reject non-string values
    ✓ should reject string with only spaces
    ✓ should allow string with non-space characters


  6 passing (118ms)
```

I'm going to save the file to rerun the test suite, and right here we have 6 passing test cases. Regardless of whether or not we use this, we can still use a custom test case.

Now that we have this in place, we can go ahead and start filling out some of these methods. We're going to fill out `getUserList` together, and you're going to be responsible for `removeUser` and `getUser`.

Filling the getUserList

Now in order to fill out `getUserList`, we're going to start by finding all of the users whose room matches the `room` argument specified. In order to do that we're going to use the `filter` method on arrays, which we've used in the past. Let's make a variable, we'll call it `users` and we'll set it equal to `this.users`, which is the array of `users.filter`:

```
getUserList (room) {
  var users = this.users.filter((user) => {

  })
}
```

Now if you remember `filter` takes a function as its argument. This function gets called with each individual user. We can return `true` to keep this item in the array or we can return `false` to have it removed from the array. I'm going to go ahead and return `user.room`, and we're going to check if that equals, using three equal signs, the `room` argument:

```
getUserList (room) {
  var users = this.users.filter((user) => {
    return user.room === room;
  })
}
```

If they are equal, `user.room === room` is going to result in `true` that value will get returned; if they're not equal it's going to result in `false` and the user will not be added to the list above. Now we can go ahead and use the shortcut for our ES6 arrow function. Instead of adding the `return` keyword and specifying the actual arrow, we'll use the shorthand like this:

```
getUserList (room) {
  var users = this.users.filter((user) => user.room === room)
}
```

It's the exact same functionality just a different technique. Now we have a list of all the users who do match the criteria. The next step in the process is to take that array of objects and convert it to an array of strings. All we care about is getting that list of names. In order to do that, we're going to use map. I'm going to create a variable called `namesArray` and we're going to set this equal to `users.map`:

```
getUserList (room) {
  var users = this.users.filter((user) => user.room === room);
  var namesArray = users.map
}
```

Now we have used `map` in the past, as we know `map` also takes a function similar to `filter`. It also gets called with the individual item. In this case, an individual user, but `map` lets us return the value we want to use instead. So we're going to get an object, it is going to have the `id` property, the `room` property and the `name` property, and all we want is the `name` property, so we're going to return `user.name`. And we can simplify that even further using the shorthand for the arrow function. `user.name` is going to be implicitly returned:

```
var users = this.users.filter((user) => user.room === room);
var namesArray = users.map((user) => user.name);
```

Now that we have our `namesArray` array, all we need to do is go ahead and return it by returning `namesArray`:

```
getUserList (room){
  var users = this.users.filter((user) => user.room === room);
  var namesArray = users.map((user) => user.name);
  return namesArray;
}
```

Now this is going to get the job done, before we simplify it any further let's go ahead and write a test case to make sure it works.

Adding test case for getUserList

Inside `users.test.js` we can add the test case below our other test case, `it ('should return names for node course')`. We're going to write the case that returns all of the users inside the Node course, we should get the two users back, `Mike` and `Julie`. We'll make a variable, we'll call that variable `userList`, and what we're going to do is call the `users` variable defined already:

```
it('should return names for node course', () => {
  var userList = users
});
```

This is the one with our seed data. We do not need to create a custom one like we do for the other test case, `users.getUserList`. And we know `getUserList` takes one argument, the name of the room you want to fetch the list for, this one is called `Node Course`. Make sure your capitalization lines up. Then we can go ahead and add a semicolon at the end:

```
it('should return names for node course', () => {
  var userList = users.getUserList('Node Course');
});
```

The last thing to do is add our assertion, making sure that what we get back is what's expected. We'll `expect` that `userList` equals, using `toEqual`, the following array. It's going to be an array where the first item is `Mike` and the second item is `Julie`:

```
it('should return names for node course', () => {
  var userList = users.getUserList('Node Course');

  expect(userList).toEqual(['Mike', 'Julie']);
});
```

If that assertion passes, we know `getUserList` worked as expected because that's exactly what we have defined up above.

Now we can go ahead and copy this test case. Doing the exact same thing for the React Course should return names for `react` course, we'll change `Node` to `React` and we're going to go ahead and update what we `expect`. The React Course has just one user, that user has `name` equal to `Jen`:

```
it('should return names for react course', () => {
    var userList = users.getUserList('React Course');

    expect(userList).toEqual(['Jen']);
});
```

Now this is a pretty good test case. If we save `users.test.js` it's going to rerun the entire test suite. We should see we have our three tests under the `users` describe block, and they should all be passing, that is indeed the case:

```
> mocha server/**/*.test.js


  generateMessage
    ✓ should generate correct message object

  generateLocationMessage
    ✓ should generate correct location object

  Users
    ✓ should add new user
    ✓ should return names for node course
    ✓ should return names for react course

  isRealString
    ✓ should reject non-string values
    ✓ should reject string with only spaces
    ✓ should allow string with non-space characters


  8 passing (20ms)
```

The next two methods that we're going to be creating are `removeUser` and `getUser`. Let's go ahead and write the `it` statements for the test cases together, and you'll be responsible for actually filling out the method and filling out the test case:

```
it('should remove a user', () => {

});
```

This method is going to take the ID of one of our seed users, whether it's 1, 2 or 3. It's going to pass it to the function `removeUser`, and your job is going to be to assert that the user was indeed removed. Next up, `it('should not remove user')`:

```
it ('should not remove user', () => {

});
```

In this case, I want you to pass in an ID that is not part of our seed `user` array, that means something like 44, 128, or basically any string that's not 1, 2, or 3. In this case, you should be asserting that the array has not changed; we should still have those three items.

Now those are the two test cases for our `removeUser` method, next up is `getUser`. We're going to add two similar test cases. First up, `it('should find user')`, you should pass in a valid ID and you should get the user object back. And the other one is going to be `it('should not find user')`, just like `it('should not remove a user')`. Pass in an invalid ID and make sure you do not get a user object back.

Filling the getUser

I'm going to start off with `getUser`, the goal here is to return the user object whose ID matches the ID of argument passed in `getUser`. To get that done, I am going to be using `filter`. We're going to return the result from `this.users.filter`, we're going to be filtering by ID, and here we filter by room. We're going to pass in our arrow function using the expression syntax, the argument will be `user`, and we are going to go ahead and return `true` if the user's `id` property equals the ID of the argument. If that is the case, we do want to keep this `user` in the array. And in the end, we should have just one user or 0 users, and all we're going to do is return the first item:

```
getUser (id){
    return this.users.filter((user) => user.id === id) [0]
}
```

If there's one user in the array we're going to get its object back; if there's no users we're going to get undefined, which is exactly what we want. Now that we have `getUser` in place we can write the test case for that. We have two test cases, `it('should find user')` and `it('should not find user')`.

Test case – should find user

For it('should find user'), I'm going to get started by making a variable called
userId and I'm going to set this equal to the ID I want to use. I need a valid ID so I'm going
to go ahead and use 2. 1, 2, or 3 would have worked here:

```
it('should find user', () => {
    var userId = '2';
});
```

Next up I am going to go ahead and make a user variable, this is going to be the return
result from getUser. I'll set it equal to users.getUser, and we're going to try to fetch a
user whose ID is 2 by passing in userId:

```
it('should find user', () => {
    var userId = '2';
    var user = users.getUser(userId);
});
```

Now the next thing we're going to do is make an assertion about what we get back, we
should have gotten our object back and we can expect that user.id equals, using toBe,
and the ID, the userId variable:

```
it ('should find user', () => {
    var userId = '2';
    var user = users.getUser(userId);
    expect(user.id).toBe(userId);
});
```

I'm going to go ahead and save the test suite, and you can see all our test cases are still
passing, which is fantastic. If it does not equal the ID, maybe the ID is 3, you're going to see
the test case fail, and we do get a pretty clear error message:

```
11 passing (23ms)
1 failing

1) Users
      should find user:
    Error: Expected '2' to be '3'
    at assert (node_modules/expect/lib/assert.js:29:9)
    at Expectation.toBe (node_modules/expect/lib/Expectation.js:66:28)
    at Context.it (server/utils/users.test.js:48:21)
```

We get `Expected 2 to be 3`, which clearly is not the case. This is the final test case though and we can move on to `it('should not find user')`.

Test case – should not find user

In this case, we're going to follow a very similar format as in case of should find user, creating the `userId` variable and setting it equal to a user ID that does not exist inside of our built-in users; something like `99` would get the job done:

```
it('should not find user', () => {
    var userId = '99';
});
```

Next up, we'll be making a `user` variable, once again to store the return result from `getUser`, `users.getUser`, passing in our `userId`:

```
it('should not find user', () => {
    var userId = '99';
    var user = users.getUser(userId);
});
```

Now in this case, we would expect that undefined comes back, `filter` should return nothing and if you try to fetch the first item in an empty array, you're going to get undefined. We can prove that over in the Terminal by running `node`, and inside our little console we can create an empty array and we can access the first item:

```
>[][0]
```

We get back `undefined`. I'm going to shut that down, restart our test suite, and over inside `users.test.js` file we are going to go ahead and make our assertion. We're going to `expect(user).toNotExist`:

```
it ('should not find user', () => {
    var userId = '99';
    var user = users.getUser(userId);

    expect(user).toNotExist();
});
```

I'm going to save the file and all of our test cases should still be passing:

```
generateLocationMessage
    ✓ should generate correct location object

Users
    ✓ should add new user
    ✓ should remove a user
    ✓ should not remove user
    ✓ should find user
    ✓ should not find user
    ✓ should return names for node course
    ✓ should return names for react course

isRealString
    ✓ should reject non-string values
    ✓ should reject string with only spaces
    ✓ should allow string with non-space characters


12 passing (18ms)
```

That's great. Next up, we need to write the `removeUser` method and we also need to fill out the test cases.

Filling the removeUser method

Over inside `user.js`, we can get started by finding the user, if any. That means, we're going to use a similar technique to what we have in the `getUser` method. I'm going to actually copy the following line from the `getUser` method and paste it just right inside of `removeUser`:

```
return this.users.filter((user) => user.id === id) [0]
```

Creating a variable called `user`, setting it equal to the preceding line. Now you could also go ahead and actually call `getUser`. I could call `this.getUser`, passing in `id` just like this:

```
removeUser (id) {
    var user = this.getUser(id);
}
```

Both of those solutions are going to work as expected. Next up, if there is a user, we want to remove it, `if(user)`, we're going to do something special, and regardless of whether or not a user did exist, we are going to return the `user` value:

```
removeUser (id) {
    var user = this.getUser(id);
```

```
    if (user) {

    }

    return user;
}
```

If it didn't exist we're going to return undefined, which is great, if it did exist after we remove user, we'll be returning the object, also what we want. All we need to do is figure out how to remove it from the list.

To do this, I'm going to set `this.users` equal to `this.users`, and we're going to call `filter` finding all users whose ID does not match the one specified up above. We're going to call filter passing in our arrow function, we're going to get the individual `user`, and all we're going to do inside our arrow expression syntax is add `user.id` does not equal `id`:

```
if (user) {
    this.users = this.users.filter((user) => user.id !== id);
}
```

This is going to create a new array, setting it equal to `this.users`, and we're going to have the item removed, if any. If there was no item that's fine; this statement is never going to run and will be able to continue on returning undefined.

Now that we have this in place, we can go ahead and write a test case that makes sure it works as expected. I'm going to save `user.js` and right inside `users.test`, we're going to fill both `it` (`'should remove a user'`) and `it` (`'should not remove user'`) test cases. Let's get started with `should remove a user`.

Test case – should remove a user

I'm going to make a variable `userId` to store the ideal ID, which would be 1, 2 or 3, I'll go with 1, then we can go ahead and actually remove it storing the return result in a `user` variable. I'm going to call `users.removeUser` passing in my `userId` variable, which is 1:

```
it('should remove a user', () => {
  var userId = '1';
  var user = users.removeUser(userId);
});
```

Now that we have the potentially removed user we should be able to go ahead and assert some stuff. We're going to `expect` that the `user` object exists. We're also going to expect that its `id` equals the `id` we have up above, and `expect` that the user removed has an `id` property using `toBe(userId)`:

```
it('should remove a user', () => {
  var userId = '1';
  var user = users.removeUser(userId);

  expect(user.id).toBe(userId);
});
```

Next up, we're going to make sure that the user was removed from the array. We're going to `expect(users.users.length).toBe)` in this case 2:

```
it('should remove a user', () => {
  var userId = '1';
  var user = users.removeUser(userId);
  expect(user.id).toBe(userId);
  expect(users.users.length).toBe(2);
});
```

It should have been 3 in the beginning and once we removed a user, it should have been 2.

Test case – should not remove user

In case of should not remove user, we're going to do some similar stuff, we're just going to tweak `userId`. I can actually copy the contents of our first test case, paste it into the second one, and all we need to do is make a few tweaks. I'm going to change the ID to an invalid ID like 99. We are still going to call `removeUser` with the ID. In this case, though instead of expecting `user` to have an `id` property, we're going to expect that `user` does not exist using `toNotExist`. Next up, we're going to `expect` the length has not changed, and we're going to make sure that the length still equals 3:

```
it ('should not remove user', () => {
  var userId = '99';
  var user = users.removeUser(userId);

  expect(user).toBe(userId);
  expect(users.users.length).toBe(3);
});
```

Now I can go ahead and save the `users.test` file. This is going to restart everything inside `nodemon`, and what we should get is a test suite that's passing. It looks like it did already run although the content didn't change so it's a little hard to figure out if anything happened. I'm going to shut that down and run `npm test` just to verify, and right here you can see all 12 test cases are passing:

```
generateMessage
  ✓ should generate correct message object

generateLocationMessage
  ✓ should generate correct location object

Users
  ✓ should add new user
  ✓ should remove a user
  ✓ should not remove user
  ✓ should find user
  ✓ should not find user
  ✓ should return names for node course
  ✓ should return names for react course

isRealString
  ✓ should reject non-string values
  ✓ should reject string with only spaces
  ✓ should allow string with non-space characters


12 passing (17ms)
```

We now have all of the methods we need to persist a user across the different event listeners; whether they're sending a message, a location message, whether they're connecting or leaving, we're going to be able to keep track of them and send the right thing to the right people.

Wiring up user list

In this section we're going to start wiring up that users class we created, and to kick things off, we're going to wire up the `People` list, which means that we need to do something when a user joins, and when a user leaves. We want to keep that list up to date and every time we update it, we want to give a fresh copy of the list to the client. This means that the server is going to need to emit an event to the client, the client is then going to listen for that event and it's going to update the markup.

Now we can view exactly where this is going to happen by starting up the server with the following command:

```
nodemon server/server.js
```

Then, I'm going to head over to localhost:3000 and open up a chat page. I'm going to enter Andrew for **Display name** and LOTR for **Room name**. Now once we're in, we have our **People** list, currently it should show us, since we are in the room, and when a new user joins it should automatically show that user:

Right now none of this is happening, but with our new event in place it's all going to happen.

Adding People list in the chat room

Now the first thing we're going to do is figure out exactly what this event is going to look like. Over inside chat.js we can add a listener figuring out what works for us, what does the client really need to get this done? Then we can go ahead and wire up the server to fulfill those needs.

Right inside of chat.js, just below disconnect, we're going to add a new listener, socket.on, and we're going to listen for a brand new event. This one is going to be called updateUserList:

```
socket.on('disconnect', function() {
  console.log('Disconnected from server');
});

socket.on('updateUserList')
```

Now updateUserList is going to need to get passed some information. We're going to need the list of users to show instead of the currently displayed ones, which means we're going to expect one argument, a users array. And this users array is going to just be an array of names exactly like what we returned from getUserList over inside of the users class.

Back inside of chat.js, for the moment, all we're going to do is log the list to the screen when it comes through, console.log('Users list'), and the second argument will be the actual users array:

```
socket.on('updateUserList', function(users){
  console.log('Users list', users);
});
```

Once we have this wired up, all we need to do is add some jQuery to update the DOM. The harder part is going to be getting an updated and up-to-date list back to the client.

Adding jQuery to update the DOM

Over inside server.js step one to that process is going to be to import the class that we've been working so hard to create. I'm going to go ahead and get this done, just below where we load in isRealString.

We can make a constant and I'm going to go ahead and pull off the users property, which is the one we export at the bottom of users.js, and we can import that using require. I'm going to require the local file ./. It's in the utils folder and this one is called users:

```
const {Users} = require('./utils/users');
```

Now that we have Users in place we can make a new instance of it. This is going to be the users instance. We need a way to run these methods, so right below our io variable, we can make a new variable called users setting it equal to new Users, just like this:

```
var users = new Users();
```

Now we're going to be able to call all of our user methods to add, remove, fetch, and otherwise manipulate that data.

Adding user to the user's list

The first step in the process is going to be to add a user to the list when they join a chatroom. We can do that right after our call to socket.join. I'm going to remove the old comments, although you can choose to keep yours around if you find they are a good reference. Just below socket.join, we're going to call users.addUser, adding our brand new user, and we need to pass in those three pieces of information, the socket ID, socket.id is where that's stored, the name, that's on params.name, and finally we're going to go ahead and pass in the room name, params.room:

```
socket.join(params.room);
users.addUser(socket.id, params.name, params.room);
```

Now as you notice this code is not supposed to run if there is a validation error, meaning that the name or the room name is not provided, but currently that's not the case. We don't actually stop the function execution, I'm going to use return to make sure none of the code down below ever fires if the data is not valid:

```
socket.on('join', (params, callback) => {
  if(!isRealString(params.name) || !isRealString(params.room)){
    return callback('Name and room name are required.');
  }
});
```

Adding users with unique ID

The next step in the process is going to be to make sure that there is already no user with the same ID. I'm going to call `users.removeUser` to get that done, passing in the only argument requires the `socket.id` just like this:

```
socket.join(params.room);
users.removeUser(socket.id);
users.addUser(socket.id, params.name, params.room);
```

That means that user joins the room, and we remove them from any potential previous rooms. Finally, we add them to the new one. Now that we have this in place we can actually go ahead and emit that event.

Emitting the event to the clients

We're going to emit the event the client expects, `updateUserList` with the `users` array. If we don't emit the event, the client is never going to get the new list and we just updated the list, so we definitely want them to get a fresh copy. This means we want to emit an event to everyone in the chat room via `io.to`. We're going to pass in the room name and then we're going to call `emit`, emitting the event.

Now we can go ahead and fill out to first, we want to pass in the room name, `params.room` has that information, and next up we want to emit the event, the event name as we just defined over in `chat.js` is `updateUserList`. And the last thing we need to do is get the user list. We already have that, `users.getUserList`, passing in the name of the room we want to get the list for. Once again, `params.room`, that's going to be the only argument we pass in:

```
socket.join(params.room);
users.removeUser(socket.id);
users.addUser(socket.id, params.name, params.room);

io.to(params.room).emit('updateUserList', users.getUserList(params.room));
```

With this call in place, we should be able to actually view this over inside the Terminal.

I'm going to save this file, which is going to restart the server in the Terminal.

Testing the users list in the chatroom

Inside the browser I can open up the **Developer Tools** to view the `console log` statements, and I'm going to give the app a refresh. If I do refresh the application we see a `Users` list and we have `Andrew` printing twice:

If I refresh the page for a second time, we have `Andrew` printing three times:

As you can see this is happening because we're not removing users from the list when they leave the chat application. That's the second goal in this section. We currently have a user list. All we need to do is update it when a user leaves as well, that's going to happen inside of Atom down near the bottom in the `disconnect` listener.

Removing users when they leave the chatroom

Inside the disconnect listener, we want to remove the user and then we want to update the list once again. I'm going to do that by doing a few separate things. First up, we're going to make a variable called `user`, storing any potentially removed users, remember the `removeUser` method does return the user removed, `users.removeUser` passing in the ID, `socket.id`:

```
socket.io('disconnect', () => {
  var user = users.removeUser(socket.id);
});
```

Now we only want to do something if we actually removed a user, if the person hadn't joined a room, there's no reason to actually do anything. If a user was removed we are going to emit two events, and we're going to emit them to every single person connected to the chatroom, which means that we're going to be using `io.to().emit`, just like we did in the preceding code. We're going to do this two times, so I'm going to copy this line and paste it, like this:

```
socket.io('disconnect', () => {
  var user = users.removeUser(socket.id);
  if (user){
    io.to().emit();
    io.to().emit();
  }
});
```

Updating the users list when someone left the chatroom

The first one is going to update the `user` list and the second one is going to print a little message, like `Andrew has left the room`. The first one is going to take the user room property as the only argument, `user.room` stores the room string, we're going to provide that for both, and now we can start emitting our events.

I'm going to emit the `updateUserList` event first, inside quotes, `updateUserList`, and we're going to go ahead and call the exact same method we did right up above, `users.getUserList`, passing in the room, `user.room`:

```
if (user){
    io.to(user.room).emit('updateUserList', users.getUserList(user.room));
    io.to(user.room).emit();
}
```

Now when someone leaves a room they're going to be removed from that list and we're not going to see those duplicates that we had over inside of the web developer console.

Emitting custom message

The next thing that we want to do is emit a message. We're going to emit a message from the admin to everybody, kind of like we did up above. We greeted the user and we told all other users that someone joined, right here we're going to `emit('newMessage')`, and we're going to call `generateMessage` like we've done in the past. We're going to pass in those two arguments, the first one is `Admin`. This is going to be an admin message, and the second one can be a template string, we're going to inject the user's name, `user.name`, and then we're going to say that user has left:

```
io.to(user.room).emit('updateUserList', users.getUserList(user.room));
io.to(user.room).emit('newMessage', generateMessage('Admin', `${user.name}
has left.`));
```

Now that we have this in place everything should be working as expected. Hopefully over inside of Chrome we no longer get those duplicates. I'm going to give the page a refresh and we see we have a users list with just one user, `Andrew`:

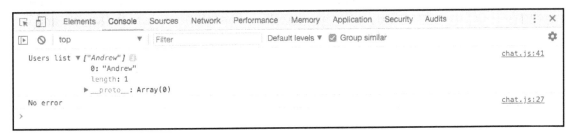

If I refresh the page, we no longer get the duplicates because when I leave I get removed and when I come back. When the page finally finishes refreshing, I get added. Now the same thing is going to be true if I add a new user. For the moment, I'm going to switch the browser to just take up half the width on my screen. I'm going to open up a second tab and drag that to the other half so we can view both of these side by side. I'm also going to open up the **Developer Tools** for this second tab, and we're going to join the exact same room.

Let's go to `localhost:3000`, I'm going to join as `Mike`, and the room name is going to be the same, `LOTR`. Now as soon as I click on **Join**, I should see an updated list in both consoles. I'm going to click on **Join**. Inside the right browser window, we get `Andrew`, `Mike`, and inside the left browser window we also have `Andrew`, `Mike`, which is fantastic:

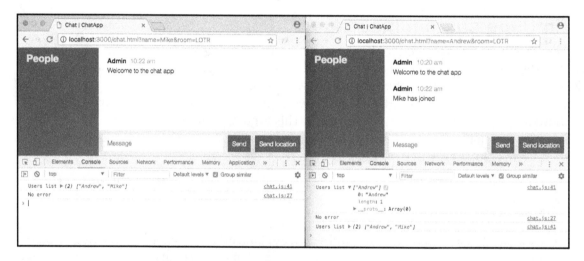

I also get a little message saying **Mike has joined**, that was in place earlier; the real test is what happens when a user leaves. I'm going to kick Andrew out of the chat room, and over here inside our other chat window, we have **Andrew has left** printing to the screen, and we have our new user list with just one user, `Mike`:

This is fantastic. We're now keeping track of users as they come and go, which lets us do really cool things like printing custom messages and updating the **People** list.

Rendering the users name to the chatroom

The last thing to get done is to actually render the names to the screen. Instead of just printing them in the console, we want to go ahead and take these names and add them to the list, that's going to happen over inside of our event listener in `server.js`. We're going to use a jQuery like we have in the past. Inside `chat.js` we're going to do something with those `users`.

Adding a jQuery to add the users to the list

First up let's go ahead and make a new jQuery element. We're going to make a variable called `ol`. This is going to store a new element using jQuery. We're going to create an ordered list. We'll create that `ol` tag:

```
socket.on('updateUserList', function(users){
  var ol = jQuery('<ol></ol>');
});
```

Now we need to iterate over every user doing something with that user, `users.forEach` is going to let us get that done. We're going to pass in our function and inside of that function we can add the individual user:

```
socket.on('updateUserList', function(users){
  var ol = jQuery('<ol></ol>');
  users.forEach(function () {
  });
});
```

The argument for the function is the name, the `user` string, and all we're going to do is append something to our ordered list up above. That's going to be `ol.append`:

```
socket.on('updateUserList', function(users){
  var ol = jQuery('<ol></ol>');
  users.forEach(function () {
    ol.append();
  });
});
```

Now what exactly do we want to append? Well we want to append a list item, the list item is going to have a `text` property equal to the name and that's going to get everything rendering just right. We can use jQuery to create a new list item by opening and closing our list item tag. Then right after the closing parenthesis for jQuery we are going to call `text` so we can safely set the `text` property equal to the user's name:

```
socket.on('updateUserList', function(users){
  var ol = jQuery('<ol></ol>');
  users.forEach(function (user) {
    ol.append(jQuery('<li></li>').text(user));
  });
});
```

Now we have an updated list but it's not actually getting rendered to the screen, the last step is to render it by adding it to the DOM.

Rendering the updated People list

Now over inside `chat.html` we do have a place for that. It's the `div` tag with an `id` of `users`, which means that we can select it, jQuery, the selector is going to start with the hash sign(#) since we're selecting by ID, and we're selecting `users`, then we can go ahead and actually add the list. I'm going to set the `html` property equal to our ordered list, `ol`, as opposed to using append, we don't want to update a list, we want to completely wipe the list replacing it with the new version:

```
socket.on('updateUserList', function(users){
  var ol = jQuery('<ol></ol>');
  users.forEach(function (user) {
    ol.append(jQuery('<li></li>').text(user));
  });
  jQuery('#users').html(ol);
});
```

Now we can save `chat.js` and test things out.

Testing the users name in the chatroom

Over inside of the browser I'm going to go ahead and close the console, refresh the page and we see the number **1** followed by **Mike**:

Now number 1 is coming from the fact that we're using an ordered list. If I add a second user we're going to see that second user. Let's create a second user, we're going to give it a display name of Jen, then we'll go to the same room, LOTR, and when we join we get a little message and we get our two users, and the same thing is showing up:

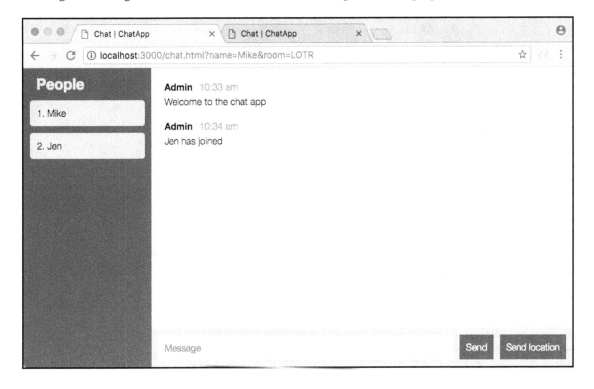

Now I'm going to go to the second tab and I'm going to close the first. When I do that your list automatically updates and we also get our message saying that **Mike has left**:

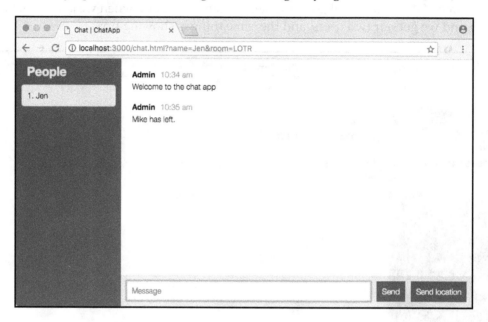

With this in place we are one step closer to being complete. The messages are still going to everybody, they're not specific to the room, but that is something we're going to take care of in the next section. For now we are done. I am going to make a commit, it has been a little while and we do have a completed feature, so let's go ahead and do that.

Making a commit for updated users list

First up, we'll run `git status`, we have some new files as well as some existing ones, I'll be using `git add .` to add all of those to the next commit. Finally, we can use `git commit` to actually make the commit, I'm going to use the `-m` flag to add our message, and right inside of quotes `Add Users class and updateUserList event`:

```
git commit -m 'Add Users class and updateUserList event'
```

We can go ahead and make this commit and push it up to GitHub, feel free to push to Heroku if you want, I'm going to hold off a little bit longer, everything should be working there as well as locally.

In the next section we're going to be making sure the messages, whether it's a text message or a location message, only gets sent to the people in the room.

Sending messages to room only

In the last section, we wired up that **People** list making sure that as new users come and go the list gets updated. In this section, we're going to make sure that our text and location messages only get sent to users in the same room. Currently, it gets sent to everybody. We can prove that by opening up a new connection, I'm going to use `Mike` and we're going to join a different room, `The Office Fans works`. When I join the room you can see that the **People** lists are indeed correct, a user in one room does not update the **People** list for a user in another room. The difference though is that the text messages do not follow those rules, neither do the location-based messages:

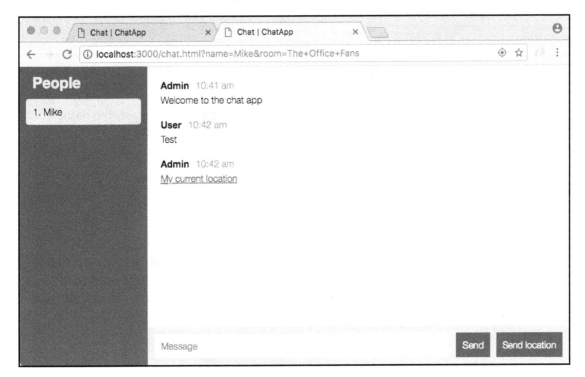

We'll have a text message and a location message as well, if I go over to the chat app for the other room we get both of those. And this is a problem. We also have the name problem, currently **User** displays for the text message and **Admin** displays for the location message, we want to make sure to use the actual user's name, whether it's Jen or whether it's Andrew. In order to get that done we are going to need to make some changes to both `server.js`. We have our event listeners for `creatMessage` and `createLocationMessage`, and we're also going to be making some updates inside of `chat.js`, and this is actually where we're going to start.

Updating the chat.js and server.js files

Currently, the name `User`, the incorrect name we see inside of the browser that comes from `socket.emit` function in `chat.js`:

```
socket.emit('createMessage', {
  from: 'User',
  text: messageTextbox.val('')
}, function() {
  messageTextbox.val('')
});
```

The client originally sent the name but this is no longer going to be the case, the name is stored by the server so we're going to remove this as a required property from `createMessage`, we're just going to be sending the text across.

```
socket.emit('createMessage', {
  text: messageTextbox.val('')
}, function() {
  messageTextbox.val('')
});
```

Now with this in place we can modify the event listener over inside of `server.js`. Inside `server.js`, `createMessage` takes those two properties and it stuffs them right in to `generateMessage`. Instead, we're going to find the user using `users.getUser` and we're going to do something with it.

Right in `createMessage` we can go ahead and delete our `console.log` statement for `createMessage`, and we're going to make a variable user, setting it equal to `users.getUser`. This is the method we created in `users.js`, `getUser`, which takes the `id` parameter. We can pass in the ID `socket.id like this`:

```
socket.on('createMessage', (message, callback) => {
  var user = users.getUser(socket.id);

  io.emit('newMessage', generateMessage(message.from, message.text));
  callback();
});
```

Now we can do something with `user`. We only want to do something if a user actually exists, which means that we're going to check if the user exists using `if` statement, and we're also going to make sure that the text that got passed along was a real string, using, after `&&`, `isRealString`. We'll then pass in `message.text`:

```
socket.on('createMessage', (message, callback) => {
  var user = users.getUser(socket.io);
  if(user && isRealString(message.text)){
  }
  io.emit('newMessage', generateMessage(message.from, message.text));
  callback();
});
```

This means if someone tries to send across an empty message or just a bunch of spaces, it's not going to get sent to everybody else. Now inside the `if` statement, all we're going to do is actually emit the message. We know it's valid so we do want to emit something, and we're going to take `io.emit` line, cut it out, and paste it in `if` statement:

```
if(user && isRealString(message.text)){
  io.emit('newMessage', generateMessage(message.from, message.text));
}
```

Now currently the `io.emit` line emits to everybody, not just the room that user is connected to, but we also use `message.from`. We really want to use the `name` property on user. We're now going to make those two changes, emit this event just to the room the user is connected to, and make sure to provide their name as opposed to `message.from`.

Emitting event to the individual room

First up, we want to emit to just a specific room and we know we can tack on a to call right in the `io.emit` line to get that done, passing in the room name, with access to that on the `user` object `user.room`. Now that we're emitting to just the individual room, we also do want to change the name we use. Instead of `message.from`, we're going to access the name on the `user` object, `user.name`, and there we go:

```
io.to(user.room).emit('newMessage', generateMessage(user.name,
message.text));
```

Now we have a much better system for sending those text messages. I'm going to refresh my first tab and my second tab, and we're going to send some text messages around. I'm going to send the number 1 from my second tab and we do get **Andrew** and we do see the number **1**:

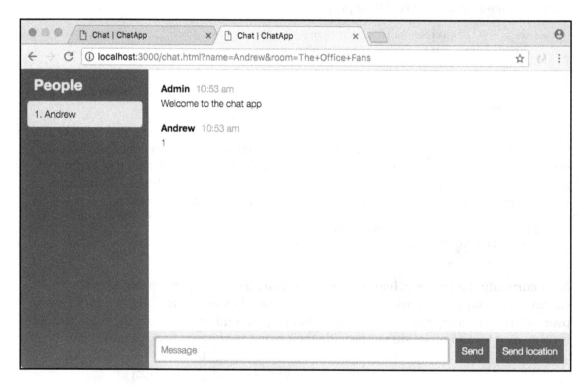

Over inside our other tab the message is nowhere to be found because we're just emitting it to users in The Office Fans room:

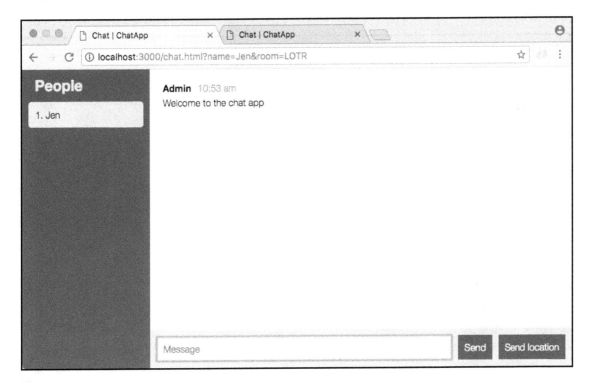

If I try to send a message from this first tab, we're going to see it there with the name **Jen**, and the second tab also looks good; we're not seeing that message from **Jen**.

Now I can go ahead and join a room again. I'm going to use the name `Mike` and we're going to join `The Office Fans` one more time. When I join the room I do see **Andrew** and **Mike** both connected:

If I send a message like `Should work` I see it there, and I also see it in the tab of the other user connected to `The Office Fans` room. Once again it's not visible to someone else connected to a different room. That is all we need to do to get our messages sending correctly. The last thing to do is to wire that up for `createLocationMessage`.

Now as we just saw we were also able to fix the validation issue, if I try to hit *enter* right now, nothing happens. I don't get moved out of the box, the focus doesn't change and no message is sent, which is great.

Wiring up createLoactionMessage for individual room

Now we're going to fix `createLocationMessage`. You're going to want to find the user just like we do above, incase of createMessage. If there is a user you're going to want to emit the location to just people in the same room. Instead of providing `Admin` as the name you're also going to want to use the user's real name. We need to make sure it still gets sent to users in the same room and make sure it does not get sent to users in other rooms.

To do this one, I am going to start by fetching the user since we are going to need to use the information on that object. We're going to make a variable user calling `users.getUser`, and we're going to pass in that socket ID, `socket.id`. This is identical to the line we used above in `createMesssage`. Now we only want to emit a message if we do find a user, so I'm going to check if the user object exists. If it does, we can take `io.emit` line, cut it out, and copy it inside the `if` statement. If it does exist, we are going to emit `newLocationMessage`:

```
if(user){
    io.emit('newLocationMessage', generateLocationMessage('Admin',
coords.latitude, coords.longitude));
}
```

Now we do still need to emit it to just a specific room by adding on a call to `to` and passing in the room name, `user.room` stores that information, and last but not least we do want to update the name. Instead of sending the static `Admin` name, we're going to use the user's real name, `user.name`:

```
io.to(user.room).emit('newLocationMessage',
generateLocationMessage(user.name, coords.latitude, coords.longitude));
```

With this in place `createLocationMessage` is now wired up to be private and to send across the correct information. Over inside Chrome, I'm going to go through my tabs one at a time giving them a refresh, and on the second tab I am going to be sending the location. This is going to take just a couple of seconds to actually fetch it, and I see it right there with the name showing up correct:

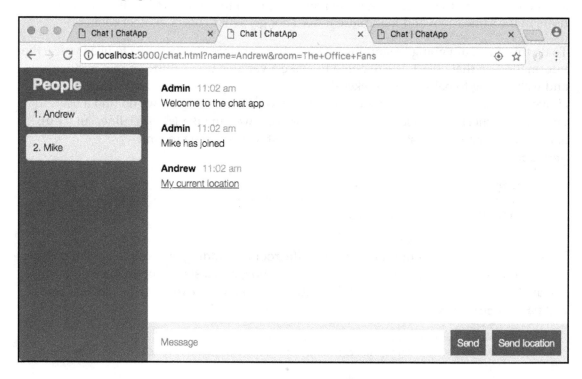

We have **Andrew** and we have a link to view the location inside of Google Maps. Now if I go to the second tab, the user who is also connected to `The Office Fans`, I see the exact same location message:

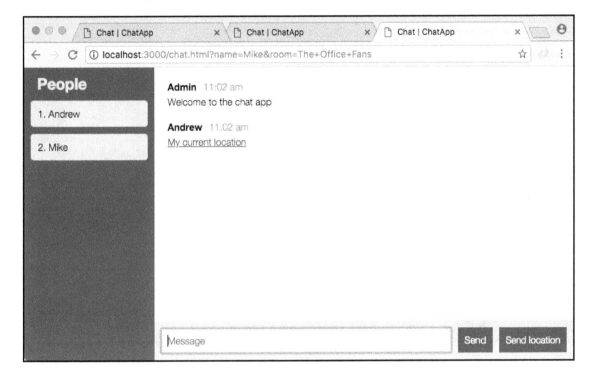

If I go to the first one, you can see that **Jen** does not have access to that message because she's in a different room:

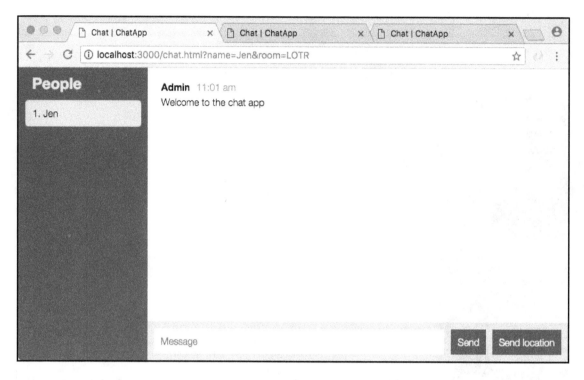

She can always share her location with anybody in her room, that happens to be nobody, this message is not going to show up anywhere because no one else is connected to LOTR.

With that in place we are now done, our messages are private, they're only going to be visible to folks in the same room. Let's go ahead and wrap this one up by committing our changes.

Committing the individual room changes

I'm going to shut down the nodemon server, use clear, and we can run git status to see what kind of changes we have:

```
[Gary:node-chat-app Gary$ git status
On branch master
Your branch is up-to-date with 'origin/master'.

Changes not staged for commit:
  (use "git add <file>..." to update what will be committed)
  (use "git checkout -- <file>..." to discard changes in working directory)

        modified:   public/js/chat.js
        modified:   server/server.js
```

Here we just have two files. They're modified, which means we can use git commit with the -am flag, whether it's separate or the same they have identical feature sets, and then we provide our message string, Send messages to only people in same room:

```
git commit -am 'Send messages to only people in same room'
```

With this in place we can go ahead and use git push to push this up to GitHub, and I'm also going to go ahead and deploy to Heroku using git push heroku master. Once it's deployed on Heroku, we can take just a quick moment to make sure all of those features we just added are still working as expected. I expect they will still work but it's definitely worth checking out because the environments are a little different and there's always a chance something can go wrong.

Now if something does go wrong, as a reminder you can always use heroku logs, this is going to show you the logs on the server, it's usually kind of cryptic but when an error occurs you're going to see a really big block. It's usually pretty easy to spot and it usually contains useful information as to what went wrong:

```
41.130.190" dyno=web.1 connect=1ms service=2ms status=200 bytes=328 protocol=https
2018-03-27T05:39:45.894411+00:00 app[web.1]: New user connected
2018-03-27T05:39:46.221256+00:00 heroku[router]: at=info method=GET path="/socket.io/?EIO=3&transport=pollin
g&t=M9b-2q6.0&sid=BNvGrIXNe5731N6DAAAC" host=rocky-sierra-37964.herokuapp.com request_id=bdb62adc-8f39-447d-
90aa-200d16e69577 fwd="43.241.130.190" dyno=web.1 connect=1ms service=1ms status=200 bytes=357 protocol=http
s
2018-03-27T05:39:46.202795+00:00 heroku[router]: at=info method=POST path="/socket.io/?EIO=3&transport=polli
ng&t=M9b-2q6&sid=BNvGrIXNe5731N6DAAAC" host=rocky-sierra-37964.herokuapp.com request_id=d1a6f212-1c16-4587-9
661-f125f9522628 fwd="43.241.130.190" dyno=web.1 connect=1ms service=2ms status=200 bytes=287 protocol=https
2018-03-27T05:39:47.429695+00:00 heroku[router]: at=info method=GET path="/socket.io/?EIO=3&transport=pollin
g&t=M9b-2ug&sid=BNvGrIXNe5731N6DAAAC" host=rocky-sierra-37964.herokuapp.com request_id=d269776d-8b78-432c-96
5b-3de965219a68 fwd="43.241.130.190" dyno=web.1 connect=1ms service=918ms status=200 bytes=225 protocol=http
s
```

It looks like our app deployed successfully, so I can use `heroku open` to open it up inside my browser, and once it's open we can actually visit some chat rooms. I'm going to close down my localhost tab and I'm going to join as `Andrew`, the room `Philadelphia`:

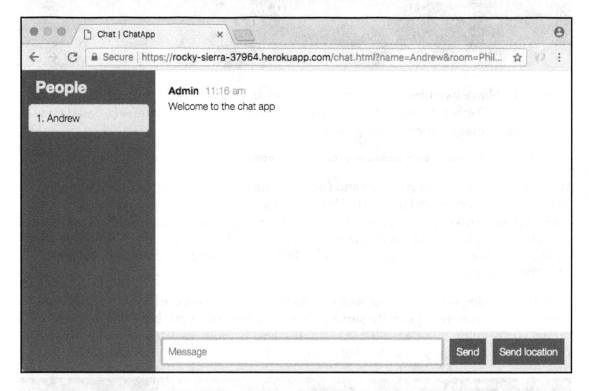

Once I'm in the room, I am going to send a message, and then I'm going to add a second user to the room. We want to visit our Heroku app website. I'm going to visit that, we'll join the room as `Vikram`, and we can join the exact same room `Philadelphia`. When I join, I see the **People** list updates for both and sending messages does still work:

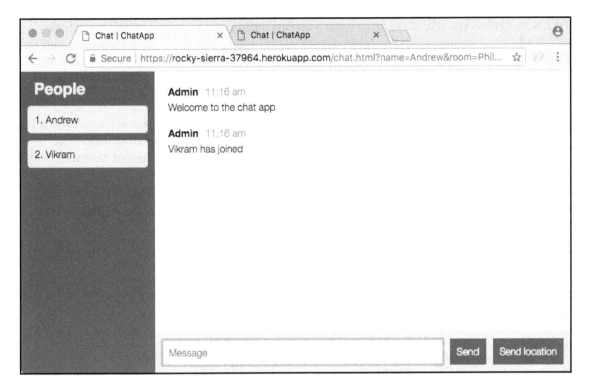

Messages from the second tab do appear in first tab, this is great. All this is possible because we wired up `server.js`, keeping track of users over time. When they first join we add them to the list, when they send messages we make sure to use their information, and when they leave we remove them from the list. This ensures that the **People** list is always up to date and that messages are only getting sent to others in the same room.

New feature ideas

Now that we have our People list in place and our messages are only getting sent to the users in the same chatroom, we are done. But that doesn't mean you have to stop developing the chat app, students always like to add on new features.

I'd like to give you a few ideas as to what you can build right now. You might get stuck while adding these features. It might be a real pain in the neck and it might take forever, but I promise you're going to learn so much along the way when you're doing something on your own. Now you have all the skills to do these features so let's just go down the list really quick.

- One awesome idea would be to make chatrooms case-insensitive. Currently, if I go to LOTr with a lowercase r, I'm not actually in the same chatroom as my friend who's in LOTR uppercase R. It would be nice if regardless of case we were all in the same room.
- Next up, I'd like to make usernames unique. Currently, I can copy the URL and paste it in a new tab, and now I have two people with the name of **Jules**:

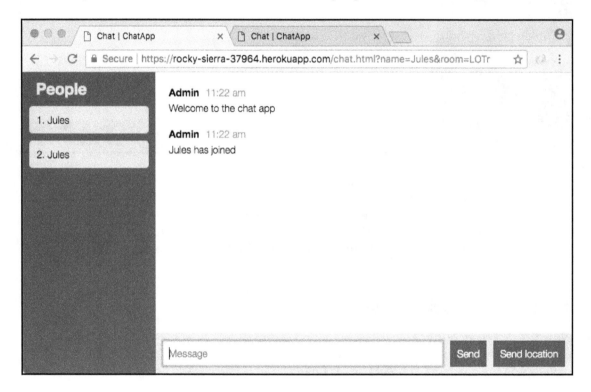

- It would be cool to reject new users who also have the same name as an existing user.
- Next up, one idea is to add a list of the currently active chatrooms down below. This could be a select drop-down, it's going to repopulate kind of like the People's list repopulates.
- This is by far the hardest feature but I think it would be really cool. That means I would see a drop-down between the **Join** button and the **Room name** input box, and it would have the two currently active rooms, LOTr and LOTR with an uppercase R, although hopefully if you implement that first feature we would only see one room. Then instead of typing in a room name, I could just pick one from the drop-down, type in a name and join that way.

These are just a few ideas of how you can continue on with the chat app.

Summary

In this chapter, we looked at how we can create classes in ES6 using the class keyword. We made a Person class, which was just an example, and we made our Users class, which we'll actually be using throughout the book. We looked at adding custom methods as well as setting up our constructor function. Then, we created removeUser, getUser, and getUserList methods in the similar manner.

Next, we looked into wiring up the users class we created and updated the People list when a user joins or left the chatroom. Then we looked into sending messages to a particular room and not to all the users. At last, we added a few ideas, which you can look into to enhance the features of the chatroom.

In the chapter, we are going to learn about Async/Await project setup.

10
Async/Await Project Setup

In this chapter, we're going to go through the process of learning how async/await works, what exactly it is, and where it's going to fit into what we know about Node already. **Async/await** is a feature that is not available in all versions of Node. You have to be using the 7.6 or greater. So if you are on V7, just make sure you are on 7.6 or greater. If we go over to `nodejs.org`, you're going to see that v9 is actually out, so we can go ahead and just upgrade to V9 right now:

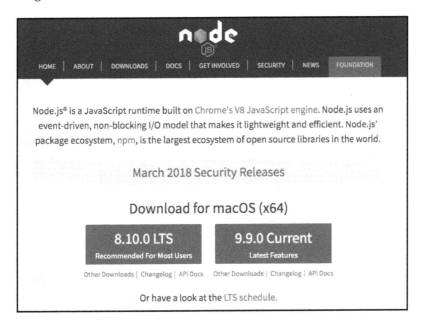

It's perfectly fine if there's a newer version. You can go ahead and grab that as well, as long as it is 7.6 or up. So 6.10, it's not going to have the syntax that we're about to dive into.

Using async/await features in promises

Now, before we actually use async/await, we're going to go ahead and run through an example that just uses promises. We're going to use techniques we already know to set up a little example project. Now, when people hear about async/await, they think that they need to forget everything they know about callbacks and promises, and that is not true. Async/await is not a third option; it is more like an enhancement for promises. We're going to go through an example using just regular old promises, things you already know how to do. Then we're going to see how async/await can enhance that code. So, to kick things off, we do need a place to put all of this. I'm going to make a brand new project on my **Desktop**, async-await.

We can crack that open in our editor and make sure to crack it open in your terminal as well. Now, the goal here is to just make a very simple project. We're not going to need any Node modules for this one and we are just going to need a single file. This file can sit in the root of the project and we'll just call it app-promises.js:

This is going to be the version of our application that just uses promises. Now, before we go any further, I do want to give you a quick idea as to what the chapter is going to look like. We're going to go through three distinct things: first up, we are going to create a very contrived example and this is going to allow us to learn how to use async/await without a lot of overhead or baggage. So, we're going to be creating constants, like users, which would just be an array of objects and constants, like grades; also an array of objects and this is going to be what a database would look like.

```
const users = [];
const grades = [];
```

Obviously, there is nothing asynchronous about accessing some property from an array, so we're going to go ahead and create some new promises to turn a synchronous process into an asynchronous one.

Setting up the getUser project

So, the first project is not very real-world, but it is going to be a great way to learn the new syntax. Then we're going to move on to another little project where you're going to be required to make two actual API calls from some APIs I picked out. Those will be asynchronous and we'll use async/await there. To wrap things up, we're going to add a little bit of async/await code back into the todo API.

So, to kick things off, we're going to go through this very contrived example and we can start by creating a few users to work with. Each user object is going to have a few properties; we'll start off with an id, just like they would have inside of a real database. I'm going to give this one an id of 1:

```
const users = [{
    id: 1,

}];

const grades = [];
```

We'll also have a name, a string name for the user. I'm going to call the first one Andrew and then we're going to move on to the final property, a schoolId, an ID that will change as the student switches from one school to another. We can just make up another id for this one. I'm going to go ahead and start at 101:

```
const users = [{
    id: 1,
    name: 'Andrew',
    schoolId: 101
}];

const grades = [];
```

Now that we have user number 1 created' let's go ahead and clone him. I'm going to copy it, toss a comma and paste it, and we'll create just one more user for this example. This one will have an id of 2. We'll change the name from Andrew over to something like Jessica and we'll give her a schoolId of 999:

```
const users = [{
    id: 1,
    name: 'Andrew',
    schoolId: 101
}, {
    id: 2,
    name: 'Jessica',
```

```
    schoolId: 999
}];

const grades = [];
```

Now that we have some users in place, we're going to create our first of three functions we'll be building in this section. This one is called const `getUser`. It is going to take the `id` of the user, find that user, and return the user object:

```
const grades = [];

const getUser = [id] => {
};
```

So, if the `id` is 1, we're going to get this object:

```
const users = [{
    id: 1,
    name: 'Andrew',
    schoolId: 101
},
```

If it's 2, I'm going to get this object back:

```
{
    id: 2,
    name: 'Jessica',
    schoolId: 999
}];
```

If it's 3 or some other id that doesn't exist, I'm going to actually have an error thrown. So, this is going to return a promise of resolve if the `id` is a match with one of the users, or reject if it's not.

Now, as I mentioned, this is a contrived example, so we're going to be creating new promises explicitly. I'm going to create a new promise, passing in that promise function which, as you remember, gets called with `resolve` and `reject`:

```
const getUser = (id) => {
    return new Promise((resolve, reject) => {

    });
};
```

Then we're going to go ahead and add a little bit of logic in the function.

The array find method

The first thing we need to do is try to find a match and I'm going to use the array find method to get that done. We'll create a `const user` to store the match, then we'll set it equal to `users.find`, passing in our function:

```
const getUser = (id) => {
  return new Promise((resolve, reject) => {
   const user = user.find(() = {
  });
 });
};
```

Now this function gets called one time for every item in the array. It's an array of users so we can call the individual item `user`. If we return `true`, it is going to consider that a match. It'll stop and it'll set that object on a user. If we return `false`, it'll continue on through the array and, if none are matched, undefined will be the value for user. So, we're just going to return `user.id`, checking if it equals the `id` passed in.

```
const getUser = (id) => {
  return new Promise((resolve, reject) => {
    const user = user.find((user) => {
    return user.id === id;
  });
 });
};
```

Now, we have a great candidate for the shorthand syntax here. We just have an arrow function that returns some value. It just provides the value and have it be implicitly returned:

```
const getUser = (id) => {
  return new Promise((resolve, reject) => {
    const user = user.find((user) => user.id === id);
```

Here we have the exact same functionality. Now, before we go ahead and use it, let's go ahead and actually call `resolve` or `reject`. If there is a user, we're going to do one thing; if there's not a user, that's fine, we're just going to do something else. In the `else` statement, we'll be calling `reject` and, in if statement, we'll be calling `resolve`:

```
const getUser = (id) => {
  return new Promise((resolve, reject) => {
    const user = user.find((user) => user.id === id);

    if (user) {
      resolve();
```

```
    } else {
      reject();
    }
  });
};
```

Now, `resolve` is just going to have the user passed in and, for `reject`, we can come up with an error message that helps the user figure out what went wrong. We can add `unable to find user with id of` ., then, we'll put the `id` next to it. Inside the template string, I'm going to reference `id`. This is the exact value that was passed in the `getUser` variable.

```
const getUser = (id) => {
  return new Promise((resolve, reject) => {
    const user = user.find((user) => user.id === id);

    if (user) {
      resolve(user);
    } else {
      reject('Unable to find user with id of ${id}.');
    }
  });
};
```

Now, before we go ahead and actually run this, let's just use `getUser` real quick. I'm going to call `getUser` with an `id` of 2, which should return `Jessica`. I'll add on then and `catch`. Inside `catch`, we can `catch` that error. We're just going to get the error and log it out, `console.log(e)`.

```
getUser(2).then().catch((e) => {
  console.log(e);
});
```

Then we can set up our `then` callback; inside `then`, we're going to get access to the user and, for now, we'll just log it out:

```
getUser(2).then((user) => {
  console.log(user);
}).catch((e) => {
  console.log(e);
});
```

Running the getUser object test

To actually run this, we're going to head over into the Terminal and make sure we do get the expected results. I'm going to be using `nodemon` to get that done. If you just updated Node, it also updated `npm` and, at the end of the day, what that means is that you no longer have access to those global modules. You might need to rerun `npm install -g nodemon` before you can use the `nodemon` command. I'm going to use `nodemon` running the `app-promises.js` file and, right here, we have our output:

```
|Gary:async-await Gary$ nodemon app-promises.js
[nodemon] 1.14.10
[nodemon] to restart at any time, enter `rs`
[nodemon] watching: *.*
[nodemon] starting `node app-promises.js`
{ id: 2, name: 'Jessica', schoolId: 999 }
[nodemon] clean exit - waiting for changes before restart
```

We have Jessica printing with a `schoolId` of 999 and an `id` of 2. That is because I passed 2 in `getUser` id:

```
getUser(2).then((user) => {
  console.log(user);
}).catch((e) => {
  console.log(e);
});
```

If I switch this out for 1, I should see `Andrew`. I do indeed see `Andrew`. Finally, let's go ahead and pass in an ID that doesn't exist like 21:

```
getUser(21).then((user) => {
  console.log(user);
}).catch((e) => {
  console.log(e);
});
```

Right here I do get the message: `unable to find user with id of 21`:

```
[nodemon] starting `node app-promises.js`
{ id: 1, name: 'Andrew', schoolId: 101 }
[nodemon] clean exit - waiting for changes before restart
[nodemon] restarting due to changes...
[nodemon] starting `node app-promises.js`
Unable to find user with id of 21.
```

So, this is the first of three projects that we're going to be building. Let's go ahead and knock out the other two real quick.

Setting up the getGrades project

This will set us up to actually explore the async/await syntax, using `const getGrades`. getGrades is going to be very similar to `getUsers` although. Instead of working with the users array, it is going to work with the grades array:

```
const getGrades = () => {

};
```

Now, we don't have any grades set up, so let's go ahead and set some up.

Creating grades for the getGrades project

We're going to go ahead and create a few grades. First up, let's create a grade with an `id` of 1. Now, this 1 is going to be attached to `Andrew`, so we'll go ahead and use the `schoolId` to do that. The `schoolId`, in this case for `Andrew`, is 101. Then, we're going to put in the actual `grade`. In this case, I'll go ahead and give myself an 86:

```
const grades = [{
  id: 1,
  schoolId: 101,
  grade: 86
}];
```

This is grade 1; let's go ahead and create three more grades. I'm going to copy it, toss in a comma, and paste it two times. This one is going to have an id of 2. We can associate this one with `Jessica`, so we'll give her the `schoolId` value of 999. She's really smart so we'll give her a 100. Finally, id of 3: we'll leave this one associated with `Andrew` and, next, we'll give him a grade of an 80:

```
const grades = [{
  id: 1,
  schoolId: 101,
  grade: 86
}, {
  id: 2,
  schoolId: 999,
  grade: 100
}, {
  id: 3,
  schoolId: 101,
  grade: 80
}];
```

So, we have some grades in place and the goal is to return all of the grades for a particular student based off of their `schoolId`. If I pass in `101`, I would expect an array to come back with the object associated with Andrew. If I pass in `999`, I would expect an array to come back with the one associated with Jessica, and if I pass in a value like `55`, there are going to be no grades for that student, so we'll go ahead and return an empty array.

Returning a new promise

Now, in the `getGrades` variable, we're going to get the `schoolId` that we're using to look things up with. Then we're going to go ahead and return a new promise; this is all part of the contrived example, `resolve` and `reject` are our two arguments:

```
const getGrades = (schoolId) => {
  return new Promise((resolve, reject) => {

  });
};
```

Then, right here, we're going to go ahead and `resolve` the filtered grades array, that is `grades.filter`. We're going to filter this one by passing an arrow function. It'll get called with the individual grade, not user, and then we'll go ahead and implicitly return something. If we return `true`, it'll be considered a match and that grade will be resolved. If we return `false`, that grade will be removed from the array that gets resolved. In this case, we want to keep the grade if the `grade.schoolId` equals the `schoolId` that the function was called with.

```
const getGrades = (schoolId) => {
  return new Promise((resolve, reject) => {
    resolve(grades.filter((grade) => grade.schoolId === schoolId));
  });
};
```

In this case, that is it for `getGrades`; we can go ahead and test it out. I'm going to call `getGrades` instead of `getUser`. I'm going to pass in a valid `schoolId` like `101` and, instead of user, we'll have `grades` and next:

```
getGrades(101).then((grades) => {
  console.log(grades);
}).catch((e) => {
  console.log(e);
});
```

If I save this, what do we get? We get an array with two objects, as expected:

```
[nodemon] starting `node app-promises.js`
[ { id: 1, schoolId: 101, grade: 86 },
  { id: 3, schoolId: 101, grade: 80 } ]
[nodemon] clean exit - waiting for changes before restart
```

We have all the grades for `Andrew`, `86` and `80`. I'm going to go ahead and pass in `999`; we get Jessica's grades and, finally, we pass in `12`:

```
getGrades(12).then((grades) => {
  console.log(grades);
}).catch((e) => {
  console.log(e);
});
```

If I pass in `12`, we get an empty array, which is exactly what I was hoping for. Just one more function left, and then we'll be done with this section and we can move on to the next one.

Setting up the getStatus project

This project is going to be called `const getStatus`. `getStatus` is going to be a function and it is going to take the `userId`, the `id` for the user whose status you're trying to fetch. Now, the goal of this project is to just return a string along the lines. We'll start off with their name, like `Andrew`, and then we'll add a little bit of information; `Andrew has a`, in this case, I have an `83` average in the class (so I take `80`, I add on `86`, I divide it by 2 to generate that average). So, we want to resolve the following string from `getStatus` after we actually run through `getUser` and `getGrades`:

```
const getGrades = (schoolId) => {
  return new Promise((resolve, reject) => {
    resolve(grades.filter((grade) => grade.schoolId === schoolId));
  });
};

// Andrew has a 83% in the class
const getStatus = (userId) => {

};
```

Resolving the getStatus string

We're going to go ahead and knock this out, and then we'll be done. That means we'll be calling `getStatus` with a `userId`. We're going to get the status back and we are going to log the status out:

```
getStatus(1).then((status) => {
  console.log(status);
}).catch((e) => {
  console.log(e);
});
```

Now to kick things off, what do we need to do? First up, we have to go ahead and `return` to keep the promise chain alive, because we attach the then and `catch` callbacks with the `getStatus` function.

Next up, we'll be calling `getUser`. Before we can actually use `getGrades`, we have to take the `userId`, find the user object, and get their `schoolId`. We also want to make sure to have access to the name for the message, so we need two pieces of information off of that object: `getUser` and `userId`. We'll add our `then` callback. In this callback, we're going to get access to that user object and this contains some useful information. One of those pieces of information is going to allow us to actually call `getGrades`. I'm going to `return` `getGrades`, right here, and we're going to pass in the student school ID, that's `user.schoolId`:

```
// Andrew has a 83% in the class
const getStatus = (userId) => {
  return getUser(userId).then((tempUser) => {
    return getGrades(user.schoolId);
  })
};
```

So now that we have `getGrades` called, we'll have access to those grades next. The success callback for `getGrades` promise will get the `grades` array. We can then go ahead and actually create an `average` variable, which we'll do in a second, and then we can `return` our `string`. So, that is the goal for this function, but this is where we run into one of the first problems you most likely have seen when working with promises:

```
// Andrew has a 83% in the class
const getStatus = (userId) => {
  return getUser(userId).then((tempUser) => {
    return getGrades(user.schoolId);
  }).then((grades) => {
    // average
```

```
        // return our string
    });
};
```

We have the `getStatus` promise chain; we have to have one promise called in order to actually start the other one and, at the end of the day, I want to do something with values from both. Well, we can't; we do not have access to user inside the second `then` function. It was created in another function, the first `then` callback, which is a pretty common problem.

So, how do we solve this? There are a few ways we could do that. Most of them are kind of ugly workarounds. Just below the `getStatus` variable, I could make a variable called `user` and I would set it equal to undefined at first.

```
const getStatus = (userId) => {
    var user;
```

Then, in the first `then` callback, I will give it a value when this function runs. Now, I can't have two variables with the same thing. If I try to type `user = user`, we're going to run into some problems:

```
const getStatus = (userId) => {
    var user;
    return getUser(userId).then((user) => {
        user = user;
```

It is going to take the `user` value and set it equal to the user value in then callback. It's not going to use the user variable at all. So we have to add another little workaround: `tempUser`.

```
const getStatus = (userId) => {
    var user;
    return getUser(userId).then((tempUser) => {
        user = tempUser;
```

Then we're going to go ahead and set `user = tempUser`, and this is going to technically work. We'll now have access to user variable and we can get some stuff done.

Calculating the average

So, we can calculate the average of our `average = 0` in the second `then` callback function:

```
// Andrew has a 83% in the class
const getStatus = (userId) => {
    var user;
    return getUser(userId).then((tempUser) => {
```

```
      user = tempUser;
      return getGrades(user.schoolId);
   }).then((grades) => {
      var average = 0;

      // average
      // return our string
   });
};
```

Now, we've been using const throughout the course. We can actually switch our `var` over to `let`; `let` is the ES6 equivalent to `var`, so this is a variable whose value we can change:

```
// Andrew has a 83% in the class
const getStatus = (userId) => {
   let user;
   return getUser(userId).then((tempUser) => {
      user = tempUser;
      return getGrades(user.schoolId);
   }).then((grades) => {
      let average = 0;

      // average
      // return our string
   });
};
```

Now we're going to start off with an average of 0 and move on to actually calculating a better average if there are grades: `grades.length`. If `grades.length` is greater than 0, we're going to go ahead and actually run a calculation.

```
   }).then((grades) => {
      let average = 0;

      if (grades.length > 0) {
      }
      // average
      // return our string
   });
```

Now, we're going to use a few array methods here. First up, we're going to set average equal to some value. We're going to kick things off by taking our array of objects and getting it down to an array of numbers.

We'll do that using map; that's `grades.map`. Here, we're going to go ahead and get access to the individual grade and all we're going to do is implicitly return `grade.grade`.

```
if (grades.length > 0) {
   average = grades_map((grade) => grade.grade)
}
```

So, we have the individual `grade` object and we're trying to access its `grade` property. At this point, we have an array of numbers. We need to turn those numbers into a sum and then we have to divide that by the length of the array. We'll be using `reduce` here, so we call `reduce` on an array of numbers. `reduce` works a little differently than some of the other array methods you might have seen in the past. This one takes two arguments, `a` and `b`;

```
if (grades.length > 0) {
   average = grades.map((grade) => grade.grade).reduce((a, b) => {

   });
};
```

So, the first time it goes through, it's going to take the first two grades and we'll be able to do something with those grades. What do we want to do? We want to return `a + b`. Then it's going to take that sum for the first two grades, it is going to call the reduce function again, putting that sum and putting the third grade. We'll take `a + b` to get that value added on to the new `b` and then we'll continue to generate that sum. Now, you can actually simplify that `a + b`:

```
if (grades.length > 0) {
   average = grades.map((grade) => grade.grade).reduce((a, b) => a + b);
}
```

Now, this alone just gives us the sum so, in the case of `Andrew`, we haven't calculated the average `83`; we've just added up the two numbers. You also want to divide this by `grades.length`; that is what's going to give us the average. We can go ahead and test this out by printing the `average` variable, `console.log (average)`.

```
if (grades.length > 0) {
   average = grades.map((grade) => grade.grade).reduce((a, b) => a + b) /
grades.length;
   }

   console.log(average);
});
```

I'm going to save it. We have `getStatus` and we have `getStatus` for 1. That is perfectly fine, we can continue to use that. In the terminal, we get 83 printing, which is the correct average.

```
[nodemon] starting `node app-promises.js`
83
undefined
[nodemon] clean exit - waiting for changes before restart
```

If I go ahead and rerun it for user 2, we get 100 printing. Everything is working really well; `undefined` is just coming up because we don't have anything returned so status equals `undefined`, which prints in the `console.log` statement. So, instead of just dumping average to the screen, let's go ahead and actually return our template string. This is the final thing we're going to do in this section.

Returning the template string

Just above the `console.log` statement for average, we're going to follow this format starting off with the name, that is, `user.name`. Then we're going to move on to the next part, has a, followed by their grade. That's the `average`. We'll toss the % after it in the class period:

```
return `${user.name} has a ${average}% in the class.`;
```

Now that we're returning something, this value will be accessible to whoever calls `getStatus`. In this case, that happens right here. In the Terminal, we see `Jessica has 100% in the class` printing to the screen:

```
[nodemon] starting `node app-promises.js`
Jessica has a 100% in the class.
[nodemon] clean exit - waiting for changes before restart
```

If I go on to 1, we see `Andrew` has an 83 and, if I type in some other `id`, we can see `Unable to find user with the id of 123` printing. So, this is it for our contrived starter example. I know there wasn't a heck of a lot of interesting stuff here, but I promise having an example to work with, it's going to make understanding async/await so much easier. So, the goal in the next section is to take the code snippet and get it down to about three lines of code using this new syntax:

```
// Andrew has a 83% in the class
const getStatus = (userId) => {
```

```
    let user;
    return getUser(userId).then((tempUser) => {
      user = tempUser;
      return getGrades(user.schoolId);
    }).then((grades) => {
      let average = 0;

      if (grades.length > 0) {
        average = grades.map((grade) => grade.grade).reduce((a, b) => a + b)
  / grades.length;
      }

      return `${user.name} has a ${average}% in the class.`;
    });
  };
```

It's going to be three lines of code that are a whole lot easier to read and work with. It's going to look like synchronous code as opposed to callbacks and promise chains.

Async/await basics

In this section, you're finally going to get to use the new async/await functionality. We're going to create an alternative version of the getStatus function and call it getStatusAlt, so we can go ahead and actually define that: a const getStatusAlt. Now, it's still going to be a function, so we're going to start off by creating an arrow function (=>). We're still going to take in an argument, so we'll define that userId:

```
    const getStatusAlt = (userId) => {

    };
```

Now, though, we're going to switch things up. Instead of working through the old example, we're going to use the new async/await functionality. To explore this, let's temporarily comment out the getStatus-then and catch block code. We'll be recreating it with a call to getStatusAlt as opposed to a call to getStatus, but I do want to leave the old code in place so we can directly compare and contrast the differences.

The new async/await functionality is going to allow us to write our old code in a way that looks like synchronous code, which means that we'll be able to avoid things like then callbacks, promise chaining, and workarounds. With async/await, we're going to able to avoid all of that stuff, creating a function that's just a whole lot easier to read, alter, work with, and test. Now, getStatusAlt is going to start off in a way that is super boring.

We're going to return a string, `Mike`:

```
const getStatusAlt = (userId) => {
  return 'Mike';
};
```

This is the JavaScript `101` stuff. You would expect `Mike` to come back. If I use `consult.log`, his name should pop out through `getStatusAlt`.

```
const getStatusAlt = (userId) => {
  return 'Mike';
};

console.log(getStatusAlt());
```

Let's just go ahead and work through this, so we're going to save the file, `nodemon` is going to restart, and there we go. We have `Mike` printing to the screen:

```
[nodemon] starting `node app-promises.js`
Mike
[nodemon] clean exit - waiting for changes before restart
```

That's exactly what we would expect. Now, with async/await, we actually mark our functions as special functions. I have a few functions here. We're going to be marking `return 'Mike'` as a special async function. So in the future, `async/await` are going to be two words `async` and `await`. These aren't just words, but actual keywords that we're going to be typing out.

Using the async function

The first one, `await`, will eventually get used inside of our `async` functions but, before we can ever use `await`, we have to mark that function as `async`, so we're going to do that first. We're going to explore it, then we'll move on to `await`. In the `getStatusAlt` variable line, all we're going to do is add `async` in front of our arguments list with a space:

```
const getStatusAlt = async (userId) => {
  return 'Mike';
};
```

Now, this is actually going to change how the `console.log` works; to explore that, all we're going to do is save the file and see what we get. Instead of getting the string `Mike` back, you can see we're now getting a `Promise` back:

```
[nodemon] starting `node app-promises.js`
Promise { 'Mike' }
[nodemon] clean exit - waiting for changes before restart
```

We're getting a promise back that resolves the string `Mike`, so this brings us to the first big difference between regular functions and `async` functions. Regular functions return strings and strings come back; `async` functions always return promises. If you return something from an `async` function, it's actually returning a promise and it's resolving the value. So this function is equivalent to the following code. You don't have to write this out; this is just to get the idea. It is equivalent to creating a function that returns a new promise where that new promise gets `resolve` and `reject`, and it then calls resolve with `Mike`:

```
() => {
    return new Promise((resolve, reject) => {
    resolve('Mike')
    })
}
```

These two are identical, they have the exact same functionality. We create a new promise, we resolve `Mike` or we use an `async` function that simply returns something.

 So, that is lesson one: when you have an `async` function, whatever you return is actually just going to get resolved, which means that we can switch up this usage.

In place of `console.log` statement, I'm going to call `getStatusAlt`. This time we're getting a promise back and we know that, so we can just use the `then` callback. What are we going to get back? We're going to get back the return value as our resolved value.

If I return to string, I'd get a string back; here a number, I'd get a number; a Boolean, an object, a function; whatever you explicitly return from this function is going to be available as if it was resolved, which means that I can create a name variable like a `console.log(name)`:

```
const getStatusAlt = async (userId) => {
    return 'Mike';
};
```

```
getStatusAlt().then((name) => {
  console.log(name);
});
```

Now, what are we going to get back inside `nodemon`? We're just going to get back `Mike` once again, the regular plain old string. Because we've added on a piece of promise-based chaining, we then get the name and we print it out, and here `Mike` prints once again:

```
[nodemon] starting `node app-promises.js`
Mike
[nodemon] clean exit - waiting for changes before restart
```

So, if returning a value is equivalent to resolving, how do we reject?

Rejecting an error using the async function

If I want it to reject an error like (`'This is an error'`), how do I go about doing that with the new `async` feature? All we do is throw a new error using standard JavaScript techniques. Throw a new error with a message, (`'This is an error'`):

```
const getStatusAlt = async (userId) => {
  throw new Error('This is an error');
  return 'Mike';
};
```

This is equivalent to using the `reject` argument in the new Promise. When you throw a new error from an `async` function, it is exactly the same as rejecting some value. So, in this case, we can go ahead and use that error by adding a `catch`, like we would if it was a regular old promise. We're going to get the error back, and I'll use `console.log` to print it to the screen, if it occurs:

```
getStatusAlt().then((name) => {
  console.log(name);
}).catch(e) => {
  console.log(e);
});
```

It's always going to occur, because I throw it on line 1. If I save the file, `nodemon` restarts and we get `Error: This is an error` printing to the screen:

```
[nodemon] starting `node app-promises.js`
Error: This is an error
    at getStatusAlt (/Users/Gary/Desktop/async-await/app-promises.js:60:9)
    at Object.<anonymous> (/Users/Gary/Desktop/async-await/app-promises.js:64:1)
    at Module._compile (module.js:660:30)
    at Object.Module._extensions..js (module.js:671:10)
    at Module.load (module.js:573:32)
    at tryModuleLoad (module.js:513:12)
    at Function.Module._load (module.js:505:3)
    at Function.Module.runMain (module.js:701:10)
    at startup (bootstrap_node.js:194:16)
    at bootstrap_node.js:618:3
[nodemon] clean exit - waiting for changes before restart
```

So, those are the first two important things you need to know about `async` functions before we go any further and use await. Returning something is equivalent to resolving, and throwing an error is equivalent to rejecting; we always get a promise back.

Using the await function

At this point, we have only used half of the feature. We've used the `async` part, which alone is not particularly useful. It gets really useful when we combine it with `await`, so let's go ahead and start taking a look at that.

The `await` function is going to allow us to introduce the other functions back into play, `getGrades` and `getUser`. We're just going to go ahead and use `await`, and then we'll talk about exactly what's happening. So, for the moment, bear with me and just type out this line: `const user =` and we're going to set it equal to the `await` keyword. We'll talk about this in just a second; we're going to call `getUser` and we're going to pass in the `userId`. So let's start breaking this line down:

```
const getStatusAlt = async (userId) => {
   const user = await getUser(userId);
};
```

We've done this before; we're calling `getUser` with the `userId`. It returns a promise. We're creating a new variable user and it's a constant; it's the `await` part that's new. So the `await` keyword, as I mentioned earlier, has to be used in an `async` function. We're meeting that criteria. We have an `async` function, which means we can use await inside it.

We use `await` just before a promise, so here we get a promise back. So, we're awaiting for that promise to either `resolve` or `reject`. If that promise resolves, the result of this expression is going to be the resolved value, which means that resolved value will get stored in the user variable. If the promise rejects, it is going to be equivalent to throwing an error, which means no user variable will ever be created. The function will stop executing and we'll get that error inside `catch`.

Let's go ahead and actually play around with this. What I'm going to do is pass an `id` into `getStatusAlt`. Let's go ahead and use `Jessica`; all we're going to do is `console.log(user)` to the screen. We want to see what user equals. Now, `nodemon` is going to restart in the background and my `nodemon` got cleared before:

```
[nodemon] starting `node app-promises.js`
{ id: 2, name: 'Jessica', schoolId: 999 }
undefined
[nodemon] clean exit - waiting for changes before restart
```

Right here, we have our object with an `id` of 2, the name of `Jessica`, and the school id of 999.

Now, without `await`, we would be getting a promise back; with `await`, we're able to actually get that value back, which is equivalent to what we did previously. It's equivalent to this stuff where we got access to the user and we did something with it but, using `async/await`, we're able to do this in a way that looks very synchronous.

Now, we can apply this exact same technique to getting the grades. Next to the user const, we're going to make a const called `grades`. We want those grades back. What we don't want to do is create stupid temporary variables, add complex chaining, and nesting. We just want to get the grades, so we're going to await the following promise, to either `resolve` or `reject`. For the one that comes back from `getGrades`, we pass in a valid school id, `user.schoolId`:

```
const getStatusAlt = async (userId) => {
  const user = await getUser(userId);
  const grades = await getGrades(user.schoolId);

  console.log(user, grades);
};
```

This is going to return the `grades` array, for that user will be able to dump them to the screen.

So, in the Terminal, we are getting the object and the grades for `Jessica`:

```
[nodemon] starting `node app-promises.js`
{ id: 2, name: 'Jessica', schoolId: 999 } [ { id: 2, schoolId: 999, grade: 100 } ]
undefined
[nodemon] clean exit - waiting for changes before restart
```

She just has one grade, so we have an array with a single object inside it. We're not getting back a promise; we're getting back a regular old array. The same thing is true for `Andrew`; he's going to have those two grades:

```
getStatusAlt(123).then((name) => {
  console.log(name);
}).catch((e) => {
  console.log(e);
});
```

They're all going to come back and, if I switch this up to an `id` that's not valid, we're going to get our error: `Unable to find user with an id of 123`:

```
[nodemon] restarting due to changes...
Unable to find user with id of 123.
[nodemon] clean exit - waiting for changes before restart
```

That is because the `await` function rejects, which is equivalent to throwing an error. We saw that when we throw an error from an `async` function with access to it via `catch`. So, at this point, we have our user, we have our grades, and we're ready to move on to the final step, which is the actual important stuff. So far, we're just getting data out, took a few lines of code that required us to nest things. At this point, we can take the code snippet for average, exactly as it sits:

```
let average = 0;

if (grades.length > 0) {
  average = grades.map((grade) => grade.grade).reduce((a, b) => a + b) /
grades.length;
}

return `${user.name} has a ${average}% in the class.`;
```

This code relies on a `user` variable, which we have, and a `grades` variable, again, we have it as well. We can take it and copy it in the `async` function like this:

```
const getStatusAlt = async (userId) => {
```

```
   const user = await getUser(userId);
   const grades = await getGrades(user.schoolId);
   let average = 0;

   if (grades.length > 0) {
      average = grades.map((grade) => grade.grade).reduce((a, b) => a + b) /
grades.length;
   }

   return `${user.name} has a ${average}% in the class.`;
};
```

Now, we set up our average variable. We calculate the average if there are grades and we return our status:

```
getStatusAlt(2).then((status) => {
   console.log(status);
}).catch((e) => {
   console.log(e);
});
```

At this point, we can use the status and we can print it using the `console.log` statement. Let's change this back to a valid `id`, either 1 or 2, some `id` that does exist. This time, when JavaScript runs through `getStatusAlt`, it is actually going to return the correct status: `Andrew has an 83 in the class` or `Jessica has a 100 in the class`:

```
[nodemon] starting `node app-promises.js`
Andrew has a 83% in the class.
[nodemon] clean exit - waiting for changes before restart
```

We were able to do all of this without a single callback, no chaining, no nesting, just regular old code that looks like synchronous code.

This code is way more readable, maintainable, and understandable than what we have up above. Using `async/await`, we're going to be able to do just that. We're going to be able to write better, more concise promise-based code. Now, you'll notice that I'm not using `await` on the functions up above. There is no need to, because we don't need `async` inside them. One more important thing to note, there is no top-level `await`. You have to use `await` inside an `async` function so, in our case, all that means is that we do use a little chaining at the end, but when we are working with complex chains, we are able to use `async/await` to get the job done.

At this point, I don't expect you to be able to use `async/await` on your own. We're going to run through another example using real APIs that's going to give us a little more real-world experience. I'm excited to get to it.

A real-world example

In this section, we're going to move on from our contrived example and we're going to look at an example using two real HTTP APIs. Before we do, it's important to note that arrow functions (=>) aren't the only functions that support `async`. I just happen to use an arrow function (=>). I could also use an ES5 function with the `function` keyword; this works as well:

```
const getStatusAlt = async function (userId) {
   const user = await getUser(userId);
   const grades = await getGrades(user.schoolId);
   let average = 0;
```

I can save the file and I'm still going to get `Jessica has 100%` printing:

```
[nodemon] starting `node app-promises.js`
Jessica has a 100% in the class.
[nodemon] clean exit - waiting for changes before restart
```

I could also `async` an ES6 object method, but I'm going to stick to an arrow function (=>) here. Now, we're going to leave this file in the dust and we're going to move on to a brand new file for our real-world example.

Creating a currency-converter using the async/await function

This one is going to be called `currency-convert.js` and, as you can probably guess by the name, we're going to create a currency converter.

Essentially, this is just a function that takes three arguments. We're going to start off with the currency code for the currency we're starting with; in this case, let's say I have US dollars. Then there's the currency code we're trying to convert to; let's say I'm going up to Canada and I want to see how much my money is worth; and the amount we want to convert by.

So, this is essentially asking for the Canadian equivalent of `23 USD`:

```
// USD CAD 23
```

We're going to be able to use any code we want and any value we want. Now, to actually get all that information, we are going to be using two APIs. We would essentially be saying `23 USD is worth28 CAD. You can spend these in the following countries:`

```
// USD CAD 23
// 23 USD is worth 28 CAD. You can spend these in the following countries:
```

Then we'll go ahead and list out all of the countries that actually accept the Canadian dollar. Now, to actually get all this information, we will be using those two APIs and I do want to explore those over inside Chrome. Then, we'll install Axios, make the requests, and integrate all of that into the currency converter.

Exploring APIs for currency exchange rate

The first API we're going to be using is at `fixer.io`:

This one is going to give us current currency numbers, so we're going to be able to get those exchange rates. If we go over to their website, they have a great usage page. You can click the URLs; it's going to show you the exact data that would come back had you made an HTTP request.

This API and the other one we're going to be using, they do not require authentication so we're going to be able to integrate them without too much trouble. Here, we see the base currency is the Euro and we can see what a Euro is worth in other currencies. So €1 is currently worth **1.2411 USD** or **1.5997 CAD**:

```
{
    base: "EUR",
    date: "2018-03-26",
  - rates: {
        AUD: 1.6048,
        BGN: 1.9558,
        BRL: 4.0932,
        CAD: 1.5997,
        CHF: 1.1739,
        CNY: 7.7924,
        CZK: 25.446,
        DKK: 7.4482,
        GBP: 0.87248,
        HKD: 9.7384,
        HRK: 7.442,
        HUF: 312.73,
        IDR: 17045,
        ILS: 4.3317,
```

This is the first end point that we're going to be using and we're actually going to be using an alternative following. Here we can specify the base query parameter that is going to start us out at the currency of our choice. This is the currency that we're converting from and then we get the exchange rate.

So, if I wanted to convert US dollars to Canadian dollars, I would get the base **USD** conversion chart. I would find this number and I would just multiply 23 by this number, or whatever value I was trying to convert. So this is API number one; let's go ahead and grab the URL, open it up in the browser and we're going to leave that up.

The other API that we're going to be using, you can find at `restcountries.eu`. This one contains some useful information about countries. If you go to the **All** example, we can get this URL:

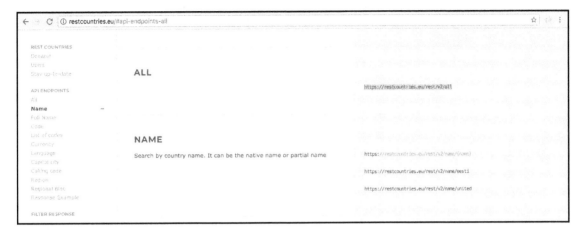

We can crack it open in the browser and we can see the extensive list of countries and country data that the API returns, starting off with `Afghanistan`: various things about it, top-level domains, alternative spellings, `regions`, lat and long, `population`, a lot of really nice information:

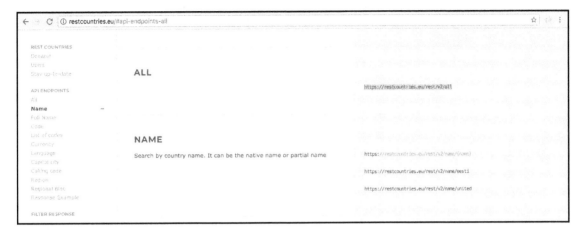

It also includes those currency codes, so we're actually going to be using a different endpoint. They support the **Currency** endpoint:

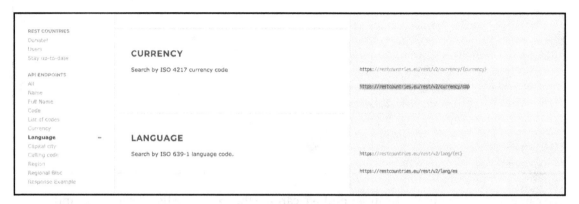

This lets you find countries that use a specific currency, so let's take this URL and crack it open in the browser. Here we're using `cop`; let's go ahead and swap that out for `usd`:

Now, there are multiple countries that use the United States dollar. We have `American Samoa`.

Down below, if we scroll way, way, way down the list, we're going to get other things; here we've got Zimbabwe, for example. Then, we have the United States of America - that's an obvious one - Turks and Caicos Islands:

```
[
  - {
        name: "American Samoa",
      - topLevelDomain: [
            ".as"
        ],
        alpha2Code: "AS",
        alpha3Code: "ASM",
      - callingCodes: [
            "1684"
        ],
        capital: "Pago Pago",
      - altSpellings: [
            "AS",
            "Amerika Sāmoa",
            "Amelika Sāmoa",
            "Sāmoa Amelika"
        ],
        region: "Oceania",
        subregion: "Polynesia",
        population: 57100,
      - latlng: [
            -14.33333333,
            -170
        ],
        demonym: "American Samoan",
        area: 199,
        gini: null,
      - timezones: [
            "UTC-11:00"
        ],
        borders: [ ],
        nativeName: "American Samoa",
        numericCode: "016",
      - currencies: [
          - {
                code: "USD",
```

So there are quite a few different places that use the US dollar. If we swap it out for `cad` -
Canada; only one there:

```
[
  - {
        name: "Canada",
      - topLevelDomain: [
            ".ca"
        ],
        alpha2Code: "CA",
        alpha3Code: "CAN",
      - callingCodes: [
            "1"
        ],
        capital: "Ottawa",
      - altSpellings: [
            "CA"
        ],
        region: "Americas",
        subregion: "Northern America",
        population: 36155487,
      - latlng: [
            60,
            -95
        ],
        demonym: "Canadian",
        area: 9984670,
        gini: 32.6,
      - timezones: [
            "UTC-08:00",
            "UTC-07:00",
            "UTC-06:00",
            "UTC-05:00",
            "UTC-04:00",
            "UTC-03:30"
```

So, using these two endpoints, we're going to be able to convert the currency and figure out,
which countries support that currency. We're going to wire all of this up together, then I'm
going to set you out on your own to actually use async/await to get that information.

Taking advantage of axios inside our application

Let's go ahead and kick things off over inside the Terminal by shutting things down, clearing the output, and installing the necessary dependencies. I'm going to run `npm init`:

```
[Gary:async-await Gary$ npm init
This utility will walk you through creating a package.json file.
It only covers the most common items, and tries to guess sensible defaults.

See `npm help json` for definitive documentation on these fields
and exactly what they do.

Use `npm install <pkg>` afterwards to install a package and
save it as a dependency in the package.json file.

Press ^C at any time to quit.
[package name: (async-await)
[version: (1.0.0)
[description:
[entry point: (app-promises.js)
[test command:
[git repository:
[keywords:
[author:
[license: (ISC)
```

We can just generate a quick `package.json` file using the defaults and they'll use `npm install axios`. The current version of Axios is `0.18.1`, and we'll toss on the `save` flag:

```
npm install axios@0.18.0 --save
```

It's going to make sure to say that as a dependency, and there we go. Everything is working, as expected. Now we can clear this output and we can actually take advantage of Axios inside our application. So, let's kick things off with the first one. We're going to go ahead and set up a function that makes the call to Fixer and gets the exchange rate.

The getExchangeRate function

To do that, over inside Atom, we're going to kick things off by creating a `const axios;` we're going to `require axios`, and then we're going to make `const` for one of our two functions. This is for the first endpoint `getExchangeRate`. Now, `getExchangeRate` is going to take two pieces of information: the `from` currency code and the `to` currency code:

```
// USD CAD 23
// 23 USD is worth 28 CAD. You can spend these in the following countries:

const axios = require('axios');

const getExchangeRate = (from, to)
```

This is going to be a function. All we're going to do is use `axios`. That's `axios.get`, and we're going to pass in that URL that I just copied from the browser:

```
// USD CAD 23
// 23 USD is worth 28 CAD. You can spend these in the following countries:

const axios = require('axios');

const getExchangeRate = (from, to) => {
  axios.get(`http://api.fixer.io/latest?base=USD)
}
```

Now we want to set the base equal to whatever currency we're coming from. So I can go ahead and use a template string, swapping out the static base value for a dynamic one, accessing `from` and `then` functions. We're going to use `then` real quick. We're going to use `then` here to just manipulate the value. This is going to return the promise from Axios with a bunch of information about the HTTP requests. The caller of `getExchangeRate` does not care about that. They shouldn't even know that an HTTP request was made. All they need back is a number, so that is exactly what we're going to give them.

In the `then` callback, we're going to have access to `response`, and on the `response` we're going to be able to get that currency code. We're going to `return response.data`. This gets us into the JSON object. Now, in here we have a `rates` object, which is key-value pairs, where the key is the currency, so we do want to access `rates` and we want to get the rate for whatever the `to` variable is:

```
// USD CAD 23
// 23 USD is worth 28 CAD. You can spend these in the following countries:

const axios = require('axios');

const getExchangeRate = (from, to) => {
  axios.get(`http://api.fixer.io/latest?base=USD).then((response) => {
    return response.data.rates[to]
  });
}
```

So, in this case, we would have USD to Canadian dollars. We would call this URL with USD and we would get this value back: `1.2889`. That is the exact value that we're going to return. Let's go ahead and test this out down below, `getExchangeRate`. I'm going to pass in USD to CAD (Canadian) dollars, then we'll get our `rate` back and we can log it out, `console.log(rate)`:

```
// USD CAD 23
```

```
// 23 USD is worth 28 CAD. You can spend these in the following countries:

const axios = require('axios');

const getExchangeRate = (from, to) => {
  return axios.get(`http://api.fixer.io/latest?base=USD).then((response) =>
{
    return response.data.rates[to]
  });
};

getExchangeRate('USD', 'CAD').then((rate) => {
  console.log(rate);
});
```

I'm going to go ahead and save this. In the background, inside the Terminal, we can start up nodemon once again, and we're going to run the currency-convert file. Right here, we get that value 1.2889 is the current currency exchange rate:

```
[Gary:async-await Gary$ nodemon currency-convert.js
[nodemon] 1.14.10
[nodemon] to restart at any time, enter `rs`
[nodemon] watching: *.*
[nodemon] starting `node currency-convert.js`
1.2889
[nodemon] clean exit - waiting for changes before restart
```

I could put EUR in code:

```
getExchangeRate('USD', 'EUR').then((rate) => {
  console.log(rate);
});
```

I could figure out what the Euro exchange rate is 0.80574, so there we go:

```
[nodemon] starting `node currency-convert.js`
0.80574
[nodemon] clean exit - waiting for changes before restart
```

We got our first one all knocked out. Now, the other one that we're going to create real quick is going to be getCountries.

The getCountries function

The `getCountries` function is going to get a list of countries, just their names, and we're going to get it by `currencyCode`:

```
const getCountries = (currencyCode) => {

};
```

This one, just like `getExchangeRate`, is also going to return a promise from `axios.get` and the URL we want to get lives over in the browser:

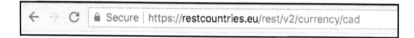

So, right here we have our URL. We have the spot where we're going to dump our `currencyCode`, so we can knock that out. It's going to be a template string and we're going to get rid of `CAD` and inject whatever the `currencyCode` argument is:

```
const getCountries = (currencyCode) => {
   return
axios.get(`https://restcountries.eu/rest/v2/currency/${currencyCode}`)
};
```

Now, at this point, once again, we do want to do a little manipulation to the data, so I could go ahead and use `then`. In the `then` callback, I can go ahead and access the `response`. What I want to do with the `response` is I just want to loop over it. I want to figure out all the countries that support my currency and then I want to return an array:

```
const getCountries = (currencyCode) => {
   return
axios.get(`https://restcountries.eu/rest/v2/currency/${currencyCode}`).then
((response) => {

   });
};
```

Now you know that we're going to get all those countries back, right? So, for `cad` we have an array with the single object inside it. For `usd`, we have an array with multiple objects inside it, so we're going to take this array of objects and convert it to an array of string.

We would start off with `American Samoa`:

```
[
  - {
      name: "American Samoa",
    - topLevelDomain: [
          ".as"
      ],
      alpha2Code: "AS",
      alpha3Code: "ASM",
    - callingCodes: [
          "1684"
      ],
      capital: "Pago Pago",
    - altSpellings: [
          "AS",
          "Amerika Sāmoa",
          "Amelika Sāmoa",
          "Sāmoa Amelika"
      ],
```

To do that, we're just going to use `map`. Back inside Atom, we can go ahead and knock this out really quickly by returning `response.data`, which is an array, which means it has access to that `map` method. We are then going to use `map`. Each individual item is going to be a `country`; each `country` has a name property, so we can return `country.name`, giving us an array of country names that support the `currency`. In this case, we can simplify that by implicitly returning `country.name`. Now, let's go ahead and test that out right here; `getCountries`. We're going to get `countries` back and we're going to dump `countries` to the screen. We only provide a single argument:

```
const getCountries = (currencyCode) => {
  return
axios.get(`https://restcountries.eu/rest/v2/currency/${currencyCode}`).then
((response) => {
    return response.data.map((country) => country.name);
  });
};

getCountries('USD').then((countries) => {
  console.log(countries);
});
```

So, if we save this and check things out over in the Terminal, we should see exactly what comes back. Here we have a list of all of the countries that we can use that currency in, in this case, the US dollar:

```
[nodemon] starting `node currency-convert.js`
[ 'American Samoa',
  'Bonaire, Sint Eustatius and Saba',
  'British Indian Ocean Territory',
  'United States Minor Outlying Islands',
  'Virgin Islands (British)',
  'Virgin Islands (U.S.)',
  'Cambodia',
  'Ecuador',
  'El Salvador',
  'Guam',
  'Marshall Islands',
  'Micronesia (Federated States of)',
  'Northern Mariana Islands',
  'Palau',
  'Panama',
  'Puerto Rico',
  'Timor-Leste',
  'Turks and Caicos Islands',
  'United States of America',
  'Zimbabwe' ]
[nodemon] clean exit - waiting for changes before restart
```

We could go over to EUR to see which countries support that:

```
getCountries('EUR').then((countries) => {
  console.log(countries);
});
```

If we save the file, we're going to get that list back in just a moment.

Here we have all the countries that support it, everything from `Belgium` all the way down to `Zimbabwe` and `Spain`:

```
[nodemon] restarting due to changes...
[ 'Åland Islands',
  'Andorra',
  'Austria',
  'Belgium',
  'Cyprus',
  'Estonia',
  'Finland',
  'France',
  'French Guiana',
  'French Southern Territories',
  'Germany',
  'Greece',
  'Guadeloupe',
  'Holy See',
  'Ireland',
  'Italy',
  'Latvia',
  'Lithuania',
  'Luxembourg',
  'Malta',
  'Martinique',
  'Mayotte',
```

All those countries are included. Next up, is CAD:

```
getCountries('CAD').then((countries) => {
  console.log(countries);
});
```

You should just have that one, Canada, and it does indeed show up right there:

```
[nodemon] starting `node currency-convert.js`
[ 'Canada' ]
[nodemon] clean exit - waiting for changes before restart
```

So, at this point, we have all the data we need to actually get things done. So, together we're going to build the equivalent of this function over in our promises and you're going to be building out the `async` one.

Over here, let's go ahead and get started: `const convertCurrency`. That is going to be the function we'll be building. It's the one that you'll eventually make `async` but, for now, we'll leave it as a regular arrow function (=>). We're going to get the currency code that we're converting `from` the one we're converting `to`, and the amount we're looking to convert.

```
const getCountries = (currencyCode) => {
```

```
    return
axios.get(`https://restcountries.eu/rest/v2/currency/${currencyCode}`).then
((response) => {
    return response.data.map((country) => country.name);
  });
};

const convertCurrency = (from, to, amount) => {

};
```

Inside here, we can kick things off by getting those countries. I'm going to `return` `getCountries`. I'm going to call that with the currency that we're converting to, then we can tack on `then` and we are going to get the `countries` list back. Next up, we're going to return a call to `getExchangeRates` - passing in `from` and `to`, and we're going to get that back as a promise as well, which means we can tack on another `then` call. Here we're going to get that rate:

```
const convertCurrency = (from, to, amount) => {
  return getCountries(to).then((tempCountries) => {
    return getExchangeRate(from, to);
  }).then((rate) => {

  });
};
```

Now, inside the `then` callback, we can go ahead and actually calculate all the stuff we're going to calculate. In this case, we're going to generate that long string I was talking about.

Let's first start off by creating a `const`; this const will be called `exchangedAmount`. All we're going to do is take the `amount` the user passed in and multiply it by the exchange `rate`; so, in this case, we would successfully convert US dollars from Canadian dollars. Now, down below, we can go ahead and start working on that string. We're going to `return` a template string and, inside here, we're going to do quite a few things.

So, first off, we're going to start off with the `amount`. The `amount` in the currency you're coming `from` is `worth`. Then we're going to put the `amount` in the currency you're going to, it's `exchangedAmount`. Then we'll toss in `to`:

```
const convertCurrency = (from, to, amount) => {
  return getCountries(to).then((countries) => {
    return getExchangeRate(from, to);
  }).then((rate) => {
    const exchangedAmount = amount * rate;
```

```
        return `${amount} ${from} is worth ${exchangedAmount} ${to}`;
    });
};
```

So, this is part one. We can actually go ahead and test this out before even moving on. Next, I'm going to switch the `getCountries` call over to a `convertCurrency` call. We're going to go ahead and convert Canadian dollars over to US Dollars. Let's go ahead and convert a hundred of those. Now we're going to get the `status` back, as opposed to actually getting back the countries list:

```
const convertCurrency = (from, to, amount) => {
    return getCountries(to).then((countries) => {
    return getExchangeRate(from, to);
}).then((rate) => {
    const exchangedAmount = amount * rate;

    return `${amount} ${from} is worth ${exchangedAmount} ${to}`;
    });
};

convertCurrency('CAD', 'USD', 100).then((status) => {
    console.log(status);
});
```

We can go ahead and save currency-convert and see what happens over inside the Terminal. Over here, we get `100 CAD is worth 73.947 USD`, and this is a great first step:

```
[nodemon] starting `node currency-convert.js`
100 CAD is worth 77.583 USD.
[nodemon] clean exit - waiting for changes before restart
```

Now, we're also going to tack on that country's list, which we do not have access to in this function. We can go through the same step we used last time. We'll create `tempCountries`. Up above, we can make a new variable called countries and we'll set countries equal to `tempCountries` like this:

```
const convertCurrency = (from, to, amount) => {
    let countries;
    return getCountries(to).then((tempCountries) => {
    countries = tempCountries;
    return getExchangeRate(from, to);
}).then((rate) => {
    const exchangedAmount = amount * rate;

    return `${amount} ${from} is worth ${exchangedAmount} ${to}.`;
```

```
  });
};
```

Now we'll be able to access those countries and do something with them. What are we going to do? We're just going to join them all together, separated by a comma, to create that nice list. That'll be the currency that we're talking about.

Then, we'll add a colon and then we will interpolate the following. So, we're going to take all those countries, we're going to take that array, and we're going to convert it over to a string using `join`. What do we want to put between all of them? We're going to put a comma and a space, we're going to create a comma separated list of countries that that currency can be used in:

```
const convertCurrency = (from, to, amount) => {
  let countries;
  return getCountries(to).then((tempCountries) => {
    countries = tempCountries;
    return getExchangeRate(from, to);
  }).then((rate) => {
    const exchangedAmount = amount * rate;

    return `${amount} ${from} is worth ${exchangedAmount} ${to}. ${to} can
be used in the following countries: ${countries.join(', ')}`;
  });
};
```

Now we can go ahead and save currency- convert and see what happens over inside nodemon when things restart, `100 CAD is worth 73 USD. USD can be used in the following countries:`

```
[nodemon] starting `node currency-convert.js`
100 CAD is worth 77.583 USD. USD can be used in following countries: American Samoa, Bonaire, Sint Eustatius
and Saba, British Indian Ocean Territory, United States Minor Outlying Islands, Virgin Islands (British), V
irgin Islands (U.S.), Cambodia, Ecuador, El Salvador, Guam, Marshall Islands, Micronesia (Federated States o
f), Northern Mariana Islands, Palau, Panama, Puerto Rico, Timor-Leste, Turks and Caicos Islands, United Stat
es of America, Zimbabwe
[nodemon] clean exit - waiting for changes before restart
```

Then we have a list of all the countries we can use it in. Let's go ahead and test out a different variation. Let's go ahead and switch US dollars over to Canadian dollars:

```
convertCurrencyAlt('USD', 'CAD', 100).then((status) => {
  console.log(status);
});
```

This time around, we're going to get a different output as follows:

```
[nodemon] starting `node currency-convert.js`
100 USD is worth 128.89 CAD. CAD can be used in following countries: Canada
[nodemon] clean exit - waiting for changes before restart
```

The Canadian dollar can be used in the following countries, in this case, just `Canada`. Everything is working as expected. The problem is we're using promise chaining in order to get everything done. We need to use the `async` function instead of that.

Creating convertCurrencyAlt as the async/await function

We are going to convert this over to async/await, and you're going to do that right here at the end of `convertCurrency` function. We're going to use `Create convertCurrencyAlt as async function`. So, just like we did over inside of app-promises, you're going to create an `async` function. Then you're going to fetch both pieces of data using `await`: `Get countries and rate using await and our two functions`. So, you're going to `await` both of these promises and then you're going to store that value in some variable. You can create a country's variable and a `rate` variable. Finally, you'll be able to take these two lines and just tack those on at the end:

```
const exchangedAmount = amount * rate;

return `${amount} ${from} is worth ${exchangedAmount} ${to}. ${to} can be
used in the following countries: ${countries.join(', ')}`;
  });
```

That will calculate the `exchangedAmount` and it will return the correct information: `Calculate exchangedAmount` and `Return status string`. You have two statements to get the data, one to calculate the exchanged amount and the final one to actually print things out.

We're going to go ahead and kick things off by creating that `const convertCurrencyAlt`. This one is going to be an `async` function, so we have to mark it as such. We can then move on to our arguments list, which is exactly the same as the other one: `from`, `to`, and `amount`. Then we're going to put the arrow and arrow function (=>), and we're going to open and close our curly braces.

```
const convertCurrencyAlt = async (from, to, amount) => {

});
```

Now we can move on to the first thing, which is getting the countries and getting the exchange rate. I'm going to start off with countries; `const countries` equals. We are going to `await` the promise that comes back from `getCountries`. What countries do we want to get? The ones where the `to` currency is able to be used. Then we're going to move on down below to rate. So, `const rate`. In this case, we are also trying to `await` something; we're trying to `await` the promise that comes back from `getExchangeRate`. We're trying to get the exchange rate, right here, `from` and `to`:

```
const convertCurrencyAlt = async (from, to, amount) => {
  const countries = await getCountries(to);
  const rate = await getExchangeRate(from, to);
};
```

So, at this point, we have all that data and we can move on to calculating the exchanged amount and returning the string. We already built that out, there's no need to recreate it. We can just copy both of those lines, paste them down below, and there we go. Everything is done:

```
const convertCurrencyAlt = async (from, to, amount) => {
  const countries = await getCountries(to);
  const rate = await getExchangeRate(from, to);
  const exchangedAmount = amount * rate;

  return `${amount} ${from} is worth ${exchangedAmount} ${to}. ${to} can be
used in the following countries: ${countries.join(', ')}`;
};
```

Now, down below, instead of calling `convertCurrency`, we're able to call `convertCurrencyAlt`, passing in the exact same arguments and getting back the status.

```
convertCurrencyAlt('USD', 'CAD', 100).then((status) => {
  console.log(status);
});
```

The difference is that our function is using `async`; a whole lot more readable, much easier to work with. We're going to go ahead and save currency-convert. That is going to run through the process of getting all of that data, converting it and then we're going to go ahead and print the status. What do we get at the end of the day? Over here, we get the exact same thing as shown in output here:

```
[nodemon] starting `node currency-convert.js`
100 USD is worth 128.89 CAD. CAD can be used in following countries: Canada
[nodemon] clean exit - waiting for changes before restart
```

In the next section, we're going to talk about a few other places we can use `async` in this example, and we're also going to talk about how we can work with and handle errors.

Handling errors and awaiting async function

We're going to kick this section off by converting both `getExchangeRate` and `getCountries` over to `async` functions. They're good candidates because we do have promises and we could just await those promises instead. Then we're going to talk about errors, how we can throw them and how we can customize errors that get thrown by other code. It's going to make it really useful and it'll make it a lot easier to actually use `async/await` in the real world where you do need to handle errors.

Converting getExchangeRate and getCountries into the async function

So the first thing we're going to do is convert `getExchangeRate` and `getCountries`. The first step I'm going to take is to make this an `async` function, otherwise we can't use `await`. Then we're going to go ahead and set up a variable, a `const` response, and we are going to set this equal to `await`. Then we're going to await the following promise, the one that comes back from `axios.get`. I'm going to copy it, paste it, toss a semicolon at the end, and the only thing left to do is to return the value. I'm going to take the `return` statement and move it right there, then we can remove all of the previous code we had:

```
const getExchangeRate = async (from, to) => {
  const response = await
axios.get(`http://api.fixer.io/latest?base=${from}`);
  return response.data.rates[to];
}
```

We now have the exact same functionality and it's a little bit nicer. Now, the benefit isn't as drastic as the benefit from going to `convertCurrency` to `convertCurrencyAlt`, but it is still indeed nice and I'd recommend using `async` anywhere you can. Now we need to convert `getCountries` using the exact same steps we just followed:

1. Mark `currencyCode` one as `async`:

   ```
   const getCountries = async (CurrencyCode) => {
   ```

2. Create that `response` variable and actually awaiting on the promise. We're going to await the following promise:

   ```
   axios.get(`https://restcountries.eu/rest/v2/currency/${currencyCode}`);
   ```

3. The last step is to just `return` the exact same thing. There we go:

   ```
   return response.data.map((country) => country.name);
   ```

Now that we have both of these converted, we're just going to test our work by saving the file and, as long as we get the exact same output, we'll move on to talking about errors; how it could catch them, how we can throw them, and how, in general, we can improve the errors that show up in our application.

Alright, the new result just showed up:

```
[nodemon] starting `node currency-convert.js`
100 USD is worth 128.89 CAD. CAD can be used in following countries: Canada
[nodemon] clean exit - waiting for changes before restart
```

It is identical to the other two, which means that we are good to go. Now, I'd like to shift the discussion over to errors.

Error handling in the async function

What we're going to do is get the endpoints to trigger errors. We're going to look at how exactly we can handle those endpoints and how we can tweak them to be something that's a little more useful, because currently we're going to get back just a whole bunch of junk.

Printing an error to the screen

Step one is to actually print the error out to the screen so we can see what we're working with. We're going to `catch` the error and we're going to print the error, `console.log(e)`:

```
convertCurrencyAlt('USD', 'CAD', 100).then((status) => {
  console.log(status);
}).catch((e) => {
  console.log(e);
});
```

Now let's go ahead and start making some things fail. We're going to kick things off by making `getCountries` fail; that's the first call.

Now, this one only uses `to`, so all we have to do to get that to fail is to send in a bad `to` `countryCode`. I'm going to use MMM:

```
convertCurrencyAlt('USD', 'MMM', 100).then((status) => {
  console.log(status);
}).catch((e) => {
  console.log(e);
});
```

Save the file and we'll see what we get over inside the browser. Now what we're going to get back is a whole bunch of junk:

```
    _headerSent: true,
    socket: [TLSSocket],
    connection: [TLSSocket],
    _header: 'GET /rest/v2/currency/MMM HTTP/1.1\r\nAccept: application/json, text/plain, */*\r\nUser-Ag
ent: axios/0.18.0\r\nHost: restcountries.eu\r\nConnection: close\r\n\r\n',
    _onPendingData: [Function: noopPendingOutput],
    agent: [Agent],
    socketPath: undefined,
    timeout: undefined,
    method: 'GET',
    path: '/rest/v2/currency/MMM',
    _ended: true,
    res: [IncomingMessage],
    aborted: undefined,
    timeoutCb: null,
    upgradeOrConnect: false,
    parser: null,
    maxHeadersCount: null,
    _redirectable: [Writable],
    [Symbol(outHeadersKey)]: [Object] },
  data: { status: 404, message: 'Not Found' } } }
[nodemon] clean exit - waiting for changes before restart
```

What's coming back here is actually the `axios` response. This has the error information; it has things like that status code. You can see it was a 404. We have a message saying not found. This is letting us know that `countryCode` we provided was not found by that endpoint. Now this is not particularly useful.

We want to come up with something that is a little more useful, like a message: `Unable to get countries that use MMM`. That'd be great. So, to do that, we're going to tweak `getCountries`. We're going to go ahead and use a regular old `try catch` block and set it up like this:

```
const getCountries = async (CurrencyCode) => {
  try{

  } catch (e){

  }
```

If the code in the `try` block throws an error, the `catch` block will run, otherwise `catch` will never run. All we're going to do is take `const response` and `return statement` code and move it inside of `try`:

```
const getCountries = async (currencyCode) => {
  try {
    const response = await
axios.get(`https://restcountries.eu/rest/v2/current/${currencyCode}`);
    return response.data.map((country) => country.name);
  } catch(e){
  }
};
```

So, what we're doing is saying anytime either of these lines throw an error, run the code in the `catch` block and provide the error. Now we know what the error is. It doesn't contain much of anything, so what we're going to do is just throw our own error; something that is human-readable: `throw new Error`. In this case, we're going to stick with a template string and we're going to go ahead and set it up: `Unable to get countries that use.` Then we'll inject, right before the period, the `currencyCode`:

```
const getCountries = async (currencyCode) => {
  try {
    const response = await
axios.get(`https://restcountries.eu/rest/v2/current/${currencyCode}`);
    return response.data.map((country) => country.name);
  } catch(e){
    throw new Error(`Unable to get countries that use
```

```
${currencyCOde}.`);
    }
};
```

Now, if we go ahead and save the currency-convert application with a bad to `countryCode`, we're going to see `Unable to get countries that use MMM` as the error. We could access the message directly using `e.message`.

```
convertCurrencyAlt('USD', 'MMM', 100).then((status) =>{
  console.log(status);
}).catch((e) => {
  console.log(e.message);
});
```

That'll improve the output even more. Now we just have a string. We could do anything we want with that string. It's very clear: `Unable to get the countries that use MMM`.

Error handling for the getExchangeRate function

Now, let's go ahead and look at the next one in our list, that is, the `getExchangeRate` function. There are actually two things that can go wrong here; the `axios` request can fail itself and we could also end up with a response that's valid, but the `to` status code is invalid. In that case, there would be no rate for it.

Now we can go ahead and actually simulate this by commenting out a few lines of code that's going to allow us to test to `getExchangeRate` in isolation:

```
const convertCurrencyAlt = async (from, to, amount) => {
  //const countries = await getCountries(to);
  const rate = await getExchangeRate(from, to);
  //const exchangedAmount = amount * rate;
  //
  //return `${amount} ${from} is worth ${exchangedAmount} ${to}. ${to} can
be used in the following`;
};
```

Now, if I go ahead and mess the USD with QWE, we can save the file and we are going to get another error request **failed with status code 422**:

```
[nodemon] starting `node currency-convert.js`
Request failed with status code 422
[nodemon] clean exit - waiting for changes before restart
```

What we're going to do again is go through that exact same process. So, we're going to wrap those two lines in a `try catch` block. Then, if `catch` runs, you're going to throw a new error using the following format: `Unable to get exchange rate for USD and CAD`. This is going to be the `from` USD currency code to CAD currency code. We're going to kick things off by setting up that `try catch` block. We are going to try to run the following code:

```
const response = await
axios.get(`http://api.fixer.io/latest?base=${from}`);
return response.data.rates[to];
```

If it runs that would be very nice but, if it doesn't, we do want to handle that as well by throwing a new error. Inside the `catch` block, we are going to provide our message; it'll just be a template string. Now, the message I want to provide is `Unable to get exchange rate for ${from} and ${to}`, followed by a period:

```
const getExchangeRate = async(from, to) =>{
  try{
    const response = await
axios.get(`http://api.fixer.io/latest?base=${from}`);
    return response.data.rates[to];
  } catch(e){
    throw new Error(`Unable to get exchange rate for ${from} and ${to}.`);
  }
};
```

Now we can go ahead and save this and see what happens over inside the browser:

```
[nodemon] starting `node currency-convert.js`
Unable to get exchange rate for QWE and MMM.
[nodemon] clean exit - waiting for changes before restart
```

We get `Unable to get exchange rate for QWE and MMM`. Now currently that's failing because `from` is invalid, but what if `from` is valid? What if we're trying to go to USD to MMM? This time around we are actually going to get something different:

```
[nodemon] restarting due to changes...
undefined
[nodemon] clean exit - waiting for changes before restart
```

Here we just get `undefined`. It comes up because the `return` statement in `getExchangeRate` has `response.data.rates`. We have a valid `from` `countryCode` so valid data comes back, but the `to countryCode` does not exist, which is where undefined comes from.

We can always go ahead and fix that by creating a variable `const rate`, and we'll set it equal to `response.data.rates[to]`. Then, well, a little bit of `if` logic. If there is `rate`, we're just going to go ahead and return it. If there's no `rate`, we're just going to go ahead and `throw` a new error, which will trigger the `catch` block, which will print the message to the screen:

```
const getExchangeRate = async(from, to) =>{
  try{
    const response = await
axios.get(`http://api.fixer.io/latest?base=${from}`);
    const rate = response.data.rates[to];
    if(rate){
      return rate;
    } else{
      throw new Error();
    }
  } catch(e){
    throw new Error(`Unable to get exchange rate for ${from} and ${to}.`);
  }
};
```

Now, if we save the code using these same codes, we get the message once again: `Unable to get the exchange rate for USD and MMM`:

```
[nodemon] starting `node currency-convert.js`
Unable to get exchange rate for USD and MMM.
[nodemon] clean exit - waiting for changes before restart
```

Now this message is going to show up if `from` is invalid, if `to` is invalid, or if both are invalid.

With that in place, we now have some little error handling set up and we can bring back the rest of the lines from our application. If we run through the app using this bad data here, `Unable to get countries that use MMM` prints:

```
[nodemon] restarting due to changes...
Unable to get countries that use MMM.
[nodemon] clean exit - waiting for changes before restart
```

Let's switch it back over to valid country codes like USD and CAD. Let's actually use the Euro, EUR, for a change and over inside the browser we should get valid values, since both of those country codes are indeed valid:

```
[nodemon] starting `node currency-convert.js`
100 USD is worth 80.574 EUR. EUR can be used in following countries: Åland Islands, Andorra, Austria, Belgiu
m, Cyprus, Estonia, Finland, France, French Guiana, French Southern Territories, Germany, Greece, Guadeloupe
, Holy See, Ireland, Italy, Latvia, Lithuania, Luxembourg, Malta, Martinique, Mayotte, Monaco, Montenegro, N
etherlands, Portugal, Republic of Kosovo, Réunion, Saint Barthélemy, Saint Martin (French part), Saint Pierr
e and Miquelon, San Marino, Slovakia, Slovenia, Spain, Zimbabwe
[nodemon] clean exit - waiting for changes before restart
```

Here we get the exchange rate, we get all of the countries that use the Euro, we aren't getting any of our error messages, which is fantastic. So by using regular techniques, things from way back in JavaScript, like try, catch, and throw new error, we're able to create a very nice setup using those async functions.

That is it for this section, and that is it for our little currency-convert example. So, at this point, we've gone through two examples: we went through the app promises example, where we had a contrived set of data; we created a few functions and we got to explore the basics of async/await. Then we went through the currency- convert example, where we used two real APIs and we added a little more robust error handling. At the end of the day, they'll both use the exact same async and await techniques. Hopefully, you're starting to see how this can fit into our Node applications. In the next and final section, we're actually going to use async and await to make some changes to the Node API.

Summary

In this chapter, we looked into a new syntax async/await. We looked into project setup, basics of async/await, and a real-world example. We also looked into error handling using async/await.

Other Books You May Enjoy

If you enjoyed this book, you may be interested in these other books by Packt:

Learning Node.js Development
Andrew Mead

ISBN: 978-1-78839-554-0

- Learn the fundamentals of Node
- Build apps that respond to user input
- Master working with servers
- Learn how to test and debug applications
- Deploy and update your apps in the real world
- Create responsive asynchronous web applications

Mastering Node.js - Second Edition
Sandro Pasquali, Kevin Faaborg

ISBN: 978-1-78588-896-0

- Create secure servers across all major network protocols
- Build an Electron desktop app using Node that manages a filesystem
- Explore Streams generally and understand how they apply to building HTTP servers
- Develop and deploy a customer-service application
- Use the Socket.IO package for rapid bi-directional communication
- Construct serverless applications with Amazon Lambda
- Implement scaling techniques and parallelize operations across multiple cores

Leave a review - let other readers know what you think

Please share your thoughts on this book with others by leaving a review on the site that you bought it from. If you purchased the book from Amazon, please leave us an honest review on this book's Amazon page. This is vital so that other potential readers can see and use your unbiased opinion to make purchasing decisions, we can understand what our customers think about our products, and our authors can see your feedback on the title that they have worked with Packt to create. It will only take a few minutes of your time, but is valuable to other potential customers, our authors, and Packt. Thank you!

Index

www.ingramcontent.com/pod-product-compliance
Lightning Source LLC
Chambersburg PA
CBHW060636060326
40690CB00020B/4417